Chicago in the World Series,
1903–2005

Chicago in the World Series, 1903–2005

The Cubs and the White Sox in Championship Play

BRUCE A. RUBENSTEIN

McFarland & Company, Inc., Publishers
Jefferson, North Carolina, and London

LIBRARY OF CONGRESS CATALOGUING-IN-PUBLICATION DATA

Rubenstein, Bruce A. (Bruce Alan)
Chicago in the World Series, 1903–2005 : the Cubs and
White Sox in championship play / Bruce A. Rubenstein.
p.   cm.
Includes bibliographical references and index.

ISBN 0-7864-2575-X (softcover : 50# alkaline paper)

1. Baseball — Illinois — Chicago — History.   2. Chicago Cubs
(Baseball team) — History.   3. Chicago White Sox (Baseball
team) — History.   4. World Series (Baseball) — History.   I. Title.
GV863.I32R83 2006   796.357'640977311 — dc22   2006009589

British Library cataloguing data are available

Cover photograph: 1907 World Series, Detroit vs. Chicago (Library of Congress)

Manufactured in the United States of America

McFarland & Company, Inc., Publishers
Box 611, Jefferson, North Carolina 28640
www.mcfarlandpub.com

To the memory of
KENNETH B. WEST
and
LAWRENCE E. ZIEWACZ
friends, colleagues,
and avid sports fans

ACKNOWLEDGMENTS

This book is largely a result of encouragement I received from Professors Peter Williams, James Vlasich, Douglas Noverr, and Joseph Price after hearing papers on World Series sportswriting I presented over the past nearly two decades at the annual Popular Culture Association Conference. Representing academic disciplines ranging from English and history to religion and philosophy, they shared my belief that baseball and its press coverage reflects the changing national social, cultural, and literary mores, and that a book on newspaper coverage of the World Series would be a valuable addition to those interested in both baseball and American culture. Without their unflagging support this project never would have reached fruition. Thanks, guys!

Thanks also go to Mark E. Harvey, State Archivist for the State of Michigan Archives, and his staff, as well as Robert Medina, Rights and Reproductions Coordinator of the Chicago Historical Society, and the research staff of that organization for their enthusiastic assistance in finding appropriate photographs for the book. As well, Library Director Robert Houbeck and the staff of the University of Michigan–Flint library were invaluable in meeting my requests for research materials housed in various libraries throughout the nation.

Friends, my wife Deborah, and colleagues who had to suffer through recitations of my latest "research treasures" deserve both my thanks and my apologies.

TABLE OF CONTENTS

INTRODUCTION

Baseball is a game of statistics. A true aficionado of America's national pastime avidly follows averages for individual batting, slugging, fielding, earned runs, and strikeouts. As well, baseball is a game of names inseparably associated with specific numbers, and virtually all fans can associate a name with the numbers 755 (Hank Aaron's home run total), 56 (Joe DiMaggio's hitting streak), and 511 (Cy Young's victory total). More important for the game's enduring popularity, however, is that even the most casual fan recognizes the numbers 60 (Babe Ruth's long standing season home run record), 61 (Roger Maris' total in surpassing Ruth), 70 (Mark McGwire's short-lived single season home run record), and 73 (Barry Bonds' current single season record for homers). In fact, the impact of a number in baseball is so ingrained in our culture that a film account of the 1961 home run race between New York Yankee legend Mickey Mantle and teammate Roger Maris was entitled simply *61**.

To fans of Chicago's Cubs and White Sox these numbers pale in comparison to two others: 1908 and 2005. These are the years in which the Cubs and White Sox, respectively, last hoisted a world championship banner over their home fields, the latter ending an 88-year drought. To further exacerbate the pain of the passage of non-championship years is the memory of the glory that once belonged to Chicago's diamond heroes.

This book is not an attempt to discuss the history of baseball in Chicago. That task has been accomplished exceedingly well by veteran sportswriters Jerome Holtzman and George Vass in *Baseball: Chicago Style* (Chicago: Bonus Books, 2001). Rather, this volume examines Chicago teams in the modern, post–1903 World Series and the manner in which the diamond action was conveyed to the millions of avid followers of the nation's foremost sporting spectacular.

In the early twentieth century, newspaper editors deemed coverage of baseball, and especially the World Series, so critical that they sent their finest writers to the ballpark. Thus, at the annual "Fall Classic" among the denizens of early press boxes were brilliant masters of the language such as Damon Runyan, John "Ring" Lardner, Irvin Cobb, Arthur "Bugs" Baer, Westbrook Pegler, Paul Gallico, and John Kieran, all of whom had other primary literary interests.

Joining them were scores of local, syndicated, and wire service reporters whose daily responsibility was covering sporting events. Among the most noteworthy of these were leg-

1

endary figures Grantland Rice, Henry McLemore, Boze Bulger, Davis J. Walsh, and New Yorkers John Drebinger, Dan Daniel, Arthur Daley, Fred Lieb, Bill Corum, Richards Vidmer, Joe Williams, Red Smith, Harry Cross, Joe Vila, and Jimmy Cannon. Other premier baseball correspondents included J. Roy Stockton, J.G. Taylor Spink, Sid Mercer, and Bob Broeg of St. Louis, James Isaminger of Philadelphia, E.A. Batchelor, Joe S. Jackson, and H.G. Salsinger of Detroit, and Ralph S. Davis of Pittsburgh. Later writers such as Ira Berkow, Jim Murray, and dozens of their wonderfully adept peers kept sportswriting alive and well in the age of television.

In the brilliance of producing sportswriters Chicago was second only to New York. I.E. "Sy" Sanborn, Hugh E. Keogh (HEK), Hugh Fullerton, Charles Dryden, Irving Vaughan, James Crusinberry, Ed Burns, Arch Ward, David Condon, Jerome Holtzman, John Carmichael, Warren Brown, Richard Dozer, and Ed Prell are but a few of the Chicago writers who made their readers laugh, cry, and tingle with excitement as they related the activities of the Cubs and White Sox. Their deft writing skills were all the more crucial to Chicago baseball enthusiasts because their teams' participation in the World Series of 1906, 1907, 1908, 1910, 1917, 1918, and 1919 took place before the popularization of radio in the 1920s. Chicago's Fall Classics of 1929, 1932, 1935, 1938, and 1945, while broadcast over the airwaves, still fell within the era of newspaper supremacy for sport coverage. Moreover, not everyone had the luxury of hearing the live broadcasts because of other responsibilities during the day, and thus written accounts remained the most popular source of coverage, especially for those who sought a permanent record of the Series. To the sorrow of followers of the North and South Side clubs, the only times a Chicago team has taken the field for a televised World Series contest were in 1959 and 2005. Therefore, the history of the post-season Cubs and White Sox must be gained primarily, if not almost exclusively, from the firsthand accounts set forth by newspapermen.

This volume seeks to recapture for a new generation of baseball enthusiasts, raised in an era of television and computer technology, not only the game-by-game history of Chicago teams in the World Series, but also the beauty of how baseball was once reported. Newspaper accounts and baseball are inseparable, and that is why this volume is primarily based on the daily writings of baseball scribes covering the World Series. Each newspaper source was selected for a specific reason: *The New York Times* because it sent a staff writer to cover each Series game and because its staff was so rich in talent; the *Chicago Tribune* because some local coverage of Chicago teams was essential; *The Sporting News* because it offered a wide range of opinions from analysts throughout the country; the *St. Louis Post-Dispatch* because of its excellent writers; and the *Detroit Free Press*, *Detroit News*, and *Detroit Times* partly because of their convenient accessibility for a Michigan author, but mostly because each carried different syndicated writers. These, coupled with wire service accounts, afforded a broad-based and thorough coverage of World Series contests from a local and national perspective.

Chicago in the World Series, 1903–2005 is meant to go beyond readily known facts and box scores. It is intended to permit readers to recapture Chicago's participation in the World Series as though they were there; to relive the local and sectional pride of Chicago, and to feel the joy and sorrow partisans felt with each victory or defeat. It is history and popular culture, highlighting some of the best sportswriting of the early twentieth century.

WHITE SOX VS. CUBS, 1906

The 1905 season was one of upheaval and disappointment for Chicago's senior major league aggregation, the Cubs. In August, Manager Frank Selee, who had guided the squad since 1902, was compelled to step down because of tuberculosis. As his illness progressively weakened him, Selee had begun relying more heavily on Frank Chance, his twenty-seven-year-old catcher and captain, to guide the team, and therefore it was not unexpected when Chance was named as Selee's successor.[1] Despite the change of leadership, the Chicagoans compiled a 92–61 record, but finished third, trailing the New York Giants by thirteen games and the Pittsburgh Pirates by four. Then, late in the year, it was announced that sportswriter Charles W. Murphy, who combined $15,000 of his own funds with a $90,000 loan from Charles P. Taft, had purchased controlling interest in the Cubs from James A. Hart.[2] Murphy, who gave 100 shares of team stock to Chance as part of the deal, immediately proclaimed that his manager would be given absolute power to assemble a squad that would dethrone Manager John McGraw's world champion Giants in 1906.[3]

Given carte blanche authority, Chance acquired Brooklyn Dodger outfielder Jimmy Sheckard, Cincinnati Red third-baseman Harry Steinfeldt, Boston Braves' catcher Pat Moran, and free agent southpaw Jack Pfiester, who had last hurled in the major leagues for the Pirates in 1904. As the 1906 season was about to get underway, Murphy took Chance aside and stated the obvious: "Frank, I think I've given you a pretty good team. McGraw says he'll win again, but you should give him a real fight."[4]

At season's end, both Murphy and his manager had achieved a level of greatness of which neither could have even dreamed. A combination of powerful batting, sterling fielding, and dominating pitching culminated in the Cubs romping to a record of 116–36, winning fifty of their last fifty-seven contests and outpacing McGraw's second place finishers by an astounding twenty games.

Offensively the Cubs led their league in runs scored (704), hits (1316), triples (71), runs batted in (539), batting average (.262), and slugging average (.339). The infield, three-fourths of whom would be immortalized by New York poet Franklin P. Adams, was without a weakness either at bat or in the field. At third was the twenty-nine-year-old newcomer Steinfeldt. The hard-hitting former minstrel show performer led the senior circuit with eighty-three runs batted in and 176 hits, batted .327, and, despite a reputation for being slow-footed, stole twenty-nine bases in his initial season with the Cubs. Joe Tinker, regarded as the slickest fielding shortstop in the game, despite a low average (.233, 1 home run, 64 runs batted in), delivered timely hits. His partner around the keystone sack was twenty-five-year-old Johnny Evers, a fiery competitor known for his knowledge of the game. Although sharing a personal animosity for each other, Evers (.255, 1, 51) joined with Tinker to demonstrate some of the most brilliant defensive work ever seen.[5] Chance (.319, 3, 71) assumed the first-baseman's duties and led the National League with 103 runs scored and fifty-seven stolen bases. Behind the plate were thirty-one-year-old Johnny Kling (.312, 2, 46), considered by most experts to be the finest defensive catcher in baseball, and Moran (.252, 0, 35).

The outfield consisted of twenty-seven-year-old, ten year veteran Sheckard (.262, 1, 45) in left and twenty-four-year-old Frank (Wildfire) Schulte (.281, 7, 60), who led the league with thirteen triples, in right. The only potential soft spot for the Cubs was in center-field where Arthur (Solly) Hofman (.256, 2, 20), a twenty-three-year-old playing in only his second full season in the big leagues, was inserted into the line-up because of a late season injury to Jimmy Slagle.

The Chicago mound corps was headlined by Mordecai (Miner) Brown, the soon-to-be thirty-year-old three-fingered right-hander who, in only his fourth year of major league hurling, compiled a 26–6 mark, with a league's best nine shutouts and 1.04 earned run average. Supporting the Cub ace were newly acquired twenty-four-year-old Pfiester (20–8, 1.51), who was the only southpaw hurler on the team, twenty-three-year-old sophomore Ed Reulbach (19–4, 165), twenty-six-year-old Carl Lundgren (17–6, 2.21), Orval Overall (12–3, 1.88), a mid-season pickup from Cincinnati, and thirty-two-year-old Jack Taylor (12–3, 1.83). Collectively, Chicago pitchers boasted a league best 1.76 earned run average and twenty-eight shutouts.

Facing this formidable assemblage from Chicago's West Side was the Windy City's American League representative, Charles Comiskey's White Stockings, or White Sox as they were affectionately dubbed. After having finished third, six lengths behind the Boston Red Sox in 1904 and a mere two games behind the pennant winning Philadelphia Athletics in 1905, the Sox seemed poised to make a run at the flag in 1906. However, in late July the team was foundering in seventh place.

Suddenly on August 2 the Sox began a nineteen game winning streak which propelled them to pennant winning final record of 93–58, enabling them to top the runner-up New York Highlanders (Yankees) by three games. The amazing feature about the Sox success was that it was accomplished with no offensive punch, as the so-called "Hitless Wonders" brought up the rear of the American League with a .230 batting average, 1,132 hits, and six home runs.

Position by position, the Sox did not match up well either in youthfulness or statistics. Around the infield, the White Sox had twenty-seven-year-old John (Jiggs) Donahue (.257, 1, 57) at first, thirty-one-year-old former Cub Frank (Issy or Bald Eagle) Isbell (.279, 0, 57) at second, twenty-six-year-old regular third-sacker Lee Tannehill (.183, 0, 33) substituting for the injured thirty-six-year-old, seventeen year veteran George Davis (.277, 0, 80) at short, and thirty-one-year-old journeyman infielder George Rohe (.258, 0, 25) assuming Tannehill's role at third. Behind the plate was Billy Sullivan (.214, 2, 33), a thirty-one-year-old veteran of eight major league campaigns.

In the outfield, the Sox were equally deficient when compared to the Cub flycatchers. In left was Patrick (Patsy) Dougherty, an early season acquisition from the Yankees, whose record of a .333 batting average, with one home run and twenty-seven runs batted in, paled alongside that of Schulte. Center-field was patrolled by Manager Fielder Jones (.230, 2,

1906 White Sox "Hitless Wonders" (Chicago Historical Society, ICHi-38990).

34), who, at age thirty-five, was completing his eleventh big league season as a player. In right was thirty-one-year-old Eddie Hahn (.227, 0, 27), a second-year player picked up from the Yankees along with Dougherty. Such anemic stickwork led New York sportswriter Fred Lieb to marvel: "It must be admitted that Fielder won his pennant with mirrors."[6]

Lieb knew, of course, that the secret of Jones' success had nothing to do with legerdemain, but rather a pitching staff which boasted a 2.13 earned run average and led the junior circuit with thirty-two shutouts. Frank Owen, a twenty-six-year-old right-hander who had won twenty-one games in each of the two preceding seasons, topped the Sox with a record of 22–13, with a 2.33 earned run average. A pair of southpaws, thirty-year-old Nick Altrock (20–13, 2.06) and twenty-seven-year-old dentist Guy (Doc) White (18–6 and a league best 1.52 earned run average) complemented Owen. However, the hurler who drew the most attention was Ed Walsh, a huge, pink-faced, twenty-five-year-old right-handed former coal miner whose mystifying spitball not only enabled him to fashion a 17–13 win-loss record, but also a 1.88 earned run average and a league leading ten shutouts. Thus, on the mound, at least, the White Sox were the equal of the Cubs.

On the eve of the Series the National Leaguers were 2–1 favorites, and many experts shared the opinion that the Sox had no chance. However, that sentiment was not unanimous. Baseball analyst Hugh Fullerton of the *Chicago Tribune* wrote a column in which he picked the Sox to win because of their pitching. His city editor, Jim Keeley, initially refused to print what he considered an insane prediction. Keeley relented only after Fullerton inserted in his story a prediction of rain after the third game so that readers would not take him seriously.[7] John McGraw, regarded as one of the shrewdest men in the national pastime, shared Fullerton's views, but surprisingly he based his belief that the American Leaguers could triumph as a result of their batting prowess. "It's hitting that wins," McGraw asserted. "They say that the White Sox won the flag without hitting, but I know better. Their grounds prevent anyone from hitting heavily, and as they played seventy-seven games there, it made their averages look very small. On the road they hit as hard as anybody."[8]

Charles Murphy dismissed such thoughts and flaunted his arrogant confidence in his team. Before the Series commenced, Murphy met with Comiskey and National Commission members Chairman August (Garry) Herrmann, American League President Byron (Ban) Johnson, and National League President Harry Pulliam to discuss rules, the addition of two extra umpires to work the contests, and division of the gate receipts. The Cub owner took the occasion to inform the Commission that his players did not care for the world championship buttons given as trophies to the Giants in 1905. The astonishment of Herrmann and Pulliam, representing the senior circuit, and the fury of Comiskey and Johnson of the junior league, increased when Murphy pronounced that the Cub players had already met and voted that they should receive diamond cufflinks as a symbol of their world supremacy.[9]

Chance assumed a far more humble public demeanor when asked by reporters if he agreed with Murphy's assessment of his club's chances. The "Peerless Leader," as he had been dubbed by Charles Dryden of the *Chicago Tribune* after the regular season ended, merely said with modesty: "The less we say now, the less we'll have to take back in case we are beaten by the White Sox. I'll say this, however. We would rather play the White Sox than any other American League team. This is not because we hold the Comiskeyites lightly, but because we know they will play fast, hard ball. They are clean players, too, and I look for no disputes during the Series."[10]

Unfortunately for players, fans, and gate receipts, the weather played havoc with the initial contest. Only 12,693 souls, bundled in overcoats and blankets, passed through the turnstiles to brave the forty degree temperature, icy drizzle, hail, twenty mile per hour wind, and gentle snow flakes that combined to plague the West Side Park during the afternoon. Charles Dryden lightheartedly said that "the air in the ballpark was ideal for putting up ice," and that the weather had determined the Sox pitching selection.[11] "Leader Jones intended to pitch Doctor White, the urbane and willowy dentist," he asserted with dry humor, "but the sudden drop in temperature made the risk too dangerous. In the chill and wintry blasts that swept across the yard the Doctor's arms and legs might have snapped off like frozen macaroni. The more rugged Altrock, reared in the pretzel districts of Cincinnati, looked good to Jones, so Nick mounted the hill in defense of his country and horse blankets. The weather also switched Big Ed Walsh out of the program. It was feared his spitball would freeze in transit to the plate. The playing rules do not permit the pitching of icicles, even in a World Series."[12] Opposing "Handsome Nick" was Miner Brown, who, Dryden said, "had been carefully hoarded away and saved in tact, like cake for company day."[13]

The enthusiasm of those present was undaunted by the football-like atmosphere, however, and the roar that greeted the players taking their position was so deafening that the megaphone man made no attempt to announce the batteries.[14] In a ceremony at home plate, silver loving cups were presented to the rival managers in recognition of the honors the two clubs had brought to Chicago.[15]

After the gifts were accepted, Chance turned to Jones and, belying his public utterances, exhibited contempt for his opponents. Referring to the decree of the National Commission that the winners would receive 75 percent of the gate receipts of the first four games, the Cub pilot sneered to Jones: "Understand, now, there must be no even splitting of the money between the two teams." Furious at the jibe, Jones snapped: "Why don't you wait until you're asked? The Sox don't want to split the coin at all, for the good reason that we will win the Series. It's one of the best bets of the year."[16] Laughing loudly, Chance headed to Murphy's box to share Jones' "joke" with him.[17]

For four innings, Altrock and Brown matched goose eggs on the scoreboard, but in the top of the fifth the American Leaguers took the lead. Rohe led off by smashing a high fastball for a triple to left. Donahue struck out attempting a safety squeeze bunt, and Dougherty came to the plate. The affable Irishman topped a soft roller toward Brown, who scooped the ball up flawlessly and tossed it to Kling for what should have been an easy force of Rohe. Kling, trying to tag the runner too quickly, had the ball bound off the tip of his mitt, and Rohe thundered over the plate.

The Sox got a second tally the following frame, and again Kling played a major role. Altrock worked Brown for a leadoff walk and was sacrificed to second by Hahn. Jones singled to right-center, and Hofman brought the crowd to its feet with a brilliant throw that cut down Altrock at the plate by a yard. Jones, who had taken second on Hofman's heave, raced to third on a passed ball by Kling and sprinted across the plate on Isbell's bloop single to left.

The Cubs fought back with their lone tally in the bottom of the sixth. Kling, trying to atone for his miscues, led off with a base on balls. After fouling off two bunt attempts, Brown chopped a high bouncer over Altrock's head into center that moved the runner to second. Both men were advanced by Hofman's sacrifice, and Kling trotted across the plate a moment later when one of Altrock's sweeping curveballs hit the ground and eluded Sullivan's mitt. Sheckard's high fly to short left-center was nabbed by Tannehill, who made an over-the-shoulder catch and held Brown at third. Schulte then hit a hard drive to Rohe, who threw it low and wide toward first. Donahue stretched, plucked the ball from the air just as it was about to touch the grass, and rolled over on his back with his heel still touching the bag. This fielding gem saved the Sox, and they went into the bottom of the ninth protecting their 2–1 margin.

With two out in the last frame, the Cubs' hopes were kept alive when Chance laced a single to center. Steinfeldt, however, was not up to the challenge and lofted Altrock's first offering high into center. Manager Jones "began a crazy war dance of joy" as he loped to where the ball would descend. Waving his arms in anticipation, he clutched the sphere tightly and jumped in the air.[18]

Thousands of Sox rooters, delirious with joy, rushed onto the field in an attempt to carry their blue-clad heroes Altrock and Rohe from the field. At least two dozen police stormed into their midst, formed a ring around the two players, and escorted them to an exit.[19]

In the safety of their dressing quarters, amid the howls of their fans outside the locked door, Jones spoke for his team. "I was not surprised by the result," he admitted cheerfully. "It seems to be our luck to have everything break right for us when it looks darkest."[20] Comiskey, beaming broadly, flatly predicted: "They'll never beat us now."[21]

Murphy, downcast over both the score and his barely half-filled stadium, tried to brush aside reporters as he left for his office. Undaunted, the ceaseless harangue continued until he abruptly halted, wheeled, and snapped: "One swallow does not make a summer."[22] Breaking suddenly into a smile, he added: "I might add that one snowstorm does not make a winter, but it keeps fans away from ball games. The Sox licked us squarely today, but we'll be at the south side grounds at 2:30 o'clock tomorrow just the same."[23]

Despite prayers from the faithful, the weather worsened for the second contest. At game time the temperature hovered near freezing and icy winds swirled snow squalls around

Comiskey's park at the corner of 39th Avenue and Wentworth, leading Charles Dryden to write sarcastically: "To a sane person, had one been present, the scene suggested an open air retreat for the feeble-minded, with a white plague cure on the side."[24] Nevertheless, 12,595 donned mid-winter gear to witness Doc White try to best Ed Reulbach and give the American Leaguers a commanding two-game lead. To the discomfort to the shivering masses, once again the beginning of the contest was delayed briefly, this time to permit admirers of Fielder Jones to gather at home plate and present him with a ninety-six piece silver service valued at $500.[25]

Neither team scored in the first, and the Cubs' second began innocently with Chance fanning. Steinfeldt singled sharply to left, and Tinker placed a perfect bunt single toward third. Evers hit a bounder to Isbell, which appeared certain to result in a double play. Isbell, however, tried to backhand the ball to Tannehill, who was nowhere near the errant toss. Steinfeldt scored on the error, and the runners advanced to second and third. Kling was intentionally passed, loading the sacks for Reulbach. The hurler laid down a beautiful sacrifice bunt, scoring Tinker and sending Evers to third. Hofman beat out an infield grounder to short, driving in the third run of the inning. On the play, however, Kling exercised poor base running by rounding third so far that he was picked off and thrown out trying to score in the run-down.

In the third, Schulte walked but was forced at second by Chance. The Cub pilot then stole second. Sullivan's wild throw on the play permitted him to move to third, and he was driven in by Steinfeldt's single to left. After that, as Charles Dryden wrote, "Doctor White was taken back to the warming pan. The air was too keen for the Doctor, who looked like a pallid icicle before he cut loose the first ball."[26]

The Sox cut into the Cub lead by scoring one run on a walk, wild pitch, and an error by Tinker, but the Cubs matched that tally with one of their own off reliever Frank Owen in the sixth. Steinfeldt opened the inning with his third single of the day but was forced at second by Tinker. Evers moved Tinker to second with a single to short left. The two runners then executed a double steal, and Tinker was sent home when Sullivan's attempt to throw him out at third sailed into the crowd.

In the seventh the Sox threatened when Rohe led off with a walk and Donahue singled to center with what proved to be the only hit off Reulbach in the game. However, the Cub twirler settled down and retired the next three batters.

In the top of the eighth, the Cubs sent two more men across the plate on a singles by Chance and Tinker, two stolen bases, and a wild pitch. Watching the Cubs coast to their 7–1 triumph, Dryden observed that once they found the range against Sox pitching "Chance and his men mounted the merry-go-round and rode it to death."[27]

Because of the lopsided score and the frigid conditions, an exodus from the park had begun at the end of the fifth inning, and there was only a small crowd of loyal Cub rooters remaining to congratulate their heroes. However, Chance and his men were escorted to their carriages and sent off to their homes amid lusty cheers.[28] Among those present at the conclusion of the contest was federal judge, and future commissioner of baseball, Kenesaw Mountain Landis, a devout Cub fan, who joined in the taunts against the Sox fans by shouting: "What league is it your team plays in?"[29] When Sox supporters replied that he was a "fuzzy haired old weasel," the Judge shook his cane at them and bellowed: "I'll take on the whole lot of you."[30]

The Series moved back to West Side Park for the third battle. The skies had cleared and, although there was no threat of precipitation, the temperature remained, as Dryden joked, "colder than a married lady's feet."[31]

For five innings Ed Walsh and Jack Pfiester matched zeroes on the scoreboard, and the only opportunity for the 13,667 fans to warm themselves through cheering came when one of the groundskeeper's pet hens escaped its coop and strutted around the outfield in the bottom of the fifth frame. Dryden captured the moment for *Tribune* readers: "Limping around on half-frozen feet in center-field, the forlorn biddy presented an odd baseball parade—a foul [sic] in fair territory. It was said that the hen escaped from the incurable ward in the hospital across the way and sought congenial company in the ball yard. Once the demented creature tried to attract the kindly notice of Joe Tinker. He owns a chicken ranch at Kansas City and has been known to adopt homeless and deserving hens of good character. But, alas! Joe was too busy toiling at his chosen profession of shortstopping to heed the mute appeals. There wasn't a spot on which the hen could perch, all the choice seats back of the diamond being taken by roosters in derby hats. Besides, she didn't have a dollar to her name. As a last resort the hen offered to go out of her class and lay cold storage goose eggs for whichever side might need her service. Nick Altrock chased the henlet off the field, but it is rumored that Mr. Comiskey later signed the homeless hen at her own terms. Her job is to lay goose eggs for him the rest of the Series."[32]

Tannehill led off the sixth with a single that just eluded Steinfeldt's outstretched glove. Trying to prevent a sacrifice, Pfiester worked too carefully to Walsh and walked him. Eddie Hahn stepped into the box with the intention of advancing the runners, but, as he squared around to bunt, the pitch hit him in the nose, "breaking the bone as if it were made of clay."[33] Dryden, one of the most literary and witty pioneer writers assigned to cover sporting events, captured the drama of the moment, writing: "Hurried calls for a doctor to diagnose the nose brought no response. All the medical men present had their legs embalmed in horse robes and furs. To unwrap would invite personal disaster."[34]

With the crowd still hushed, teammates helped Hahn to his feet, took him to the bench, wrapped him in sweaters, and then received assistance to take him to a nearby hospital.[35] Amid loud cheers and applause as he passed behind home plate on his way to receive medical attention, Hahn, his bloodied face partially hidden by a towel, was blocked by a group of photographers who asked him to smile for a picture. To break through their lines, he managed a wan grimace.[36]

Bill (Tip) O'Neill took Hahn's place at first, filling the bases. With two strikes on him, the next batter, Manager Jones, popped a low foul behind the plate. Kling dashed back, leaned far over into the stands, and grabbed the ball just as it was about to drop among the first row spectators. Isbell than fanned on three outside curves, leaving it up to Rohe not to squander the opportunity.

As Rohe stepped to the plate, Kling looked up and sneered: "So the lucky stiff is up again. I guess you're going to look for another high fast one. Busher, you don't get another pitch like that if the Series lasts until Christmas."[37] Kling, confident he had outwitted the inexperienced opponent, then signaled for a high fastball toward the inside of the plate. Rohe swung and the ball traveled on a line over Steinfeldt's head to left. Sheckard vainly raced after it but could only watch it bound over the wall and into the seats for a ground rule triple.

The day's laurels belonged to Rohe and Walsh. Of the former, Joe S. Jackson, sports editor of the *Detroit Free Press*, predicted: "If the Sox win the Series, Rohe is assured of a lifetime job with Comiskey, as Isbell has been holding one for his work in past big races. Perhaps Rohe will replace Issy as the family pet. The big second-sacker is about done. His work today was again uncertain in the field, while he struck out three times, once with the bases full, and hit a long fly good for the first run. Without Davis he is of no use."[38] The latter, whose two-hit, twelve strikeout hurling led the Sox to their 3–0 triumph, was eulogized by those who covered the contest. Typical of the praise was the observation from one writer who marveled that, "from first to last Walsh had the Cubs marooned in a cloud of doubt. He flimflammed the Cubs with his misty vapor ball. They didn't know where they were at."[39] Another scribe concurred, stating: "When the game began the Nationals swung viciously at Walsh's delivery, but before the contest was half over they were fishing for the ball, seemingly trying merely to touch it."[40] Comiskey and Ban Johnson were vociferously optimistic. The "Old Roman," as the Sox owner was known, told Sox rooters as he was entering his automobile after the game: "There is nothing to it now."[41] Johnson, accompanied by Chairman Herrmann of the National Commission, beamed and said: "It was one of the grandest battles I ever saw anywhere. There is nothing more to it now than the shouting."[42]

For the Cubs, Murphy, picking up on his opening game remark, told newshawks: "Two swallows do not make a summer, nor do two games win a world's championship. We'll be out at the south side once more tomorrow to repeat our previous performance there."[43]

The Cub owner proved a prophet, as the Cubs' Mordecai Brown bested Altrock in a masterful pitching duel 1–0 witnessed by 18,385 fans basking under a warm autumn sun. On hand to bring the Sox luck was the hen from the previous day. White Sox rooters had outfitted her with white stockings on her legs and a white ribbon around her neck. After the loss, Dryden jested: "Back to the coop with the hoodoo hen is the wail of the southsiders. She is low-browed and dotty and doesn't know her lines. After Mr. Comiskey had imported her from the west side at severe expense, the hoodoo hen laid goose eggs for the wrong party. So much for the perversity of the female species in general."[44] The deciding tally came in the seventh. Chance opened the inning with what should have been a harmless fly to right. Isbell misjudged the ball, and Hahn, courageously back in right with white plaster holding his nose in place and breathing through straws inserted into his nostrils, lost the ball in the sun. Steinfeldt moved Chance to second, and Tinker sacrificed his manager over one more base. Evers then drove Altrock's first pitch to left for a single, and Chance crossed the plate.

Gamely, the Sox tried to rally in the ninth. With two out, Jones drew a walk and moved to second on a passed ball by Kling. Isbell lined a shot straight up the middle of the diamond headed towards Brown's face. In self-defense the pitcher threw up his hands and was knocked flat on his back by the force of the ball hitting his glove. Brown scrambled to his feet and fired a strike to Chance, ending the game and preventing the next batter, Rohe, from another opportunity to be a hero.

After the game, Fielder Jones railed at his club, pointing out that they were lucky that the Series was tied. The Sox, he noted, had gone 11–113, a puny .096 average, in the four games. Jones singled out clean-up hitter Frank Isbell, who like Jones had only one hit in the Series, for a verbal tongue-lashing. "Issy, you're a white-livered so-and-so. You've choked up to here," he screamed, running his fingers across his neck, "and you have less guts than a gnat."[45] Some writers thought Jones was trying to ignite a fire under his players by this tirade, but most thought his anger was inspired by the morning's announcement that the winning share of the purse would be nearly $1,300 per man, while players on the losing end would get but $450.[46]

With the visitors winning each of the first four games, the White Sox did not mind returning to the Cubs' domicile for the fifth contest. Again the sun afforded warmth, and more than 30,000 spectators witnessed Walsh, dubbed by Dryden as "The Human Spitz," face Reulbach.[47] Of those watching, 23, 257 paid Murphy for the privilege of sitting in his park, while the remainder were outside the grounds "packed on adjoining roofs, clinging to telegraph poles and wires like monkeys, or fretting behind locked gates trying to gain from the incessant yelling some idea of how the tide of battle was going."[48] Fans were so eager to get inside the lot that just before the game started, they smashed down the guard fence in front of the left-field bleachers and had to be repelled by police.[49]

Cub loyalists and even Chance tried to bring the National Leaguers luck on their home grounds. Chance ordered the Cubs to don their traveling gray uniforms instead of the prescribed white suits because they had not lost while in the darker garb.[50] The Board of Trade purchased a pair of black bear cubs and presented them to Chance before the game, after they had been paraded around the field.[51] In their dugout was a huge horseshoe made by former heavyweight boxing champion Bob Fitzsimmons, who donated it to the cause of helping his favorites.[52] Even the "Hoodoo Hen" had been welcomed back and was in her familiar coop.[53]

The game itself was characterized by Joe S. Jackson as "a mixture of everything that ought not to be seen in a game of ball on which a title hangs, but with dabs and splashes of brilliant doings without which a championship cannot be snatched."[54] Dryden echoed that sentiment, saying "but for the size of the crowd, the game might have been played in a loose back lot of a livery stable."[55]

Brown was tapped for a run in the first on Hahn's leadoff single to center, which Tinker might have flagged down, Jones' sacrifice, and a ground rule double to right by Isbell. With a runner perched on second and the heart of the order coming to the plate, Sox fans dreamed of putting the game quickly out of reach. Such was not to be, as George Davis, making his first appearance in the Series, hit a weak grounder to Reulbach. Isbell, who had broken for third, was caught in a rundown. Ignoring the basic rule in such an instance of giving the batter time to advance an extra base, Isbell opted for a futile attempt to return to second, thereby sacrificing himself and forcing Davis to stay at first. This mental error cost the Sox a run, as Rohe promptly drilled a line drive past Steinfeldt into the left-field crowd for another ground rule two-bagger. Had Davis been on second, he would have scored, rather than being forced to stop at third. Donahue was intentionally passed, filling the bases, to bring up Dougherty. The Irish lad chopped a high bounder, which looked like a sure safe blow, over the pitcher's head, but Evers raced in, snared the ball, and fired it to first, the throw barely beating the runner to the bag.

Having escaped the Sox threat with minimal damage, the Cubs struck back in their half of the frame. Hofman singled to right and moved to second on Sheckard's sacrifice. Schulte beat out a grounder to third, but Hofman could not advance. Chance was hit by an errant spitball, filling the sacks for Steinfeldt, who drilled a drive to short. Davis came up with the ball cleanly and tossed it to Isbell in plenty of time to start a double play. Issy, however, heaved the ball past Donahue and into the crowd, permitting two unearned runs to cross the plate and Steinfeldt to perch safely on second. Tinker tried to catch the Sox off guard by laying down a bunt. Walsh charged in, fielded the ball cleanly, and his throw would have caught the on-rushing Tinker had Donahue not dropped it. Steinfeldt trudged home safely, but the uprising ended when Tinker was cut down trying for second.

The Sox drove Reulbach to the showers in the third when the first two batters, Isbell and Davis, laced ground rule doubles into the crowd in left-field and right-field respectively. Reliever Pfiester rose to the challenge and struck out Rohe but hit the next batter, Donahue, in the middle of his back. Dougherty forced Donahue at second, but moved Davis to third. With Sullivan at the plate, Pfiester took a full windup and the two runners pulled off a double steal, Davis sliding across the plate with the tying marker.

In the fourth, the Sox unloaded more slugging power, driving four more runs across the plate. Walsh opened the inning with a walk but was forced at second by Hahn. Jones blooped a single to left that advanced the runner a base. Isbell drove Hahn across and moved Jones to the opposite corner bag with his third consecutive double, this one into right-center. Davis sent both his teammates home with a double just inside the bag at third. Sensing the game was getting out of reach, Chance yanked Pfiester and waved Orval Overall to the mound. Rohe worked the new hurler for a pass. Donahue then doubled to left, driving in Davis. Dougherty lofted a fly which Sheckard speared with a lunge, wheeled, and fired a strike to Kling, who ended the inning by tagging Rohe.

The Cubs got one run back in the bottom of the fourth on Rohe's throwing error, a walk, double steal by Tinker and Evers, and a wild pitch by Walsh. The Sox, however, regained their four run lead in the sixth when Isbell drilled another double to right and scored on Rohe's single to right.

In the bottom of the sixth, the Cubs launched what proved to be their final assault. Evers and Kling both grounded weakly to Davis at short to start the frame, and it seemed that Walsh had finally gained control over his spitter. The erratic Walsh then issued passes to Overall and Hofman, bringing Sheckard to the plate. The hard-hitting outfielder swung mightily and topped a roller to Rohe, who committed his second error. With the sacks now loaded, Schulte lined a blast over Jones' head in center for a ground-double, driving in the final two Cub tallies and leaving them on the short end of an 8–6 score. Thus, as I.E. Sanborn wrote, "in spite of the rankest exhibition of fielding a team of champions ever gave in public," the Sox overcame their six errors and inched within one victory of the championship of the diamond world.[56]

On a bright, sunny Sunday afternoon, 19,249 baseball fanatics crammed into South Side Park to see if Three-Finger Mordecai Brown could come back on one day's rest and best Doc White, who had hurled three scoreless innings the previous day to save the game for Walsh. Outside the stadium, at least an equal number of people milled on the streets and vacant lots pleading for obliging spectators in the top rows to yell down accounts of the events on field. Seeing the enthusiastic throng inside and outside of the ball field, Dryden marveled: "What Mr. Comiskey needs is a rubber park warranted to stretch a mile in each direction."[57]

The drama seemed to engulf the entire city. Residents gathered outside the *Tribune* office to await bulletins. As it was the Sabbath, some ministers cut their services short so their parishioners would not miss the game, while others arranged to have bulletins delivered so that they could read them to the worshippers.[58]

In the clubhouse before the contest, Chance put his arm around Brown's shoulders. "We're all relying on you," he said earnestly. "You've got to keep us in this thing, so we can beat them in a seventh game."[59] The arm-weary hurler, simply nodded, but less than thirty minutes later they was trudging back to the bench, head bowed, after surrendering eight hits, a walk, and six runs while only retiring four batters.

The Cubs came out snarling, with Hofman starting the game with a single and moving to second when Dougherty fumbled the ball. He moved to third on Sheckard's sacrifice and finished his trip around the sacks on Schulte's double into the right-field crowd.

With even greater ferocity, the home team retaliated in its half of the opening frame. Hahn began the attack by lining a one-hop grounder off the glove of Evers, but he was forced at second when Jones' sacrifice attempt went awry. Isbell, still fuming from Jones' castigation, continued his hitting streak with a single to right that moved his manager up one base.

George Davis then skied a deep drive to right. Schulte drifted back to the edge of the crowd, patted his glove, and waited for the ball to settle harmless in his hands. Suddenly, he wobbled and stumbled awkwardly, and Davis' drive bounced on the turf for a run scoring double. Schulte and Hofman, the latter having witnessed what had happened, raced in to lodge a protest with Umpire Silk O'Loughlin, claiming that a policeman stationed along the edge of the crowd had interfered with the play by jostling Schulte.[60] The arbiter dismissed the allegation, and ordered the contest to proceed.

Donahue then doubled in two more Sox, giving them a 3–1 lead. As Dryden observed cynically: "This one swift kick in the bloomers applied to Mr. Schulte in the opening round wrestled the world's championship from the Spuds. Anyhow, it helped some. This disaster upset the sanguine temperament of the men who had picked the diamond cuff buttons ... and once [the Sox] had started they went through the Cub lines like a thirteen inch shell tearing new mesh."[61]

In the second, the American Leaguers put the championship in their back pockets by scoring four more times and giving White a 7–1 margin. The assault against the great Brown was all the more stunning because it occurred after the first two batters had been retired on easy grounders. Hahn singled to left, and Cub rooters grew increasingly uneasy when Jones worked Brown for a pass. Isbell then hit what appeared to be an inning ending grounder to the right of second-base. As Evers set himself to make the play, Tinker raced in front of him in a vain effort to cut off the ball. This caused Evers momentarily to lose sight of the ball, and it skipped off his glove for a single. Davis then tore a liner toward short. Tinker leaped high into the air, but the ball tipped off his fingers and two runs crossed the plate. After Brown reloaded the bases by walking Rohe, Chance brought in Overall. Donahue greeted the reliever with a single off Evers' glove, sending Isbell home and keeping the sacks filled. Dougherty then concluded the scoring by drawing a pass, forcing in Davis.

The National Leaguers got one run back in the fifth on Kling's infield roller, Overall's double, and a ground out by Sheckard, but the Sox matched it in the eighth when Hahn led off with his fourth hit of the game, a single to left, and scored on Isbell's single to center. Battling to the end, Chance's men tried to rally in the ninth. With one out, Evers doubled to right. As he stood on second, his team hopelessly beaten, in a show of sportsmanship Evers reached out and shook Isbell's hand, congratulating him on the Sox victory.[62] Evers was sacrificed to third, and pinch-hitter Harry (Doc) Gessler drew a pass. Gessler moved to second on Hofman's run scoring single to left. The bases became loaded again when Rohe booted Sheckard's roller, but Schulte grounded to first to end the threat and the Series.

As thousands of American League partisans poured onto the field, the players raced to the safety of the clubhouse. In Comiskey's box behind first-base, the Sox owner and Ban Johnson exchanged a hurried embrace and congratulatory kiss before being escorted away by police to protect them from adoring fans, while on the other side of the diamond Murphy was surrounded by good-natured Sox fans demanding a speech.[63] The Cub owner waved a Sox banner that had been thrust into his hand and said graciously: "The best team won because they played better ball and deserved to win. I am for Chicago and will say that Chicago has the best two ball teams in the world. The contests have been well contested, and Chicago people should be proud of both clubs. If we had to lose, I would rather lose to Comiskey's club than any other club in the world."[64] He then offered three cheers for the victors and added: "Chicago now has the world champions and also the club which won the greatest number of games on record."[65] This elicited three cheers for the Cubs, after which Murphy praised the city's fans, saying: "These contests have been made possible by the excellent patronage which Chicago has given to its two ball clubs, thus enabling the management to go out and secure good players. The games of this Series have been fought fairly and squarely, and we accept defeat gracefully."[66] Amid shouts of "Murphy, you're all right," the Cub owner headed to Comiskey's private office to offer his congratulations.[67]

Inside his sanctuary, Comiskey was savoring his seventh league title and third world championship, the last of which had been achieved exactly twenty years previously to the day, when his St. Louis Browns defeated the Chicago Nationals. Comiskey responded to Murphy's knock and admitted his friendly adversary. The portly Murphy strode toward the graying "Old Roman," extended his hand, and said: "Commy, I want to shake hands and congratulate you. If I had to lose, there is no one I'd rather lose to than you." Comiskey replied: "Well, Charlie, I'd rather beat any other club in the country than yours. Maybe we'll get another whack at each other next year. I've only evened up for [the Sox defeat in the intra-city series] last fall, you know." Smiling, Murphy concurred: "That's right. I hope both teams win again next year and that we'll have another meeting next fall."[68]

Meanwhile, outside the victors' clubhouse door at least a thousand screaming admirers were demanding souvenirs from their heroes. Frank Isbell courageously opened the door a crack and tossed out several pairs of socks. A wild scramble ensued in which the lucky survivors of the battle, although bloodied, bruised, and clothes torn to shreds, left clutching their trophies.[69]

After the mob was finally herded away by police, late that afternoon and into the evening reporters sought statements from both winners and losers. Comiskey was still so overjoyed that he found it hard to speak coherently, rambling: "Happy? I'm happier over this victory than any other pennant winning proposition I was ever mixed up in. Give all the credit to Fielder Jones and the grand, game boys in the white stockings. I never saw a ball club with half their gameness. Whoever heard of a team making an uphill fight from seventh position in its league to be the baseball champion of the world. They are the best in the world, and I am proud of every mother's son of them. There is nothing too good for them, and every member of my team knows that I am, and will be, his friend after his playing days are over. My share of any glory rests entirely upon discovering and developing the greatest manager of his time. Fielder Jones is a leader and a general. I got him the players, and he did the rest."[70] Pausing briefly to catch his breath, he continued: "My admiration for Chance as a manager, player, and man is unbounded. He takes defeat manfully, and while I rejoice at our success, I regret that Chance's men were our opponents."[71]

Jones echoed Comiskey's tribute, stating: "I can't say too much about the Cubs. They are the finest bunch of ball players I ever played against. There never was a time during the Series they were not dangerous opponents. I did not consider the championship won until I saw Schulte go out at first in the ninth inning."[72]

Not unexpectedly, Ban Johnson, belligerently reveling in the joy of humbling the National League not only in the World Series but also in the intra-city series between the Yankees and Giants, uttered no conciliatory remarks. "From the first, I have been absolutely confident that the Sox would win," he asserted, "and their well earned victory pleased me more than I can say."[73]

National League officials were generous in their praise of the new champions. President Pulliam candidly admitted: "I was mistaken in my judgment of the strength of the White Sox. I never dreamed that Manager Jones' men could down a club that had made a runaway race of the National League pennant battle. They beat the Cubs at their own game — batting — and won the championship fairly and squarely."[74] John Heydler, secretary and future president of the senior circuit, offered an obvious analysis, saying: "The

Series was fairly contested. The team that we expected to bat well did not do so, and the team we expected not to bat well did the slugging. That's baseball for you."[75] National Commission Chairman Herrmann, owner of the National League Cincinnati Reds and supposedly an unbiased observer, let his prejudice show only slightly when he stated: "Those who figured on the result undoubtedly figured the White Sox entirely too low. The best team won simply because it outplayed its opponents. The games were the greatest in the history of the national pastime, and had it not been for the extreme cold on the first two, and possibly the third, days the crowds that would have been played to would have likewise been the greatest. The Series was a grand success from my standpoint, and there is honor in defeat by such a foe. Saluting the world champions, I attest my admiration for, and pride in, the Cubs."[76]

The Cubs, privately seething at their embarrassing loss and at receiving only $437.50 per man from the gate receipts, vainly attempted to assume a sportsmanlike public demeanor.[77] Murphy issued a press release, which implied that the best of seven game format for the World Series contributed to the Cubs' downfall. "The White Sox defeated us in the short series and are entitled to all the honors and usufruct which goes with victory," he wrote. "The games were conducted admirably under the supervision of the National Commission — the Supreme Court of baseball — and not a word of fault can be found with the work of the umpires. Our team won more games of ball this year than any club ever did, and I naturally thought it would win the Series. But it is a consolation to myself, as well as to the baseball enthusiasts of Chicago, to know that the greatest honor in organized baseball — the championship of the world — remains in this city. I extend the hand of congratulations to the victors, as much as the vanquished can gracefully do that."[78]

After reading Murphy's statement and a subsequent letter to the National Commission, acerbic *New York Sun* sportswriter Joe Vila, an ardent supporter of the American League, replied: "Well, well! Chubby Charlie must have tumbled through the earth when the Sox won! He didn't object to the length of the Series before the games were played, did he? Oh, no! But now he has informed the National Commission that in the future the World Series should consist of thirteen games instead of seven, in order to 'eliminate all chances for luck.' Well, the National League is a minor league organization. It is a joke, and the public is now onto it with both feet."[79]

A grim-visaged Chance permitted his disappointment, as well as a hint of bitterness, to intrude into his comments. "It was the greatest Series ever played," he said, "and we've got to give it to Comiskey's champions. The Sox played grand, game baseball and outclassed us in this Series. But there is one thing I just never will believe, and that is that the White Sox are a better ball club than the Cubs. We did not play our game, and that is all there is to it. The Sox, on the contrary, were fighting us in the gamest kind of a way. They fought so hard that they made us like it and like it well. We played our hardest to win, but in this Series we did not show we were the best club, but we are, just the same. It was a hard Series to lose, but you can't win all the time. Next year you will see the Cubs come back again for another battle, for I think we will once again win the pennant. We are coming back next year, remember that."[80]

Late that night, long after the news conferences had ended but the street dancing and drinking were still at their peak, admiring fans carried George Davis to the home of Manager Jones, who was entertaining Doc White. In response to their demands, Jones made a brief speech lauding the team and its fans. Then he pulled from his pocket a slip of paper. "Look at this," he said proudly. "A certified check handed me by President Comiskey after the game. He said to me, 'Take this and divide it up equally among the boys, share and share alike.' That's one sample of appreciation."[81] Another such example came when Comiskey announced that each player's souvenir of the championship would be a charm, made of fourteen carat gold, valued at $75, which could be worn either as a fob or on a vest chain.[82] Comiskey noted proudly that the presents were much finer and more expensive than the buttons distributed to the Giants the preceding year, which had cost only $50 apiece.[83] The charms, designed and manufactured by a Chicago jeweler, had one side representing the globe encircled by a band marked "World Champions" in black enamel and White Sox" in white enamel. Over the globe was the raised team insignia of a winged foot over which was the lower limb of a player in white socks and blue trousers, the team colors. The winged foot rested on a platinum "home plate," which was grouped by two crossed baseball bats below which was a platinum baseball. Above the globe were eagle's wings between which was a diamond. Two full-color waving American flags entwined the entire grouping.[84]

Only mildly discordant notes were raised. Some critics, doubtless who had lost money betting on the favorites, questioned Chance's handling of his pitching staff, especially his refusal to utilize either Lungren or Taylor. I. E. Sanborn quickly rose to Chance's defense, saying that Lundgren had been batted hard by the Sox in the 1905 intra-city series and that Taylor still was tainted by his alleged throwing of games in the 1903 intra-city series.[85] Others, such as New York baseball writer W.M. Rankin, attributed the Cubs' defeat to Chance's managerial inexperience in all phases of the game. Unfairly comparing the Cub pilot to Connie Mack of the Athletics and John McGraw of the Giants, Rankin wrote: "While Chance did exceedingly well during the past season, he will know more after he has handled his ball team a few more years. His mistakes were of such a serious nature that no veteran manager would have been guilty of them, and they cost him dearly. He has lots to learn before he can be classed with the best and shrewdest managers of the game."[86] In response, *The Sporting News* editorialized: "The leader of the Cubs may have erred, but his grand record in the first full season of his managerial career should shield him from charges of incapacity founded solely upon conjecture."[87]

Rankin and Joseph M. Cummings, a Baltimore scribe, also fumed that the inclement weather demonstrated that the season needed to be reduced. "Unless a race is so heated that it requires a final game to decide the question of supremacy, the public does not care to witness games when overcoats and ear mufflers are an actual necessity," Rankin raged. "Just as good results in a financial way could be obtained if the regular season began about May 15 and ended about September 15. Four months of baseball, played on every clear day of the week before large crowds, should suffice for one season. If the post-season Series could be started early in the third week of September it would certainly prove more satisfactory to all concerned."[88] Cummings chose to broach the problem in a lighter vein, suggesting: "Either the schedule ought to be cut to 140 games or only clubs that can show a decent temperature this time of the year be declared eligible to win the pennant. As a settlement to the whole difficulty, since there seems so much disinclination to cut the list of games down from 154, I suggest that Baltimore be admitted to the National League and that it be the National League's perpetual pennant winner, while Washington be 'promoted' to the rank of perpetual American League winner. Between the two cities I believe we could guarantee at least a decent height of the thermometer until Thanksgiving Day."[89]

Statistics and cold weather aside, what should be remembered as the lasting legacies of the 1906 World Series are Chance's promise to return to the Fall Classic the following year, which he fulfilled, and an act of treachery by Comiskey regarding the $15,000 to be distributed among his players. This apparent uncharacteristic generosity on the part of the notoriously frugal Comiskey was revealed for what it actually was during contract negotiations during the winter. At that time, Comiskey informed "his boys" that the $15,000 was not a bonus for winning the championship, but rather an advance on their 1907 salaries.[90] The resultant discord among the team over this deception dropped the Sox into third in 1907, and it was not until 1917 that the Pale Hose captured another league title, while the Cubs became a perpetual diamond power during those same years.

CUBS VS. TIGERS, 1907

When the Chicago Cubs assembled to prepare for the 1907 season, Chance made sure that they had not forgotten their post-season debacle of the previous fall. "You're a bunch of stiffs," he bellowed. "Maybe you so-and-sos have learned your lesson in overconfidence, and what happens when you underrate the other so-and-sos."[1]

Despite taking their manager's message to heart and giving themselves an opportunity for post-season atonement by amassing a 107–45 mark and romping to the pennant by seventeen games over the second-place Pittsburgh Pirates, the Cubs were beset with criticism. Fielder Jones spoke for the skeptics when he noted that only the Philadelphia Phillies and New York Giants joined the Cubs and Pirates as having winning records, and that playing such weak competition did not adequately prepare the Cubs for the world championship struggle. "The Cubs are at a great disadvantage in not having gone through enough hard battles during the season," the White Sox manager explained. "They outclassed the rest of the National League so far that they didn't have to fight enough to prepare for a hard series. The Cubs are not at all representative of the National League, being in a class above that organization, as shown by the ease with which they won their pennants."[2]

Although the Cubs had clinched the pennant by August 1 and did not have to exert themselves for the last two months of the season, no one could question their fierce determination and competitive spirit. Led again by their fabled infield of "The Peerless Leader" Chance, a ten-year veteran who batted .293 with a lone home run and 49 runs batted in at first, fiery Johnny Evers, who hit .250, with two round-trippers and 5 runs driven in, at second, steady Joe Tinker (.221, 1, 36) at short, and Harry Steinfeldt (.266, 1, 70) at third, the Cubs were nearly flawless in the field. With Johnny Kling (.284, 1, 43) behind the plate, the Chicago inner defense was considered by baseball analysts to be the best in the major leagues, despite the fact that two of its members had not spoken to each other throughout the season.

Early in the campaign, Tinker fired a ball from ten feet away as hard as he could to Evers and broke a finger on the second-sacker's right hand. Evers cursed at Tinker and received laughter in response. Evers, who related the event nearly three decades later to Joe Williams of the *New York World-Telegram*, added: "We still took signs from each other, but we didn't speak. What one guy thinks about another guy on a ball team doesn't mean a thing. Tinker and myself hated each other, but we loved the Cubs. We wouldn't fight for each other, but we'd come close to killing people for our team. That was one of the answers to the Cubs' success."[3]

Two-thirds of the outfield was the same as in the previous year's World Series, with Frank (Wildfire) Schulte (.287, 2, 32) in right and eleven-year veteran Jimmy Sheckard (.267, 1, 36) covering left. Patrolling center-field was Jimmy Slagle (.258, 0, 32), who had missed the previous year's Series because of an ankle injury. Ironically, Artie Hofman, who bad batted .304 in the 1906 classic as Slagle's replacement, hurt his knee in the final week of the 1907 season and was forced to witness the Series from the bench, relinquishing his role back to Slagle.

Chance's pitching staff again topped the senior circuit with a 1.73 earned run average and thirty shutouts. Right-handers Mordecai Brown (20–6, 1.39) and Orval Overall (23–7, 1.68, and a league best eight shutouts) combined for 501 innings pitched. Supporting these workhorses were right-handers Carl Lundgren (18–7, 1.17) and Ed Reulbach (17–4, 1.69) and southpaw Jack Pfiester (14–9, 1.15).[4]

The American League race had been spirited, with Philadelphia, Chicago, and Detroit still in contention entering the final week of the season. However, the Athletics' pitching faltered, and White Sox owner Charles Comiskey's "bonus fiasco" ultimately came back to haunt him as his team faded in the stretch and finished third. This enabled Manager Hughie Jennings' Tigers to seize the pennant in a late rush with a 92–58 mark and finish 1½ games ahead of the A's and 5½ ahead of the defending champion White Sox.

I.E. Sanborn, Comiskey's friend and apologist, bemoaned the fate of the "Old Roman." Writing for *The Sporting News*, Sanborn stated bitterly that the Sox owner had been "thrown down by a trio of players who owed him a huge debt of gratitude and repaid him by keeping themselves so far out of condition they were of little use during the race."[5] While refraining from publicly naming the guilty parties, Sanborn was referring to infielders Frank Isbell and George Davis, whose batting averages plummeted thirty-six and thirty-nine points respectively, and Nick Altrock, whose victories dropped from twenty to seven while his earned run average rose from 2.06 to 2.57.

A thin, freckle-faced, jocular Irishman, Hugh Jennings had played with John McGraw on the fabled Baltimore Orioles teams in the 1890s and won universal plaudits among diamond experts for lifting the Bengals from a dismal sixth place finish in 1906 to a league title. New York scribe Joe Vila characterized the thirty-eight-year-old, red-headed Tiger pilot as "a natural born leader, a plucky, enthusiastic hustler, who has accomplished more in one year than any other manager in a decade."[6]

While Jennings did bring fire to the Detroit team, what lifted them to the championship was a combination of youth, hitting strength, steady defense, and solid pitching. At the plate the "Tiges," as they were dubbed by *Detroit Free Press* sports editor Joe S. Jackson, led their league with a .266 batting average, 696 runs scored, seventy-five triples, and a .355 slugging average. Like the Cubs, the Tigers were paced by two fierce competitors who barely spoke to each other — Ty Cobb and Sam Crawford.[7] The heart of the Tigers was twenty-year-old right-field sensation Cobb, who paced the junior circuit with his .350 batting average, .473 slugging average, 212 hits, 119 runs batted in, forty-nine stolen bases, and a club-high five home runs. Joining Cobb in the outfield were twenty-seven-year-old Nebraska barber "Wahoo Sam" Crawford, the brilliant center-fielder who batted .323 with three homers and 81 runs batted in to go with a league-leading 102 in runs scored, and twenty-seven-year-old Davy Jones (.273, 0, 27) in left. The infield, while not as potent, was sure-handed and lightning fast. Bill (Rowdy) Coughlin (.243, 0, 46), who at twenty-nine was one of the oldest Tigers, guarded third. The middle of the infield consisted of twenty-six-year-old shortstop Charley O'Leary (.241, 0, 34) and former Cub second sacker Herman (Germany) Schaefer (.258, 1, 32), who was approaching his thirty-first birthday. First-base was manned by twenty-five-year-old Claude Rossman (.277, 0, 69).

The only weak spot among the Tigers' position players was behind the plate, where a trio of second year men — twenty-seven-year-olds Charlie (Boss) Schmidt (.244, 0, 23) and Fred Payne (.166, 0, 14) and twenty-four-year-old Jimmy Archer (.119, 0, 0) — demonstrated neither offensive nor defensive prowess. Fully aware that the Cubs had pilfered 235 bases during the season, Jennings wistfully admitted to Joe S. Jackson before the initial contest: "I'd give a million dollars if I had a Kling behind the bat."[8]

The Detroit mound corps boasted an impressive 2.33 earned run average and a pair of twenty-five game winners in thirty-one-year-old right-hander "Wild Bill" Donovan (25–4, 2.19) and thirty-year-old southpaw Ed (Twilight) Killian (25–13, 1.78). Rounding out Jennings' five man staff were erratic twenty-seven-year-old right-hander George Mullin (20–20, 2.59), thirty-year-old lefty Ed Siever (19–10, 2.16), and little used twenty-three-year-old right-hander Ed Willett (1–5, 3.70), the latter of whom accounted for a mere forty-nine of the 1,371 innings hurled by Tiger boxmen.

At five o'clock on the afternoon of the day before the Series opened, players from both squads, club owners, managers, and umpires met in Chicago's Congress Hotel with the National Commission to discuss rules and distribution of gate receipts. After selecting Hank O'Day of the National League and John Sheridan of the American to officiate the Series and determining that Manager Jennings could not use a police whistle to give signals, but could emit his famous "E-e-yah" cry from the third-base coaching box, Commissioner Chairman Garry Herrmann addressed the matter of money.[9]

The portly brewer, who spoke with a thick German accent even though he had lived in Cincinnati his entire life, reiterated an earlier Commission ruling that the gate receipts for the first four games played would be divided among the players on the basis of the winners receiving 60 percent and the losers 40 percent. Wanting to leave for dinner, Herrmann then asked wearily: "Has any player any questions to ask before the meeting is adjourned?"

To his surprise, Germany Schaefer, known for his clowning and practical jokes, stood up and proclaimed: "I have. I have a very important question."

"Yes, Schaefer," Herrmann said impatiently, "there are nine men on a side, three bases and a home plate, and over the fence is not out. Anything else you want to know?"

"Yeah," Schaefer said earnestly. "I wanna know whether the Commission considers a tie game a legal game?"

"What do you mean, Herman?" the Commissioner snapped.

"The players share in the first four games," Schaefer explained. "I now wanna know is a tie game a legal game as far as us players is concerned, or do we share in the Series until four games are played to a decision?"

"There is no chance whatsoever for a tie game in a championship series," Herrmann pontificated, obviously not knowing that there had been such an occurrence in 1885 between Chicago and St. Louis and another in 1890 between Brooklyn and Louisville.

"I don't care," yelled Schaefer, "I still want a ruling right now."

Herrmann then huddled with league presidents Ban Johnson and Harry Pulliam. After a brief conversation, Herrmann announced his decision: "Yes, Mr. Schaefer, it is the opinion of the National Commission that if a tie should occur it does not constitute a game. Our rules for playing a World Series decree that the players shall get all the receipts for the first four games played. So, if one contest results in neither side being the victor, the players will be awarded the gate receipts paid for the first five attendances."

"That's all I wanna know," snorted Schaefer.[10]

After the meeting, most of the owners laughed over the episode, but Frank Navin, secretary of the Detroit club, muttered: "Maybe it's all right, but just supposing it happens?" Cub President Charlie Murphy agreed that the chances were slight, but added that Herrmann was certainly being generous with other people's money.[11] Meanwhile, asked by his teammates and newsmen why he had brought the issue before the Commission, Schaefer explained that earlier in the week he had dreamt that the first game would end in a tie and thought he had better ask what might happen if, indeed, his dream came true.[12]

That evening the hotel lobbies were filled with diamond gossip and predictions. New York Giant ace Christy Mathewson, the hero of the 1905 Series when he shut out the Athletics three times, said in an interview: "I pick the Cubs to win the Series easily. There is nothing else to it. Chicago has the pitchers. Jennings' pitchers are good, but let me tell you those on Chicago's staff are superb. The past three or four weeks Detroit has had to make a good many runs to win. In other words, Jennings' pitchers have been hit hard. Even with Donovan in the game, the Tigers, in order to win, have had to do very heavy batting stunts. Wild Bill, in my opinion, is the only man who can win for Jennings—and baseball luck may turn against him in the Series. Kling will stop them in their attempts to steal bases, while the Cubs are apt to run wild and gain many points by their base running."[13]

Reaching the Tigers for comment was a more arduous task for scribes because upon the Detroiters' arrival at their downtown hotel, they were met by a jeering mob wielding clubs and stones and had to be escorted through the hostile forces by police.[14] Tiger Owner William Yawkey, a millionaire playboy who had inherited the team upon the death of his father in 1904, had been informed of possible violence by Cub fans, and responded by stationing Doc "Six-Gun" Crowe, a massive, powerful sheriff from Arizona, in the lobby to protect his employees.[15]

Waiting for Jennings to appear in the lobby of the Tigers' hotel to issue a statement, reporters, under the watchful eyes of Crowe, sought out team captain Bill Coughlin, the only vegetarian in the major leagues. During July and August, Coughlin had told scribes that he limited his diet to onions and cabbage. Asked what his winter regimen would be, Coughlin smiled and said that with the winner's share he and his mates would dine on "broiled squabs."[16]

Jennings, flashing the broad smile which had graced his countenance throughout the season, was flanked by two other Tigers known for their sunny dispositions, Donovan and Mullin, as he met writers.[17] "I won't say we're going to win," he said, "but we are going to try our hardest, and I think that will be hard enough to win. They are a grand set of ball players, those boys of mine, and they deserve all the credit for what they have done, for they have done it not I. They are as confident as I am that we can beat any team that walks, but they would rather prove it on the diamond than in the newspapers. If we do lose, we will take our hats off to a better team than we are just as gamely as we have fought for first place in the greatest race I ever went through."[18]

Although 8 to 5 favorites, the Cubs, having learned from the experience of the previous October, were modest regarding the potential outcome of the Series. "We are going into the game believing we are the better team and that we can win it," Chance said, quickly adding, "but with the knowledge that we must play every point out to the limit to win it."[19] Mordecai Brown, still recovering from a severe cold that had caused his arm muscles to tighten and made him doubtful to pitch in the upcoming battles, refused to comment, but displayed with pride a diamond scarf pin presented him by friends. The pin was gold and enamel and made in the shape of a baseball field with a green infield and white base lines encircling an initial B formed from diamonds.[20]

Local newspapers, however, were certain of a hometown triumph and even ran poetry submitted by Cub partisans. Typical was a limerick in the *Chicago Daily Journal* ridiculing Jennings' habit of chewing grass while coaching:

> We are waiting for grass-eating Hugh,
> Who eats timothy washed down with glue.
> We will welcome him here
> With a jovial cheer,
> And send him back home sad and blue.[21]

On a crisp, partly cloudy day, 24,377 eager fans jostled their way to their seats in Murphy's stadium at Polk and Lincoln Streets to witness a battle between Bill Donovan and Orval Overall. In an effort to reduce the number of ground rule doubles that had been hit in the West Side Park in the 1906 Series, Murphy had constructed temporary stands close to the foul lines and all around the field, except in right. Chance had requested a deep opening remain in that area to increase the difficulty for left-handed batters Cobb and Crawford to reach the crowd for a double or clear the fence for a home run.[22]

Shortly before Umpire O'Day was scheduled to call for the first pitch at 2:30 p.m., Ty Cobb was presented with a diamond-studded gold medal for winning his league's batting crown. Charles Dryden of the *Chicago Tribune* playfully noted that the crowd found it difficult to decide which was more dazzling, Cobb's shiny medallion or the wardrobe of O'Day, whom Dryden claimed was "the only living umpire who knows how to dress for the part."[23] According to Dryden's fashion report: "O'Day's blue serge suit did not cost a cent less than sixty dollars. More likely the price exceeded that figure. New and unbroken creases extended down the legs, sleeves, and the side seams of the coat. The hang of the trousers was perfect. A window dresser could not have draped Hank's legs more artistically. Above the well-fitting coat at the back peeped a real collar — none of your cheap celluloid. Some of the slob umpires wear the near-collar that is washed and ironed with a sponge, but not Mr. O'Day. Just a shade less in sartorial elegance was Mr. Sheridan, who did not have his suit built expressly for the occasion, but neither did he appear in the outfit that enveloped his manly form during the season."[24]

Once the contest got underway, spectators were treated to what I.E. Sanborn described as "a rank exhibition of two teams wearing the laurels of championship, and it was meritorious chiefly for the gameness and unbeaten spirit exhibited by both teams at times."[25] For the first 3½ frames the teams were scoreless, but in the last of the fourth the Cubs struck for a run. Chance led off with a walk, was sacrificed to second by Steinfeldt, and was driven home by Kling's single to left. The potential for an outburst of tallies was thwarted, however, when the Cub receiver vainly attempted to stretch his hit for an extra-base.

The score remained 1–0 until the eighth, when the Bengals exploded for three runs. With one out, Jones beat out his third infield hit of the afternoon and stole second. Tinker, overly anxious to nip the lead runner at third, fumbled Schaefer's slow roller, putting Tigers at the corners. Chance drew the infield in to cut down the tying run, but Crawford foiled the strategy by lining a drive over the heads of Evers and Chance. Jones scored easily and Schulte made a wild heave to the plate to try to nail the on-rushing Schaefer. His throw was wild and bounded into the crowd, permitting Schaefer to score and Crawford to take third. The Cubs then mishandled Cobb's bounder to Overall. Seeing Crawford breaking for the plate, Overall threw to Kling. Crawford skidded to a stop and headed back to third, but Kling made a late, low throw that permitted the runner to arrive safely.

Meanwhile, Cobb had sped to second. Rossman then sent Crawford across the plate on his long sacrifice fly to Slagle in center, but the inning ended when Coughlin fanned.

With Donovan leading by two runs going into the bottom of the ninth, hundreds of Cub fans streamed toward the exits believing the game was lost. Chance, refusing to concede defeat, led off with a single to right and moved to second when Donovan's fourth pitch hit Steinfeldt's arm. As the departing spectators stopped and began heading back toward their seats, their hopes again dropped when Kling popped out to first. Evers hit a sharp grounder to third, which might have resulted in a game-ending double play had not Coughlin misplayed it so badly that every Cub runner was safe. Chance cut the deficit to a single run when he scored on Schulte's grounder to first that moved all the runners up a base.

Then came the turning point of the contest. Tinker, who had fanned three straight times, was called back by Chance, who inserted left-handed batter Del Howard, a .230 hitter who had been acquired from the Boston Braves in mid-season, as a pinch-hitter.

Tiger captain Bill Coughlin called time to confer with his catcher. Throughout the season Coughlin, who believed Schmidt was too stupid to call a game for himself, always had flashed pitch selection signs to Schmidt from third-base. Following that practice, Coughlin now told Schmidt: "This fella is a sucker for that low one on the outside. He's missed it twice now and won't be expecting it again."[26]

Following instructions, Schmidt, signaled for a low, outside curve. Howard swung harmlessly and struck out for what should have been the third out. However, Schmidt, who was playing with a broken bone in his throwing hand, let the ball tip off the edge of his mitt, and Kling scored the tying run.[27] The rally and hopes of victory were dashed a moment later when Johnny Evers was thrown out trying to pilfer home.

For the next three innings, Donovan and reliever Ed Reulbach refused to permit a score. With the field rapidly becoming engulfed in darkness, Umpire O'Day signaled an end of the nearly three hour struggle at the conclusion of the twelfth frame.

In the Tiger dressing quarters, Schmidt was viciously assailed verbally, his ears ringing with cries of: "Damn, you, why didn't you hang onto that pitch, you dumb Dutch so-and-so!"[28] The berating, although not short-lived, never attained the level of physical conflict because Schmidt, a burly 215 pound ex-coal miner from Arkansas, was known as the strongest man in baseball and a good pugilist. When angry, Schmidt was known to drive spikes into the clubhouse floor with his bare fists, and he once had taken on heavyweight champion Jack Johnson in a boxing match.[29]

Chicago writers also singled out Schmidt, who had permitted seven stolen bases, as the reason for the Tigers' failure to take the initial game. Sanborn sneered that "if Schmidt had given many such exhibitions during the championship season the Tigers never would have cut into the Series' watermelon," while veteran *Tribune* scribe Hugh E. Keogh, who wrote columns bylined as H.E.K., wrote insinuatingly that "if catcher Schmidt were not worrying what to do with all the money he is going to get he might have a better line on second-base."[30]

Many fans, picking up on Keogh's suspicion, began to wonder aloud if the catcher's muff was part of a players' plot resulting from the National Commission's ruling the previous day regarding tie games. Even Ban Johnson, still raging over the American Leaguers' failure to hold a two run margin, joined in, telling writers: "I don't like it!"[31] After deliberating for several hours, the Commissioners concluded that the tie was merely a coincidence, but they also stated that in future World Series players would share in the receipts of only the first four games, regardless if one or more resulted in a deadlock.[32]

The National Commission also had to rule on two other issues. The first dealt with a sartorial matter. The Cubs chose to play the opener in their traveling gray uniforms, which was in violation of baseball rules. Chance said that it had been done because his team had lost the previous year's home opener wearing the prescribed white garb, and his players were superstitious.[33] The Commission informed Chance that he must conform to the rules, if for no other reason than having both teams wearing the same color was confusing to fans, especially those sitting at a distance from the infield.[34] Second, it was ordered that the starting time should be moved up a half hour to 2 o'clock in order to minimize the possibility of another postponement.[35]

Putting on his best face for the public, Jennings spoke for his players after the game. "Why the Cubs couldn't win a game like that from us in an entire season," he joked. "I told the boys to forget that tie, and that I didn't want to hear any more about it. We didn't win it, but we didn't lose it. I'm going out with some friends for an automobile ride, and then the players, all twenty-five of them, are joining me at the Studebaker Theatre as guests of the *Detroit Free Press* for a performance of 'The Man from Home.'"[36]

The second contest drew only 21,901 to the West Side Park, even though the field was basked in warm sunshine. Jennings gambled on George Mullin, who, like the little girl with a curl of nursery rhyme fame, either was very good or was horrid, as his record of 62–59 during 1905–1907 attested. Opposing him for the Cubs was bellicose Jack Pfiester, known for his fastball and even faster temper.

The visitors jumped off to a one-run lead in the second on Rossman's leadoff grounder past Tinker, who made little effort to stop the ball. By the time Sheckard raced in to make the play, Rossman was on third with a triple. After Coughlin fanned, Payne, who had been inserted in place of Schmidt behind the plate, lifted a short fly to left that Tinker should have caught but left for Sheckard. The left-fielder, however, could not make the play and the ball dropped in for a run scoring single.

The Cubs evened the count in their half of the inning, with consecutive singles by Kling, Evers, and Schulte loading the sacks. Tinker drew a pass, forcing in Kling with the tying run. Mullin then suddenly reclaimed his control and struck out Pfiester and Slagle and retired Sheckard on a grounder to second.

In the fourth the Cubs sent two runs over the plate. Tinker began by bouncing a grounder off Mullin's glove into center for a single. After Pfiester sacrificed him to second, Tinker stole third when Coughlin failed to cover the bag. Slagle then singled off O'Leary's glove, sending Tinker home with the go-ahead tally. The Cub outfielder then stole second, the fourth Chicago larceny off Payne, and trotted home on Sheckard's double down the first-base line. That made the score 3–1 and marked the end of the run- making for the afternoon.

An obviously disappointed Jennings refused to speak with anyone except Joe S. Jackson of the *Detroit Free Press*. "The result of today's game has only caused the boys to feel all the scrappier. It was a tough one to lose, but the luck broke against us," the Tiger pilot said, sounding the loser's knell of bad luck. "It can't always break that way. Watch our smoke tomorrow. I'm not predicting, but a barbecue of bear flesh at the West Side Park tomorrow is just our meat."[37]

Game three saw a decline in both the temperature and attendance. Driven by a chilling, damp wind, temperatures dipped into the upper forties and only 13,114 fans witnessed the contest. Attempting to salvage Chicago's reputation as the finest baseball city in the west, I. E. Sanborn blamed the tie game for the steady decline in attendance. "That tie disarranged the schedule which the rooters had committed to memory so they could not forget it even in their sleep and by which they had made all their plans," he explained, almost pleading diminished mental capacity for Windy City enthusiasts of the national pastime. "In consequence, many did not know yesterday's game was to be played here instead of Detroit and could not get off from work for it even if they knew of it."[38]

Hoping to change his team's fortunes, Donovan brought a striped kitten to the park as a mascot.[39] Tiger faithful also sang a new tribute entitled "The Tigers Went A-hunting and Came Home With the Bunting," which had been penned and put to music by local Detroit musicians.[40] The charms proved futile, however, and the Cubs laced into what Cobb referred to as Ed Siever's "Lady Godiva ball," because there was never anything on it, and cruised to an easy 5–1 victory behind Ed Reulbach's six-hitter.[41]

Reulbach, whom Dryden described as "the whole cheese, imported from Germany, where they make them large and strong," took only an hour and thirty-five minutes to dispose of the Tigers.[42] "He toiled," added Dryden, "like a man who had a certain stint or stunt to perform, after which he could go fishing or otherwise enjoy himself."[43] Only in the fifth did Reulbach falter, surrendering three singles, the last by Cobb, which drove in his team's lone tally.

The Cubs scored once in the second on doubles by Steinfeldt and Evers, and three more runners crossed the plate in the fourth on consecutive singles by Kling, Evers, and Schulte, an error by Jones, and a single by Reulbach. As the dejected, sore-armed hurler trudged from the mound, a Cub fan tossed a lemon at the feet of Siever. Coughlin pounced on the sign of disdain and carried it with him to the dugout, leading Dryden to ponder if the Tiger captain was planning to use it to season the broiled squabs he had promised he would be eating.[44] On a serious note, Dryden condemned the practice of fans throwing lemons, musing sarcastically: "Think of the profound study and preparation and sleepless nights required to train the human intellect sufficiently to roll a lemon at an athlete doing the best he can. No wonder baseball has taken such a grip on the American people."[45]

The final Cub tally came in the fifth off reliever Ed Killian, whom many thought Jennings should have named as the starting hurler. Chance doubled to center and rode home on Steinfeldt's single to the same part of the field. Killian shut down the Chicagoans for the next three frames, but the contest was long decided.

Chicago scribes ridiculed the "wretched Tigers," and singled out Cobb, who left the Windy City sporting a .167 batting average and no attempted steals. Dryden was especially cruel, saying derisively: "The slump of the wearer of the diamond swat medals, the sensation of the century, is quite a puzzle to Cobb himself. To the Cubs, the situation is as plain as the bat in Ty's fist. The Cub pitchers are too dadgasted intense for him. As to his failure to steal bases, Cobb can elucidate on that point himself. He thinks the diamonds in the National League are larger than in the newer organization. At least they look bigger. Until he gets used to the increased distance between bases and the haunting shadow of J. Kling, the young phenom would be foolish to take chances."[46]

As the Cubs and Tigers boarded their shared special train to Detroit, the Cubs claimed that the Tigers were playing dirty ball. Chance soothed them with the pledge that "we'll make it four straight."[47] Jennings dismissed the Cub allegations, saying both teams were playing the same type of baseball and turned the conversation to the remaining games of the Series. "It will be harder to win, of course," he admitted, "but that only means we will have to work a little harder to land. The Tigers never quit. A couple of victories for the Detroit team at home will change the aspect entirely. There will be no changes in the line-up. The team that won the American League pennant is good enough to defend that league's honor. Some of the boys are showing the effect of the hard finish of the pennant race, seeming a little stale. The encouragement of the home crowd will ginger them up and get them going. Then they'll have to look out for us."[48]

Anticipating the first World Series game in their city in twenty years, Detroiters were in a frenzy, which, as H.E.K. noted snidely, should surprise no one because "Detroit can turn itself inside out just for an Elks convention."[49] Sanborn, exhibiting a more sophisticated snobbery than his fellow Windy City writer, wrote derisively: "This large village [with a populace of slightly less than 300,000] resembled smaller ones on circus days and county fairs. Stores were closed and factories closed down to let their employees see the big show."[50]

It was left to the deft pen of Dryden, however, to give readers of the *Chicago Tribune* an objective account of the extent of Detroit's civic enthusiasm. "Everything in Mr. Yawkey's town partakes of the Tiger," he wrote admiringly. "He is the one supreme beast in this region. Group pictures of the team and portraits of the immortal Jennings flash in shop windows and on the whatnot at home. No fireside is complete without some Tigers. Local furriers have bought full-page ads in the newspapers. The meek and lowly seal and the pensive otter have been supplanted by the tiger, with a long and handsome tail. Up-to-date toy dealers unloaded the Teddy Tiger upon the absorbed public, and the supply is several laps behind the demand. All puppies born here in the last month have been named 'Tige,' regardless of sex. One dotty citizen, it is said, christened his twins 'Tiger' and 'Tigerine.' The latest sensation was sprung this morning in large type. A sweet and beautiful maiden of blonde habits, aged twenty-two years, has offered to marry the first Tiger who makes a home run in this bug-house Series. While this is romantic, unfortunately, most of the local boys are married, which state of connubial felicity puts them out of the running."[51]

Such enthusiasm belied long-standing concerns that Detroit's population was not large enough to sustain a major league team. Criticism of Detroit being one of the charter members of the American League had intensified annually because of low attendance. Even winning a pennant could not quiet the incessant cries from leading baseball writers pleading with Ban Johnson and his associates to transfer the Tigers to "a more populous and appreciative community."[52] The opinions of the critics, however, were outweighed by the influential editorial support for Detroit from *The Sporting News*, which stated: "The Detroit club will in 1908, if it has not already done so, demonstrate that the American League will, as a whole, profit by having its championship team in one of its smallest cities. Jennings and his Tigers have almost doubled their home attendance [to 300,000] and will start next season as they ended this—the best drawing card in the country."[53]

Unfortunately the optimism of *The Sporting News* was undermined when the enthusiasm of Detroit's residents did not carry over to parting with the National Commission mandated price of $2.50 for reserved seats and $1.50 for bleacher and standing room locations, the latter of which sold for only 50 cents during the regular season.[54] The Tigers' home, Bennett Park, a wooden structure located on the corner of Michigan and Trumbull Avenues, was the smallest edifice in the major leagues, seating slightly more than 10,000 patrons. Moreover, it was uncomfortable for fans and players alike. It possessed a single dreary and shabby dressing facility, which was used only by the home team; visiting teams were compelled to dress in their hotel rooms before coming to the park. To make going to the park even more of an expensive inconvenience was the presence of a row of "wildcat stands" erected in an alley behind a row of houses along National Avenue. These ramshackle, rickety structures, while offering no comfort, were priced at from a nickel to fifteen cents, for an outfield perch with an unobstructed view. Unfortunately, the low admission cost lured many undesirables who seized the opportunity to disrupt games with verbal outbursts and hurling of various objects at opposing players, thereby creating another detriment to lure the more respectable citizenry to Bennett Park.[55]

Added to such negative factors, reluctance of Detroiters to come to the ballpark to witness the first contest was compounded by overcast skies with a threat of rain, and temperatures hovering in the upper forties. Consequently, only 11,306 fans paid to enter antiquated Bennett Park, and while that was the largest throng ever to witness a baseball game in Detroit, it was smaller than those present in Chicago.

Before the contest could begin, the obligatory ceremonies had to be concluded. Detroit Mayor William Thompson summoned Jennings to home plate and presented him with an immense floral tiger, as big as a horse, draped in an American flag, and a diamond-studded gold watch.[56] While this was occurring, a fan led a black Great Dane, on which yellow stripes had been painted to give the appearance of tiger, onto the field. As the dog was dragged reluctantly around the field many in the audience, feeling sympathy for the poor creature's obvious embarrassment, voiced their displeasure with a chorus of jeers.[57]

Chance stalked over to view the huge tiger. Turning to Jennings, he snorted: "What are going to do with that, Hughie? Eat it?"

"No," snapped the Tiger manager, "we'll ram it down your throats."

"Who, you and Cobb?" Chance taunted, his temper growing more heated. "I thought you told me he was a hitter."

"He'll hit plenty before it's over," Jennings promised.

"That's what you say," the Cub manager laughed as he strode to his bench.[58]

Tempers continued to flare in the first inning. In the top of the frame, Wild Bill Donovan fired a fastball that dislocated the middle finger of Chance's right hand and ripped off the nail. After the wound was bandaged, Chance, targeted by the Tigers with taunts of "Oh, does the big man's finger hurt?" remained in the game and immediately gained a measure of revenge by stealing second.[59] In the bottom of the inning, Chance was again the target of Tiger fury. Cobb grounded slowly to short and made a vicious slide into first in an effort to beat the throw from Tinker. Cobb's spikes dug into Chance's foot and ankle, leaving a bloody gash in the Cub leader. The two had words, but Umpires O'Day and Sheridan quickly interceded and restored order.[60]

The home team finally broke the scoreless deadlock in the fourth when Cobb lined a two-out triple to right and scored on Rossman's single to left. Coughlin singled and Schmidt drew a pass, but Orval Overall worked out of the jam by fanning O'Leary.

Evers opened the fifth for the Cubs by grounding to short, but he reached first safely when O'Leary threw wildly past Rossman's outstretched glove. As Schulte stepped into the box, the light drizzle that had been falling steadily since the second inning turned into a downpour, and the game was delayed for fifteen minutes. Donovan's arm tightened during the wait, and when the game resumed he walked Schulte. Tinker sacrificed the runners ahead a base, and Overall sent both home with a line single to center, giving himself a 2–1 lead.

In the seventh, the Tiger defense collapsed behind the hapless Donovan. Schulte dropped bunt along the third-base line and beat Donovan's toss to first. Tinker laid down a perfect bunt in front of the plate, and Donovan's throw to second arrived too late to cut down Schulte. Overall sacrificed both runners up a base, bringing Slagle to the plate. The Cub outfielder grounded weakly to short, but O'Leary's heave to the plate was off line. Schulte scored and Tinker took third, setting the stage for yet another Tiger fielding lapse. Sheckard bunted toward first. Rossman charged the ball and, seeing that he had no chance to throw out Tinker at the plate, wheeled to toss to first. However, neither Donovan nor Schaefer had moved to cover the bag and Sheckard was safe. Chance forced the runner at second, with Slagle advancing to third. The Cub manager gave the sign for a double steal. Schmidt, the slow-witted Tiger receiver, threw toward second and inexplicably Donovan made no effort to cut it off. As a result, Chance permitted himself to be caught in a run-down long enough to allow Slagle to cross the plate with the third run of the inning.

The visitors added another run in the ninth when Tinker walked, moved up a base on Overall's sacrifice, and scored on Slagle's single to center. That made the final score 6–1, as Overall, who was "steaming the wet ball across the plate so hotly it sounded like a cannon cracker when it met Kling's mitt," tamed the Tigers with a five-hit, six-strikeout performance.[61]

Sensing the inevitable, a mere 7,370 faithful braved even colder temperatures than the day before to see if George Mullin might salvage at least one game for the Bengals. As game time neared, speculation was rampant among sportswriters huddled in the press row atop the roof of the first-base pavilion that Charles Murphy would instruct his team to give a lackluster performance and lose, thereby necessitating a lucrative sixth game in Chicago, for which 25,000 tickets already had been sold.[62] Hearing the rumor, Mordecai Brown, who was scheduled to pitch for the Cubs, angrily told reporters: "To blazes with that crowd in Chicago tomorrow. I'll finish it today."[63]

True to his word, the "three-fingered wonder" stifled the Tigers with a seven-hit, 2–0 masterpiece that, as Sanborn wrote, "put four knots in the Tiger's tail that will never come out, besides drawing the claws from all four of their paws."[64] The Cubs, playing without Chance, struck in the first as Slagle walked, pilfered second for his sixth steal of the Series and scored on Steinfeldt's single to center. Evers led off the following inning by tapping a soft roller to Coughlin at third, but he reached first safely when Rossman dropped Coughlin's throw. Tinker's single to right moved Evers to second, and both advanced on a double steal, giving the Cubs their fifteenth and sixteenth stolen bases for the Series. Evers then crossed the plate on Slagle's force play, giving the Chicagoans their final margin of victory and making them the first team never to lose a game in a World Series. The triumph also enabled Chance to inch ahead of the revered Adrian (Cap) Anson in the hearts of Chicago fans, for Anson had failed in his two bids to bring a world title to the Windy City.[65]

Recalling the previous year's embarrassment, Murphy had refused to claim victory until the final out, telling reporters light-heartedly, "Remember the *Maine* and cuff buttons."[66] However, once surrounded in the Cubs' dressing room by his cheering team and Manager Chance, who wore "a grin that a barber couldn't remove with his sharpest razor," Murphy was ebullient.[67] The owner announced that there would be an intra-squad exhibition game played in West Side Park the following day, with Brown and Chance manning the ticket windows, and all gate receipts would be divided among the players.[68] When the cheering for this act of unexpected generosity died down, Murphy elicited even greater shouts of approval by adding that he would donate an additional $10,000 to the players' receipts.[69] When all the monies were finally distributed, each Cub received the unprecedented amount of $3,342.10.[70]

Not to be outdone, William Yawkey contributed $15,000 to his team's receipts, as well as giving Manager Jennings a $1,000 bonus and a diamond tie stud. The losers thus each took home $1,945.96.[71] This marked the last time any owner would contribute to the players' financial pool.[72]

The Cubs returned to Chicago as conquering heroes, being bestowed with a parade, banquets, and roles in theatrical productions. The local idols were acclaimed musically as well, being featured in a lively march entitled "Cubs on Parade" and in a song "Between You and Me," purportedly written by the non-speaking duo of Johnny Evers and Joe Tinker.[73]

Baseball analysts blamed several factors for the Tigers' poor showing. Many targeted Cobb, who, before the Series, was predicted by so-called experts to "steal the uniforms off the Chicago players," but finished the Series with a .200 batting average and no thefts.[74]

The hot-tempered "Georgia Peach," who New York columnist Bozeman Bulger claimed "was possessed by the Furies," was enraged to read remarks by Joe Vila in *The Sporting News* proclaiming that "the wonderful Ty Cobb dwindled from a world beater to a lame amateur," and he even dismissed Yawkey's bonus with the terse statement: "He's one of the richest men in Michigan. He can afford it."[75] Fuming also that teammate Sam Crawford was spared all blame despite swatting only .238, Cobb left for home pledging to come back next spring and prove that he was not the "bust" Chicago writers had dubbed him.[76] Ban Johnson hinted that Jennings was a major contributing factor, saying: "I must say that I do not think Manager Jennings during the Series followed the generally well-defined rules of baseball entirely in handling his team."[77] The American League president quickly added: "But there is no criticism of him for that. Mr. Jennings is a great manager and achieved wonderful results this season."[78] Others agreed with the comment of Vila that: "The fact that Jennings' men could not hit a balloon, couldn't run the bases a little bit, and actually lacked ginger after the first game of the Series has convinced us American Leaguers that there was something radically wrong with the Tiger crowd."[79]

All writers agreed, however, with Ban Johnson's assessment that the Tigers' collapse might have been caused more by Detroit's fatigue than Chicago's superiority. In his post-Series statement, Johnson said: "The Detroit team took the field for the Series in the same condition as an over-trained race horse. They jumped into this World Series right on the heels of the greatest championship race in baseball history and without any opportunity to recuperate from the strain of the season's fight."[80] This theory was seconded by the *Detroit Free Press*, which editorialized: "Our team was simply worn out. There is a limit to human endurance."[81]

While strain and weariness might have played a role, this argument conjured up a column on the same topic written by crusty New York scribe W.M. Rankin for *The Sporting News* following the 1906 Series. "It is news to me," he observed sarcastically, "that the players on any ball team cannot get into form and be as fresh as daisies after two nights and a day's rest. Just think it over. Two solid hours out of every twenty-four for five and a half months in a year, and then paint them as overworked and exhausted men who would require from ten to fifteen days rest before starting in on another series of say from five to seven games. They would make fine soldiers if a little thing like that would exhaust them. During the late Civil War the Army of the Potomac, with knapsacks and other paraphernalia, marched twenty miles a day for three days, and without any rest worth mentioning, then met and defeated the southern armies after three days of the hardest kind of fighting that has ever been witnessed. That was the Battle of Gettysburg. Oh, fudge! Do not try to make our ball players appear like lawn tennis or croquet players. They are built on different plans."[82]

Perhaps two lasting judgments can be derived from the 1907 World Series. First, it demonstrated the truth of the adage that an older and more experienced team has an advantage over a younger and less experienced one. Second, and more importantly, as sportswriter Hamilton J. Hamilton of Cincinnati observed: "If ever there is any argument advanced as to the crookedness of baseball, this Series can be referred to with convincing effect. For if ever there was a temptation to throw a game, it was there yesterday. A win by Detroit meant close on to $15,000 in the pockets of each of the club owners, and as Manager Chance is a heavy stockholder in the Chicago Cubs, it must have been a double temptation for him. But the Cubs never wavered."[83] In short, the World Series between the Tigers and Cubs accomplished the most important service a championship contest can hope to achieve by reaffirming the integrity of the national pastime in the collective minds of the sporting public.

CUBS VS. TIGERS, 1908

The 1908 season witnessed two pennant races that were so hotly contested that they made the World Series anti-climactic. In the American League, entering the final week of the season, Detroit, Cleveland, and Chicago were battling neck and neck for the championship. The White Sox were the first to lose ground when Ed Walsh suffered a heartbreaking 1–0 defeat at the hands of Cleveland's Addie Joss. The big Chicago spitball artist single-handedly had kept the weak-hitting Sox in the pennant chase by compiling a record of 40–15, 1.42 earned run average, and 464 innings pitched, including taking the mound in seven of his team's final nine contests. In this crucial battle, Walsh hurled a four-hit, fifteen-strikeout masterpiece, giving up his only run on a passed ball. However, Joss did even better, twirling not only a no-hitter, but also a perfect game. As a result of Joss' triumph, the Indians, who referred to themselves as the "Naps" in tribute to their playing manager Napoleon Lajoie, had only to win their final three games from the fourth place St. Louis Browns to win the flag. However, they could only manage to capture two. Meanwhile, the Detroit Tigers swept a series from the lowly Washington Senators and, on the final day of the season, rode Wild Bill Donovan's two-hitter to a 7–0 victory over the White Sox to defend their league title, finishing the season 90–63 and edging out Cleveland and Chicago by ½ and 1½ games respectively.

As close as the junior circuit struggle was, that of the National League was even more bitterly contested and thrilling. Entering the stretch drive, Pittsburgh, Chicago, and New York were all in contention for the title, but the course of the season was altered on September 23 when Christy Mathewson of the Giants squared off against Jack "the Giant Killer" Pfiester of the Cubs at the Polo Grounds. The score was 1–1 as the Giants came to bat in the bottom of the ninth. With two out and Harry (Moose) McCormick on first, nineteen-year-old substitute first-baseman Fred Merkle drove a single to left, sending McCormick to third. The next batter, Al Bridwell drove an apparent single to center to win the game. The ensuing scene is vividly recounted by veteran New York baseball writer Joe Vila:

"Merkle, losing his head, never went near second-base, but made a beeline for the clubhouse, thinking the game had been won. [Johnny] Evers called for [Artie] Hofman to throw the ball to second-base for a force out, but [Joe] McGinnity [of the Giants], who wasn't in the game at all (the pitcher had been coaching at third-base), rushed out on the field and intercepted the throw. Mathewson, meanwhile, hustled after Merkle and told him to run to second-base. The crowd was all over the field by that time and McGinnity, in a tussle with several Chicago players, threw the ball into the crowd back of third-base.

"Not knowing just what was in the wind, a wild-eyed mob surrounded Umpires [Hank] O'Day and Bob Emslie, but luckily the regular police, who had been sent to the battlefield by Police Commissioner Bingham, kept the judges of play from being killed, perhaps.

"The ball (perhaps the one McGinnity had fired into the stands, perhaps a substitute), by this time, had been thrown to Evers while Merkle was fighting his way through another mob to the bag. Half a dozen fistfights were soon going on, and it looked as if somebody would soon be seriously injured. The cops took the umpires under the grandstands, where O'Day declared that the run did not count and that the game was a tie—1 to 1."[1]

O'Day later reported to National League President Harry Pulliam: "I did not ask to have the field cleared, as it was too dark to continue play."[2] This was a critical decision as had the field not been able to be cleared, baseball's rules mandated that the Giants would have been forced to forfeit the contest to Chicago, by a score of 9–0. Pulliam chose to support the umpire's decision and ordered the game to be replayed, if it would affect the final standings of the pennant chase.[3]

While Pulliam prayed that such a game would not be necessary, the gods of baseball decreed otherwise. In the last game of the regular schedule for both of their teams, Mordecai Brown of the Cubs faced Vic Willis of the Pirates. The "Three-Fingered Wonder" outdueled the Pirate ace for his twenty-eighth season triumph by the score of 5–2. This left the Cubs with a record of 98–55 and dropped Pittsburgh out of the race, finishing with a 98–56 mark. However, the Giants still had three games to play with the sixth place Boston Braves, and their resultant sweep brought about a tie with the Cubs for first and the need for a replaying of their earlier tie.

On October 7, the night before the playoff game at the Polo Grounds, young Bill Klem, who had been assigned as one of the umpires for the big game, was walking along Madison Avenue when a man approached him and tried to shove a wad of cash into his hands, muttering "the Giants gotta win."[4] Klem shoved him aside, but the following morning, as the arbiter was walking through the tunnel to the playing field, another similar attempt was made, with Klem screaming at him: "Get away from me, you dirty bum."[5]

Such attempts to influence the outcome of the game, which created greater excitement than any other sporting event in New York history, resulted in extreme security measures. Police sealed off the Polo Grounds two hours before game time, and even ticket holders who arrived after that were denied entry. Those fans lucky enough to arrive before the security lines were established witnessed Mordecai Brown defeat Mathewson 4–2 to earn the Cubs their third consecutive berth in the World Series.

As might be expected, the Giant organization was furious. Owner John T. Brush threatened to seek an injunction to prevent the playing of the world championship series, but, at the urging of the National Commission, recanted, saying: "We are too good sports for that. We shall not contest the matter further. But we believe the pennant is ours technically. There is not a doubt about this."[6] To reaffirm his conviction, Brush had a medal struck for each of his twenty-eight team members. The token depicted a ball player holding a bat and another throwing a ball, and bore the inscription: "The Real Champions, 1908."[7] Catcher Roger Bresnahan sneered to reporters then, and maintained until his dying day, that: "Johnny Evers hasn't completed the force out on Merkle yet."[8] Manager John McGraw expressed his anger in a telegram to his old comrade, Tiger Manager Hugh Jennings: "If justice had been done, you would be playing it off with the Giants. My hearty congratulations. May you always prosper as you have this year."[9] Tired of listening both to

McGraw's whining and his apparent desire to see the American League triumph, "Chubby Charlie" Murphy, president of the Cubs, explained his team's victory by referring to Merkle and sneering: "We can't supply brains to the New York club's dumb players."[10]

The bitter aftermath of this pennant race lingered for months. To reassure the public of the honesty of the national pastime, a National League Commission, consisting of Brush, Brooklyn Dodger owner Charles Ebbets, and Cincinnati's Garry Herrmann, was established to investigate the attempted bribery of Klem. After hearing witnesses, they ordered Doc Cramer, a part-time Giant trainer, banned from National League ballparks. On the personal level, Merkle went down in history with his name becoming synonymous with a "bonehead" play. Pulliam, however, paid the ultimate price. Unable to escape the shadows that haunted him over his decision in the tie game, the Klem affair, and the disputed loss of the pennant by the Giants, on July 29, 1909 the brooding league president committed suicide by firing a shot into his head.[11]

With the Series commencing only two days after the playoff concluded, the Cubs had little time either to rejoice or recover. Fortunately for them, only one member of the squad was injured going into the first game with the Tigers. Frank Chance, while departing the Polo Grounds, had been assaulted by an irate Giant fan who struck the Cub manager in the throat, bruising both cartilage and his vocal chords.[12]

The reigning world champions boasted the same line-up that had brought them victory over the Tigers the previous year. Around the infield from first to third were Chance (.272, 2, 55), Johnny Evers (.300, 0, 37), Joe Tinker (.266, 6, 68), and Harry Steinfeldt (.241, 1, 62). Acid-tongued John (Noisy) Kling (.276, 4, 59) was behind the plate, and Jimmy Sheckard (.231, 2, 22), Artie Hofman (.243, 2, 42), and Frank Schulte (.236, 1, 43) patrolled the outfield from left to right.

While the Cubs led their league offensively only in stolen bases (212) and doubles (197), their mound corps once again was dominating, leading the senior circuit with 1,434 innings pitched, 668 strikeouts, and twenty-seven shutouts. Mordecai Brown (29–9, 1.47) paced the staff, with Ed Reulbach (24–7, 2.03), Orval Overall (15–11, 1.92), and Jack Pfiester (12–10, 2.00) rounding out the starting rotation.

Although hampered by his sore throat, Chance addressed local supporters as he and his wife boarded the club's special train to Detroit. "I don't expect a repetition of last year's four straight victories," he said in a hoarse whisper. "Detroit's team is too strong to suffer any such a defeat again. I expect this Series to be hard fought, but the Cubs will win it, I believe, because they have the class of the two teams and the confidence of one victory to help them. We respect the Tigers, but we think we have a team that can beat them."[13]

The American League champions, and especially Manager Jennings, were disappointed on not meeting McGraw's contingent. As the *Detroit Free Press* editorialized: "So our Tigers must stay their whetted appetites with Cub meat this fall after all. It is rather a pity, too. Our feline tribe had been cultivating other tastes during the last few days. Their dainty palates had been watering for the delicate flavor of Giant meat. It is all one, however, in the end. The Tigers will hibernate just as well on ursine flesh as that of overgrown men."[14]

As in 1907, the Detroiters boasted an impressive offensive machine, leading their circuit in batting average (.264), slugging average (.347), hits (1,347), runs (645), doubles (199), and runs batted in (520). Right-fielder Ty Cobb's .324 led the league in batting for the second time in what would prove to be a nine consecutive year string of swatting titles. The "Georgia Peach" also ranked first with 108 runs batted in, .475 slugging average, 188 hits, thirty-six doubles, and twenty triples, as well as stroking four home runs. The remainder of the outer defense was nearly as impressive, with Sam Crawford (.311, 7, 80) in center and Matty McIntyre (.295, 0, 28) replacing Davy Jones in right. The infield during most of the regular season consisted of Claude Rossman (.294, 2, 71) at first, Germany Schaefer (.259, 3, 52) at second, Charley O'Leary (.251, 0, 17) at short, and Bill Coughlin, in the tenth and final year of his major league career (.215, 0, 23) at third, with Charlie Schmidt (.265, 1, 38), despite defensive lapses caused by a lingering injury to a finger on his throwing hand, remaining behind the plate.

During the final twenty-five games of the season, twenty-year-old, switch-hitting Donie Bush had replaced O'Leary at short. Bush not only fielded his position brilliantly, but also compiled a .294 batting average. Most baseball analysts agreed that Detroit could not have won the pennant without Bush's contributions. However, because he had not been on the major league roster prior to September, the National Commission declared him ineligible to participate in the World Series. Even a sportsmanlike plea from Charlie Murphy to waive the rule failed to reverse the decision, so Detroit entered the postseason battle without one of its most valuable players.[15]

The Tiger pitching staff was topped by twenty-three-year-old rookie phenom Ed (Kickapoo) Summers. One of the first knuckleball pitchers in major league history, the right-hander hurled 301 innings and compiled a record of 24–12 with a 1.64 earned run average. Wild Bill Donovan, who was hampered by chronic rheumatism throughout the season, finished 18–7, with a 2.07 earned run average. George (Wabash) Mullin (17–13, 3.10), Ed Willett (15–8, 2.28), and (Twilight) Ed Killian (12–9, 2.99) completed the starting mound corps.

Jennings was his usual buoyant self on the eve of the opener, telling his players: "The Cubs wouldn't be as fresh and rested as they were last year. We'll wipe those 1907 defeats off our slate."[16] Nor was he less restrained with the press, informing newsmen: "I'm not claiming victory, but I have no fear of the outcome. The last game in Chicago [against the White Sox] showed me the boys are still the gamest and greatest team in modern baseball. The big fellows are back in their stride at the plate. The pitchers are working right. The catchers are there now, and the infield will show its real merit under fire."[17] Talk such as this led the *Chicago Tribune* to note sarcastically: "Judging from the boastful manner in which Detroiters are talking they must have forgotten what happened to them a year ago."[18]

The first game, witnessed by 10,812 at Bennett Field, was played under the worst conditions imaginable. The contest began in a steady rain that turned into a downpour which left the field a soggy swamp and the baselines almost two inches of mud.[19] Making the drenched locals even more uncomfortable was that Jennings decided to start Killian rather than Summers against Reulbach and inserted second year reserve Jerome (Red) Downs (.221, 1, 35) at second, moved Schaefer to third, and Coughlin to the bench.

Killian struggled through the first two innings, holding on to a 1–0 lead given him as the result of a first inning single by McIntyre, a stolen base, and Cobb's run-scoring single. However, in the third the visitors struck the southpaw with a vengeance. Sheckard doubled to right and moved to third on Evers' attempted sacrifice, which turned into a single when Schaefer slipped in the mud trying to field the ball. Schulte singled, scoring Sheckard and moving Evers to second. The lead runner was cut down at third on Chance's failed sacrifice bunt, but Steinfeldt drove in the second run of the frame with a single to left. Hofman drew a base on balls, filling the sacks with Cubs and driving Killian off the hill in favor of Summers. Tinker stroked what should have been an inning ending double play grounder to Downs, who tossed perfectly to O'Leary, but the relay to first went wild and another tally crossed the plate. On the next pitch, Tinker "waddled down to second like a duck in the mud," beating Schmidt's belated throw.[20] Steinfeldt scored when Schaefer again fumbled an easy grounder, this time off Kling's bat. The inning came to an end when Kling was caught trying to steal, but the visitors had assumed a 4–1 lead.

The Cubs scored again in the top of the seventh on a single by Evers, a sacrifice, Downs' error, and a sacrifice fly by Steinfeldt. In the bottom of that frame, however, the home team finally demonstrated the form that had brought them their pennant. Cobb drove a line drive off Reulbach's glove for a single and went to third on Rossman's shot to center. After Schaefer fanned, Schmidt grounded to short, scoring Cobb. Downs slammed a double into the crowd in left, scoring Rossman. Summers blooped a single over Tinker's head, and Downs crossed the plate, cutting the Chicago lead to a single run. Overall was quickly summoned to quell the uprising, which he did, but only after he hit McIntyre with a pitch.

After walking leadoff man Crawford in the eighth, Overall was removed in favor of Mordecai Brown. The reliever, chilled to the bone by the rain and wind, immediately hurled a wild pitch, which sent Crawford to second. Cobb bunted toward the mound and was safe when Chance dropped Brown's throw. Rossman singled over the pitcher's head into center, sending the tying run across the plate. Cobb also tallied when Evers made a wild throw on the Tiger outfielder's daring try to reach third on the hit. With their team now in front 6–5, Tiger rooters shrieked with glee and threw their most treasured possessions—hats and umbrellas—in the air and onto the field in anticipation of gaining their first World Series triumph.[21]

Before the start of the ninth, Jennings put his arm around Summers and told him: "You can do it, Eddie, just take your time."[22] After getting Evers on an easy roller to start the inning, Summers induced Schulte to rap a grounder to O'Leary at short, but his throw was too late to beat the fleet-footed Cub to the bag. Chance moved the runner up a base with a single to center. Amid the crowd calling for a pitching change, Steinfeldt looped a single to short left, filling the bases. As the crowd's pleas grew louder, Hofman put his team ahead again with a single to center. Tinker's perfect bunt sent Steinfeldt home and the local fans streaming toward the exit. To further humiliate the deflated Tigers, Hofman and Tinker executed a double steal, and Kling drove them both in with a single to center, making the final score 10–6 for the Chicagoans.

Following the victory, Murphy was exuding confidence. "Today's game confirms my opinion that I have the best ball club in the world," he bragged in his usual boisterous fashion. "There is not the slightest doubt in my mind that the Cubs will win the Series, but the Tigers showed so much more aggressive form this year than they did last that they may take a game or two."[23]

Chance was only slightly more gracious, saying: "It is a hard matter to express an opinion on the relative merits of the two teams playing under such conditions as today's game was pulled off in. Either team might have won today's game under such conditions. We consider ourselves fortunate to have stirred up such a rally in the final inning. But, on the whole, it seems to me that the Cubs have proved themselves the classier team of the two, and, of course, with one game stowed away I am more confident than ever of winning a second world's championship. On dry fields our pitchers will not be hit as hard as they were today."[24]

For the losers, Jennings tried to assume a positive outlook, although it was obvious the defeat stung him deeply. "We'll win yet," he pledged. "Of course, I wanted today's game, but the loss of it does not discourage the Tigers. They're the gamest lot of ball players I ever knew, and we're going after tomorrow's game just as if we had won today's hands down. I thought we had today's won in the eighth, but the Cubs started on a batting streak in the ninth inning that just could not be stopped. Summers did not lose his nerve, though the wet ball might have bothered him some. It was one of the accidents of baseball we all have to put up with."[25]

Writers were not as forgiving of the Tiger boss as he was of his pitcher. The *New York Times* said that if "Jennings had exercised some acumen, he would have relieved Summers when that twirler weakened in the ninth and let some of the other five eager Tiger pitchers finish up."[26] Horace S. Fogel, veteran Philadelphia scribe, cruelly wrote: "Jennings must have been rattled. He knew Brown had pitched a hard game in New York and that Chance would not put him in again to start the opener. Hence, there was his chance to run in Donovan and cop the first game, and the first game in a short series means a whole lot. It practically means the Series. If Killian was really a good left-hander it would have been the proper caper to start him against the Cubs, who do not like southpaws, but he isn't first class. If Summers had been started in the opening game he most likely would have won it. From this end, it looked as if Jennings was displaying very poor judgment."[27]

Even the fans came under attack as a cause for the day's disappointment, as a local writer bemoaned the fate of Detroit's baseball future unless the populace underwent a change in attitude. "Maybe sometime in the future the public will realize what it means for a team representing a city to win a major league baseball championship twice running. The Detroit public didn't show this appreciation," scolded Will B. Wreford in the *Detroit Free Press.* "To say that the attendance, numerically, at the opening game of the World Series at Bennett Park was disappointing would be touching it mildly — it was a dismal failure. The threatening weather probably kept away a thousand or two, but no such difference between the attendance and 20,000 can be laid to the fault of the weatherman. Go out to Bennett Park and root. Root until the last inning is finished. What is more, be there sure and show the army of newspapermen that the city where life is worth living is a baseball town and can at least go above the lowest World Series attendance and also show the Detroit players that what they have done for the city is appreciated."[28]

The second game was played at Chicago's West Side Park before only 17,760 spectators. That the crowd was nearly 8,000 below stadium capacity was not a reflection of Chicago's lack of enthusiasm for their National League heroes, but rather a display of disgust toward team owner Charles Murphy. Past practice had been to double the normal twenty-five and fifty cent admission prices for postseason contests, but Murphy, as avaricious as he was pompous, raised prices to five times that of the regular season. Moreover, Murphy was rumored to have sold large blocks of choice tickets to scalpers at an even higher rate. To demonstrate their disdain, fans boycotted the game, and the space roped off in the outfield to contain the anticipated overflow crowd was empty.[29]

Clear skies and a stiff, but mild, breeze toward right-field created an ideal setting for Bill Donovan to match his pitching talent against that of Orval Overall. For seven and one-half innings the two right-handers permitted no runner to cross the plate, making "the most dependable sluggers of both teams look as helpless as soap bubbles in a gale of wind."[30] In the bottom half of the eighth, however, "Wild Bill" unexpectedly succumbed to a barrage of Cub hits. After Steinfeldt led off by fanning, Hofman beat out a bunt along the third-base line. Joe Tinker then approached the plate swinging his slender "toothpick" bat menacingly. Donovan threw a waist-high fastball, which was so far inside that Tinker was stepping back as he swung. Somehow his bat met the ball squarely and sent it soaring over Cobb's head. The Tiger right-fielder went back until he reached the rope barrier in front of the stands and then watched it go over the screen for what home plate umpire Bill Klem, representing the National League, ruled a two-run homer.

Instantly, Jennings, Cobb, Donovan, Schaefer, and the entire Tiger team surrounded

Klem to protest, saying that it had been agreed in the pre-game conference that any ball hit behind the rope barrier would be a ground rule double. "That ground rule doesn't cover the bleachers when there is no overflow crowd," bellowed Klem, never one to tolerate criticism of his rulings. "I've been calling balls that land in that bleacher home runs all season, and that rope out there don't change it!"[31]

After fifteen minutes the game resumed, but during the delay Donovan's rheumatic arm had stiffened in the late afternoon chill. Kling belted a ground rule double to left and advanced a base on Overall's sacrifice. Sheckard followed with a run-scoring single to left and promptly stole second. At that point, as I.E. Sanborn of the *Chicago Tribune* wrote, "the Tigers went off their feet altogether and for several minutes were pressed in pursuit so hard that they looked like veritable minor leaguers."[32] Evers dropped a sacrifice bunt between Donovan and Schmidt but reached first safely when neither of the Tiger battery went for the ball. Evers then stole second, and both runners crossed the plate on Schulte's triple to left. Broken in spirit, Donovan uncorked a wild pitch that sent Schulte home with the sixth, and final, Chicago tally of the afternoon, as Overall, despite surrendering a run in the ninth, gained a 6–1 triumph.

As might be expected, National League adherents could not resist the temptation to gloat over their two-game margin in the race for the championship. Chance told reporters: "That makes two. We now have some reason to expect a repetition of last season's four straight against the Tigers, but baseball is so uncertain we will not count our chickens yet."[33] Murphy expressed pleasure with the outcome, but he urged fans not to slight his players monetarily by staying away in the future. "Of course, we are pleased. We expected to win, but in baseball realization is better than expectation," he said sternly, adding: "I hope the baseball loving public will understand there will be room for all at tomorrow's game. The players get 60 percent of the receipts as compared with slightly more than 15 percent for each club, and I want them to get all the money the fans want to pay to see the great contest."[34] Clark Griffith, former pitcher in both leagues and ex-manager of the New York Highlanders, lavished praise on the day's hero, Joe Tinker, asserting: "That little fellow is the toughest fellow to come up in a pinch of any man on the team, if not in the whole league. His drives are hard, they are long, and they are timely. I don't care if the rest of the team are batting .300, I'd rather have Tinker up in a pinch than any of them, if it were my team. He is on his toes all the time, and he's all nerve."[35] Of all the comments, however, it was Hugh E. Keogh, the acerbic baseball writer of the *Chicago Tribune* known as HEK, who put into words what most observers were thinking after witnessing another exhibition of futility by the Tigers: "Honest, now. Can you figure out how this willing to be kidded, ingenuous bunch from Detroit ballyhooed Fielder Jones' White Sox out of the American League championship?"[36]

American League President Ban Johnson issued a statement trying gamely to shore up the flagging spirits of the followers of the junior circuit. "We are not willing to give up yet, but certainly our boys are not playing their game against the Cubs," he stated. "We should have won the game at Detroit. Possibly a change of pitchers would have staved off defeat. Donovan was pitching magnificent ball — as well, if not better, than Overall — up to the eighth inning. Then Hofman's bunt was followed by Tinker's drive into the right-field seats. How greatly the wind affected the ball was shown by the fact that Cobb first ran in on the hit, only to see it finally sail far over his head. That hit turned the tide."[37]

Manager Jennings publicly offered the standard pep talk to the press, promising better days for his squad. "Don't think for a moment the boys have given up the fight," he warned newsmen. "They're mad clear through at losing today's game and will battle hard to the finish. The Cubs are a good team, but the Tigers are just as good. Baseball's a peculiar game. You can say the Tigers will be there tomorrow full of fizz and pepperino."[38]

However, speaking candidly to I.E. Sanborn in the lobby of the team headquarters at the Lexington Hotel, the Tiger leader was uncharacteristically somber and introspective as he attempted to explain the play that lost the game for his team. "We're two to the bad," he said softly, "but baseball is such a funny game. That little scratch hit by Hofman started all our trouble. I kicked over that hit of Tinker's into the bleachers because we had a special agreement that hits that reached the boundary were to be two-baggers. I am well aware that under ordinary circumstances a hit over the fence is a home run, but we were playing under special rules. With a two-base hit, Hofman would have been on third, with a chance to get him out. After a man scores, you have no chance at him. I thought I had a legitimate kick and so made it."[39]

The third contest was perhaps the low point of the Series for Murphy. First, Cub fans remained unforgiving toward his price gouging, and, despite ideal weather conditions, another less-than-capacity crowd of 14,543 passed through the turnstiles. Second, he was forced to miss the game because of a severe cold and was advised by his physicians not to accompany the team back to Detroit.[40] Third, he infuriated the local press corps, which included such literary luminaries as Sanborn, Charles Dryden, Hugh Fullerton, and Ring Lardner, by compelling them to join their out-of-town compatriots and cover the game from the last row of the grandstand.[41] Finally, and almost as painful as the loss of revenue, his team suffered its first postseason setback in two years.

In an effort to revitalize his squad, Jennings juggled his line-up, inserting veteran Bill Coughlin at his familiar third-base post, moving Germany Schaefer back to second, and putting Downs on his familiar place on the bench. To fortify the defense, Ira Thomas replaced Schmidt, who had given up eight stolen bases in the first two contests. To face Jack Pfiester on the hill, he surprised most observers by nominating erratic George Mullin instead of Summers.

Detroit scored in the first on Steinfeldt's error and a run-scoring single by Cobb, but the Cubs tallied three unearned runs in the bottom of the fourth as a result of Coughlin's error to take what seemed to be a commanding 3–1 lead. However, in the sixth, the Cubs, whom many observers said did not appear to be trying very hard to win, collapsed.[42] Mullin led off with a walk and moved to second on McIntyre's single to left. O'Leary then dropped a bunt toward the mound. Pfiester raced in and threw to third for a force, but, as I.E. Sanborn noted sourly, "the play miscued because Mullin was not quite such an ice wagon as Jack thought" and beat the throw.[43] Crawford singled a run across, leaving the bases loaded for Cobb. The American League swat king tapped a slow roller to Tinker, whose throw to Chance was late, and McIntyre crossed the plate with the tying run. Rossman drove home two more runners with a single to right, and Cobb sped into third.

By that time, the crowd, which had been yelling for the removal of Pfiester, broke into a chorus of lusty booing. However, as the *New York Times* noted insinuatingly, "Manager Chance, who failed to show any traces of embarrassment or displeasure at the way in which the Detroits came up from behind and went ahead, smiled cheerfully and ignored the request."[44]

Schaefer popped a fly to short center. As Hofman trotted in for the ball, Cobb stood on the bag "poised like a bird."[45] As soon as Hofman made the catch, Cobb broke for home, but the strong-armed Cub outfielder rifled the ball to Kling, who slapped the tag on the sliding runner to complete the double play. Ira Thomas, however, drove in Rossman with the fifth, and final run, of the frame with a long double to right-center.

In the eighth, the gray-clad visitors added their final two runs of the afternoon. Cobb doubled to left to start the inning and moved to third on Rossman's bunt single. Thomas walked to fill the sacks for Coughlin, who lofted a sacrifice fly into left to score Cobb. Mullin followed with a single, driving home the final run of the day and making the score 8–3.

In the ninth, Cobb, who had been bristling under the barbs of the Cub bench jockeys for his previous feeble showings against them, singled with two out off reliever Ed Reulbach. Standing on first, Cobb cupped his hands and bellowed: "Kling! I'm going on the next one!" As Grantland Rice described the ensuing action: "Speedy Tyrus went into second as he'd boldly promised so hard that he knocked the bag from its moorings and was safe as he sent baseman Joe Tinker flying."[46] Sneering, Cobb kicked at the bag a few times, as if to see if it was defective; in truth, he was moving it ever so slightly toward third.[47] As Reulbach set himself, the brash runner again yelled: "I'm going on the next one!" Unnerved, Kling threw late to Steinfeldt, and the laughing Cobb dusted himself off.[48] Rossman walked, and when the two runners attempted a double steal, Cobb was tagged out in a rundown to end the inning.

Years later, at the age of seventy-three, Cobb recalled the incident and why he was not concerned about alerting the Cubs to his plans. "I knew Kling's mind," he explained, "how he'd be shook up by it and would have to collect himself before throwing. All I needed was inches."[49]

After the game, Jennings encouraged his players, saying: "We've started to hit. Now let's show 'em what we can do on home cooking."[50] The *Detroit Free Press* waxed eloquent in a gushing editorial: "The hoodoo is broken. We've learned that the Chicago Cubs are only human after all. Four times last year and twice this fall these ball tossers had toyed with our vaunted athletes. They seemed to win as they pleased. Then arose one Mr. Mullin and life took on a new look. Surely never lighted this on this orb a more delightful vision. The world became a glad place. The skies were bluer than we had known. The grass we had thought to be faded turned bright green before our eyes. The sober faces all about us gleamed into sudden smiles, and thoughtful visages blossomed into joy. Men at some time, we discovered, are masters of their fate. To your positions, O Tigers! Nothing less than four straight will satisfy us now!"[51]

In Chicago, however, such elation as seized "The City of the Straits" over a lone victory was viewed with disbelief. Keogh, his words dripping with cynicism, wrote: "They tell us that the genuine Detroit gloat over winning a ball game has the New Orleans Mardi Gras, the Los Angeles Fiesta, and the Chinese New Year stripped to the pelt, but it has been our misfortune to have never been able to mingle with it. They tell us that the Fourth of July and the fall of the Bastille never provoked anything like it. The frenzied populace seized upon express wagons, piano boxes, ash barrels, and other properties to make fuel for bonfires; that the town was shot up from the Windsor ferry dock to Highland Park, and that is a goodly stretch of paved streets."[52] Even Sanborn was moved to dismiss the game's final score, explaining haughtily: "It was Detroit's first meal of Cub steaks in two seasons of hungry waiting, and the feline tribe gorged itself against a possible famine for years to come."[53]

Apparently Detroit fans shared the *Tribune*'s belief that the Tiger's showing was an aberration, as a mere 12,907 were willing to pay to see Ed Summers take the mound against Mordecai Brown on a beautiful Indian Summer afternoon at Bennett Park. Unfortunately for the hometown team the weather was the only thing ideal for them, as they fell victim to Brown's four-hit, 3–0 masterpiece. Chicago batters pounded out ten hits, including run-scoring singles by Steinfeldt and Hofman, and, with Schmidt inexplicably back behind the plate again for the Bengals, the Cubs pilfered four bases.

To most diamond observers, the Series was now all but over. HEK gloated: "It's the same old Tinker and the same old Cobb and the same old Jennings on the same old job."[54] The *New York Times* was equally certain of the Tigers' inevitable doom, stating: "Should the Cubs not seize the opportunity of profiting by Detroit's inferiority there will still remain a ray of hope for the outplayed Tigers, but that hope is hanging by a slender thread, and that delicate fabric is more likely to give way under the weight of Chicago's crafty, powerful, and resourceful baseball team than to withstand the tremendous odds against it."[55]

The fifth game at Bennett Park set a record for the smallest attendance at a World Series contest. A mere 6,210 fans witnessed Orval Overall send Bill Donovan down to a 2–0 defeat to capture the Cubs' second consecutive world title. The Tigers were feeble in support of their ace, fanning ten times while garnering only three safeties. Shortly before his death in 1947, Overall recounted his meetings with Donovan in 1907 and 1908 and lavished praise upon the Tiger hurler. "In the two Series, I met Donovan four times and got out of it with three victories and a tie," Overall said, "but Donovan was a great pitcher and a grand fellow. He was a real artist on the mound. While I am proud of those Series victories, I don't hesitate to say that if Donovan had had the Cubs behind him, and I had pitched for the Tigers, the verdict could easily have been reversed."[56]

The Tigers were gracious in defeat, trotting over to the Cub bench to congratulate them.[57] Jennings tried to console his downcast men by saying: "Don't feel too badly about losing. We were beaten again by a great team. A great team!"[58] He then met the press and offered the same alibi for defeat as in the previous year: "We were beaten because the Chicago team played better ball. I freely admit that our opponents played better baseball than we did, but I will not admit they are a better team. Detroit did not play the game it is capable of. There was not the old-time Detroit dash and ginger to our work, and we didn't measure up to our full ability either at the plate [batting an anemic .203] or in the field [nine errors]."[59]

As he prepared to board the train to Chicago, Chance called Detroit writers to his side. "I want you to say for me," he told them, "and you can't make it too strong either, that I think the Tigers are the strongest team the Cubs were stacked up against, and that if they had met any other team in the National League they would have beaten them and beaten them easily. They have proved themselves to be the best of the American League, having won the title twice hand-running, and, my Cubs excepted, they are the best ever. What is more, the Tigers individually and as a team are the finest lot I have ever met. They are gentlemen, and never once during the five games of the Series just closed did one hasty word pass between the two teams. I can't also help but give you my hand when I say that Detroit, as a ball town, is a little dandy. The fans are sportsmen, and the contrast between it and New York is as vivid in my mind as day and night. They give visiting players credit and take their defeats like sportsmen. While it is an absolute fact in my mind that the Cubs are the best in the world, let me say for the Tigers that each time they have stacked up against us they have hit us when we were playing our very best ball. In the third game we made one slip, and you remember what they did to us. Just one slip in any of those games we won, and we would have been beaten. We could have made those slips against other teams and won, but not against the Detroits. While the Cubs are a good team, we had to play our best to win."[60]

Neither the Chicago nor the national press corps were nearly as gracious as Chance, with most concurring with the sentiment expressed in a *Chicago Tribune* editorial: "Well, who expected anything else?"[61] Keogh was his usual insulting self, writing a derogatory, anti-Semitic verse regarding Detroit, Jennings, and the Tiger manager's famous cry of "Ee-e-yah":

> The shades of night were falling fast
> As through the subdued village passed
> A Kike who bore, mid snow and ice,
> A banner with this strange device:
> 'Ee-e-yah.'
> He pleaded with the passing throng
> To help the goodly cause along.
> He pleaded with the passing throng.
> He pleaded long and pleaded loud
> Unto that day's besaddened crowd:
> 'Ee-e-yah.'
> But no one seemed to heed his call,
> And no one cared a thing at all,
> And none would pay a nickel for
> The emblem of a losing war:
> 'Ee-e-yah.'
> 'I'm long upon my stock,' he cried,
> While time upon his losing trade he plied.
> 'Now I deserve some recompense.
> Here take the bunch for thirty cents:
> Ee-e-yah.'[62]

The usually reserved Sanborn was moved to exercising poetic license, gushing: "Not in a thousand years has a team been compelled to fight as hard for its titles as the Chicago team which won the National League pennant twice inside of five days under the most trying circumstances. But once assured of the National League banner, the rest proved comparatively easy. At the gait they were going in the World Series just closed, they wouldn't lose a game in a month. What those gray-clad modest young warriors have accomplished will be remembered longer than any of them lives, for in this Series, as never before, they demonstrated the perfection of their machinery. That stonewall infield has never been better, and Chance, Evers, Tinker, and Steinfeldt have written their names above those of Cap Anson, Fred Pfeffer, Ned Williamson, and Tom Burns, Chicago's original and long famous stonewall defenders [of the 1880s]."[63] However, the cruelest, but most accurate, remark came from an editorial writer of the *Chicago Tribune* who encapsulated the Series succinctly, stating: "The Cubs simply made monkeys of the Tigers."[64]

Since the owners were no longer permitted to give cash bonuses to their players and the low attendance resulted in the winning team receiving only $27,662.11 and the Tigers $13,584.90, the combatants agreed to play an exhibition in West Side Park in lieu of the scheduled sixth game. The Tigers won 7–3, but the featured attraction was a series of field events presided over by Umpire Hank O'Day. Mordecai Brown won the fungo hitting contest, defeating Overall and Mullin with a 265 foot belt. Cobb bested teammates Davy Jones and George Winter, as well as Cubs' Johnny Evers, Del Howard, and Mordecai Brown, in the bunt and run event, covering the distance from home to first-base in 3.5 seconds. Cobb outpaced Evers and Winter in the base-running race, circling the sacks in 13.8 seconds. The "Georgia Peach" also captured the 100 yard dash, nosing out Jones and Artie Hofman. The 6,700 spectators roared their approval, and the players pocketed an additional $145 apiece to supplement their Series checks. The Tigers also received a $50 suit of clothes from their owners and a custom-made club bag from the Detroit City Council.[65]

In retrospect, the 1908 World Series was memorable for several reasons. First, it marked the innovation of having four umpires assigned to the Series. Only two worked in each game, however, with the duo of Bill Klem and Tom Connolly alternating with Hank O'Day and Jack Sheridan.[66] Second, the terrible accommodations for the press both in Detroit and Chicago resulted in the creation of the Baseball Writers' Association of America, whereby scribes could not only control press boxes, but also strive for uniformity in scoring procedures and suggest rule revisions.[67] Third, it marked the pinnacle of achievement for the wonderful Cub machine.

Without question, Chance's squad was one of the greatest diamond dynasties of all time, and, as Sanborn predicted, the names of Tinker, Evers, and Chance became synonymous with the national pastime. Yet the heart of the team was neither its hitting nor fielding, but rather the pitching staff. During the 1906–1908 league championship seasons, the starting aggregation of Brown, Overall, Reulbach, and Pfiester compiled an astonishing record of 232–85, leading the Cub mound corps to club earned run averages of 1.76, 1.73, and 2.14. With such mound aces, it seemed that the Chicago juggernaut could not be stopped.

The *Detroit Free Press,* however, offered wise counsel to those fearing perpetual Cub dominance. "The Chicago Cubs are a great team," it editorialized. "It is doubtful if any of the famous nines of the past was its equal. If they are kept together, will any other city have a chance for next year's honors? Probably the future will take care of it. The fate of other three-time winners may come to the Cubs. Another season or two may find them broken up and scattered."[68] Little did the gloating Chicago players, press, and fans realize the truth of this prophecy, for throughout the remainder of the twentieth century and into the twenty-first another world championship banner would never fly over the Cubs' home field.

CUBS VS. ATHLETICS, 1910

Despite compiling a 104–49 record in 1909, the Cubs were foiled in their bid for a fourth consecutive National League flag as they finished 6½ games behind the Pittsburgh Pirates. The following year Chance directed the Cubs to another 104 victory season, but this time the Chicagoans were rewarded with a return to postseason play. They took first place on May 25 and did not surrender it throughout the remainder of the campaign, finally outpacing the second place New York Giants by 10½ lengths.

The Chicago squad was basically the same as that which had humbled the Detroit Tigers in 1907 and 1908, with one significant change. Johnny Evers, a mainstay at second-base, had broken his leg sliding into home in a late season game and was relegated to watching the Series from the press box as a newspaper columnist. Although his replacement, twenty-three-year-old Heinie Zimmerman, was touted by his teammates as a "wonder" who "has the advantage of being so versatile at bat that no pitcher knows what to serve up to him," the third-year player could not match the injured veteran's fiery field leadership.[1] Fielder Jones, ex-manager of Chicago's American League White Sox, offered sage wisdom regarding the situation, telling reporters: "Zimmerman may be the greatest ball player in the world. I haven't seen enough of him to know, but I will say that Evers' absence will weaken the Cubs."[2]

The fabled Chicago assemblage, although aging, was still a formidable force both at the plate and with the glove. Chance (.298, 0, 36) patrolled first, Zimmerman (.284, 3, 38) was at second, Joe Tinker (.288, 3, 69) covered short, Harry Steinfeldt (.252, 2, 58), dubbed the "forgotten Cub" because he was not mentioned in the recently published poem extolling the other Cub infielders, handled third, and Johnny Kling (.269, 2, 32), remained a mainstay behind the plate. In the outfield, the Cubs boasted, from left to right, returning veterans Jimmy Sheckard (.256, 5, 51), Arthur Hofman (.325, 3, 86), and league leading home run slugger Frank Schulte (.301, 10, 68).

The mound corps was anchored by thirty-four-year-old Mordecai Brown (25–14, 1.86), who had hurled 295 innings and amassed a league best twenty-seven complete games, and rookie sensation Leonard (King) Cole (20–4, 1.80), who pitched 240 innings.

Supporting these aces were a quartet of double-digit winners, Harry McIntire (13–9, 3.07), Orval Overall (12–6, 2.68), Ed Reulbach (12–8, 3.12), and Lew Richie (11–4, 2.70). The only weakness of this staff was a lack of balance, as all were right-handers.

Facing the Cubs were Connie Mack's Philadelphia Athletics, who had compiled a 102–48 record to outdistance the New York Yankees by 14½ games. The Athletics, also known as Mack's "White Elephants," were a skillfully blended mix of youth and experience. The team revolved around twenty-three-year-old second-baseman Eddie Collins, whom Mack had signed off the diamond at Columbia University.[3] The "college boy" batted .322, with three home runs and eighty-one runs batted in, but more important to the A's were his league leading eighty-one stolen bases. Rounding out the infield were fifteen-year veteran Harry Davis (.248, 1, 41) at first, twenty-three-year-old shortstop Jack Barry (.259, 3, 60), and twenty-four-year-old Frank Baker (.283, 2, 74), who, only in his second full season, had not yet earned his famous "Home Run" sobriquet. The weak link in the inner defense, especially when compared to his Cub counterpart, was Yankee and Tiger castoff Ira Thomas (.278,1, 19), a weak-armed backstop who had shared the catching duties with Jack Lapp, Paddy Livingston, and Pat Donahue during the regular season.

Like the Cub infield, Mack's outfield entered the Series minus a key veteran. Center-fielder Rube Oldring (.308, 4, 57) suffered an injury near the end of the season, which necessitated Mack juggling his outer defense. Little used twenty-one-year-old Amos Strunk (.333, 0, 2), who had only forty-eight at-bats during the season, was inserted into center replacing Oldring. Flanking the youngster were Briscoe Lord (.280, 1, 20), a mid-season acquisition from the Cleveland Indians, in left and eleven year veteran Danny Murphy (.300, 4, 64) in right.

As was Mack's practice, he utilized a four-man pitching staff, relying on each to pitch 200 or more innings. The heart of the 1910 mound corps was Jack Coombs, a strapping twenty-seven-year-old right-hander from Colby College, who finished 31–9, with a 1.30 earned run average and 353 innings pitched. Joining Coombs were veteran right-handers Charles Albert (Chief) Bender, the Carlisle Indian School educated, one-quarter blood Chippewa (23–5, 1.58), pitcher/coach Cy Morgan (18–12, 1.55), and venerable thirty-five-year-old southpaw Eddie Plank (16–10, 2.01).

On the eve of the Series, most baseball scribes shared the view of their Windy City compatriot Hugh Fullerton, who predicted: "These green Athletic kids will show their inexperience when they grapple with the tested, battle-scarred Chicago veterans."[4] Not unexpectedly, most National League players and managers shared in Fullerton's assessment. Even Fielder Jones of the American League, while admitting that the Athletics were "one of the best home teams that ever played baseball," concluded that "if Chance's pitchers are as good as they were in 1907 and 1908, Chicago should have the edge."[5]

What impressed most observers was the supreme confidence exuded by the National League representatives. Ring Lardner, who rode with the Cubs on their special train to Philadelphia, wrote: "These Cubs are acting like a bunch of school kids just out for recess. The Cubs would be more surprised than anything else if the Athletics trim them. They just can't see a chance of losing."[6] Fielder Jones, who also was aboard the special train, shared Runyan's astonishment at the Cubs' nonchalant attitude. "In all my experience as a ball player and a manager, I never saw a ball team as unconcerned before entering a crucial series as are the Cubs on the eve of the first battle with the Athletics for the world championship. They talk of everything in the world but baseball. They may be thinking a lot of baseball, but they aren't talking it and are not nervous about it. Unless the Athletics are just as unconcerned, the Cubs will have an advantage over them regardless of the actual merits of the two teams.[7]

This supreme confidence on the part of the Chicagoans, which bordered on indifference, was typified by outfielder Hofman in his ghosted columns for the *Chicago Tribune*.

"We're going into the World Series to win four straight if possible. It doesn't seem just right for a ball player to praise his own team, but I must say that I believe that we have the best ball club ever put together," he gushed. "I may be prejudiced. I probably am. But I will say that I think our ball club is better than Philadelphia's, and I think we will win the World Series because the better ball club usually does win when it comes right down to a pinch. I firmly believe Mack has a great pitching corps. I'd be sorry if he had a poor pitching staff, for that would make the Series uneven. But however great the Philadelphia pitchers may be, I don't think there is one of them greater than Christy Mathewson, and we've beaten him not once, but many times. I think we have it over Philadelphia in infielding, pitching, and catching. Philadelphia can't win if it can't score, and I believe Mack's men will have a lot of trouble scoring, especially against Overall."[8]

Chance and Cub owner Charles W. Murphy were only slightly more cautious in their optimism than was their star outfielder. The "Peerless Leader" told reporters on the eve of the Series: "From what I have heard of the Athletics, they are a great ball club and will give us a harder fight for the world championship than Detroit did in 1907 and 1908. Of course, I expect to win, but I'm not looking for an easy time. I got over that long ago. We'll fight our hardest, and, if we lose, Connie Mack's players will know that they have been in a battle. I wouldn't be surprised to see the Series go six games or even seven, but I think we'll come out on top, and I'll have to hand it to the Athletics if they beat us."[9] Murphy echoed his manager's remarks, adding: "I don't want to take anything away from Connie Mack or [Philadelphia owner] Ben Shibe, but I really can't say that I consider the Athletics as strong as we are, and I believe my opinion will be proven correct in the next four or five days. I'll be satisfied with a victory in any number of games, but I can say conscientiously that I hope the Cubs take the first four."[10]

By contrast, Mack and Shibe were remarkably subdued. The manager dismissed questioning scribes with the terse observation: "I hope we will win. We have a chance."[11] Shibe was even more reserved, stating meekly: "I hope we can win it in four games, but I do not think we can quite do it."[12]

Under a cloudless sky, the initial contest was played before 26,891 baseball enthusiasts, the largest assemblage ever to witness a game in Philadelphia, and a contingent of hostile writers. Ben Shibe, who was notoriously frugal, had declined to add extra spaces in the press quarters for visiting newspapermen. Instead, out-of-town writers were assigned to the highest row of regular box seats and were compelled to use their knees as desks.[13]

In an effort to minimize illegal sales of tickets, Philadelphia officials decreed that everyone buying a general admission ticket had to immediately pass through the turnstiles and enter the park. The club had set a limit of ten tickets per customer and hoped that by compelling immediate entry, scalpers would not purchase tickets and then peddle them to those not wanting to stand in line. This did not stop unscrupulous purchasers, however, as they took their ducats, entered the park, and dropped the extras from the stands to waiting confederates. One scalper, who obviously did not trust his cohorts in crime, went so far as to jump twenty feet off a wall to personally deliver the tickets to partners.[14]

To the consternation of the fans, the opening pitch was delayed because of a long conference over ground rules and allowing motion picture cameramen on the field while the game was in progress. Umpire Hank O'Day of the National League, who was working on the bases, ordered the photographers off the field, but they refused to leave and appealed to American League President Ban Johnson. Tom Connolly, an American League arbiter who was umpiring behind the plate, was summoned to Johnson's box and informed that the National Commission had given permission for cameras on the field. Manager Chance then rushed over to object to cameras being placed behind home plate. Only after the crowd began impatiently chanting "Play ball!" was the crisis settled by consenting to place cameras along the grandstand behind first and third base.[15]

Once the contest finally began right-handers Chief Bender and Orval Overall each hurled a scoreless first inning, but in the second the home team tallied twice. Muscular Frank Baker led off the inning for the A's. Swinging his thick-handled, fifty-two ounce bat effortlessly, the Maryland farm boy drove an opposite field line drive past Sheckard into the crowd for a ground rule double. Davis sacrificed the runner to third, and he was driven in by Murphy's shot past Steinfeldt into left. Murphy then stole second, having taken such a long lead off Overall that Kling did not attempt to throw him out. Murphy went to third on Barry's ground out and, after Thomas drew a pass, scored on Bender's bad hop ground single over Zimmerman's head.

The Athletics added another run in the third on a long double into the crowd in right-center by Lord and a single to left by Baker. The White Elephants' final score came in the eighth off reliever Harry McIntire. Collins led off with a single and went to third on McIntire's wild pickoff attempt. Baker, who once innocently remarked that he "never saw a reason why a man with a bat in his hand should be unable to hit a ball thrown towards him," met one of McIntire's moist slants and lofted a high drive which landed a foot short of clearing the right-field wall.[16]

Meanwhile, Bender, "American Indian by birth, ball player by profession, and pitcher by grace of a strong right arm, clear head, and stout heart," was spinning one of the best games in World Series history, retiring the Cubs "with the regularity of the swing of a pendulum."[17] Through eight innings Bender had faced the minimum of twenty-four batters. Two Cubs had reached base, one on a single and the other on a walk, but both had been retired trying to steal. In the ninth, as E.A. Batchelor of the *Detroit Free Press* wrote, the Athletics, "probably in an excess of joy that victory was within their grasp, grew careless and the Chicago tribe, game to the last, managed to bunch a couple of hits [by Tinker and Kling] with as many errors [by Strunk and Thomas] to slip over the run that broke the shutout."[18]

After the 4–1 victory, which marked the first time since 1906 that the American League captured the opening game in the World Series, the Athletics lauded Bender's heroic effort. A beaming Ben Shibe, showing none of the previous day's concern, now exuded confidence. "I can't say how pleased I am at the showing of Bender and the rest of the boys. I knew they had it in them. We're perfectly confident now," he stated. "I can say sincerely that I believe we will win three out of the next four games, if we do not win the next three."[19] Mack, usually noted for his graciousness, was uncharacteristically blunt in his comments to reporters, stating: "The great Chicago machine showed us nothing. We have had much harder battles in our own league against pitchers such as [Walter] Johnson and [Eddie] Walsh. Overall wasn't the marvel of former seasons, that's true, but the victory gained right off the mark has given my boys resounding confidence. I won't say how many games will be needed, but the Series isn't going to be a long one."[20]

Among the losers there was grudging admiration for Bender, mingled with grim determination, disappointment, and defiance. Murphy, refusing to face newsmen, merely issued a terse press release: "I have to take my hat off to Bender for the work he did today, but if we could have hit him just a little bit we would have won. A defeat in the first game of the World Series is an unpleasant dose to swallow, but we'll get over it and show them something tomorrow. I still believe we have the greatest ball club in the world, and I'm not worrying about that defeat. I have great confidence in Manager Chance, and I don't expect him to lose a World Series as long as he is head of the Cubs."[21] Overall was candid in his self-assessment: "I couldn't do anything I wanted to do today, and that's all there is to it. Bender pitched a wonderful game and looked all the better because I looked bad. I know the weak points of most of their hitters, but somehow I just couldn't pitch to them."[22] Chance was seething over his club's dismal performance. "We had the best pitching we will get from the Athletics. Bender was almost invincible, but we have struck better twirling all year in certain National League boxmen, and we came out ahead. Mathewson is so much better than the Indian Bender that there is no comparison," he sneered. Then as an added insult, Chance stated: "I want to say that even [Louis] Drucke [of the New York Giants who went 12–10 during the regular season] right now is a better man than Bender. I made a mistake by not taking Overall out in the second inning. He did not show anything. But we'll cop the Series sure as shooting. The Athletics have shot their bolt."[23]

In his column, Hofman put forth the players' view of the Chicago debacle. "That's about the least discouraging defeat we've ever suffered," he wrote. "Of course, there wasn't one of us who wasn't sore about losing the first game, but there isn't one of us who doesn't believe we'll take tomorrow's game and the next three after that. The Athletics looked better than we did, but a team always looks bad when it isn't hitting — and we certainly weren't hitting."[24]

Hofman also offered an alibi for the fielding lapses of himself and Zimmerman that led to Athletic runs. "The sun bothered me a good deal in the outfield. Ordinarily I would have caught Lord's fly in the third without a bit of trouble. I saw it when it first left his bat, but when I reached up to pull down my goggles I lost it. When I started back after it, it was too late," he explained. "Also, the infield here must be hard to play for one who isn't used to it. Ground balls take peculiar bounds, and it is mighty hard to judge them. The diamond is a kind of turtle-back affair. I think today's experience will help a lot in tomorrow's game."[25]

On the way to Shibe Park for the second contest, five Chicago players were involved in a traffic accident. Johnny Kling, Harry McIntire, Ed Reulbach, Mordecai Brown, and utility man John Kane were thrown from their taxi, which was traveling at thirty miles per hour, when it collided with a mail car. Only Kane was injured seriously, twisting his left leg, but all were badly shaken and bruised by the incident.[26]

Once again the start of the contest was delayed, this time for the National Commission to present automobiles to Ty Cobb and Napoleon Lajoie for leading the major leagues in hitting. Normally only one automobile was awarded, but because Lajoie finished only a fraction of a point behind Cobb (.384944 to .384084), Hugh Chambers, founder of the automobile company which bore his name, announced he would donate a Chambers' "30" to both men. Cobb, who was covering the Series as a correspondent for the *Detroit Free Press,* accepted his award in person at home plate and, accompanied by Chambers and teammates "Germany" Schaefer and "Wild Bill" Donovan, drove the car around the outfield and out through a gate.[27] Lajoie, who felt the batting title had been stolen from him on a scoring decision in the final game of the season, did not appear, and his car was accepted for him by the secretary of the National Commission.[28]

When the call of "Play ball!" at last echoed through the stadium it brought joy to a disappointingly small crowd of 24,597 who had assembled to witness Jack Coombs face Mordecai Brown in what Cobb later called "the most spectacular game that has ever been played in a World Series."[29] The visitors scored in the first frame, as a result of walks to Sheckard and Hofman, an infield single by Chance, and a sacrifice fly off the bat of Zimmerman. In their half of the third, the Mackmen took advantage of two errors by Steinfeldt, a bunt single, and a double by Collins to take a 2–1 lead. The A's tallied again in the fifth, but the Cubs came back to within one run in the top of the seventh when Sheckard doubled into the crowd in right and scored on Chance's single to center.

In the bottom of the seventh, however, as E.A. Batchelor wrote, "the Athletics changed what had been a close and exciting game of ball into an utterly hopeless rout and sent Mordecai Brown to the bench a battered wreck."[30] Collins opened the inning with a pass and went to third on Baker's single to right. Davis drilled a ground rule double into the left-field crowd, scoring Collins and sending Baker to third. Murphy then duplicated Davis' performance, sending two more runners across the plate. After Barry's sacrifice, Thomas singled to left, scoring Murphy. Coombs moved Thomas to second on a fielder's choice to Chance, and Strunk sent him home with the Athletics' record setting fourth double of the inning. Johnny Evers, watching shell-shocked from the pressbox, murmured to a nearby writer: "How can you expect to beat a team that makes doubles, triples, and home runs off wild pitches!"[31]

The devastation was all the more pronounced because Chance had announced before the game that he had been saving Brown for the second contest and that his ace was in the best form of his life. This led E.A. Batchelor to muse: "If this be so, the Athletics must be a collection of great batsmen, for they thumped the miner with stout-hearted enthusiasm. It was rather surprising that Manager Chance left Mordecai in to assimilate such a walloping, but the Chicago leader probably had nobody handy on whom he could count for anything better."[32]

Lew Richie finished the game without permitting further damage, and the Cubs, showing spirit, scored a run in the ninth off Coombs, making the final score 9–3. Ironically, this was one of Coomb's worst efforts of his career. He walked nine, gave up eight hits, and was rescued repeatedly by brilliant fielding plays behind him. In the dressing room, the victorious hurler admitted his poor form. "My nerve won me the game," he said, with a hint of embarrassment. "I felt sure I could beat Chance's men before the game and had perfect control then, but when I walked on the field and took up pitching I felt my control slipping. Never did I lose my head though, and when I was in the tight places I worked my head as well as my arm. Their batters did not seem to be such a hard bunch, but they make a pitcher work hard. I owe much to my defensive support and the great work on the offensive by my teammates."[33]

Mack praised his hurler, stating: "I had confidence in John, and he finally came around. We're going to Chicago brim full of confidence. I'm delighted with the showing we have made against the Chicago club. I know Brown is one of the greatest pitchers the game has ever known, and to beat him is indeed quite a feather in our caps."[34] Ben Shibe gave his manager, rather than the players, credit for the Athletics' success. "Connie Mack is the greatest manager on earth," Shibe proclaimed proudly. "His brain made it possible for the Athletics to win the championship of the American League, and his brains will make it possible for the Athletics to win the world championship. This team is equally balanced, and by teamwork they will defeat the Cubs."[35]

Among the Cubs there was an air of "whistling through a graveyard at night." Murphy, seemingly oblivious to the dire straits in which his team now found itself, issued an unbelievable press statement, in which he asserted: "Two games is just the proper handicap for us to give the Athletics, and I believe we will take the next four straight. We will look different when we have them on our own grounds. All our boys tried their best, but luck was against them. The luck must break our way soon, and then you will see a difference."[36] Chance was just as blind to reality, echoing Murphy's excuse of "bad luck" being his squad's only nemesis. "Brownie was going along so well in the early part of the game that I thought sure we were going to win," he explained to queries by writers as to why he left his starter in for such a pounding. "Coombs didn't show up nearly as well as Bender, and I can promise you that we will give him all the trouble he wants the next time he works against us. If we could have hit in the pinches today we would have won hands down, for we would have taken all the fight out of the Athletics. The latter had luck enough to last them a whole season."[37]

As always, Hofman's column set forth the purported views of the Cub players. "While we were trimmed badly this afternoon, we certainly didn't look much worse than the Athletics," he whined, the clarity of his vision of the game perhaps still dimmed by his smoked sunglasses. "Brown had it on Coombs in every way up to the seventh inning. There is no mistaking that they hit the life out of the ball in that inning, hit it far away and in all directions. However, if we could have scored runs when we had chances earlier in the game, the Athletics wouldn't have been so full of pepper, and I don't think they would have done all that hitting in the seventh. If we had as much luck today as the Athletics had, it would have been nearly even. We certainly didn't have any of the better of the breaks. The balls seemed to bound wrong every time the Philadelphia batters hit them. They also bounded wrong when we threw them. The outfield was an awfully hard place to play because of the sun."[38] Amazingly, Hofman concluded this sob-story by saying: "I don't want to offer any excuses. I will let our showing in the next two games speak for itself."[39]

A more honest appraisal came from Barney Dreyfuss, the outspoken president of the Pittsburgh Pirates. "I never saw a team present a more demoralized appearance than Chance's outfit showed in the Quaker City," he told Pittsburgh scribe Ralph S. Davis. "They did not play real baseball for a single moment, and there is no denying that they showed up 50 percent below their real form. Miner Brown didn't look good. He appeared hog fat and lacked his usual speed, depending almost entirely upon his hook curve, which was properly murdered. It was rumored pretty freely in Philadelphia that some of the Cubs were not keeping themselves in the best condition. The way some of them played seemed to bear that out."[40]

On the train to Chicago, Mack was asked if Eddie Plank would take the mound in game three. The Athletic pilot, notorious for not naming his pitchers until just before game time, winked at the handful of writers eagerly hoping for a scoop. "You know, boys," he said softly, "Coombs did such a great job in Philadelphia for us yesterday, I think I'll come back with him again."[41] Thinking he was pulling their collective legs, the writers departed for the club car laughing at Mack's little joke.

The Cubs' train pulled into Chicago's Union Station an hour after that of the Athletics' and hundreds of loyal rooters gave their heroes a warm welcome. The scene was not entirely sanguine, however, as I.E. Sanborn related in the *Chicago Tribune:* "Only one untoward incident marred the homecoming, and that was the attempt of a misfit bug who not only got into the wrong pew, but the wrong church as well, by trying to hand a lemon to the Peerless Leader of that gallant band. It was so raw that even those in the crowd who were attracted by curiosity instead of sentiment resented it. They were no quicker than Chance was, for he smashed the would-be joker in the face and it took a large part of the crowd to keep the manager from changing the fellow's map so that his best friends would not recognize it, while the majority of the law, represented by the blue-coats, was all that kept the other half of the crowd from making pulp of the intruder."[42]

As a further show of their displeasure, and perhaps a prediction of the future, disgruntled Cub fans draped the door of club president Murphy's office in the Corn Exchange

National Bank Building with black crepe paper. They then barricaded the door and prevented janitors from removing it. Rather than incite public sentiment against himself and his team by calling in the police, Murphy permitted it to remain.[43]

An early morning rain that turned into a relentless cold mist by early afternoon, coupled with a strong northwest wind, helped to limit attendance to a smaller than expected gathering of 26,210 hearty souls. Shortly before game time, the shivering fans were warmed by the announcement of the starting line-ups. The temperature of those writers who had inquired about Mack's pitching choice on the train ride to Chicago also soared as they learned that the venerable gentleman's "joke" with them was that he was being truthful: it would be Coombs facing Ed Reulbach in the Windy City inaugural.

The A's took an one run lead in the top of the first on walk to Strunk, a sacrifice by Lord, and a single to center by Baker. The Cubs tied the count in their half of the frame on a walk to Sheckard, Schulte's ground rule double into the right-field crowd, and a sacrifice fly by Hofman. Each team scored twice in the second, the Athletics putting together a walk to Davis and doubles by Barry and Coombs and the Cubs getting a two-run double by Schulte.

In the third, however, the Mackmen launched one of their fabled assaults. Harry McIntire, who had come into the game to relieve the ineffective Reulbach at the start of the inning, got leadoff man Lord on a deep fly to left. Collins beat out an infield grounder and sped around the bases on Baker's three-bagger to deep right. Davis was hit by one of McIntire's underarm curves, and Danny Murphy followed with a towering three-run blast over the screen into the right-field bleachers.

Chance rushed onto the field screaming at Umpire O'Day that the ball should have been ruled a ground rule double. Connolly, who had made the call, charged in to explain his decision. Chance, who as I.E. Sanborn wrote, "would not have carried his protest so far if his big, strong heart had not been nearly breaking with the death of almost his last hope to win the 1910 world pennant," cursed Connolly for partisanship and called him, among other epithets, a liar.[44] In return, Connolly emphatically thumbed the Peerless Leader out of contest.

As he departed, still berating his nemesis in blue, Chance yanked McIntire in favor of southpaw Jack Pfiester. E.A. Batchelor noted sarcastically, this was perhaps done because "the Public Safety Committee had got out an injunction in response to the fans in the outfield stands complaining that their lives were being risked unnecessarily."[45] Pfiester gave up a double to Barry, and Tinker's wild throw to first on Thomas' slow roller permitted the fifth run of the inning to score. Coombs then hit into a double play to end the frame.

After this, neither team tallied until the seventh, when, once again, the Philadelphians demonstrated that any attempt to silence for very long their bats was as futile as "trying to stop a landslide with a toothpick" or "a steel projectile from a sixteen inch gun with so many pounds of butter."[46] After two had been retired, Baker reached base on Steinfeldt's error and moved to second on Davis' single to right. Murphy beat out an infield grounder, loading the sacks. Barry drove in two of his mates with a single to left, and Thomas walked to reload the bases. Coombs then helped his cause with a two-run single to center, giving him three runs batted in for the day.

The Cubs scored twice in the eighth, though both runs were a gift from the Athletic hurler. Sheckard led off with a base on balls and went to third on Hofman's single to left. Hofman took on Lord's vain attempt to cut down the lead runner. Both Cubs then scored on Coombs' wild pitch, making the final score 12–5, the worst beating any team had ever suffered in a World Series.

After witnessing the third consecutive exhibition of Cub ineptness, writers could contain their cynicism no longer. E.A. Batchelor poetically wrote: "As the waters of the Great Lakes go over the cataracts of Niagara, ceaseless and irresistible, so did the Athletics go over the helpless Cubs this afternoon. The crash of Mackmen's bats meeting the ball sounded like the roll of a snare drum, and the patter of feet as the Philadelphians swarmed around the sacks in squads was like unto the rattle of rain on a tin roof. If the first game of the Series had been a defeat, and the second a rout, today's affair was a massacre that, like the Alamo, knew no survivors. Connie Mack could have taken the mound himself and won with all that kind of hitting behind him. The Cubs were about as bad as their pitchers today, which is all that can be said about them in a paper that goes through the mails. They played raggedly in the field, ran bases without judgment, and in general gave the appearance of being totally demoralized."[47] I.E. Sanborn led off his game commentary stating: "The Cubs are in their last ditch now, and if it was anybody but Frank Chance and his grim warriors, no man on earth would give them a ghost of a show to rally after the terrific beating they got today."[48]

Former Cub owner and president James Hart blamed age for the National Leaguers' performance. "Like the man whose afternoon pleasure was ruined because he was compelled to ride to his wife's funeral in a carriage containing his mother-in-law," he wrote in an attempt at macabre humor, "my enjoyment today was blasted when Murphy of the Athletics in the third inning put the ball into the right-field seats for a home run. The icy cold fact remains that our favorites were out-pitched, out-batted, and out-fielded, and, as usual with a losing team, they looked weak in comparison with their opponents. It seems to me that the decisive result of the three games already played gives more or less a reminder that in test of skill in athletics youth must be considered as an all-important factor. Chance's men have the experience, the brains, the nerve, but it may be they are lacking the important quality of youth, which is so emphatically a part of the American League champions. It has been the most aged of the Cub team who thus far have failed to deliver the goods, which their friends and admirers know have been there in the past."[49]

No one was more vicious in his condemnation of his hometown club than the caustic H.E.K of the *Tribune*. "Is there any excuse for further dissembling? Is there any reason for encouraging a hope that was knocked down on Monday, stepped on on Tuesday, and run over by a truck on Thursday?" he asked angrily. "Wouldn't it be just as well to let the old cat die without attempting to prolong its life through another edition by shooting it full of digitalis and oxygen? It's hard to sustain a line of salve, especially when it is adulterated, if not out and out spurious. To look a friend in his sunken and filmy lamps and tell him that he is looking first-rate when his ears are set far, far off listening for the flutter of wings and the tinkling of harp strings is rather irksome, to say the least."[50]

Having thus dismissed the Cubs' future, H.E.K. analyzed why they were lying in their coffins being lowered into a mass grave. "The Cubs were overpowered, crushed, and humiliated in the third game," he wrote bitterly. "The young and gamesome Athletics, schooled and trained in every department of the game, including courage, by one whom we all must now acknowledge as a master craftsman, a superlative organizer and tactician, demonstrated before a crowd, vast and critical, that this wonderful machine we have been boasting about as the *ne plus ultra* of baseball combination was nothing more than a magnificent shell, a glittering reminder that it must have owed its prowess and prestige during the late season, at least, to the effect on the minds of its opponents of the dazzling glamour of past performances. There is a compelling reminder in that game, and the two that preceded it, of [John L.] Sullivan against [Jim] Corbett, [Jack] Dempsey against [Bob] Fitzsimmons, and [Jack] Johnson against [Jim] Jeffries—a record against a reality, age and mocking confidence against youth and enthusiasm. A man who is glutted with the glory of past achievement never feels himself slipping until he has slipped, and a ball club is but the embodiment of many men with a single impulse."[51]

Despite these attacks on their ability, no one in the Cub organization would concede defeat, although a disgusted Overall did announce his retirement effective after the World Series.[52] Murphy kept on his rosy public mask, saying: "The Athletics have outplayed us in these three games, but I don't think they can keep it up forever. I have seen the Cubs win four straight often, and it would not surprise me a bit if they did it now."[53] Chance brought out all the hackneyed phrases used by losers. "A World Series is never over until one club has won four games," he fumed to newsmen after the game. "It would be foolish to say that I am not sorry about the results of the three games we have played, but I can say that we will not quit until we have won the Series or lost it. I still think we have the better ball club, and I won't admit that the Athletics are world champions until they have won the title."[54] Even the usually ebullient Hofman was subdued but still hopeful. "You can bet we will try hard to win the next game, for it isn't the pleasantest thing in the world to lose a World Series," he wrote. "We won't give up until it's over."[55]

Sensing the opportunity to become the first team to win the championship in a four game sweep, the Athletics radiated smugness. Speaking for his players, Connie Mack could not contain his enthusiasm, telling reporters: "I'm not at all surprised at the way the Series has gone so far. I will admit that I didn't expect that we would take four straight before the first game was played, but I believe we will do so now. I'm anxious to make a clean sweep and get it over with."[56]

Joy was so pervasive among the youthful A's that even being the victim of a "loaded cigar" prank could not dampen the spirits of Cy Morgan. Amid howls of laughter from his mates, the thirty-one year old pitcher and coach peered through the smoke, holding the shattered end of the exploded cigar between his teeth. "I'm used to seeing things blow up," he chortled. "So, I'll finish this cigar just the way we will finish the Cubs tomorrow!"[57]

The day of the scheduled fourth game dawned as dark as Cub fans' spirits, and by early afternoon a steady downpour had flooded the field, causing the contest to be postponed. The rain delay gave critics a chance to continue their ridicule. I.E. Sanborn's column was headlined "It is Seldom That a Funeral is Postponed Because of Mean Weather," and the *Detroit Free Press* editorialized: "Rain saved the Cubs from dropping the fourth game in a hurry. Chicago has nothing but its census returns to be proud of."[58]

For the first time, however, a scribe dared offer a somewhat half-hearted defense, which read more like an obituary, of Chicago's battered bruins. "Chicago fans now find humor in mailing lemons to Manager Chance and suggesting the substitution of a 'D' for the 'C' in spelling the nickname by which the club is known and in hurling jibes and jeers at the players they formerly honored. Overconfidence, if there was any; cocksuredness, if there was any; even enthusiastic egotism, if there was any, are not crimes. Too much may prove costly, but it does not indicate yellowness," wrote the *Chicago Tribune*'s sports editor Harvey Woodruff. "The disintegration of former greatness, whether in baseball or anything else, is pitiable. If the Cub machine, our proud boast of former years, is disintegrating, its members deserve sympathy, not reproach, as their years of active diamond work near an end. Why not give the Athletics their share of credit. Admit that their batting and pitching have been superior. Manager Chance and his club deserve better treatment than they are receiving at a time when their own spirits and hopes might well have been crushed by the unexpected reverses they have suffered. All the world professes to hate a quitter, but Manager

Chance's Chicago Cubs, four times National League champions and twice world champions, have not QUIT."[59]

Ring Lardner used the diamond respite to interview the besieged Peerless Leader, who proved unexpectedly forthright in his evaluation of the Series. "We have one thing in our favor," he said, mustering an attempt at humor. "There isn't a chance for us to play worse ball than we've played, and there is a big chance for us to play a great deal better. I don't feel at all good about our three straight defeats. I wouldn't have cared so much if they had whipped us 1–0, 2–1, or by any close score, for then we would have known that we had been in some battles. As it is, we haven't had a chance to play any ball, let alone the ball of which we are capable. I regret that our pitchers weren't at their best. If they had been, the Athletics wouldn't have had such a picnic. I can take defeat gracefully, but I don't like to have our club shown up. The Athletics have played great ball, but I have seen the Cubs play even better. It is unfortunate that they haven't done themselves justice in this Series. However, there is another game coming, and there may be four more. We'll try to make it four, but you won't hear us squeal if we're trimmed."[60]

Charles Comiskey, president of the Chicago White Sox, stole the day's sporting headlines, however, by asserting that the balls used in the World Series were different than those used during the regular season. The suspicions of the Old Roman had been aroused by comments made by Fielder Jones following the first game in Philadelphia. The former Sox manager had told Comiskey: "They're using a different ball than the ones we had when I was in the game. It bounds differently and looks livelier. I have never played with the new cork core baseball, but I have read about them. That probably explains why they look different. It's a different ball."[61]

Comiskey then decided to do his own research and called a press conference to reveal his findings. "The balls used in that [third] game yesterday were not like the balls batted by the White Sox this season," he stated. "They were livelier. That's the only way I can explain to my own satisfaction the amount of clean, hard hitting, which was greater than I have ever seen in one game between two high-class team. I've been watching ballgames a good many years. It seemed to me that those balls did not bound as I expected them to. They bounced higher than seemed natural, and they left the bats of the players differently. The only way I can understand it is that they were livelier than the ones the American League used this year. Of course, it is just as fair for one club as another, and it is my explanation of why so much good hitting was done off good pitching."[62]

Immediately, the Albert J. Reach Company, which manufactured the official baseballs used by the major leagues, denied Comiskey's allegation. A company spokesman explained that two baseballs were produced, one for each league, but the only difference was the color of the thread used to sew the covers and the official stamp and signatures placed upon them. The cork core, he insisted, was identical for both leagues and was the same used during the regular season. This ended the furor, and the public, reassured of the integrity of the national pastime, returned their thoughts to what might be the final game of the diamond season.[63]

Decades later, George Reach, Albert's son, confided to sportswriter Fred Lieb that Jones and Comiskey had been correct. The 1910 World Series participants were being used secretly as guinea pigs to try out a new baseball, which had a layer of corrugated rubber wound tightly around the cork center. "We had been experimenting with this ball for some time in our Philadelphia factory," related Reach, "and with the consent of the old National Commission decided to try it out in the 1910 World Series. Only a few were in on the secret. Ban Johnson, [National League President] Tom Lynch, 'Uncle Ben' Shibe, my father, and maybe a few others. And those young Athletics really feasted on that new ball."[64]

Under partly cloudy skies and a cool breeze, 19,150 diehard Cub faithful passed through the turnstiles silently praying for a miracle that could keep Chicago's slim hopes alive for another day. To their surprise, Manager Chance, demonstrating both a superstitious nature and desperation, opted for several changes in his team. First, he ordered the squad outfitted in new uniforms of white from caps to hosiery. Second, he sent Leonard (King) Cole, a Bay City, Michigan barber who was only a year removed from toiling in the South Michigan League, to take the mound to face Chief Bender. Finally, he benched Johnny Kling, who was batting .087, and inserted Jimmy Archer behind the plate.

The manager's maneuver's seemed to pay instant dividends as the home team took a 1–0 lead in the bottom of the first. Sheckard led off the frame by drawing his seventh pass of the Series and then stole second. A sharp single to left by Hofman sent him home. The A's evened the count in the third when Bender drew a pass and scampered across the plate on Strunk's triple to right. The Athletics took the lead with two runs in the fourth on a single by Collins and doubles by Baker and Murphy. The Cubs, however, countered for one run in their half of that frame on consecutive singles by Schulte, Hofman, and Chance.

Bender nursed his slender lead and entered the bottom of the ninth maintaining that narrow one-run margin. Schulte brought the crowd to its feet with a leadoff double to right. Hofman moved him to third with a neat sacrifice bunt down the first-base line. Chance then lined a triple to the deepest sector of center, driving home the tying run. Bender then bore down and retired the next two batters, leaving the winning run stranded on third.

Mordecai Brown, who had come in to relieve Cole in the top of the ninth, retired the Mackmen in the top of the tenth. In the bottom of that inning, Manager Chance's intuitive genius came to the fore as, with one out, Archer doubled to left and moved to third on Brown's ground out. Sheckard lopped a single to right, and the Cubs had earned their first victory by a score of 4–3

Mack was stunned that his team, which had out-hit, out-fielded, and out-pitched the Cubs, left the field with the short end of the score. However, he quickly smiled and told the gathering of writers who crowded around him: "I'm disappointed in not being able to win four straight, but four out of five will be almost as good. I have no complaint to make about the showing of our boys. They played good ball, but things went against them. We've used only ten men in the four games played so far., and it would have been a proud record if we could have taken four straight without altering the batting order in any of the contests. But tomorrow will be another day."[65]

The Cub dressing room was filled with laughter and cries of "now we'll get 'em." A beaming Murphy congratulated the team and personally told reporters: "That's a lot better than a defeat. It shows the whole world that the Cubs are not in the quitting business. We have only three games to win instead of four. We will win here and in Philadelphia, and I hope the deciding game will be played at the West Side Park so Chicagoans will see it."[66] Chance yelled: "We beat their best pitcher, and I don't believe he can come back. I hope we convinced everybody that we are not outclassed in this Series. We haven't won the Series by any means, but we are lots nearer the world championship than we were last night. We'll give them another battle tomorrow afternoon, and I'll have my grip packed ready to start for Philadelphia sometime tomorrow night."[67] The "fighting spirit" theme was carried on by Hofman, who declared: "I'm tickled to death over that victory, not only because it was a victory, but because it was a blow in the face of the fans who said that the Athletics had our goat. I don't think you will find many ball clubs that will fight as hard to the last ditch as we did. Instead of giving up because we looked bad, our players played all the better ball."[68]

A beautiful autumn sun favored the 27,374 fans who jammed into the West Side Park to see if their three-fingered hero, Miner Brown, could send the Series into a sixth game by defeating Coombs. Mack, sensing either an easy triumph or a need to rest some of his regulars, inserted Jack Lapp behind the plate for Ira Thomas and Tully (Topsy) Hartsel in left for Amos Strunk.

There were groans when the A's took a one-run lead in the first, but cheers erupted in the bottom of the second when Chance doubled and scored on Steinfeldt's infield hit. Boisterous hometown fans yelled at the top of their lungs in the fourth when, with one out, the Cubs loaded the sacks on a walk, single, and an error by Baker. Mack called time and called Coombs to the bench. "Just take your time, Jack," Mack said softly, trying to reassure his hurler. "Nice and easy. Just don't walk anybody. Don't give 'em a run. Let 'em work for it."[69] Coombs stared at his manager, twirled the ball in his hand, and replied: "Don't worry Mr. Mack. I'll take care of this situation."[70] Waiting at the plate was veteran Joe Tinker, who entered the game batting .429. The shortstop fanned on three curves. Archer then went down swinging at three fastballs.

As Coombs' final pitch to Archer thumped into Lapp's mitt, the Philadelphia reserves jumped up, waving their arms and shouting. They became so wild in their gesticulations that Mack, wearing his traditional blue business suit and starched collar, was knocked off his seat and sent sprawling into the dirt. Horrified, the players looked down in stunned silence, as Mack rose and brushed himself off. Breaking into a broad grin, he told his men: "It's all right, boys. I'm pretty excited myself, and I have another suit back at the hotel."[71]

The excitement of Mackmen increased in the top of the next inning when they regained the lead on an error by Steinfedlt, a sacrifice, and a single to left-center by reserve catcher Jack Lapp. The A's clung to their narrow margin, with Coombs and Brown matching each other in a brilliant pitching duel, until the eighth, when once again the Philadelphia sluggers erupted.

Coombs started the frame with a single to right, but was forced at second by Hartsel. A moment later, Hartsel made a dash for second and slid hard into the bag. The play was extremely close, and when American League arbiter Jack Sheridan ruled the runner safe Zimmerman "rushed at the umpire like a grizzly crazed by mortal wounds."[72] Chance raced to the scene and pulled Zimmerman away in a bearhug.[73] Amid the steady outpouring of booing and hissing aimed at Sheridan, Lord stepped to the plate and doubled to right, sending Harsel across the plate. Collins followed with a double over the bag at first, which O'Day ruled fair, and Lord scored easily. Chance argued to no avail that the drive was foul. On the next pitch Collins picked up his fourth steal of the Series but was cut down at the plate in his attempt to score on Baker's grounder to Zimmerman. Davis drew a pass and scored on Murphy's single to short center. Murphy steamed into third on the play when Zimmerman made a wild relay to the plate trying to cut down the slow-footed Baker. Brown, clearly unnerved and exhausted, uncorked a wild pitch, permitting Murphy to lope home with the fifth run of the inning.

Although the Cubs scored one run in the eighth on a double by Sheckard and a single by Chance, the rally fell far short and the Athletics took the world championship game by the final score of 7–2. When Kling, pinch-hitting for Brown hit into a force play for the last out, it seemed as though everyone in the stands had become an Athletics fan. Hundreds of spectators singing "What's the matter with Connie? He's all right!" rushed the Philadelphia bench and cordons of police had to storm the field to escort the besieged players and Mack to waiting taxicabs. In an effort to placate the cheering throng, and doubtless to buy enough time for the police to restore order, several players tossed belts, caps, shoelaces, and other paraphernalia into their midst.[74]

On the other side of the field, the Cubs dejectedly made their way to their clubhouse to face what they knew would be a steady stream of second-guessing and criticism. Angry and embarrassed, no one from owner Murphy down to the lowliest reserve was a completely gracious loser. Murphy snorted: "I want to give Connie Mack and his players all the credit due them. They outplayed us and out-pitched us. The Series gave the impression to the world in general that we were beaten by a better ball club. I will admit the Athletics were better when they played us, but I can't believe they have anything on us when we are at our best."[75] Chance somberly stated the obvious: "There is really not anything to say. I've said often enough that we wouldn't do any squealing if they beat us, and I don't intend to do any now. We were beaten four games out of five, and I'll let the figures talk for themselves. If anyone wants to say that Connie Mack has a better ball club than I have, I'll let him say it and I won't try for a comeback. The Cubs were beaten. They have been beaten before, but I think they have made a record of which anyone would be proud. I hope the Athletics will win the American League next season, for I want another chance at them."[76] Brown was disconsolate, saying: "I didn't have the stuff that is usually mine. I'd like to face Mack's club when I'm at my best, and I hope I'll have another chance before I'm out of baseball — and I have no intention of quitting for a while."[77] Hofman remained the most combative of the Cubs, stating: "I don't want to take anything from the Athletics. They outplayed us in the Series. There isn't a doubt about that. I will admit. We don't want to squeal, but I would give everything I have in the world to see them play us when we were right and our pitchers were right. Without saying a word about our outfield, which I believe is better than theirs, I will say that any intelligent manager would think a long while before he would trade any infielder we have for anyone they have. We have catchers we wouldn't give for their catchers no matter what they offered us in return. I think even Connie Mack will admit that we have the better ball club in many respects. But don't take this as a knock at them. They outplayed us all around and deserved to win the world championship. If they win out the next season, however, I'll bet all that I have that we'll beat them."[78]

Whispering among the Cubs laid much of the blame for the defeat on Johnny Kling, whose sloppy glovework they believed had permitted Athletic coach Topsy Hartsel to steal the catcher's signs. Pitcher Jack Pfiester openly vented his frustration, asking a Chicago scribe rhetorically: "How can you expect a guy to win with his catcher giving the signs so the coaches can read 'em and tip the batters?"[79] The notoriously hot-tempered Kling, being told of the remark against him, confronted his accuser and shot back: "And you can't expect a catcher to win a game for you if you haven't got anything on the ball."[80]

A few days later, Kling, who subsequently was traded to the Boston Braves before the 1911 season, defended himself to Christy Mathewson. "Why, I changed signs every three innings, Matty," he said bitterly. "Some of the boys said that I gave the old bended-knee sign for a curve ball. Well, did you ever find anything to improve on the old ones? That's why they are old."[81]

While the losers wallowed in recriminations, the victors, once safely ensconced in their quarters, "carried on like schoolboys" and, as E.A. Batchelor, a veteran observer of American League baseball, noted: "Connie Mack was actually seen to laugh, the first time in history that this phenomenon has been recorded."[82] The beaming Philadelphia manager made no effort to conceal his delight, boasting: "I knew we would win and was not the least bit afraid of the Cubs. We outclassed the Cubs in every department and hammered their pitchers at will. Only for a few tough breaks in the luck in the fourth game and we would have made it four straight. Chance and his men put up a fine fight and were game to the last, but they couldn't hold up their end against the aggregation that represents Philadelphia. We won because we had the better team, and I'm proud to be manager of the Athletics."[83]

Coombs, who matched Christy Mathewson's perfect 3–0 record achieved against the Athletics in the 1905 classic, was overjoyed. "I have achieved my life's ambition," he exclaimed. "I felt confident that I could beat the Cubs and was fortunate enough to make good. Great fielding and great hitting made it easy for me to win my games. We beat the Cubs fairly and squarely. I would have been happier if we had taken four straight, but I'm happy enough now."[84]

Following the Series, Mack, who was about to end his years as a widower and remarry, returned to his home in Philadelphia. As he was sitting in his favorite chair talking with his elderly mother, he glanced out his front window and was horrified by what he saw. Local fans were bringing him a present: a full grown, live elephant, which had been given a coat of whitewash to make it symbolic of the Athletics. Mack grabbed his coat, dashed out the rear door, and hurdled the backyard fence to safety. Mrs. McGillicuddy, with tears in her eyes, had to argue with the gift-bearers for an hour before she convinced them that her son had no room for an elephant and that they should give it to a zoo. Disappointed, they led the beast away, so that Mack could slip back into his house.[85]

In retrospect, this World Series was significant for several reasons. First, it established Connie Mack as the American League's equivalent of John McGraw of the New York Giants as a master strategist. Second, it set the stage for the youthful Athletics to begin Connie Mack's first diamond dynasty, as they returned to the Fall Classic in 1911, 1913, and 1914, capturing the world championship from the Giants in 1911 and 1913 and losing to Boston's "Miracle Braves" in 1914. Third, it reaffirmed that Chicago, the nation's second largest city, was the greatest sporting metropolis in the country. As E.A. Batchelor wrote: "There was nothing resembling a real demonstration when the Athletics won their first two games at home. The players walked off the field without being obliged to fight their way through a mob of enthusiastic rooters, and nobody seemed to think to give the winning pitchers a ride on their shoulders. In Chicago when the Cubs came to life for a moment and won a ball game it was altogether different. The fans went fairly mad, mobbing the Cubs in an effort to get at them and shake hands and giving those whom had taken a prominent part in the struggle cheer after cheer. The next day the fans packed the ballpark as it had never been packed before and, as long as there was anything to shout for, kept up their clamor. We have to hand it to the Windy City for enthusiasm in the face of many discouragements.[86] Fourth, it marked the beginning of a rebuilding phase for the aging Cubs, and it would not be until 1918 that a National League pennant would again flutter in Chicago.

However, it was *The Sporting News* which set forth the true meaning of the 1910 Fall Classic and what James Hart referred to simply as "America's grand game."[87] "Another World Series has passed into memory," it editorialized, "and while some may question an assertion that it has fully measured up to the forecast that it would be the greatest ever known, there can be no question that it possibly proved the very greatest and, assuredly in many respects, surpassed its predecessors. It is certain that no previous World Series, or, in fact, any sporting event, has previously commanded the universal attention and interest that this battle between the Athletics and Cubs has. It is no exaggeration to say that in a nation of 15,000,000 persons, young and old, men and women, were almost were almost breathlessly awaiting results last week or following in the mind's eye two steel-clad deluxe trains speeding between Philadelphia and Chicago on the off day."[88]

"The great interest aroused is an abject lesson in itself," the "Bible of Baseball" continued. "No other sport commands it. But, after all, the lesson is the same old one to which attention is often called — the confidence the nation has in the absolute honesty of baseball, the knowledge that it is the cleanest, grandest game ever known, in addition to its intrinsic merits as a thrill producer. Chicanery, incited by the gambling element having large sums of money involved in the issue, is unknown. Baseball is the one game of which it can be safely said that skill and chance alone decide the issue, and as long as that can be said without fear of contradiction so long will baseball continue to show its wonderful prosperity of the present time."[89]

WHITE SOX VS. GIANTS, 1917

Baseball, with its promise of springtime hopes and summer excitement, was unceremoniously shoved from the limelight before the first pitch was thrown in 1917, when on April 6 the Congress of the United States consented to President Woodrow Wilson's request and declared war on Germany. The entire season, which many observers had expected to be cancelled before its conclusion, had been played under the ominous cloud brought forth by headlines of bloody battles in unfamiliar regions an ocean away and the certain knowledge that soon Americans would be dying in combat. Yet, to the faithful, the national pastime maintained its lure, even if now it merely assumed the role of a momentary diversion from the spectre of the horrible reality sweeping the world into turmoil.

At the close of the season, the Chicago White Sox, who had fallen two games short of catching Boston the previous year, won 100 games and romped to a nine length victory of the defending world champions. The White Sox, piloted by Clarence (Pants) Rowland, the first manager with no major league playing experience to win a pennant, led the junior circuit with 219 stolen bases, 81 triples, and 657 runs scored, while compiling an amazing 57–20 record on their home field.[1]

Chicago's easy triumph surprised most diamond experts because, despite some selected impressive statistics, the Sox were far from being a mighty offensive aggregation like the Red Sox and Athletics. Because of their woeful team batting average of .253, even their most faithful followers sarcastically dubbed them the "new Hitless Wonders." Only the outfielders possessed respectable numbers, led by center-fielder Oscar (Happy) Felsch's .308, with 6 home runs and 102 runs batted in. In left, "Shoeless Joe" Jackson, hampered all year by nagging injuries, batted a mere .301, with 5 homers and 75 RBI. Right-field was patrolled by John (Shano) Collins (.234, 1, 14) and Nemo Liebold (.236, 0, 29). Around the infield, third-sacker George (Buck) Weaver (.284, 3, 32), rookie shortstop Charles (Swede) Risberg (.203, 1, 45), second-baseman and team captain Eddie Collins (.289, 0, 67), and Arnold (Chick) Gandil (.273, 0, 67) had sub-par years, while backstop Ray Schalk (.226, 2, 51) added little punch.

Moreover, the Sox were riddled with dissention, much of it aimed at the cocky, well educated, high salaried team captain Eddie Collins. His fellow infielders refused to throw the ball to the former Athletic in pre-game warm-ups, and Weaver viciously denounced the gentlemanly demeanor of Collins while running the bases and fielding his position.

"He figured they might come back at him [if he slid hard into a fielder] and he'd get hurt playing there in the infield," Weaver sneered. "He was a great guy to look out for himself. If there was a tough guy coming down to second, he'd yell for the shortstop to take the ball."[2]

Therefore, the Chicagoans triumphed because of team speed, intelligence, and a superior cast of moundsmen, who crafted a league leading earned run average of 2.16, led by thirty-three-year-old Eddie Cicotte. The veteran right-handed "shine" ball artist led the league with a 28–12 record, 347 innings pitched, and a 1.53 earned run average. His success led Philadelphia Athletics' manager Connie Mack to observe: "I don't understand it. Two years ago Cicotte appeared on his way out. Now he looks faster than ever because of the shine ball. One side is darkened, the other light, and it is like looking at two pitches."[3] Nor was Mack alone in his concern about the legality of Cicotte's doctoring of the ball, which caused it "to break like the course of a flying pigeon just after a shot had been fired."[4] During the season the pitch, which, according to *Detroit Free Press* writer E. A. Batchelor, made a "baseball perform stunts that it is hard for a sober man to believe possible," had been protested in virtually all of his outings and had been subjected to a chemical analysis.[5]

Despite all the uproar, according to veteran *Chicago Tribune* scribe I.E. Sanborn this mysterious pitch did not exist. Before the Series opened Sanborn informed his readers: "It is my belief that the 'shine' ball is mostly a myth. Cicotte has perfected his knuckleball and his control of it to such an extent that his opponents have imagined it was uncanny and also illegal. None of the attempts of rivals to discredit his performance has been successful, and none of the American League umpires or players has been able to discover anything illegal in his delivery."[6] Cicotte, not unexpectedly agreed, revealing to writers: "Hap Felsch and I framed it on a training trip. The idea was to rub the ball in a peculiar way to make batsmen think I was doing something to it. I wasn't really, but others thought I was. Felsch started the talk, and the first thing we knew the 'shine' ball was an established fact."[7] Fact or fiction, Giant skipper John McGraw refused to believe anyone from Chicago and

1917 White Sox team photograph (Chicago Historical Society, ICHi-20696).

ordered Fred Anderson, a spitballer, to throw a similar pitch to his mates in batting practice.[8]

The remainder of the Chicago starters consisted of Urban (Red) Faber (16–13, 1.92), Claude (Lefty) Williams (17–8, 2.97), and Ewell (Reb) Russell (15–5, 195). Dave Danforth (11–6, 2.65), Jim Scott (6–7, 1.87), and Joe Benz (7–3, 2.47) rounded out the White Sox staff.

Because of their pitching, defense, and daring on the base paths, the American League champions were the darlings of both Chicago and team owner Charles Comiskey. At the onset of the campaign the notoriously frugal Comiskey had promised his squad a bonus if they captured the pennant. Priding himself on his honesty, if not his integrity, the "Old Roman" kept his pledge, and on the day his club clinched the flag he presented the players a case of cheap champagne, which, according to sportswriter Ring Lardner, "tasted like stale piss."[9]

Facing the White Sox in the World Series were the New York Giants, who had finished fourth the previous season. The New Yorkers had rebounded to 98 victories, finishing ten games ahead of the second-place Philadelphia Phillies and giving McGraw his sixth league title. The pennant was not only a personal triumph for McGraw, but also for club president Harry Hempstead, who had inked the pilot to a new contract giving him $40,000 and a percentage of the team's profits for the year, thereby making McGraw the highest paid person in Organized Baseball.[10]

McGraw's evaluation of his handpicked squad seemed effusive even given his reputation for self-adulation in his ability to mold a winning club. At the conclusion of the regular season, the New York leader immodestly informed reporters: "This is the strongest and best balanced team I have ever managed. It is the product of a combination of much thought, time, and money. I never had such a lot of hard and conscientious workers. I wanted, and worked to get, a team with the punch. I have it. I am also able to say the same of the Giants' defensive work. I do not think there was ever a team its equal for steadiness in that respect or in sensational fielding. Together with the Giants' rare batting and fielding ability and speed on the bases, they are, too, imbued with a true fighting spirit to win. They have been invariably at top speed when they have the most at stake."[11]

Undoubtedly the Giants were a solid club, but McGraw's opinion notwithstanding, they hardly represented diamond perfection. Like the White Sox, the strength of the New Yorkers was its pitching staff, which compiled a league best 2.27 earned run average. The ace of the starting hurlers was Ferdie Schupp (21–7, 1.95), closely followed by Harry (Slim) Sallee (18–7, 2.17), Will (Pol) Perritt (17–7, 1.88), John (Rube) Benton (15–9, 2.72), and 6'2", 218 pound "Big Jeff" Tesreau (13–8, 3.09). Fred Anderson (8–8, 1.44) and Al Demaree (4–5, 2.64) completed the mound corps.

At the plate the Giants were less awe-inspiring. The infield consisted of Walter Holke (.277, 2, 55) at first, second-baseman Charles (Buck) Herzog (.235, 2, 31), shortstop Art Fletcher (.260, 4, 56), and Heinie Zimmerman (.297, 5, 102), while Bill Rariden (.271, 0, 25) shared the catching duties with Lew McCarty (.247, 2, 19). From left to right the outfield was made up of George Burns (.302, 5, 45), flamboyant Benny Kauff (.308, 5, 68), and Dave Robertson (.259, 12, 54). By leading this group of "Punch and Judy" hitters to the league crown, McGraw had exhibited, according to many baseball analysts, the finest exhibition of his managerial skill.[12] Unfortunately for McGraw, his ego led him to believe that he had accomplished the most difficult part of his goal an that winning the World Series would be easy because the "busher," as McGraw scornfully referred to Rowland, would be no match for his bench wizardry.[13]

Because the White Sox and Giants seemed so evenly matched on the field, most baseball experts chose to emphasize the contrast between the opposing managers, giving the edge to McGraw. I.E. Sanborn, however, penned a series of columns to conjecture that the importance of the manager had increased proportionally to the decrease in the intelligence of the modern ball players. Sanborn, who had been covering the national pastime since before the turn of the twentieth century, stated that in "the old days" players had to be thick-skinned, self-reliant, and not require minute instructions from the bench as to what to try and when to execute certain tactics. These players, Sanborn recalled, were "supposed to know enough about the ABC's of baseball to use their own judgment in details sometimes of vital importance, while the manager was responsible for the generalship and broader scope of attack and defense."[14]

Unfortunately, lamented Sanborn, those days were past. "Today the average player has come to rely upon his manager for almost everything in the way of tactics," he asserted. Perhaps targeting the rift between Collins and his comrades, Sanborn added: "Because of this unwillingness to act on his own initiative, the modern player has become thin-skinned and unaccustomed to sharp criticism either from his leader or his teammates. Where old-school players, like the famous Cub machine, would fight each other and play all the harder for it, the player of today is more likely to sulk or be upset entirely by such tactics."[15] As a consequence, Sanborn explained, McGraw, who was often condemned for his tyrannical rule, was, in reality, compelled to take such action because his players lacked the ability and wisdom to act on their own.[16]

By contrast, Sanborn continued, Rowland had developed his leadership style in the "modern" game and refused to give orders lest it harm a fragile ego, but rather merely offered advice and suggestions to his men.[17] The problem with this method, Sanborn wrote sarcastically, was that while it might have a chance to be successful with an intelligent squad "no championship team in memory has shown poorer judgment, on the whole, than the White Sox," who were "constantly trying to devise ways to beat themselves."[18]

As expected, on the eve of the contest both teams were supremely confident of the Series' outcome. McGraw brashly predicted an easy victory. "The best thing I can say before the championship series is that the New York Giants are fit for a fight, and that I think I have as great a ball team as I have ever had in New York and one of the greatest ball teams the National League has ever had," "Muggsy" gloated. "I feel confident the boys will play as great baseball as they ever did, and that we will win. I feel certain that the Giants will bring the world championship back to the National League. We had a great team in 1912, but it wasn't as strong as this one, except in the pitching, and that was because in that department at that time Christy Mathewson was still on the slab."[19] Team captain Buck Herzog echoed his skipper and then explained why the Giants would triumph. "Nearly every one of the last half dozen World Series has been won by a long hit," he reminded assembled writers. "Don't you remember 'Home Run' Baker, Harry Hooper, Duffy Lewis, and Hank Gowdy? In a short series the long hit is the most effective weapon a club can have. I believe we have the better array of hard hitters. Burns, Kauff, Robertson, Zimmerman, Holke, and McCarty are liable to smash out an extra-base crack at any time. I think we have the edge on the Sox in this feature of the game, and I think it will be the thing that will win."[20]

For the American Leaguers, Sox President Comiskey was guardedly optimistic, but seemed to be more concerned with assuring prospective ticket buyers that his ball yard was in perfect condition for the opener despite the on-going heavy rain that had drenched the city. "I expect the White Sox to win the World Series and feel confident that they are going to. They are in perfect condition and will have no alibis," he stated, adding: "While I regret the fact that it was impossible to get any final practice on account of the rain, the diamond has been protected by the big cover and will be fit for the opening game."[21] Rowland seemed almost awestruck at his upcoming role, but he expressed complete confidence in his players, telling reporters: "The two greatest ambitions in my life have been realized in winning the American League pennant and getting into a World Series, particularly with John McGraw, recognized as the greatest manager in the National League. We are going into battle with plenty of confidence. Every one of my players feels that he has been in harder series during the pennant race than this one will prove."[22] Only grizzled Kid Gleason, a Pale Hose coach, sounded a note of danger, warning the Sox not to "hold the Giants too cheaply," and that they should not be overconfident because they would have to be "at their very best to beat the New Yorkers."[23]

Before the diamond hostilities began, each of the participants sought to demonstrate its patriotism as American Expeditionary Forces were preparing to move into combat along the Western Front. McGraw announced that all his players had participated in the first Liberty Bond drive and would continue to provide financial support for the war effort. "Every one of the Giants will put his shoulder to the second Liberty Loan with as much as he did in the first campaign," the New York pilot promised. "If anything, we will be better fighters in this big world series than we hope to be in our own World Series in Chicago and New York."[24]

Not to be outdone, Comiskey reminded reporters that he had donated 10 percent of his team's earnings, which amounted to slightly more than $200,000, during the regular season to the American Red Cross and that he would contribute 1 percent of his squad's post-season revenue to Washington Senators' President Clark Griffith's Bat and Ball Fund for American soldiers in France.[25] He also announced that for the Series he was changing his team's colors from black broadcloth and white socks to white uniforms with a huge red, white, and blue S over their hearts and red, white, and blue leggings."[26] Then, to prove that his patriotism and generosity went beyond just helping the troops—and to assure that he and his boys would receive favorable newspaper coverage—he declared that for Series games at his park he would provide the working press with a daily feast of ham, tongue, roast beef, potato salad, and green onions.[27]

The day before the initial contest Chicago was at the height of baseball frenzy. Despite the continuing downpour and temperatures so frigid that one wit remarked "only those qualified to serve on a polar expedition would enjoy sitting in Comiskey's ball yard," hundreds of fans stood in line throughout the night to purchase bleacher seats.[28] Speculators were selling $5 box seats for twenty times their face value, and the city was so thronged that E.A. Batchelor noted it was "as easy to get a room in a Chicago hotel as it is to cross the German frontier wearing Scotch kilts."[29]

Game day, however, dawned sunny, and mild temperatures created a perfect setting for the first encounter between the representatives of the nation's two largest cities. Huge red, white, and blue streamers fluttered in the gentle breeze, and several military bands stood and played patriotic tunes in front of flag draped field box railings. In the box seats behind first-base were thousands of uniformed service men, the invited guests of Comiskey, who led the cheering when the strains of the national anthem ended and "the flag that the boys are someday going to hoist over Mr. Hohenzollern's residence in Berlin" was raised.[30] Amid these festivities, Clark Griffith's volunteers, who included virtually every member of the Chicago Cubs, as well as Johnny Evers of the Phillies, Duffy Lewis of the Red Sox, and George McBride of the Senators, passed collection buckets among fans to raise money for his Bat and Ball Fund.[31]

Approximately one-fifth of the capacity crowd of 32,000 were women. While their finery added a welcome splash of color to contrast with the drab blue, black, and brown suits of the men in the stands, their presence also elicited sexist observations from baseball writers. One New York scribe reported that a female fan, after witnessing Rowland and McGraw shake hands for photographers, innocently remarked: "Oh, I thought these men knew each other before. How interesting."[32] A Chicago writer related that several of the women he interviewed said that their female friends who had tickets to the game bartered them to their husbands or male acquaintances in return for new hats or theatre tickets.[33]

Before taking the field, Comiskey gathered his players in the clubhouse and tearfully told them that his lifelong ambition was at stake, but that deep in his heart he knew they could fulfill his dream if only they would play the type of ball they were capable of playing.[34] Doubtless motivated more by the winner's share of the receipts than their owner's speech, the Sox dashed onto the field.

As expected, Eddie Cicotte took the mound for the home team to face the Giants' Slim Sallee, a ten-year veteran who had been obtained the previous year from the St. Louis Cardinals. The 6'3" 180 pound left-hander matched Cicotte for two innings. Then, in the third, Cicotte singled to center, but was thrown out trying to reach third on Shano Collins' single

Posed handshake between John McGraw of the Giants and "Pants" Rowland of the White Sox before first game of the 1917 World Series. Following the final Series game, a bitter McGraw refused to shake the victorious Rowland's hand (Chicago Historical Society, ICHi–38991).

to right. Collins, who had taken second on the throw in, scored when Benny Kauff misjudged a pop fly off the bat of Fred McMullin turning it into a two-base hit. The following inning, "Hap" Felsch, a German-American from Milwaukee, drilled a prodigious home run deep into the left-center field bleachers, prompting E.A. Batchelor to write: "These Germans aren't so bad at all, if you catch 'em young enough and remove them from the baneful influence of the Kaiser and his pals."[35]

The Giants tried to stage a comeback in the fifth, as Lew McCarty led off with a long triple to right-center and scored on Sallee's single. However, a double play ended that threat. For the rest of the afternoon Cicotte had the Giants "groping around for his knuckler like myopic old maids" and in their frustration they "folded up like accordions," losing 2–1.[36] In the stands, songwriter/singer George M. Cohan summed up sentiment of most Giant rooters, by sneering disgustedly: "After having seen the Giants, I am more enthusiastic than ever about the Yankees."[37]

In their dressing quarters the Giants put on a brave front, saying: "Wait until Cicotte faces us again. He'll be driven off the rubber before four innings have been played. We were surprised to learn that he really didn't have a thing."[38] This confidence and "we have just begun to fight" attitude in the wake of defeat prompted E.A. Batchelor to make a wartime analogy. "The Germans have been saying that ever since the retreat from the Marne. Every time they are driven back a few yards or a new country declares itself in on the side of the Allies the Kaiser has the official state printer tear off a few lines about how it looks practically a cinch for his brave soldiers, providing that 'Gott' doesn't loaf on the job."[39] Batchelor then rubbed more salt into the New Yorkers' wounds, adding: "The Giants may be as confident of beating Cicotte the next time out as they say they are, but it would be worth a small bet that if Eddie should break both legs before next Tuesday McGraw and his party would be able to bear up bravely under their load of grief."[40]

Among the victors, Comiskey was a picture of unbridled joy. "It is one of the happiest days of my life," he bubbled. "I think there was never a better game of ball played in the opening game of a World Series. I am sure that McGraw's team is one of the best the National League ever put out. New York has a great team, but we won! The boys stood up and were steady. I was proud of them individually and as a team."[41] Rowland expressed similar pride in his players. "At all times the Sox were up on their toes and wide awake," he beamed. "I am well satisfied with the first victory, for we won a tough and brilliant game of ball. I now feel assured that the world championship will belong to the White Sox."[42] The man in the dressing room with the biggest smile, however, was the aptly nicknamed "Happy" Felsch. In appreciation for his game-winning homer, fans bestowed upon the outfielder two $50 Liberty Bonds, a certificate for a new suit, several dozen pairs of socks, a new pair of shoes, neckties, and a pledge for a bloc of stock in a new airplane company.[43]

The weather once again cooperated for the second contest, with summer-like temperatures and a cloudless sky welcoming another capacity crowd of 32,000 Chicago partisans. Spitball artist Red Faber took the hill for the "Red, White, and Blue" Sox against Ferdie Schupp in the first World Series game ever played on a Sunday. The Giants' ace was staked to a 2–0 lead in the second on singles by Robertson, Holke, and McCarty and an error by Schalk. However, in their half of that frame the Sox tied the score on four consecutive singles and drove the shaken right-hander from the mound, leading a New York writer to note disdainfully that "Schupp had everything but experience."[44]

In the fourth, the rout began. Weaver beat out a bunt and moved to second on a single by Schalk. After Faber fouled out, Liebold singled one run home. McMullin followed with another run producing single, which drove reliever Fred Anderson from the mound.

Eddie Collins greeted new hurler Pol Perritt with a single, which drove in Liebold with another tally. To add to the Giants' misery, catcher Lew McCarty injured his throwing arm and shoulder when, in an attempt to tag the sliding Liebold, he lunged over him and crashed awkwardly on his right side. Jackson then sent a shot to right, which Dave Robertson, "panting like a deer which had been chased about twenty miles," could not catch, and two more Sox runners scurried across the plate, making the count 7–2 and ending the day's scoring.[45] When the McGraw's men finally retired the side, a Gotham scribe noted that "as they walked to the bench the Giants looked just as jolly as a crowd of invalids taking their constitutional on the lawn of Dr. Killum's sanitarium."[46]

In the fifth the crowd, already delirious with joy over their heroes smashing the "smarty effete easterners" into "tottering wrecks," were treated to some comic relief courtesy of Faber.[47] Weaver was safe on Fletcher's error and took second on a ground out. Faber singled to right. Robertson's throw held Weaver at third, but Faber advanced to second. Suddenly, Faber sped toward third with larceny in his heart. Giant reserve catcher Bill Rariden fired the ball to third-sacker Heinie Zimmerman. Weaver, who thought the Giants were trying to pick him off, dove back to the bag only to see Faber sliding in from the other direction. Zimmerman tagged both runners, looked up at Umpire Silk O'Loughlin and barked: "I got 'em both. What about it?"[48] Laughing, O'Loughlin replied to Heinie: "You're like the German Kaiser. You want too much for your own good. It's Weaver's bag until he leaves it. Faber can't run him off it. Faber's out!"[49]

Weaver, still clutching the bag, screamed at his teammate: "Where the hell are you going?" Without hesitation, the nonplussed Faber dusted himself off and said: "I'm going out to pitch."[50]

In the dressing room, amid the ribbing of his teammates, Faber gave his version of the play. "Rowland had instructed us to steal on Perritt if McGraw used him. We were to run bases wild. Well, Perritt was pitching, and when I went all the way to second on my hit into right I naturally concluded that Weaver scored, since Weaver only had to go from second," he explained with mock seriousness. "I didn't see Weaver on third — didn't think about looking for him because my mind was all set on stealing third. On the first ball he pitched I dug out for third. It was a bone, that's all."[51] Breaking into a wide grin, he added: "Hey, give me credit. I had the throw beaten."[52]

Once again, Comiskey was bubbling with praise and confidence. "I never felt happier in my life than in the fourth inning when the boys went out and knocked in those five runs. That clinched the ball game for us, and I figure just about clinched the world championship. The Sox proved their mettle in that attack, and it now seems that nothing can stop us. I'm proud to be president of such a grand ball club," he gushed to newsmen.[53] "I also want to thank the people of Chicago for their patronage," he continued. "I want them to know that I did everything possible to take care of them and am glad I have given them a team that looks like a world champion."[54]

Rowland, his right hand bandaged as a result of turning on a hot shower carelessly and being scalded by the steam, was equally ebullient. "I'm afraid to say for publication just how I feel about the Series now," he told reporters. "However, I can't help but feel absolute confidence in the final result, and I really am hoping to take four straight. The White Sox are the greatest short series team in the world."[55]

The Giants headed home with the jeers of Chicago fans of "Where oh where was John McGraw's wonderful galaxy of diamond stars" and "Where was the great baseball machine?" still ringing in their ears.[56] A *New York Times* baseball expert told his readers that McGraw's "extravagantly praised" champions had "become a laughing stock" which had been "thrashed into a limp, lifeless ruin," while humorist Arthur "Bugs" Baer described them as looking "like an accident going somewhere to happen."[57]

New York writers were unusually critical not merely because of the two unexpected losses, but also because of the Giants' lackadaisical performance. The players, they noted with dismay, "acted as though they were stale, and the lifeless, colorless games they played were nothing like the performances they had put up during the championship season" and that they "took defeat in an indifferent, matter-of-course way."[58] Gotham scribes even went so far as to put forth the unthinkable. "Even in strategy and generalship, Rowland has had the edge on McGraw," they admitted. "With Rowland coaching on the first-base line at Comiskey Park, and with Kid Gleason handing out advice along the third-base line, there has not been a single move by McGraw which has not been met and solved."[59] The Giants and their leader had to revive their pennant winning spirit or else, as the New York Times grimly predicted, "the World Series of 1917 will go down as a disastrous explosion of one of the most overrated clubs in the history of the game."[60]

Despite the Giants' having endured their dismal exhibition on the field, having their desire questioned by the press, and a one-day rain delay, the initial contest in the Polo Grounds was played before a sellout crowd of 33,616 hopeful fans. Some of the younger enthusiasts who were unable to purchase a ticket climbed to the roof of the elevated railroad station to catch a partial glimpse of the field, while the more daredevil ascended two nearby steel towers and clung there perilously watching the events below.[61]

Club president Harry Hempstead was determined to outdo his Chicago counterpart in patriotic trappings and raising funds to support the million dollar war loan drive. He had the day of the contest named by the mayor as Liberty Loan Day and doubled Comiskey's two tons of red, white, and blue streamers decorating the stadium.[62] Traditional commercial signs along the outfield walls had been removed and replaced by huge billboards proclaiming: "Buy Liberty Bonds and Help Knock the Kaiser out of the Box," "The World's Heaviest Hitter is Uncle Sam," "Our Boys are Fighting in France. Don't Let Them Fight Extra Innings," and "Buy Liberty Bonds and Help Win the European World Series."[63] Amid stirring tunes blared forth by three military bands, Clark Griffith used former Series heroes Nick Altrock and Hank Gowdy to raise funds for his Ball and Bat Fund, and during the game patriotically attired young men and women were dispatched through the crowd every three innings with red, white, and blue collection plates to, in Hempstead's words, prompt those in attendance to "disgorge their bank notes" for the cause.[64]

At home plate ceremonies before the game, Corporal Hank Gowdy, wearing his army uniform, was honored by his Manhattan admirers. The star of the 1914 World Series, who had been the first active major leaguer to enlist for military duty, was presented with a silk American flag and a new $4.50 gold Swiss wristwatch.[65] As well, dapper Giant outfielder Benny Kauff, whose wardrobe made "a rainbow look like a triumph of the camouflager's art," was presented by his fans with a gold-headed walking stick even though he was in the throes of an 0–8 slump in the Series.[66]

Once the festivities were concluded, the Giants treated the assembled faithful to a magnificent exhibition, with stocky Rube Benton twirling a five-hit 2–0 triumph over Cicotte. The Pale Hose hurler deserved a kinder fate, as he pitched better ball than he had in the opener, striking out eight and walking none, but he was victimized by bad luck in the fourth inning when the New Yorkers tallied the only runs of the game. Robertson started that frame by lofting a deep drive to right. The ball "traveled with all the deadly accuracy of the stone which whizzed from the sling of David of old when he won the decision over Goliath," and by the time Shano Collins, slipping in the muddy turf, had retrieved it, Robertson was headed into third with a triple.[67] Holke followed with a Texas League fly into left. Jackson dove for the sinking sphere but missed it by inches, permitting the run to score and Holke to reach second. Rariden sacrificed the runner to third, Benton fanned, and Cicotte seemed to be out of the inning when Burns chopped a ball slowly down the third-base line. Cicotte raced in, cleanly fielded the ball on the soggy grass, but then fired the ball wildly over Gandil's outstretched mitt at first, and Holke tallied the final run of the game. Given this cushion, Benton finished the game "as cool as an Artic breeze" and never permitted a runner to reach third-base.[68]

Despite having his dream of a sweep dashed, Comiskey was gracious, giving "John McGraw's boys credit for coming back and playing ball in high-spirited style from start to finish."[69] He added optimistically: "Barring a few bad breaks that went against the White Sox they might have won, for Eddie Cicotte pitched good enough ball to have won or at least tied any pitcher in the game. I don't think being defeated today disheartened the boys any."[70]

Rowland was equally sanguine in the subdued clubhouse. "Rube Benton was a great pitcher today, and he beat us. I wouldn't want to take away any credit he gained from his great victory. He was great all the way and deserved everything he got," the Sox manager admitted. Smiling, he added: "However, the defeat hasn't hurt the boys one bit so far as I can see. I look for them to come right back and wind it up in two more battles."[71]

Under a sunny sky dotted with fleecy clouds, a disappointing crowd of only 27,746, the lowest attendance at a world championship game in New York since 1905, gathered to see if their heroes could repeat the previous day's magic. Before the contest, McGraw and several of his players, each bearing a flag of one of the Allies, paraded around the field. E.A. Batchelor, exhibiting his typical midwestern cynicism of all things New York, scoffed at the scene, informing his readers: "The day was not completely spoiled for some of us when we noticed that the Siamese banner was not borne in the parade, and that Patagonia had been overlooked also. McGraw carried the Stars and Stripes because someone beat him when they matched for the privilege of displaying the Harp and Shamrock. The parade almost bogged down before it started because there was only one Irish flag and about twenty players who wanted to be its custodian."[72]

On the sidelines while Faber and Schupp were warming up for their rematch, Christy Mathewson was spotted by fans, and a murmur quickly spread through the stands. Soon a tremendous ovation was raised for the legendary "Big Six," who had spun three shutouts for the New Yorkers in the 1905 World Series against Connie Mack's Philadelphia Athletics.

For three innings Faber and Schupp were deadlocked in a scoreless battle, but in the fourth, with two out, the diminutive 5'8" 157 pound Kauff lifted a high fly over Felsch's head in center. The ball rolled through a clump of hollyhock along the center-field terrace and disappeared under a roll of canvas at the base of the fence. While Felsch was "wading among the posies, Benny was legging it around the paths" and crossed the plate standing up with an inside-the-park home run, ending his 0–13 drought.[73]

The Giants tallied single runs in the fifth and seventh before Kauff drilled a two-run homer into the lower right-field stands off reliever Dave Danforth, making the final score 5–0. While the *New York Times* reported that Kauff smote a "mighty belt," the *Detroit Free Press*' E.A. Batchelor was closer to the truth when he wrote: "Home run number two was just an ordinary fly ball that went into the trick right-field stands. In a man-sized park it would have been an easy out, but they wear the baseball stockades—like the girls' skirts— very short in the metropolis, and it cleared the retaining wall."[74]

Against Schupp's seven strikeout, one walk performance, the Sox managed only seven scattered hits, and did not advance a runner to third until the ninth inning, leading a *New York Times* writer to assert smugly that they couldn't have squeezed a runner home with a dark lantern and a kit of burglar's tools."[75] Batchelor sneered that the Chicago attack "was about as useful as Uruguay's will be in the war," and added that it must have been anything but inspiring for Faber, who also hurled a seven-hitter, "to watch his comrades go up to the plate and give an exhibition like an old lady in a roomful of mice."[76] To those who defended the Sox, saying that everything but their hitting was sound, Batchelor retorted: "That's true, but it is like saying a man is perfectly well except for a couple of broken legs and a fractured skull."[77]

As the Sox left the diamond, jeering Giant supporters taunted them with cries of "bush league, bush league" and "Three-I," referring to Rowland's previous managerial experience.[78] As a horde of admirers crushed around McGraw, he pushed through them, grumbling: "I told you I had a real ball club, and maybe now the White Sox are aware of it!"[79]

Comiskey, whose club was in the midst of a twenty-two consecutive inning scoring drought, displayed bitterness for the first time in his meetings with reporters. "The Giants gave us a good licking today all right and deserved to win because they outplayed the Sox," he stated, adding with disdain: "We can't win ball games without runs, and we haven't had a run since we arrived here."[80]

Perhaps the most optimism for the sinking Sox came from I.E. Sanborn, who reminded his *Chicago Tribune* readers that all season the Chicagoans "did not fight until they were hurt or stung out of their complacency."[81] He then explained without sentimentality why he expected the mercenary Sox to regain their victorious spirit: "It is old-fashioned anymore to speak of the world's pennant as the reward for which teams are playing, for nobody thinks of that old rag as cutting any figure in the doings. It is the mazuma in the National Commission's strongbox that counts."[82]

On the eve of the fifth game, snow squalls and sub-freezing temperatures blew into the Windy City. Only a few fans braved the cold to stand in line overnight for bleacher tickets, and those who did kept warm by building bonfires fueled by wood stolen from a neighboring lumberyard.[83] Conditions had not improved by game time and only a hearty band of 27,323 fans huddled against the wintry blasts at Comiskey Park to see Reb Russell square off against Slim Sallee.

Russell, a fan favorite, proved to be "wild as a hawk" and faced only three men, meting out a walk, single, and double before being rescued by Cicotte, but the home team trailed 2–0 before they ever came to bat.[84] The Sox cut the lead to a single run in the third, but the Giants rebounded with two tallies in the fourth aided by three Sox errors. Chicago added a run in the six, but the Giants matched it in the seventh with a run off Lefty Williams, and the Sox trailed 5–2 as they came up in the home half of that frame.

Having endured booing and hissing all afternoon because of their weak stickwork and six miscues in the field, the Sox, suddenly realizing "there was a pile of money at stake," came to life, and McGraw's team "crumpled up like tissue paper."[85] With one out Jackson and Felsch singled, and Gandil drove both in with a double. After Gandil had moved to third on a ground out, Schalk drew a pass and promptly took off for second. Giant backstop Rariden thought it was a bluff and threw the ball to Sallee in case Gandil broke for home. The Giant hurler, however, seeing that only Schalk was moving, rifled the ball to second-sacker Herzog, who missed it entirely, and Gandil then crossed the plate with the tying run.

As the crowd roared, Buck Weaver forgot his three egregious errors and danced in front of the Chicago dugout, tossed his hat in the air, and soon afterward heaved his sweater, a dozen bats, and several of his teammates' caps heavenward.[86] An amazed writer recorded the scene: "The players threw everything portable into the air, screamed, cried, kissed one another, rolled on the ground in glee, laughed with the abandon of madmen, and did everything else that's supposed to denote that the human mind has gone off key completely. When a man gets so far gone that he insists on implanting a chaste salute on Kid Gleason's ruby lips, there isn't much use trying to keep track of his actions, and when another born in North Carolina hugs a Negro trainer in public and is hugged in return without noticing that his companion is of the unbleached race, the powers of description simply foul out to the catcher."[87]

To amazement of virtually every baseball analyst, McGraw not only permitted the obviously exhausted Sallee to get pummeled in the seventh, but also to take the mound in the eighth. As one writer noted sarcastically, this was the equivalent of "leading a turkey up to the chopping block the day before Thanksgiving."[88] Shano Collins led off with a single, was sacrificed to second, and scored the go-ahead run on a single by Eddie Collins. Jackson singled to center, moving Collins toward third. Kauff foolishly tried to cut down the speedy Collins at third, but his throw to Zimmerman was too late. The third-sacker then compounded the mental mistakes on the play by heaving wildly to second in an effort to cut down Jackson. The ball rolled into right, and Collins and Jackson each moved up another base. Finally, McGraw lifted Sallee in favor of Perritt, who surrendered another run scoring hit, making the score 8–5, before retiring the side. The shell-shocked Giants, numbed by the realization that the game was now lost, went down in order in the ninth before the slants of the third Sox reliever, Urban Faber, who earned his second Series win.

From a New York perspective the game was an avoidable disaster. Veteran baseball writer Walter Trumbull, using military parlance, summarized the contest perfectly: "It was a wild, hair-raising, soul-stirring, nerve-breaking melee, filled with terrific hitting, spectacular plays, foolish errors, and a savage fighting spirit seldom displayed in post-season games. Yet, in the end, it was if a parade of soldiers, having gone over the top and passed the perils of no-man's-land had hurled their enemy from their trenches, only at their moment of triumph to be scattered and annihilated by a sudden flame of death from batteries hidden and unsuspected. There was no chance to rally or reformed the battle line. The onslaught was too deadly and too sudden and too unexpected."[89]

Other writers belittled McGraw's decision to stick with Sallee for so long, while Chicago mobsters and New York gamblers who had wagered large amounts on the game spread ugly and unfounded rumors that McGraw had personal monetary motives for his action.[90] Furious at the impugning of his integrity, an irate McGraw snarled to reporters that the loss should be blamed on second-baseman Buck Herzog, whose sloppy, and often lackadaisical, glovework had led to several Chicago scoring opportunities.[91] After the Series, McGraw told sportswriter Fred Lieb that he believed Herzog had thrown the game, and in the post-season he traded his field captain to the Boston Braves.[92]

In the victors' clubhouse, happiness was tempered with seriousness and anger. Chicago players resented what they considered an excessively hard tag by Art Fletcher on Hap Felsch in the eighth. When Rowland remarked to Fletcher about it after the inning, the Giant shortstop tried to punch the Sox pilot and had to be restrained by the umpire.[93] As well, Weaver and Eddie Collins complained of Herzog and Fletcher blatantly interfering with their running by body-blocking them on the base paths.[94] When told by writers that the Giants were threatening to use their spikes in the next game, they said they would not be intimidated.[95]

Manager Rowland, still upset over the defensive tactics used by the Giants, snarled to reporters: "We finally got them. It took a long time, but I think the rest of the way to the world championship is easy."[96] Comiskey concurred with his manager, but did admit to some apprehension before the game, stating: "I think the rest is easy. The boys suffered from overconfidence after beating the Giants in the first two, and it took them a long time to get back into their stride. I was afraid they weren't going to get into it until next season, but they finally awoke and went through in great shape."[97] However, it was Eddie Collins, sitting by himself in a corner and mopping himself with a towel, who best put the contest into perspective. "I have been in many a World Series game," he smiled, "but never in one like this."[98]

After the game, club presidents Comiskey and Hempstead met with National Commission Chairman Herrmann to have a coin toss to determine the site of the seventh game, if necessary. Herrmann flipped a half dollar into the air and Comiskey called "tails." When the coin came up "heads," Hempstead said, "You're unlucky, Mr. Comiskey." The Old Roman laughed, and replied prophetically: "There won't be a seventh game, so it doesn't matter."[99]

Balmy, summer-like weather welcomed the teams back to the Polo Grounds for the sixth contest, and 33, 969 partisans, the largest crowd of the Series, went through the turnstiles hoping to see the Giants prolong the classic for one more game. On the hill for the visitors was Urban Faber, seeking his third triumph. Opposing him was New York's hero of the third game, Rube Benton.

The two matched three shutout innings, but in the fourth the White Sox tallied three runs, primarily as a result of shoddy Giant fielding. Eddie Collins led off with a hot smash to Zimmerman at third. Heinie made a fine stop, but his throw was "wilder than any prairie flower that ever grew."[100] The ball skipped past Holke at first, rolled to the grandstand, and Collins sped into second on the error. Joe Jackson followed with a pop fly to right, but Dave Robertson tried to squeeze the ball in his glove too soon and it dropped safely for an error, Collins taking third. Felsch then tapped a one-hopper to Benton, who promptly threw to third, trapping Collins halfway between the bag and home plate. Collins hesitated for a moment, signaling the other runners to keep moving. Then he darted toward home. Rariden, the catcher, had moved thirty or forty feet toward third and first-baseman Holke inexplicably remained rooted at his station, leaving the plate unguarded, except for Umpire Bill Klem. In a panic, the slow-footed third-sacker vainly tried to overtake Collins, but the Sox captain beat him to the plate by two strides. Watching the spectacle helplessly, Herzog turned to American League umpire Billy Evans at second and asked in wonderment: "Did you ever see anything like that? I have $1,700 riding on this ball game, and that's the shortest run for $1,700 that I ever heard of!"[101]

While the crowd was still showering curses upon the hapless Zimmerman, Benton, who was livid with rage, fired a fastball straight across the plate to the next batter, Chick Gandil. The first-baseman laced a single along the right-field line, driving in both Jackson and Felsch. Benton then retired the side, but the Giants were badly shaken by the three unearned tallies. Moreover, they now had to battle the crowd, which deserted the home team after the fourth inning "faster than rats leave a ship that they think is going to be submarined."[102]

Amid the jeers of their former adherents, who seemed ready to form a posse and haul Zim to the tar barrel, the Giants attempted to rally in the fifth.[103] Herzog tripled home two runs, but Kauff left him, and any hope of victory, stranded on third. In the visitors' ninth, Weaver led off with a single, and Faber sacrificed him to second. As Weaver approached the bag, Fletcher deliberately tripped him. After a heated exchange, Fletcher ran over to cover the bag on an attempted pickoff and Weaver belted him in the ribs. Only hasty intervention by Umpire Evans prevented a full-scale brawl.[104] Weaver ultimately got his revenge by scoring, and Faber, who was "as steady as a chronometer and almost as intangible as a myth," set the Giants down in order to preserve the 4–2 victory that made Chicago the world champions.[105]

In the frenzy following the final out, Rowland raced to the New York manager, whom he truly admired, extended his hand, and said graciously: "Mr. McGraw, I'm glad we won, but I'm sorry you had to be the one to lose." Humiliated and boiling with anger, McGraw refused the proffered handshake and growled: "Get away from me, you goddamned busher!"[106] Ironically, the *New York Times,* which prided itself on accuracy, vainly tried to salvage something of McGraw's tarnished image by totally fictionalizing this scene for its readers, stating: "Here was a picture: McGraw, one of the oldest, craftiest leaders in the game, squeezing the outstretched mitt of the bush league manager from Peoria — the same Clarence Rowland, a mere novice in the major leagues, who was said to be so young and inexperienced that the Giants would play horse with him. There were tears of happiness in Rowland's eyes as McGraw grasped his hand, and he was happier still when McGraw told him he had won with as game and fair a team as he had ever played against."[107]

In the clubhouse, an elated Rowland reflected on his accomplishment and, indirectly, on McGraw's snub. "Now that it is all over, I admit that I feel dazed," he said, a wide grin brightening his face. "I know that only a few years ago I was a busher, but even then I had ambitions, even though I never expected to be manager of the world champions. Charlie Comiskey gave me the chance, and I owe everything to him. I would have done anything in the world to win this championship for him. He gave me the players, and the players went out and won it. I want to give all the credit in the world to the boys who worked with me and to Kid Gleason, who helped me day after day. It was a great Series, even if we didn't play as good baseball as we should. The boys never felt for a moment they would lose, and they beat a great team in the Giants, without a doubt the best team the National League has had in many years."[108]

Shoving through the noisy celebration, Giant Captain Buck Herzog reached Rowland's side and congratulated him. "You played it right," he stated. "I have to admire you for the way you handled the fifth game. You played all of your cards to win that game, regardless of the future. And you won that game."[109] Showing his contempt for the man who had blamed him for the loss of that game, Herzog continued: "If McGraw had managed as well, I think we would have beaten you in the Series. He held his good cards back, and he is still holding some of them even though the game is all over."[110]

A tearful Comiskey poured out his heart to eager newsmen. "I wanted to win one more time before I got too old, and the boys this year have gone out and turned the trick. It was a wonderful victory, and no one in America can be as happy as I am. Clarence Rowland has turned out to be a great manager, and the boys with him have fought so hard and so faithfully that they deserve all the honor coming to a world champion," he said softly. In the spirit of graciousness and generosity, which was his trademark among everyone but his players, who knew they would receive more "honor" than money for their accomplishment, "Commy" proceeded to lavish praise upon his defeated foe. "It has always been my wish to play New York for the championship of the world, and now that we've played it and won, I feel as if my life in baseball is completed," he confided to his listeners. "I wish to give McGraw and his players credit for putting up a great fight. I really feared the outcome of this Series because I knew McGraw had a strong team, the best, I think, the National League had put out in many years."[111]

Not unexpectedly, American League President Ban Johnson took the occasion to gloat. "McGraw and his Giants aren't so tough anymore," he shouted. "They just talk tough. They're our meat."[112]

In the New York locker room, writers crushed around Zimmerman, repeatedly asking why he had not thrown the ball home instead of chasing Collins. His face flush, "The Great Zim," as his fickle detractors had previously referred to him, finally posed his deathless query to them: "Who the hell was I going to throw the ball to, Klem?"[113] McGraw, smarting from his fourth World Series setback in seven years, refused to speak to reporters, except to defend Zimmerman. "It wasn't Zimmerman's fault," he fumed, saying that the goat's horns should be placed on first-sacker Walter Holke, "who stood at first base watching Heinie instead of covering the plate."[114]

Some scribes, especially in New York lampooned Zimmerman mercilessly. One wag penned a lengthy paraphrase of Rudyard Kipling's *Gunga Din*, ending with the refrain: "I'm a faster man than you are, Heinie Zim," and another predicted: "When the men in olive drab get over to France they will amuse the armies of all the Allies with Zimmerman's famous play. In a few months Zim's notorious bonehead play will be known in every corner of the earth."[115]

Most baseball experts, however, agreed with McGraw and defended the Giant thirdsacker. Eddie Collins, who was in the best position to understand the situation, exonerated Zimmerman, implying that catcher Bill Rariden was the culprit who permitted him to score. "I don't know how I got past Rariden, but I didn't see him ahead of me. The one thing I do know is that when I actually started to run there was nobody at the plate to take a throw from Zimmerman, and he had to make it. His only chance then was to chase me, and I won the race."[116] George McCoy, sports editor of the *Pittsburgh Leader,* concurred, writing: "Why should Zimmerman be charged with making a bone-headed play when the fault was clearly Rariden's? Had Big Bill been in his place it is almost a certainty he would have tossed the ball so as to head off Collins at the plate. But he was not in position to receive the pill, and therefore Zim had to do the next best thing. He did all he could."[117] Learning of these charges, the Giant receiver retorted defiantly: "I yelled to Heinie to throw the ball, and he told me to 'get out of the way — I got him.'"[118]

Veteran Pittsburgh baseball writer Ralph S. Davis said that Zimmerman should be excused because of the strain under which he was laboring. "In Chicago he was the butt of a thousand ribald jokes and was cursed, booed, and hissed all the time the games were in progress— simply because he formerly had been a member of the Cubs. In New York he was unfortunate enough to make a couple of slips and the fans there began to ride him. He is more deserving of pity than shame."[119] Davis then singled out Art Fletcher as the Giant who deserved censure, not because of his errors but rather because of his conduct throughout the Series. "Fletcher has been brought up in the McGraw school," Davis stated accusingly, "where everything goes in the way of roughhouse methods. He made no friends for himself or his team when he started to 'ride' Clarence Rowland or when he went into second-base in a manner which left little doubt as to his intention to injure or maim any opposing player who might be in his way."[120]

Jimmy Isaminger of the *Philadelphia North American,* however, best explained why, even though Rariden, Holke, and Benton should receive the "gold bones" on the play, it would be Zimmerman who would forever be blamed. "Zim is a cave man, the product of the abysses of the dark Bronx," he wrote. "He says 'youse' and 'nuttin.' So the more culpable malefactors of the New York inner cordon will make the most of their superior standing in society and shift the blame on poor Heinie."[121]

The "Zimmerman boner" aside, the World Series of 1917 was memorable. While it was not, as Comiskey gushed, "the greatest of all World Series," it did provide sterling plate performances by Eddie Collins (.409), Buck Weaver (.333), and Dave Robertson (.500), and the team batting marks of .274 for Chicago and .256 for New York were the best combined averages in World Series history to date.[122] On the mound, Faber (3–1, 2.33), Cicotte (1–1, 1.95), and ill-fated Rube Benton, who finished 1–1 despite a perfect 0.00 earned run average, were sensational, even though the team marks of 2.77 for the Sox and 3.00 for the Giants paled in comparison to those compiled two years earlier by the Red Sox (1.84) and Phillies (2.30). Moreover, the fielding on both sides was atrocious with the Sox committing twelve errors and the Giants eleven.

I.E. Sanborn best captured the essence of the post-season clash in terms of execution of the fundamentals of the game. "The Series of 1917 was the poorest played of any of similar modern vintage," he observed. "Yet it was the most exciting because of that fact. The unsteadiness of both teams and the quality of ivory displayed increased the uncertainty of the games and added to the excitement furnished the crowds. The bonehead plays and bobbles kept increasing the interest because of the additional uncertainty in which the issue was shrouded on account of the inability to guess what was going to happen next or who was going to pull it."[123]

It was *The Sporting News,* however, which set forth the real significance of this World Series. "Above all," it editorialized, "considering the times and the state of the public mind, the contests have proven a diversion that is undoubtedly beneficial. That, in the highest sense, is the purpose of playing the games, whether we are at war or merely going through the grind that peaceful pursuits are likely to develop into."[124]

CUBS VS. RED SOX, 1918

After their humiliation at the hands of the Philadelphia Athletics in the 1910 World Series, Cub owner Charles Murphy became disenchanted with Manager Chance and several players whom he felt had not given their best effort. In 1911, despite winning 92 games, the Cubs finished second behind John McGraw's great New York Giant squad, and Murphy openly criticized Chance's handling of the team. The owner's wrath toward Chance intensified during the following season when his manager not only sold his one-tenth interest in the club, but also vainly requested a long-term contract as field general. At the close of the campaign, the Cubs had compiled a 91–59 record, but again failed to capture the pennant, finishing third behind New York and Pittsburgh. Thus, Murphy was in a foul mood when the Cubs faced the White Sox in their annual post-season intra-city series. When the Sox scored six runs in the first inning of the initial game, Murphy went into a rage, raced onto the field, fired his manager, and named second-sacker Johnny Evers to pilot the team. To further insult Chance, Murphy gave his new manager the four-year contract that he had denied the "Peerless Leader."[1]

Missing also were Joe Tinker, traded by Murphy to Cincinnati after the 1912 season, Ed Reulbach, dealt to Brooklyn early in 1913, and Mordecai Brown, whom Murphy humiliated by shipping to the minors to reduce the payroll, even though he had a 21–11, 2.80 record the previous year. Evers won 88 games in 1913, but he also was canned by Murphy for finishing third and losing the intra-city series.

The wisdom of Murphy came under additional scrutiny when he chose as his new manager Hank O'Day, the former umpire whom McGraw charged had stolen the 1908 pennant for the Chicagoans by his ruling in the famous tie game with the Giants. O'Day led the depleted Cubs to a 78–76 record, finishing a distant fourth behind the Boston Braves. What made this all the more distasteful to Cub fans was that the player/manager of the National League champions was Johnny Evers, who not only led his team to the pennant and world championship, but also batted .279 and was named the league's most valuable player.

By his irresponsible dismantling of the once-proud Chicago dynasty, Murphy earned the ire of Chicago fans and his fellow baseball magnates. American League President Ban Johnson had targeted Murphy for years as being a detriment to Organized Baseball because of the infamous ticket scandal of 1908, his refusal to treat players fairly, and his insincere promise to construct a new ballpark. Pittsburgh Pirate owner Barney Dreyfuss publicly referred to Murphy as a "rat" and a "sneak," while Cincinnati owner Garry Herrmann stated that the Cub owner was constantly trying to "stir up trouble and strife."[2] Yet nothing was done to eradicate this thorn in their sides until the two-year old upstart Federal League declared itself a major league in 1914.

Entering the Windy City baseball market in 1913, the Federal League's Chicago Whales, owned by local millionaire restaurateur Charles Weeghman, gained instant credibility with local baseball enthusiasts by inking both Tinker and Brown to contracts. With the fan base of the established Chicago teams now threatened, John K. Tener, the new President of the senior circuit, joined with his American League counterpart to pressure Cub minority owner Charles P. Taft, who had been bankrolling the team, to purchase Murphy's 53 percent of the team's stock. When the deal was consummated, Murphy's exit from the national pastime was mocked in *Sporting Life* magazine, which published its own updated version of Franklin P. Adams' famous poem:

> Brought to the leash and smashed to the jaw,
> Evers to Tener to Taft.
> Hounded and hustled outside of the law,
> Evers to Tener to Taft.
> Torn from the Cubs and the glitter of gold,
> Stripped of the guerdons and glory untold,
> Kicked in the stomach and cut from the fold,
> Evers to Tener to Taft.[3]

At the end of the 1915 season, in which the Whales won the championship, the Federal League signed a truce with Organized Baseball that included a provision to permit Weeghman and millionaire oilman Harry Sinclair to obtain from Taft controlling interest in the Cubs. His two teams would then merge and move to Weeghman Park, a $250,000, modern 16,000 seat stadium on Chicago's North Side, which had opened in 1914.[4]

Despite the new ownership, the Cubs' diamond fortunes continued to decline, as they finished nineteen games under .500 in 1916 and six below that mark the following year. Moreover, the nation had entered a recession in 1916, and Weeghman could avoid bankruptcy only by selling shares of his stock in the team to minority partner William Wrigley, the chewing gum tycoon.[5]

In 1918, however, the fortunes of Manager Fred Mitchell's Cubs soared, not because of an infusion of new talent, but a diminution of skill on other teams caused by American participation in the Great War. By mid-season only three regulars and one starting pitcher remained on John McGraw's defending league champion New York Giants, and, as a result, the Cubs, playing in a war-dictated abbreviated season, captured the pennant with an 84–45 record, finishing 10½ games ahead of the New Yorkers.

Offensively, the Cubs were a solid, if not spectacular, group of castoffs, batting .265 and boasting some power with twenty-one home runs, fifty-three triples, and 164 doubles. The infield consisted of former Giant and Brooklyn Dodger Fred Merkle (.297, 3, 65) at first, former Washington Senator and Philadelphia Athletic Charlie Pick (.326, 0, 12) at second, twenty-two-year-old rookie Charlie Hollocher (.316, 2, 38) at short, former Tiger, Boston Brave, and St. Louis Brown Charlie Deal (.290, 2, 34) at third, and ex-St. Louis Brown, Philadelphia Phillie star backstop Bill Killefer (.233, 0, 22). In the outfield from left to right were ex-Brave Leslie Mann (.288, 2, 55), and former Cincinnati Red and Phillie George (Dode) Paskert (.286, 3, 59), and homegrown Max Flack (.257, 4, 41).

On the mound, the Cubs, although also mostly retreads, dominated their league with a 2.18 earned run average, twenty-three shutouts, 472 strikeouts, and 1,197 innings pitched. The ace of the staff was former New York Yankee and Washington Senator James (Hippo) Vaughn, a 6'4," 215 pound, thirty-year-old left-hander who went 22–10 and led the league with a 1.74 earned run average, eight shutouts, 148 strikeouts, and 290 innings pitched. Closely behind Vaughn were ex-Pirate right-hander Claude Hendrix (20–7, 2.78) and former Boston Brave George (Lefty) Tyler (19–8, 2.00). Right-hander "Shuffling Phil" Douglas (10–9, 2.13), who had been with the White Sox, Dodgers, and Reds during his five years in the major leagues, rounded out the starting staff.

The war also opened the door of opportunity for several teams in the American League as well, as pre-season favorite Chicago lost stars Red Faber, Hap Felsch, Joe Jackson, Swede Risberg, and Lefty Williams either to military service or war-related industry. As a consequence of the new parity, the Boston Red Sox, with a record of 75–51, nosed out Cleveland (73–54) and Washington (72–56) in the last week of the season to capture the pennant, while the depleted White Sox tumbled to sixth at 57–67.

When Manager Jack Barry enlisted in the United States Navy, Ed Barrow stepped down from the front office to assume field control of the Red Sox. A tough man who demanded complete obedience from his players, Barrow had numerous run-ins during the season with his star player, the fun-loving George Herman Ruth, occasionally having to engage him in a fistfight to prove who ran the team.[6]

Barrow's squad did not have much offense, hitting only .249 with fifteen home runs, but was unbelievably gifted defensively. First-base was manned by either ten-year veteran John (Stuffy) McInnis (.272, 0, 56) or George Herman (Babe or Tarzan) Ruth, the left-handed pitcher who topped the team with a .300 batting average, eleven home runs, and sixty-six runs batted in. At second was journeyman Dave Shean (.264, 0, 34), playing with his sixth team in eight seasons. Slick-fielding Everett Scott (.221, 0, 43) covered short, and rookie Fred Thomas (.257, 1, 11) patrolled third until he enlisted in the United States Navy late in mid-season. The catching duties were shared between Wally Schang (.244, 0, 20) and Sam Agnew (.166, 0, 6). The outfield was only slightly more threatening at the plate, with Harry Hooper (.289, 1, 44) in right, eleven year veteran Amos Strunk (.257, 0, 35), in center, and George Whiteman (.266, 1, 28), who had only forty-four previous at-bats in two major league trials dating back to 1907, in left.

Boston hurlers, who compiled a 2.31 earned run average, were led by right-handed submarine ball artist Carl Mays, who had a league-leading thirty complete games and eight shutouts to complement his 21–13 record and 2.21 earned run average. Rounding out the starting staff were southpaw Babe Ruth (13–7, 2.22) and right-handers "Sad Sam" Jones (16–5, 2.25) and "Bullet Joe" Bush (15–15, 2.11), who, along with McInnis, Schang, and Strunk, had been dispatched to the Red Sox by Connie Mack after the 1917 season to reduce the Athletics' expenses.

Because of the short season, the World Series was scheduled to begin on September 5 in Chicago, the first time a post-season contest was scheduled before October. However, Chicago was "shrouded by the haze of the great struggle for democracy," and was not even mildly excited on the eve of what under normal circumstances would have been the sporting event of the year.[7] As an effort to increase gate receipts for the two participants, Charles Comiskey volunteered to permit the Cubs to borrow, free of charge, his 32,000 seat stadium for their home games, and Weeghman readily accepted his gracious offer.[8]

Larger turnouts would not benefit the Series participants, however, because prior to the season the National Commission altered the formula for distribution of revenue. As in the past, the players would receive 60 percent of the revenue from the gate receipts of the first four games, but under the new rules each member of the winning club, no matter what the gate receipts were, would receive $2,000 and each loser $1,400. The remainder of the 60 percent of the players' pool would then be distributed proportionally to members of the second, third, and fourth place teams in each league.[9] This revision was instituted partly because of a potential negative reaction to players gaining a huge monetary reward during wartime, and partly because the owners did not want to share so much money with their players, thinking it would encourage higher salary demands in future years.[10]

Another pre–Series ruling by the National Commission distressed Boston's owner, Harry Frazee. It had been decided by a coin toss that the first three contests would be played in Chicago, and the remaining games in Boston. Frazee believed that it was unfair to his players that they might have only one contest on their familiar grounds at Fenway Park. Commission Chairman Herrmann, always courteous and usually patient, reminded Frazee that wartime travel restrictions mandated that the teams not only make a single trip, but also that they ride on the same train. When Herrmann also recounted that Frazee had no complaints until his team lost the coin toss, the Boston owner ceased his protest.[11]

A torrential rain, driven by a stiff northeast gale-force wind, caused the first contest to be postponed, but the following afternoon the sun intermittently peeked through the clouds and Comiskey Park's diamond was in perfect condition for Babe Ruth to face Hippo Vaughn to inaugurate the Series. A sparse gathering of 19,274 witnessed the Boston south-paw best his rival 1–0 on an run-scoring single by Stuffy McInnis in the forth inning of a contest that, as I.E. Sanborn of the *Chicago Tribune* sagely noted, was "from the ball players' standpoint a great game because of its proximity to perfection, but from the rooters' viewpoint was tame and monotonous because there were so few tense moments."[12]

One of the strangest occurrences of the afternoon not surprisingly involved Babe Ruth. Before the game, Barrow had taken Ruth aside and warned him: "Watch out for this fellow Mann. Don't let up on him. Don't ever let him dig in at the plate. Drop him in the dirt!" Ruth replied cockily: "Don't worry. I'll get him."[13] In the first inning, Ruth brushed back Max Flack twice before striking him out. Then in the third, Flack singled, and in the fifth Ruth fired a fastball which thumped off the top of the stocky outfielder's head. As the *New York Times* reported: "Three doctors and half-a-dozen undertakers forgot about the game and were on their toes in a second, thinking that an important case was at hand. However, Max jumped up and walked down to first-base without even rubbing his head. A top-piece like that would hardly need a steel helmet on either side."[14] When the inning was over, Ruth strode into the dugout and said smugly to Barrow: "Well, I guess I took care of that guy Mann for you, didn't I?" Barrow, disgusted and trying not to laugh, muttered: "Not yet you haven't. You've been knocking down poor Max Flack!"[15]

The greatest highlight for the spectators did not occur on the diamond, but rather over their heads in the sky. Several times during the game as many as six army biplanes flew over the field, and occasionally one or more would elicit a gasp from the crowd by going into a nose dive or tailspin to demonstrate they were ready to fly over Berlin.[16]

Perhaps, the most emotional moment of the day occurred during the seventh inning stretch. Spontaneously the Cubs' Claws Band, seated behind the Chicago dugout, broke forth with "The Star-Spangled Banner." Fred Thomas, who had been granted permission by the Navy to play for the Red Sox in the Series, snapped to attention and saluted the flag fluttering from the pole in right-center field. Other players stood and removed their caps, and the crowd slowly but steadily joined in the singing. At the conclusion of the song, which was not yet the official national anthem, thunderous cheering and applause rumbled throughout the park.[17]

This, more than anything else, demonstrated that the World Series was merely a diversion for the nation's baseball fans, who were primarily concentrating on the outcome of the "the great game for democracy being played overseas."[18] As the *New York Times* observed: "There was no getting away from the fact that there was a touch of sadness in the clash today. Empty seats, rows and rows of them, brought home to every man and woman in the crowd that the lads who sat in these seats in the past were far, far from home on the world's grimmest mission. The far-reaching hand of war has thinned the ranks of the fans; it has thinned the ranks of the players; and even the most enthusiastic of today's onlookers could not help but realize that this will probably be the last World Series for a long, long time."[19]

For the players, however, the low attendance planted a worrisome seed in their minds. They had already pledged to give 10 percent of their share to war charities, and they wondered what would happen if the remainder would not meet the guaranteed payoff for each player. Simply put, the players cared little why the stands were half empty, but they cared greatly about the monetary results of the fans' lack of interest.[20]

A warm, sunny day raised player hopes for a box office bonanza, but only 20,040 fans paid the cut-rate prices of $3 for grandstand and $1.50 for bleacher seating — a 40 percent reduction from the previous year — to witness the show.[21] Harry Bullion of the *Detroit Free Press* captured the mood of Chicago's diamond patrons, writing: "There is no use trying to fool anybody about this Series. It can't be done. Interest may be centered in it, but not sufficiently to pull the people into the gates, even though grand opera prices no longer prevail and the cost of seats is within reach of the poor man's pocket."[22]

The game itself was over in the second inning when the home team battered "Bullet Joe" Bush for three runs. Merkle led off with a walk and moved to second when Pick beat out an attempted sacrifice down the third-base line. After Deal popped to second, Killefer doubled to right, scoring Merkle and moving Pick to third. Cub hurler Lefty Tyler then helped his own cause by singling over second to drive in both runners.

At the end of the inning, the cheering of the fans for their favorites as they took their defensive positions was momentarily stilled as their attention turned to an unexpected outbreak of fisticuffs. Jim Crusinberry of the *Chicago Tribune* described the scene for his readers: "It happened just after the second inning was completed. Heine Wagner walked to the third-base box to assume his tame duty of directing the Boston offense, and [Cub coach] Otto Knabe shot a few of his choicest words to him from the bench. Wagner took exception to some of them and leaped into the dugout, apparently intent on planting a couple of rights and three or four lefts to emphasize his disapproval of Otto's words, whatever they were. There was some rolling among the feet of other players and some deranging of uniforms and hair before other players of the Cubs succeeded in separating the chief assistants and convincing them that they weren't supposed to demonstrate their athletic prowess, but to confine their efforts to brainy things during the Series. Four or five Red Sox players, seeing the affair from their bench made a run for the Cubs' dugout, for to them it looked as if the entire gang of Chicago benchwarmers had jumped upon their Heine with intentions of destroying him. Complete details of the scrap were difficult to obtain, but it seemed the pair were about evenly matched, as Otto is about twenty pounds overweight and Wagner has a busted finger. The only evidence of the row appeared on Wagner's back when he returned to the coaching lines. It was easily seen that it had been in contact with a dirty and wet floor."[23]

It was symbolic of the afternoon's festivities that Wagner could not land a solid punch and ended on his back, for that was the story of his club's efforts as well. Tyler entered the ninth with a four-hit gem, but back-to-back leadoff triples by Strunk and Whiteman deprived him of his shutout, although the Cubs triumphed 3–1.

The final game scheduled to be played in Chicago until world peace was restored elicited the first real enthusiasm of the Series. Despite leaden clouds that oozed a light shower intermittently throughout the game, a crowd 27,054, including many sporting military uniforms, eagerly anticipated the meeting of two giants of the mound — Carl Mays and Hippo Vaughn.

After matching three scoreless frames, Boston broke through in the fourth. With one out, Whiteman was hit by a pitch and moved up a base on McInnis' single to center. Schang lined a single over second, scoring Whiteman and moving McInnis to third. Everett Scott laid down a bunt toward the mound. Vaughn stumbled going for the ball, picked it up, and froze. As the *New York Times* recounted the event: "Vaughn was within a half a dozen feet of McInnis as he scored from third and was facing toward first-base, but he held the ball as if it were a chunk of gold. Did he throw it home to try to cut off McInnis? Not so. Did he throw it to first-base to cut off Scott? Not so again. He stood there like a man of bronze, without a sign of life in any part of his huge, statuesque frame."[24]

In the fifth the Cubs cut the lead in half, scoring a run on a double by Pick and single by Killefer. However, Mays' underhand deliver had the Chicagoans mystified. Then, with two outs in the bottom of the ninth, Pick slammed a single between first and second. On the first pitch to pinch-hitter Turner Barber, Pick broke for second, hurled himself head first into the bag, and, amid a cloud of dust, was ruled safe by Umpire Hank O'Day, who was once more donning his umpire's togs. Mays' next pitch skipped past Schang and Pick broke for third, arriving at the same time as the catcher's throw to third-baseman Fred Thomas. Pick's spikes jarred the ball from Thomas's glove, and it rolled slowly toward the Chicago dugout. With the crowd screaming hysterically, Manager Mitchell, coaching at third, implored his runner to head for home. Thomas retrieved the ball and fired to the catcher, just as Pick was beginning his slide, his spikes high and threatening. Schang grabbed the throw and tagged the runner in a simultaneous sweeping motion. Hesitating for dramatic effect, Umpire Bill Klem thrust his right-arm in the air and yelled with the appropriate air of finality: "You're out!"[25] The arbiter then hobbled from the field seeking medical assistance, as Pick's spikes had torn into his right leg.[26]

In the dressing room after the game, Vaughn was disconsolate, but he refused to blame his teammates for again not giving him any offensive support. "It was my fault," he candidly told reporters. "They gave me one run, and that one should have been enough to win for us. Do you remember that one that McInnis hit in that bad [fourth] inning? Well, that was supposed to be a bean ball. You see, it was a bad enough mistake to let the curve get away and hit Whiteman in the ribs before McInnis came to bat. But that probably wouldn't have beaten me. I got the first two past McInnis for strikes and had all the best of it, but I wanted to drive him back from the plate. So I intended to shoot the next one close to his bean. My control was bad, and it almost got over the plate, just where he likes them, and he hit it to left-field for a single. I think that one pitched ball beat me. If I hadn't missed my aim on that one, I think they never would have scored, and the one run the boys got for me would have been enough."[27]

During the train ride to Boston, players from both teams exchanged concerns regarding the players' pool and rumors that the National Commission had stated privately that the actual amounts would not reach the pledged $2,000 and $1,500, but rather would be closer to $1,200 and $800 per man.[28] The players agreed to send representatives to meet with Ban Johnson, Garry Herrman, or John Heydler, who only a month earlier had been elected to succeed Tener as president of the National League and inform them that they would not take the field unless their monetary concerns were addressed.[29]

Reporters accompanying the teams got wind of the threat and used it to portray them in the most unfavorable light possible. Of these accounts, the most vicious, but also the most accurate, came from the pen of Harry Bullion, who warned his readers: "Wait until you hear the squawk unleashed by the World Series participants when the money split comes. Talk about the shot heard round the world! The howl that is certain to be sent up by the athletes when the truth dawns on them will shake Berlin to its foundations. Those feted persons are doomed to the keenest sort of disappointment before this thing is finished, and there are a lot of doubts whether the spiked-toed knights of the diamond will get any sympathy. In the past World Series it has been customary for the ball players to merely hold out their hands and receive rewards which often exceeded the pay of a working man for a year. But conditions are entirely different now, and the athletes are destined shortly to real-ize the truth of the situation, and it will hit them right where it hurts them the most — in the region of their bank accounts."[30]

The players' committee sent word to the National Commission before the fourth game and issued their strike ultimatum. The Commission refused to meet that day but prom-ised to confer with the players before the fifth game. Reluctantly, the player representatives of the two teams consented to the agreement and took the field for the fourth contest before 22,183 spectators, including sixty wounded veterans of the Marne battlefield.

On the mound for the Red Sox was Babe Ruth, who had injured the middle knuckle of his pitching hand while engaging in horseplay on the train. While he struggled with his control throughout the cloudy, threatening afternoon, Ruth managed to blank the Cubs through the first seven frames, enabling him to run his consecutive scoreless innings to a record twenty-nine and surpassing by one the former mark held by Christy Mathewson. Moreover, his two-run triple to deep center in the fourth had driven in the game's only runs throughout the first seven innings.

Ruth faltered in the eighth, however, as he walked Killefer to open the inning. Claude Hendrix, pinch-hitting for starter Lefty Tyler, moved the runner up a base with a single to left, and both advanced on a wild pitch. Killefer then crossed the plate on a ground out by Hollocher, and pinch-runner Bill McCabe tied the score on a single by Mann.

Boston regained the lead in the bottom of the eighth off reliever Phil Douglas. Wally Schang, pinch-hitting for Sam Agnew, began the inning with a single and moved to sec-ond on a passed ball. With hard-hitting Harry Hooper at bat, Douglas prepared to deliver a heavily loaded spitball. However, Hooper was not deceived and laid down a bunt toward the pitcher. Douglas raced in and tried to scoop up the ball, but it was so wet with saliva that as he threw to first the ball slipped from his grip and his throw sailed into right-field.[31] Schang loped across the plate with the go-ahead run, and Bush relieved Ruth in the ninth to preserve Boston's 3–2 lead and give the Red Sox a commanding two-game lead in the Series.

At 10 o'clock on the morning of the fifth game, Harry Hooper and Dave Shean of the Red Sox and Leslie Mann and Bill Killefer of the Cubs arrived at the umpires' room at Fen-way Park to keep their appointment with the National Commission. Herrmann and Hey-dler were present to meet them, but Ban Johnson was absent, having decided to stop at the Copley Plaza Hotel bar to drink his lunch with a friend.[32] Hooper, who already had threat-ened a team strike if Boston owner Harry Frazee did not pay them an extra half-month's salary on the grounds that the season ended early, was designated by the players to act as their spokesman. He reminded the commissioners what they had been promised, and Her-rman responded by stating that the smaller than anticipated crowds and reduced ticket prices made keeping the pledge was impossible. Hooper offered a compromise of $1,500 and $1,000 apiece for each winner and loser, but Herrman said revenue generated would be insufficient to cover such a payoff.[33] Herrmann also reminded Hooper that Mann had been informed in a telephone conversation the previous day that the Commission would not change the rule that stated: "If for any reason the players' fund for 1918 shall be less than $152,894.48 [the minimum amount required to meet the $2,000 and $1,400 shares], the respective shares of the players participating shall be scaled in proportion."[34]

When Hooper began to argue, Herrmann silenced him and stated firmly: "I further told Mann that if the players did not propose to play, we would inform the public at once at the gates, and that we would end the Series at that point and divide the money that was coming to the players equally among the club owners, and that we would take care of the players' share of the Red Cross contributions."[35] The meeting then adjourned until Johnson arrived.

Unaware that, as I.E. Sanborn wrote, the players were engaged in a "wrangle over the pennies on the corpse's eyes," 24,694 fans passed through the turnstiles in expectation of seeing their local favorites capture their fifth world championship.[36] By the scheduled 2:30 starting time, only Stuffy McInnis had appeared on the field, and, despite the attempts by the band to keep the mood festive, a buzz of discontent over the rumored strike becoming a reality spread through stands. Former Boston Mayor John F. (Honey Fitz) Fitzgerald silently slipped from his seat near the Red Sox dugout and used his influence to have four wagonloads of police and four mounted policemen sent to Fenway Park to quell any potential riot if the players went on strike.[37]

Meanwhile, under the stands Ban Johnson finally strode unsteadily into the umpires' room, accompanied by his fellow Commission members, all of whom had imbibed a bit themselves during the interlude between meetings.[38] When Hooper and the other player representatives arrived, they reiterated their instance that they would strike if their demands were not met. Johnson, tears streaming down his face, made a slurring oration. "If you don't want to play, don't," Johnson said, "but, Harry, you fellows are putting yourselves in a very bad light with the fans. There are going to be wounded soldiers and sailors at the game again today. With a war going on and fellows fighting in France, what do you think the public will think of you ballplayers striking for more money?" He then threw his arm around Hooper's neck and implored the outfielder: "Harry, go out and play the game. You know I love you, Harry. Go out and play. For the honor and glory of the American League, go out and play the game."[39]

Hooper, although telling scribes anxiously waiting outside the door, that the Commissioners were "not in a condition to hear our argument," realized that Johnson doubtless had a valid point regarding public relations and said that the decision on whether to play or not would be left with the players.[40] After a brief consultation, Hooper and Mann returned and said the game could be played, but only if two conditions were met. First, a statement written by Hooper on behalf of the players would have to be read to the crowd. Second, a guarantee had to be given by the Commission that no punishment would be meted out against the players for the threatened strike.[41] Johnson said there was no time to put the promise into writing, but again hugged Hooper and said: "Go out and play, Harry. Everything will be all right."[42]

Shortly after 3:30 Fitzgerald entered the field, picked up the public address announcer's megaphone, walked to home plate, and asked for quiet while he read the statement from the players, which said in part: "We will play not because we think we are getting a fair deal, because we are not. But we will play for the sake of the public, which has always given us its loyal support, and for the wounded soldiers and sailors who are in the grandstand waiting for us."[43] At the conclusion of the reading, the players trotted onto the diamond amid cheers and a generous smattering of booing.[44]

Once the cry of "Play ball!" was finally uttered by Umpire Brick Owens, Sam Jones took the hill to face the thus far unfortunate Hippo Vaughn. Fate smiled on the big left-hander that afternoon, however, as his mates scored three times and he held the Red Sox to five scattered hits en route to a 3–0 triumph.

As might be expected, the story of the contest was not the game but rather the impact of the proposed walkout. In a society moving into a period of irrational fear of the spread of communism bred by the Bolshevik Revolution in Russia, the word "strike" had become synonymous with "Leninism." Consequently, accounts in the New York Times spoke of "Comrade Harry Hooper" and "Leon Trotsky Mann, the leader of the baseball Bolsheviki," and said that because the contest marked "baseball's valedictory" it should have been played to "the weary strains of Chopin's funeral march."[45] A Chicago Tribune staff writer noted sadly that the actions of the greedy players sounded "the death knell of the World Series for all time," while another began his story with: "Hats off to the Red Sox! Professional baseball is dead! Vive la amateur baseball!"[46] In his Tribune game analysis, I.E. Sanborn sneered that the game was played "under the sinister shadow of the dollar sign, which would have killed professional baseball in another year if the war had not already done so."[47] Thomas S. Rice of the Brooklyn Eagle was livid, especially with Hooper and the Red Sox for their leadership role, saying: "[The threatened strike] was another blow to the professional sport by the boneheaded performers who derive a living therefrom. It is to be hoped that the draft boards will cherish that action if there is a question of exempting any of the Red Sox from immediate induction into the military service.[48]

Disheartened by the avarice of their tarnished heroes, only 15, 238 fans, the lowest attendance at a Series game since 1909, were present to witness the sixth game of the Series. The melancholy atmosphere of Fenway was captured by a New York Times' scribe, who observed: "The gleaming sun of admiration did not shine this afternoon on the professional ballplayers. He was hidden behind the murky clouds of indifference. Silent was the trumpet voice of the ribald fan, and still were the thundering echoes which the ball tosser has always held as his own."[49] The somber mood even continued after the final out, as there was no wild demonstration of joy on the part of the winners, and "the crowd filed out of the gates with about as much enthusiasm as a party of home folks trooping out of a poor moving picture show."[50] This prevailing gloom was all the more meaningful because it occurred even though the Red Sox, behind Carl Mays' sparkling three-hitter, had defeated Lefty Tyler and the Cubs to capture the world championship.

The turning point of the battle occurred in the third inning when, after walks to Mays and Shean, Whiteman lofted a high fly to right. Flack loped in, planted himself under the falling sphere, and let it slip through his hands, and Boston had its only runs of the game. The New York Times could not resist a final jab, saying sarcastically that "the players are unanimous in the belief that if Whiteman had hit a silver dollar out to Flack, instead of a baseball, Boston would never have won the championship today."[51]

Victorious manager Ed Barrow tried vainly to exude typical winner's demeanor. "It was a wonderful Series," he gushed. "The Red Sox played machine-like baseball and presented a defense the Cubs could not break down. We made only one error in the six games. The Cubs gave us a great battle. No two gamer teams ever fought for the championship. I wish to congratulate the Cubs for the fight they made."[52]

Manager Mitchell was equally gracious in defeat, saying: "All the glory that goes with winning the world championship belongs to Boston. It scored the most runs. It was a contest between two clubs playing tight baseball. The pitching was the best in World Series games in years. It was a tough Series to lose."[53] Bill Killefer expressed the team's attitude more succinctly, candidly snapping: "I'll never forget this Series, even if I'm in 'No Man's Land.' No doubt we should be sportsmen enough to give the winners credit, but I cannot say that the better team won the Series. They were just lucky."[54]

Financially, Manager Barrow and fourteen regulars received $1,108.45, and Fred Thomas, who missed most of the season, was awarded $750. Among the Cubs, each regular received $671, and five members of the team who missed the season because of military duty were granted $140 apiece. Even more galling to the Boston players than the paucity of the purse, however, was that the National Commission broke its pledge not to institute punitive action against them for the threatened strike. Shortly before Christmas, each Red Sox received a letter from National Commission Chairman John Heydler stating that because of "the disgraceful conduct of the players in the strike during the Series, each Boston player will be fined the World Series emblems" normally awarded to the world champions.[55]

Were there to be a eulogy for the 1918 World Series, it might well be taken from a column by Harry Bullion, who placed the game and its players into perspective for the readers of the *Detroit Free Press*. "Today baseball is as dead as the proverbial herring," he wrote. "It passed out when the gates of Fenway Park, where the last game of the last World Series until after the war was played, closed on the spectators who had lost their interest. Greed to the very last was manifested, however, and gave the sport a setback that at any other time would have brought down the curses of the populace upon the heads of the guilty. Permitted to play out of sufferance, the athletes, feted and petted these many years, couldn't see their position and 'struck' for more money. While the flower of the nation was giving up its life for the cause for which the country is fighting, two groups of ballplayers, whole in body and soul, objected because they thought in their own selfish minds that the reward for their efforts was too small. They didn't stop to realize that the government who had transported millions of young men to Europe to be maimed for life, perhaps killed, to protect them and theirs had granted the privilege they were exercising at the very moment. Blind to all causes but their own, they 'struck' and were promptly, and most correctly, turned down. Heroes of the diamond won't rank with the heroes of the war. Their own tactics only can be the cause."[56]

WHITE SOX VS. REDS, 1919

The gloom that pervaded the 1918 World Series and darkened the future of the national pastime was short-lived. On November 11, 1918 an armistice was signed ending the Great War, and by the following spring the military heroes of baseball again had donned the uniforms of their profession and were training to recapture their diamond glory.

While every team was strengthened by the returning veterans, none benefited more than did the Chicago White Sox. All of the key White Sox 1917 world championship team were reunited, except for Manager Clarence Rowland, who had been blamed by Comiskey for the team's precipitous fall to sixth place in 1918. After the season, the White Sox owner fired his former favorite and replaced him with fifty-two-year-old William "Kid" Gleason, who had ended his twenty year major league playing career with the White Sox in 1912 and had served as a coach under Rowland.

Displaying all the skills that had made them champions before the war, the White Sox claimed the American League flag with an 88–52 record, finishing 3½ games ahead of Cleveland. Possibly the greatest team in the history of baseball, the Chicagoans were adept in every aspect of the game. Offensively, they led their league with a .287 batting average, 1,343 hits, 668 runs, 571 runs batted in, and 150 stolen bases. As well, they swatted 218 doubles, seventy triples, and twenty-five home runs. Around the infield, from first to third, were Arnold (Chick) Gandil (.290, 1, 60), Eddie Collins (.319, 4, 80), who led the league with thirty-three steals, Charles (Swede) Risberg (.256, 2, 38), and George (Buck) Weaver (.296, 3, 75). Behind the plate was scrappy Ray Schalk (.282, 0, 34). Not only was each of these men a threat with a bat, but also each fielded his position with precision. The outfield consisted of Harry (Nemo) Leibold (.302, 0, 26) in right, Oscar (Happy) Felsch (.275, 7, 86) in center, and "Shoeless Joe" Jackson (.351, 7, 96) in right. Like the infielders, each was superb defensively.

On the mound, the White Sox compiled a 3.04 earned run average, a league leading eighty-seven complete games, and fourteen shutouts. The ace of the staff was right-hander Eddie Cicotte, who finished 29–7, with a 1.82 earned run average. A control pitcher, Cicotte issued a paltry forty-nine bases on balls, while leading the circuit in victories, twenty-nine complete games, and 307 innings pitched. Nipping at Cicotte's heels for hurling honors was Claude (Lefty) Williams (23–11, 2.64), who led the league with forty starts. Another excellent control pitcher, Williams gave up only fifty-eight passes in 297 innings.

Rounding out the starters were rookie southpaw Dickie Kerr (13–7, 2.88) and Urban (Red) Faber (11–9, 3.83), who saw limited duty during the season, and none in the World Series, because of injuries.

Despite all of this talent, the White Sox salaries were among the lowest in baseball, with the payroll only at $85,000. The notoriously frugal Comiskey paid star second-sacker Eddie Collins $15,000, but the remainder of the team members were grossly underpaid. In fact, the combined salaries of Gandil, Felsch, and Jackson did not equal that of Collins. White Sox players remembered the insulting "rewards" given by their owner after capturing the 1917 pennant and world championship, and their scorn for Comiskey festered throughout the 1918 and 1919 campaigns. Were it not for the winning share of the World Series payoff, many White Sox players would have enjoyed finishing second simply to witness Comiskey's humiliation.[1]

In the National League, the surprising Cincinnati Reds, who had finished only eight games over .500 in 1918, amassed a 96–44 mark and won the pennant by a nine game margin over the New York Giants. Pat Moran, known to Cincinnati fans as "Dot Irishman" and to opposition players as "Old Whiskey Face," had been hired as manager on January 30, 1919 to replace Christy Mathewson, who was still in the military. By finishing first with a solid, but not exceptional squad, Moran earned yet another nickname — "Miracle Man."[2]

Offensively, the Reds batted .263 as a team and led the league only in triples with eighty-three, and although their inner defense contained some veteran talent, none could match the skills of their Chicago counterparts. Jake Daubert (.276, 2, 44), who had been traded to the Reds just before the season opened after nine years with Brooklyn, manned first-base. Diminutive Morrie Rath (.264, 1, 29), a former White Sox who was also in his first year with the Reds, was at second, teaming with shortstop Larry Kopf (.270, 0, 58) to guard the middle of the infield. Eight-year veteran Heinie Groh (.310, 5, 63) was stationed at third, and another first year member of the Reds, former New York Giant Bill Rariden (.216, 1, 24) was the backstop. The outfield boasted the team's only superstar, center-fielder Edd Roush, who had broken into the major leagues with the White Sox in 1913. Leading the National League in batting for the second time in three years with a .321 average, Roush also contributed nineteen doubles, thirteen triples, four home runs, and seventy-one runs batted in to the Reds' offensive output. Flanking Roush were left-fielder Pat Duncan (.244, 2, 17), another first-year Red, and right-fielder Alfred (Greasy) Neale (.242, 1, 54), who later gained distinction by being the only man ever to participate in a World Series, be the head coach of a Rose Bowl team, and be admitted to the National Football League Hall of Fame as a coach.[3]

On the hill, Cincinnati was led by a pair of twenty game winners, former St. Louis Cardinal and New York Giant left-hander Harry (Slim) Sallee (21–7, 2.06), in his initial season with the Reds, and right-hander Horace (Hod) Eller (20–9, 2.39). Joining them were southpaw Walter (Dutch) Ruether (19–6, 1.82), and three right-handers former New York Giant Ray Fisher (14–5, 2.17), also in his first year with the Reds, Jimmy Ring (10–9, 2.26), and Adolfo Luque (10–3, 2.63).

These were the participants who prepared to face each other for the ultimate diamond honors for 1919. Yet, on the eve of the opening game of the Fall Classic, unbeknownst to most observers, there actually would be two concurrent World Series. One would be witnessed and written about by innocent fans and sportswriters, while another would be cloaked in suspicion, deceit, and corruption.

For several days before the Series opener in Cincinnati on October 1 rumors about a "fix" were spreading, as one wag crudely said, "like a wind strong enough to blow an egg back up a hen's ass."[4] Jack Doyle, the "betting commissioner" of New York whose Billiard Academy was the gambling center of the city, confided to associates: "You couldn't miss it. The thing had an odor. I saw smart guys take even money on the Sox who should have been asking 5 to 1."[5]

Fred Lieb of the *New York Morning Sun,* after spending time wandering through the lobby of the Hotel Sinton, where the White Sox were quartered, bumped into Edd Roush, who related that earlier a fan had grabbed him and said earnestly: "Do you know what the hell is going on? It all looks and smells funny. It's in the bag. So put all your dough on the Reds. You'll get great odds. The Series is in the bag. The Sox are going to throw it."[6] Roush told Lieb that he stormed away from the fellow, thinking to himself: "Damned if you don't hear the strangest things at World Series time. The Series is fixed. I wonder how in hell those rumors get started?"[7]

Lieb then strolled over to the Metropole Hotel, whose lobby was filled with gamblers telling everyone to put their money on the Reds. Meeting fellow writer Hugh Fullerton of the *Chicago Herald and Examiner,* Lieb related his morning's activities, and Fullerton replied: "Something's wrong, Freddy. I don't like it. Every dog in the streets knows it smells. Keep your eyes open. A lot of strange things may happen before this Series ends."[8]

Later that morning, Fullerton saw Dan Daniel, another New York writer, in an elevator in the Metropole. "Dan, the Series is fixed," he whispered. "The gamblers have gotten to some of the White Sox." Daniel replied incredulously: "Hughie, I'm surprised that an old stager like you should fall for such bunk." Fullerton flashed his famous grin and warned his young colleague: "The gamblers have got to the White Sox. Take it or leave it."[9]

Such talk generally was dismissed as simply part of the usual pre-Series banter, however, and was lost amid the gushing admiration of Cinncinatians bursting with pride over their first championship team in fifty years. To celebrate the occasion, club president Garry Herrmann had Redland Field repainted and fitted with temporary stands to increase the seating capacity. The field had been manicured to perfection, and to assist fans to find their proper places without confusion, numbers had been painted on the seats to correspond with those printed on the tickets.[10] It was as if the "Queen City" was polishing every gem in its baseball tiara to assure that nothing would mar this great civic occasion.

As the record-setting throng of 30,511 paying customers filed into the stadium to take their seats and bask under a warm autumn sun, they were treated to a concert by a local band. When the Sox, wearing new gray pinstriped uniforms and white stockings, took the field for batting practice, the musicians serenaded them with "I'm Forever Blowing Bubbles," and an appearance of Pat Moran elicited "The Wearing of the Green."[11] About a thirty minutes before game time, an elderly gentleman wearing the uniform of a Navy Lieutenant stepped onto the field from a box near the White Sox dugout and walked toward the band. When the musicians recognized that he was John Philip Sousa they immediately rose and saluted him with "The Star-Spangled Banner." Sousa stood at attention until they had completed their tribute, then stepped forward, took the baton, and led a spirited rendition of "The Stars and Stripes Forever," which was met with prolonged cheering and applause from the crowd.[12]

The most attentive fans also spied Eddie Cicotte, the Chicago starting pitcher, moving among the Reds, shaking hands, and engaging in friendly conversation during the home team's batting practice. Cicotte spent several minutes watching the Reds before returning to his own dugout.[13] Meanwhile, Fred Lieb, heading to his seat in the press box, overheard two gamblers remark: "Nothin' to worry about, boys. Nothin' to worry about. It all will be over in the first inning."[14]

Kid Gleason was also aware of these rumors, but he discredited them until his friend John (Ring) Lardner of the *Chicago Tribune,* usually ebullient and ready with a quip, wandered into the Chicago manager's office and said somberly: "Just came to wish you luck, Kid. That's all."[15] Sensing the underlying message being conveyed to him by Lardner, Gleason left his room, gathered his players, and stated accusingly: "Now some of you fellows on this club have arranged to throw the Series."[16] Dick Kerr later recalled that all the innocent players looked at each other and muttered, "What the hell is this?" and that it was easy to spot the conspirators because they kept their heads down.[17]

Following this brief meeting, all of the players except Joe Jackson headed for the field. The star outfielder approached Gleason and with bowed head said softly: "I don't wanna play. You can tell the boss [Comiskey], too!" Glowering, Gleason replied threateningly: "You'll play, Jackson. You'll play!"[18]

After Ruether had retired the visitors in the first inning, Cicotte, who reputedly was suffering from a sore pitching arm, strode slowly, almost thoughtfully, to the mound to face Morrie Rath, the Reds' 5'8" leadoff man. Cicotte wound up and fired a pitch that struck Rath in the ribs under his shoulder blade. As Rath trotted to first, Cicotte rushed to him. Learning that the pitch had caused no harm, he patted Rath on the back and returned slowly to the hill.[19]

Daubert's single to right-center moved Rath to third. A long sacrifice fly by Groh sent the Reds into a 1–0 lead, but, despite giving up another walk, Cicotte escaped further damage.

The Sox tied the score in the second when Kopf booted Joe Jackson's soft tap to second and the Sox outfielder gambled by trying for an extra base. He should have been an easy out, but Kopf had trouble picking up the ball and his throw was too late to beat Jackson. Felsch sacrificed the runner to third, where he scored on a checked-swing bloop single into short left by Gandil. The prospective rally was thwarted, however, when Gandil was thrown out trying to steal second, and, after a walk to Risberg, Schalk flied to center.

In the bottom of the fourth, the Sox folded like an umbrella. After Roush had flied to center, Duncan singled over second. Kopf topped a bounder back to Cicotte, who turned to throw to Risberg. However, instead of leading the shortstop with the throw so that Risberg could touch the bag and fire to first for a double play, Cicotte held the ball until Risberg was standing on the bag, thus turning a sure twin-killing into a simple force. Watching the play, the sports editor of the *Detroit Free Press,* Joe S. Jackson, remarked that Cicotte and Risberg "handled the ball like the Associated Press sometimes handles a cablegram from Russia —'delayed in transmission.'"[20] Youthful Grantland Rice, writing a syndicated column for the *New York Tribune,* shared in the veteran Jackson's suspicions, writing that "Eddie, instead of jumping swiftly for the ball, took his time with all the leisure of a steel striker."[21] Sitting next to Fullerton, Ring Lardner leaned over and sighed: "I don't like what these old owl eyes are seeing."[22]

Neale then hit a grounder that Risberg knocked down at short but attempted no play on either runner. Reserve catcher Ivy Wingo drove in Kopf with a single to right, and both Neale and Wingo advanced on Shano Collins' futile heave to the plate to cut down Kopf. Ruether, never known for his prowess with a bat, drilled a triple to the base of the left-center field wall, driving in two more of his mates.

Collins called time and went to the mound to talk to Cicotte. Gandil and Buck Weaver raced to join in the conversation. After the conference, Cicotte lobbed a mediocre fastball straight across the plate to Rath, who slapped it past third for a double. Jake Daubert's single to right drove in Ruether with the fifth run of the frame. Gleason, his face white with rage, strode to the baseline, angrily kicking dirt, and bellowed: "Cicotte, you're finished! That's all, goddammit! That's all!"[23]

Roy Wilkinson was summoned to the mound, and Cicotte, his head bowed and his eyes avoiding those of his manager, shuffled from the hill.[24] Summing up the Chicago performance in the inning, Lardner wrote sarcastically: "The White Sox' only chance at this point was to keep the Reds hitting until darkness fell and make it an unfinished game. But Heinie Groh finally hit a ball that Felsch could not help from catching and gummed up another piece of stratagem."[25]

The Reds scored two more runs in the seventh, aided by an error by Gandil. They added another in the eighth when Ruether belted one of Grover Lowdermilk's pitches deep to left for his second triple of the game, making the final score 9–1 in favor of the Reds.

The White Sox, whom the *New York Times* sneered "looked like bush leaguers," found little solace in their dressing quarters.[26] Fiery Ray Schalk screamed at Gleason: "That dirty louse, Cicotte, shook off my curve ball signs. He didn't want to throw a curve ball. Now why in hell did he do that? Keep shaking me off!"[27] Gleason, knowing in his heart the reason for Cicotte's behavior, was furious, telling Fullerton and James Crusinberry of the *Chicago Tribune* in confidence: "Those miserable sons of bitches aren't playing the kind of ball I know they can. Something's rotten here, and I'm gonna do something about it."[28]

To the remainder of the press corps, however, Gleason dutifully put forth the standard speech of losing managers. "We will even the Series up tomorrow," he stated confidently. "When Cicotte hit Rath in the first inning, he was unnerved and was not himself thereafter. I could have taken him out then, but I trusted that luck would enable Eddie to regain his control. Ruether had a world of stuff today and pitched a really remarkable game. He should have all the credit for the victory. His batting stamps him as a second Babe Ruth. Today's defeat has not disheartened my players. I am sure that the defeat will act as an incentive to win tomorrow. There are nine games to be played, and one defeat does not mean that the Series is lost."[29]

Asked specifically why White Sox not only lost, but also looked so bad, Gleason had another stock answer. "The boys never got started today, and, anyway, we never should have scored a run, so there's no use worrying over that game. A beating like that is just what my gang needed. You'll see them fighting out there tomorrow. Just wait and see. There were a lot of mistakes made in that game of ball."[30] He paused and then added, insinuatingly: "Maybe I made one myself in starting Cicotte. We know several places where he should have used a spitter instead of a fast one."[31]

Gleason dressed and went to dinner, but when he returned to the Sinton he saw Cicotte and Risberg sitting in the lobby joking with some men. Enraged, the manager strode to his players and said loudly: "Cicotte! Whattaya laughing at, eh? You two think you can kid me? You busher, Risberg! You think I don't know what you're doing out there? Cicotte, you sonovabitch! Anyone who says he can't see what you're doing out there is either blind, stupid, or a goddam liar!"[32] As hotel patrons listened and gaped in startled silence, Gleason abruptly stopped his vituperations when Hugh Fullerton hooked his arm and led him away, saying gently: "Come on, Kid. Tomorrow's another day."[33]

Later that evening, Lardner visited Cicotte's room at the Sinton and confronted the pitcher. "What was wrong, Eddie?" he inquired accusingly. "I was betting on you today." Cicotte mumbled something about it being "bullshit" and changed the subject.[34]

In his subsequent testimony regarding the Series, Cicotte admitted that the suspicions of Lardner, Fullerton, Rice, and the handful of other writers who were watching for questionable plays and marking them in red on their scorecards, were true. "It's easy to throw a game," he confessed, adding that he had received $10,000 for his participation in the scheme. "Just the slightest hesitation on the part of the player will let a man get a hit or score a run. I did it by giving the Cincinnati batters easy balls and putting them right over the plate with nothing on them. A child could hit them. Ray Schalk was wise the moment I started pitching. I double-crossed him on the signals.... Just before I took the mound in the fourth, Gandil told me to lob them over. Duncan got on first by a walk, which brought up Kopf. I fed him a straight ball, and he dribbled it to me, and I fielded it like an amateur. If I had been playing on the level a double play was a cinch and the inning would have been over. I kept right on feeding straight balls, and before the inning was over five runs were across."[35]

For the victors, however, there was nothing but elation. Dutch Ruether, the hard-drinking hurler with a reputation for being "as wild as a Borneo headhunter," was hailed as the day's hero for his six-hit, one walk performance.[36] Manager Moran praised not only his hurler, but also his entire squad of battling underdogs. "We got away to a flying start," the smiling Irishman told reporters, "beating Cicotte, Gleason's best bet, and it makes no difference to my men what pitcher Gleason starts tomorrow. They said before the game that the Reds couldn't hit. Fourteen hits tell the story. The same batting drive will carry them through to victory. The Reds entered the Series a cocky lot of players, and this victory has given them a lot more confidence. Ruether deserved a shutout, and the Chicago players will find it just as hard to hit our other pitchers. Ruether deserves great credit for the victory, and his batting was a surprise to me."[37]

Throughout the evening Gleason had been receiving telegrams from people throughout the country claiming to know about gamblers fixing the Series, and shortly before 1 a.m. he was summoned by Comiskey to come to the owner's suite at the Sinton. Comiskey blurted: "Do you think they're throwing the Series?" Gleason offered a noncommittal response, and Comiskey shouted: "Answer me!" When Gleason still was evasive, saying that he had no proof, Comiskey dismissed him with the command to see him after the second game.[38]

His mind whirling over the possibility that the Series was dishonest, the Old Roman went to see John A. Heydler. "Gleason tells me there's something fishy going on," Comiskey said. "He doesn't know exactly what it is; he can't put his finger right on it, but he knows things aren't right. I can't go to Herrmann; he's president of the rival club; and you know how I am with Johnson. So, I'm coming to you, the president of the National League."[39]

Heydler listened and brusquely dismissed the White Sox owner, saying: "You're wrought up too much, Commy. You're just a bum loser. Your team was too confident and the Reds rushed them off their feet. They were taken rather by surprise. You can't fix a World Series."[40]

Comiskey, who had not been on speaking terms for two years with Ban Johnson because the American League president erroneously thought the White Sox owner had intentionally sent him some spoiled fish as a "gift," pleaded with Heydler to visit Johnson. Heydler reluctantly consented, and slightly before 3 a.m. he knocked on the door of Johnson's suite at the Sinton. Furious at being awakened, Johnson listened in stony silence as Heydler related Comiskey's fears. At the conclusion of the recitation, Johnson bellowed, before slamming the door, "John, what he [Comiskey] says is the whelp of a beaten cur!"[41]

The second game, played before 29,698 on yet another sunny and warm afternoon, pitted Lefty Williams against Slim Sallee, who had lost twice to the White Sox in the 1917 Series. As Williams walked to the mound, Gleason pulled Schalk aside and ordered: "Watch Williams closely."[42]

The stylish White Sox southpaw, who had begun his day by accompanying Chick Gandil to demand $20,000 from gamblers "Sleepy Bill" Burns, Abe Attell, and Billy Maharg, unintentionally blanked the weak-hitting Reds for three innings. Meanwhile, Gandil and Risberg managed to keep the score even by their inability to deliver a timely hit in the clutch. In the second, Jackson doubled to center and was sacrificed to third by Felsch. Gandil tapped weakly to short, forcing Jackson to stay at third, and Risberg flied to short right to end the inning. Two frames later Weaver and Jackson led off with consecutive singles and were advanced by Felsch's sacrifice bunt. Gandil chopped a slow bouncer to first, and Weaver was cut down trying to score. Once again, Risberg ended the threat by popping to Daubert in short right.

As in the initial contest, the play of the White Sox was so blatantly inept that it could not avoid comment from scribes. The New York Times reporter said of the first four innings: "Miss Opportunity carried on a shocking flirtation with the White Sox. She coyly winked at them, nodded her head, pouted her lips, and smiled. Like a bashful country bumpkin the Sox stubbornly refused to be vamped. Miss Opportunity was turned down cold and was so much hurt by the inattention that she shifted her wiles toward the Reds. They gave her a chance."[43]

In the bottom of the fourth, Williams, doubtless frustrated by his opponents' inability to get a hit off him in the first three innings, decided to take matters into his own left hand. He walked Rath, who was sacrificed to second by Daubert. Groh drew a pass, and Roush followed with a single that scored the lead runner and moved Groh to third. Roush was out trying to steal second, but Duncan drew another pass. Kopf followed with a triple, driving in two more runs and making the score 3–0.

Williams' sudden attack of wildness led Harry Bullion of the Detroit Free Press to sneer that the hurler "soared so high today that it became necessary to adjust toe weights to get him back to earth."[44] Grantland Rice wrote that "Williams was wilder today than Tarzan of the Apes, roaming the African jungle from limb to limb."[45] The New York Times was the most cynical, and accusatory, stating: "No sailor ashore after a six months cruise was ever more generous than Williams was this inning. Williams established himself as the World Series Santa Claus of all times. His philanthropy was unbounded, and if he had money to distribute instead of bases on balls he would probably flood the country with public libraries. When Williams gets back to Chicago they probably will appoint him as head of the Department of Charities. When the epitaph of Williams is written it will have to be admitted that Lefty Williams was a liberal guy when he had it. You would think that would be a lesson for Williams, and he would profit by his bitter experience and would try to lead a better and more upright life. Yes, neighbor, you'd think so. But that isn't the way of left-handers. They are incorrigible folks. No one ever knows when and where they will spill the beans."[46]

The Reds scored in the fifth when Risberg dropped an easy pop fly near the mound, and the White Sox avoided being whitewashed only because of poor Cincinnati fielding in the seventh. After Gandil grounded out, Risberg singled to left. Schalk followed with a single to right, and Risberg scored when Neale's throw to third sailed over relay man Kopf's head and rolled to the stands. Schalk also scored on the play when Groh's throw hit him in the back and rolled away from catcher Rariden. This made the final score 4–2 and gave Sallee a victory despite giving up ten hits to Williams' four. Gleason glowered at his players as they filed into the locker room, but maintained a stony silence as he stalked into his office. Shortly, a livid Schalk barged into Gleason's room, slammed the door behind him, and again verbally accosted his manager.[47] "The sonovabitch! Three fucking times, three times," the feisty 150-pound backstop fumed, "he crossed me in that lousy fourth inning. He wouldn't throw the curve! He never did that all season! Goddamit, Kid, you gotta do something about this!"[48]

Having tried in vain to calm his catcher, Gleason's own temper flared when he saw Gandil sitting on a stool smiling smugly. "You sure had a good day today," Gleason said icily. "So did you, Kid!" Gandil replied. The manager lunged at Gandil and began to throttle him with such fury that it took two players to pry his hands loose from Gandil's throat.[49]

Schalk, who had also verbally assailed Risberg for his sloppy play, waited for Williams under the grandstand. When the dapper, smiling pitcher emerged, Schalk bushwhacked him and kept punching him until he was pulled away by other team members.[50]

Masking his fury, Gleason gamely faced the press to rationalize a second inexplicable defeat. "We out hit them nearly three to one, but the breaks of the game went against us," he said somberly. "The Sox are far from out of the race. We have the greatest comeback ball club in the world, and these two beatings will make my players fight all the harder to even it up. The Reds' victory was almost given them on a platter. We have too good a ball club to be licked until the Reds have won the fifth game, and they'll never win the fifth one unless they continue to have that phenomenal luck."[51]

For the winners, Manager Moran, who had promised to win the Series "by hook or by crook," was unbridled in his joy.[52] "We have beaten Cicotte and Williams and have nothing to fear of the other pitchers on Gleason's staff," he stated gleefully. "I will admit that the victory was a lucky one and that we got the better of the breaks, but winning ball games is the thing that gives players confidence. With two games to their credit, my players are brimming over with it."[53]

Managers Pat Moran and Kid Gleason meet with umpires before game three, 1919 (Chicago Historical Society, ICHi-31480, photograph by *Chicago Daily News*).

Some of that confidence was shattered that evening, however, when Edd Roush and some of his teammates were gathered at the Sinton waiting for cabs to take them to the train station for their trip to Chicago. A man sidled over to Roush and said in hushed tones: "I want to tell you something. Did you hear about the squabble the White Sox got into after the game this afternoon. Schalk accusing Lefty Williams of throwing the game. Well, they didn't get the payoff, so from here on they're going to try to win."[54] Roush later said, "I didn't know whether this guy made it up or not. But it did start me thinking."[55]

Also that evening, at a roadhouse saloon on the outskirts of Cincinnati, Lardner and fellow baseball writers Tiny Maxwell, Nick Flatley, and James Crusinberry, were meeting to discuss the Series over dinner and several drinks. Many rounds later, the scribes, led by Lardner, had penned a parody of "I'm Forever Blowing Bubbles" that they dedicated to the White Sox:

> I'm forever blowing ball games,
> Pretty ball games in the air.
> I come from Chi.,
> I hardly try,
> Just go to bat and fade and die.
> Fortune's coming my way,
> That's why I don't care.
> I'm forever blowing ball games,
> For the gamblers treat me fair.[56]

A sunny, cold day greeted the smaller than anticipated crowd of 29,126 who paid to see if "Wee Dickie" Kerr could defeat Ray Fisher and put the White Sox back into contention for the world championship. The hopes of the Chicago faithful doubtless would have been dimmed had they known that early that morning, Chick Gandil had entered Bill Burns' hotel room to meet with the gambler regarding that afternoon's contest. Gandil, who was still livid that he had received only $10,000 of the $40,000 promised for losing the first two games, was told to come back after the game to get the remaining money. Asked by Burns if the team was going to play legitimate ball behind Kerr, Gandil sneered: "If we can't win for Cicotte and Williams, we're not gonna win for no busher."[57]

Gandil and his cronies were stymied, however, as Kerr, whom the New York Times said "looked like the White Sox batboy," hurled a three-hitter en route to a 3–0 whitewash of the Reds.[58] Watching from a box behind the White Sox dugout, heavyweight boxing champion Jack Dempsey was reminded by newsmen that Kerr formerly was a former bantamweight professional fighter. Dempsey laughed and retorted: "It's too bad that kid didn't stay in the ring. He packs an awful wallop in that left hand."[59]

Ironically, it was Gandil who drove in the winning runs for Chicago in the second inning. Jackson had led off with a single to left, and Felsch followed with an attempted sacrifice bunt. Fisher raced in, fielded the ball cleanly, but threw wildly past second, thereby permitting Jackson to reach third and Felsch second. With the infield pulled in for a play at the plate, Gandil took a weak swing and chopped a bouncer over second scoring both runners.

Angry at his success, Gandil still managed to prevent his team from blowing the game wide open in that frame by sloppy base running. Risberg drew a pass, moving Gandil to second, and bringing Schalk to the plate. The suspicious nature of what ensued was recounted by the Chicago Tribune: "Schalk laid down as pretty a bunt toward third as one ever would see. It didn't look like there was a chance for anyone to get it, and Gandil seemed to feel that way about it for he slowed up in his dash for third. Fisher, however, skidded over in some way and scooped the ball to Groh in time for a force play. If Gandil had gone through, the bases would have been filled with no outs and two runs already in. It would have looked like a five-run inning, but the break stopped the assault."[60]

As imposing as Kerr's performance was, certain writers posed the subtle hint that perhaps the Reds looked so powerful in the first two games only because the Sox hurlers had been so uncharacteristically inept. Harry Bullion raised this suspicion in the *Detroit Free Press,* observing: "The same players who almost earned a jail sentence by mangling Eddie Cicotte and who ran roughshod over Claude Williams were as helpless as so many infants against the little side-wheeler's wiles. They curled up in a manner which left no room for doubting Kerr's complete mastery of the situation."[61]

In the dressing room of the losers, Manager Moran retained his air of confidence. "The fellows didn't hit," he said. "Of course, it takes hits to win games."[62] Then, without knowing the truthful implication of his words, Moran analyzed the game succinctly, blaming the loss on his team's play rather than the skill exhibited by their opponents. "That wild throw to second-base by Fisher upset everything in that second inning," he explained. "Without that, I don't think the Sox would have counted in that round. The three-base hit by Risberg in the fourth that enabled the Sox to squeeze him home for the other run should have been held to a single. It took a bad bounce and got past Neale and let Risberg go on. If that had been held to a single, there would have been no run that time. There were too bad breaks against us and both proved costly."[63]

Later that evening Burns met with Gandil and his fellow conspirators and told them there was no more money, and that he wanted to receive his $1,000 fee from them for his past services. Gandil told him to go to hell and that the fix was off. Angry, Burns stormed out of the room threatening to go public with what he knew about the bribery.[64]

The following morning, another gambler, John (Sport) Sullivan, telephoned Gandil and wanted to know why the betting was suddenly switching to Chicago. Gandil said the fix was off, but Sullivan promised to deliver $20,000 before game time and another $20,000 before the fifth game if the fix was reestablished. Gandil told Sullivan that he would do so only after he received the money. Sullivan came through, and a smiling Gandil gave $5,000 each to Risberg, Felsch, Williams, and himself, leaving the others to share in the next day's payoff.[65]

The amount of money previously being placed on the Reds and now an even larger amount on the White Sox before the fourth game was known throughout sporting circles, and it caused the first public intimation of a potential scandal. Even the *Chicago Tribune,* whose editor had refused to print any of Hugh Fullerton's accusations of dishonesty, was compelled to admit that the betting "has been so heavy as to give concern to those interested in the sport."[66] It concluded, however, with the reassuring admonition that "the difficulty of fixing a baseball game, aside from the honesty of the players and the almost sure detection even if it were possible to find one black sheep, is so great as to be almost negligible."[67]

The fourth game, played under threatening skies and a nearly seventy degree temperature, was witnessed by 34,363 fans eager to see their hometown heroes even the Series. On the mound for the Reds was Jimmy Ring, opposing Cicotte, whom the *New York Times* reported had "implored and beseeched" Gleason for this opportunity to redeem himself before the local fans.[68]

Through four innings the game was a scoreless deadlock, but in the fifth Cicotte again single-handedly assured the Reds of victory. With one out, Pat Duncan grounded sharply to the mound. Cicotte knocked the ball down with his glove, swatting it a few feet away from him. Picking up the elusive sphere, Cicotte still had time to retire the runner. He took aim and heaved it low and wide past Gandil to the field boxes, and Duncan raced into second. Larry Kopf, the next batter, was the recipient of what Cicotte later called "an easy one," and stroked a single to short left.[69] Jackson charged the ball and let loose a prefect throw to Schalk. Cicotte moved directly in front of the throw and cut it off, permitting a startled Duncan to cross the plate uncontested and Kopf to reach second.

Ring later said that he always recalled that play with sadness, even though it put his team in the lead. "That's when we knew for sure there was some horseshit going on," he confessed years later, "when Cicotte cut that ball off. Up till then we'd heard a lot of talk which we tried not to pay attention to. I'll never forget Schalk standing there in front of the plate staring at Cicotte. Eddie went back to the mound and was standing there with his back to the plate, staring out to center-field and rubbing the ball up very slowly, like he didn't want to turn around and face Schalk."[70]

Cicotte then grooved another pitch to Neale, who slapped it high into left. Jackson, who was out of position by playing too shallow, let the ball drop over his head, giving Neale a run scoring double. Having deliberately given the Reds the only two runs of the game, Cicotte suddenly "settled down" and limited the Reds to a lone single over the remainder of the contest.

In the Chicago dressing room, Gleason once again was forced to pretend luck was the cause for his team's downfall and to alibi for a pitcher he was convinced was intentionally throwing games. "They shouldn't have scored on Cicotte in forty innings," he snorted in disgust.[71] Choosing his words carefully to assure they would not completely mask his true

Cincinnati players watch Chicago pitchers, 1919 (Chicago Historical Society, SDN-061910. photograph by *Chicago Daily News*).

meaning, Gleason continued: "It was a downright shame for Cicotte to be beaten. He was so set upon winning that he was a bundle of nerves. However, he was responsible for his own beating. You remember that play when he intercepted a throw from Jackson to the plate? It was in the fifth when they got the two runs. Duncan was on second and Kopf hit one to Jackson on the first bound. Jackson pegged to the plate. There wasn't any occasion for Cicotte to intercept that throw. He did it to prevent Kopf from going to second. But Kopf had no more intention of going to second than I have of jumping in the lake. You see, Cicotte figured he was playing against a club that would do things, and he wasn't. Kopf stopped at first, and Cicotte tried to intercept a throw when he wasn't set for it. That play gave the Reds their two runs. Kopf scored when Neale hit one over Jackson's head for two bases. Jackson wouldn't have been in so close if Kopf hadn't been on second."[72] Pausing to rub his hand over his head, Gleason blurted: "What makes me mad is to be licked by a team that plays baseball that way. The Reds haven't taken a chance on a play in the whole Series."[73]

Moreover, the erratic play of Gandil and his cronies was becoming so blatant that it could not be discounted as a prime factor for the White Sox performance. One of the foremost diamond scribes, Joe S. Jackson of the *Detroit Free Press*, wrote sourly after witnessing the third Chicago defeat: "Gandil is either in or out in this Series. He failed twice in Cincinnati, broke up the [third] game on Friday, and today in the second inning, with Jackson on third and one out, lifted a weak fly to Groh. You can say this without making any mistake. The Sox on the offensive at no time during the season played as badly as they have in this Series. A minor league team would have been ashamed at some of the stuff they have shown."[74]

Rain caused the postponement of the scheduled fifth game, and Gleason took the occasion to call together his squad for a meeting. When asked by reporters what was discussed, the Sox pilot replied: "We just talked things over among ourselves."[75] He added somberly: "It's the best team that ever went into a World Series, but it isn't playing the baseball that won the pennant for me. I don't know what's the matter; the players don't know what's the matter; the team has not shown itself thus far."[76] Another writer asked Gleason if Williams would be his pitcher in the fifth game. The Kid scowled and momentarily let his emotions burst forth, blurting: "No, I think I'll go in myself."[77]

In direct contrast to Gleason, Pat Moran was flashing his best Irish smile. "I have never allowed our boys to become overconfident," the gray-haired Cincinnati leader stated to newsmen, "but I have been very sure all along that we would win the Series, and win it rather easily. Many critics underestimated our ball club. We have half a dozen first-class pitchers, and the rest of the team lives right up to them. How are they going to beat neat pitching like Ring displayed yesterday? Not a chance in the world."[78]

Before fielding practice the following morning, however, the smile vanished from Moran's face when Edd Roush asked to speak to him in private. "I've been told that gamblers have got to some of the players on this club. Maybe it's true and maybe it isn't. I don't know. But you sure better do some finding out. I'll be damned if I'm going to knock myself out trying to win this Series if somebody else is trying to throw the game."[79] Moran then conferred with team captain Jake Daubert, who was shocked at the revelation, and the two men decided upon a course of action.

At the pre-game meeting, Moran stared at Hod Eller, his starting hurler, and said: "Hod, I've been hearing rumors about sellouts. Not about you, not about anyone in particular, just rumors. I want to ask you a straight question, and I want a straight answer. Has anyone offered you anything to throw this game?" To everyone's amazement, Eller replied: "Yep, after breakfast this morning a guy got on the elevator with me and got off at the same floor I did. He showed me five thousand-dollar bills and said they were mine if I'd lose the game today. I said if he didn't get damn far away from me real quick he wouldn't know what hit him. And that the same went if I ever saw him again."[80]

Moran remained deep in thought after this revelation. Finally he told Eller: "OK, you're still pitching, I'm gonna watch your every twitch out on the field. One wrong move and you're out of the game."[81]

In the opposing clubhouse, Gleason, despite harboring serious misgivings, had decided to send Lefty Williams back to the hill. Like Moran, the White Sox skipper also was planning to keep a watchful eye on his mound choice.

A throng of 34,379, comprised mainly of die-hard White Sox faithful, were on the edge of their seats throughout five scoreless frames. In the sixth, however, Williams served up a fat pitch to Eller, who lifted a high fly deep to left-center. Jackson, who was described by *Reach's 1920 Official Guide,* as "day-dreaming" let the ball drop between himself and an equally nonchalant Hap Felsch for a two-base hit.[82] To compound his guilt, Felsch then threw wildly to second, and Eller moved to third. Rath lined another fastball over the heart of the plate to right for a single, driving in the first run of the day. Rath was sacrificed to second by Daubert, and Groh drew a pass on a close pitch. Schalk was furious over the call and spit at home plate umpire John (Cy) Rigler. From then on, as the *New York Times* stated, Williams "began to wilt like a morning glory."[83]

Edd Roush followed with a booming drive to deep center. Felsch raced for the ball, hesitated a moment, and then made a futile two-handed lunge for the ball. As it rolled away from his outstretched arms, Felsch rose, fell, and rose again. Rath had crossed the plate and Groh was rounding third when Felsch fired the ball toward home plate. Roush was heard by some of his teammates to exhort Groh on with the less than flattering cry: "Get running, you crooked son of a bitch!"[84] Schalk tagged the sliding runner, but Rigler ruled the runner safe. Swearing, Schalk jumped up and down in anger and bumped into the umpire, who promptly ejected him.[85] Duncan then drove in Roush with a sacrifice fly, making the score 4–0. The Reds tallied again in the ninth off reliever Erskine Mayer to give a fifth and final run to Eller, who shut out the White Sox on three hits.

Disgusted at what they were seeing, scribes became more critical of the Chicagoans. Harry Bullion described the Sox as "whipped to a frazzle" and engulfed by the Reds "like a tidal wave would erase a canoe from the surface of the Atlantic Ocean."[86] As to the Chicago defense, Bullion wrote: "The Hose seemed to wander at random in the meadows like a lot of fellows who trust more to prayers for deliverance than their own ability to avert trouble."[87] Even Christy Mathewson, who had joined Lardner, Fullerton, and others in watching for suspicious plays, finally was moved to criticism, writing: "The fielding of Felsch and Jackson was not up to the advertisement. Jackson allowed one to get over him without even seeming to get started after the ball until it was past him. Felsch misjudged one hit by Roush that put an end to all doubt about the result."[88]

After the game, Moran was unable to contain his joy. "It's all over but the shouting," he told the press. "We'll win again tomorrow no matter whom Gleason selects as his pitcher. My players feel that world's championship already within their grasp. The Reds have played championship ball all the way through, and I am proud of being their manager. Eller pitched one of the greatest games that ever won a World Series battle. He couldn't be touched, that's all. His feat of striking out six in a row [Gandil, Risberg, Schalk, Williams, Leibold, and Eddie Collins] will go down in World Series history as one of the greatest achievements on a ball field."[89]

For the losers, Kid Gleason was simply despondent. He dressed slowly and refused to speak with reporters. As he left the park, Gleason met his friend James Crusinberry of the *Chicago Tribune,* and the two shared a taxi to Gleason's hotel. He invited Crusinberry to his room and poured out his feelings about the Series.[90]

"They aren't hitting," Gleason began wearily. "I don't know what's the matter, but I do know something's wrong with my gang. The bunch I had fighting in August for the pennant would have trimmed this Cincinnati bunch without a struggle. The bunch I have now couldn't beat a high school team. We hit something over .280 for the season. That's the best hitting any ball club ever did in the history of baseball. The way those .280 hitters acted against Eller, they couldn't make a place on a high school team. I am convinced that I have the best club that was ever put together. I certainly have been disappointed in it in this Series. It hasn't played baseball in a single game. There's only a bare chance they can win now. The gang I had in August might do it. The gang that has played for me in the five games of the World Series will have to have luck to win another game."[91]

As he spoke, he grew less weary and more angry. Crusinberry recalled: "He clearly indicated he was mad enough to lick a lot of people and go to jail for it. He clearly indicated there was something wrong and that he intended to find out what it was."[92]

The Chicago manager went on, telling Crusinberry: "You know, it doesn't seem possible that this gang that worked so great for me all summer could fall down like this. I tell you, I'm absolutely sick at heart. They haven't played any baseball for me. I felt like a schoolteacher might feel toward his pupils. I loved those boys for the way they fought for me this summer. I wouldn't let any guy in the world cut into things the way I had them going. I didn't need any help. Those fellows were right around me like a lot of kids all summer, and I would have staked my life that they would have gone through for me in the World Series. But they aren't playing baseball. Not the kind we played all summer. If they had, the Sox would just about have the world championship clinched by this time. Something has happened to my gang. If they would just play baseball for me the rest of the Series they might pull it out yet. The team I had most of the summer would do it."[93]

In another part of town that evening, the conspirators were gathered watching for Sport Sullivan to arrive with the promised second installment of $20,000. He never came, and the grumbling about ending the "fix" again arose.

With the Series back in Cincinnati, the sixth game pitted Kerr against Ruether. While 32,006, the largest crowd ever to see a game in Redland Field, paid more than $101,000 to see a world championship struggle, the *New York Times* remarked snidely: "They could have seen lots of better played games on a bush league park for two bits. The Reds' infield slipped around at times as if it were on roller skates."[94]

Cincinnati got off to a four-run lead by scoring twice in both the third and fourth innings, but the Sox cut into the margin by scoring a solo run in the fifth on two walks, an infield single, and a sacrifice fly. The Sox teed off on Ruether in the following frame, with Weaver leading off with a pop fly back of short, which turned into a two-base hit when Duncan and Kopf each pulled away and the ball dropped safely. Jackson's single to center sent Weaver scampering across the plate. Felsch's double into left-center drove Jackson home and Ruether to the showers. Jimmy Ring retired Gandil and Risberg, who were still doing their best to lose, but Schalk singled past shortstop Kopf's glove and Felsch crossed the plate with the tying run.

The score remained deadlocked through the next three innings, but the Sox broke through in the tenth. Weaver laced a double to left and moved to third on Jackson's bunt single. Felsch struck out, but Gandil became the unlikely hero when his checked swing soft liner eluded Rath at second and drove Weaver home with what proved to be the winning run, as Kerr retired the Reds in order in the bottom half of the inning.

The defeat was the culmination of what already had been a bad day for Pat Moran, as on the way to the park from his hotel a pickpocket lifted his gold watch and diamond studded charm, which had been given him by the Cincinnati Knights of Columbus.[95] Obviously disappointed that his club had blown a four-run lead and given Chicago renewed life, the Cincinnati pilot lamented to reporters: "Today's game was a heartbreaker for the Reds to lose. We should have won it a half dozen times, but the strain of the World Series is beginning to tell on my players, and they were a bit unnerved."[96]

Gleason, who had left his usual position on the third-base coaching box to view the game from the bench, did not disagree with the Reds perhaps cracking under pressure, but he had his own explanation for the offensive turnaround by the Sox.[97] "I never took my eyes off the batter," the Chicago manager related. "I knew little Dick Kerr would be in there with the pitching, and I knew they could hit. I have watched them hit all summer. Consequently, I let some others do the coaching, and I watched every move the fellow at bat made. I didn't mind it when a fellow failed, just as long as I was satisfied that the fellow gave his best effort. The best effort of the Sox will beat any ball club in the world. No matter what happens from now on, I will feel all right because the boys played at least one good game."[98]

The seventh game brought forth brilliant sunshine, a cool breeze, and an unexpectedly small crowd of 13,923 to witness Cicotte duel with Slim Sallee. By this time, Cicotte had become guilt-ridden and decided that he had to pitch one honest game in the Series, and against an honest Cicotte the Reds were helpless.[99] Chicago tallied once in the first and third innings, and drove Sallee from the hill with a two-run salvo in the fifth. Sitting dejectedly in the dugout after removing his starting hurler, Moran nervously tore a piece of paper into tiny pieces. Bewildered at what was happening to his team, the Cincinnati manager looked, as the *New York Times* described him, "like a distracted old schoolmaster who wanted to keep the whole class after school and give them a licking."[100]

For the White Sox, Gleason savored Cicotte's seven-hit, 4–1 triumph. Sitting in his hotel with James Crusinberry, Gleason, for the first time in the Series, was truly excited about his team and its effort. "They are licked sure," he said to his favorite sportswriter. "I don't see a chance for the Reds to win another game. I feel absolute certain we can take the next two, and then it will be over. This isn't the same ball team that was playing for me in the first three or four games. My gang that went through the summer and knocked everybody down in the American League race is back with me. I was the sickest man that ever walked when we left Chicago to come back here. I hadn't had a wink of sleep in two nights and felt as if I would never be able to sleep again. It wasn't because my fellows were beaten. It was because they weren't playing any baseball. Well, tonight I expect to sleep like a schoolboy on the train ride to Chicago. I haven't felt so good in years. My gang is back playing ball again. Honestly, I could have hugged every one of them after that game today, and we haven't won the championship yet. But I could hug the fellows because for the last two days they have hustled and fought and come through for me as I know they can come through. The Reds never had a chance, and I can't see where they'll have a chance in the next two games with that gang of mine fighting."[101]

At virtually the same time Gleason was lauding his team's effort, plans were being laid in New York City to seal Chicago's fate. Arnold Rothstein, one of the most notorious of Gotham's gambling contingent, had placed $375,000 on the Reds to win the fixed Series. Concerned that the White Sox were now playing honestly, Rothstein met with Sport Sullivan and ordered him to assure that the World Series ended the next afternoon. Sullivan telephoned Chicago and later that evening a man approached Lefty Williams and his wife as they were returning from a local restaurant. Williams, who was the scheduled starter for the eighth game, was told that if he made it through the first inning something would happened to him and his wife.[102]

Amid rumors that more than $2,000,000 had been wagered on the Series in New York City alone, the crowd of 32,930 began to file into Comiskey Park confident that Williams would defeat Hod Eller and even the Series.[103] Hugh Fullerton, however, did not share in their sanguine hope, for in a Comiskey Park men's lounge a well-known local gambler confided to the scribe: "All the betting is on Cincinnati. It'll be all over in the first inning. Watch for the Reds' big first inning. It'll be the biggest first inning you ever saw."[104]

In the Reds' clubhouse Moran gathered his men and gave them a fatherly talk. He assured them that in his mind they were a far better club than the White Sox, and if they failed in this crucial game it would only be a result of self-doubt and a lack of fighting spirit, not inferior ability.[105]

In the White Sox dressing quarters, Gleason was also addressing his troops, but his tone was far from fatherly. "The minute I think any one of you ain't playing to win — if I think you're laying down — I'm gonna pull you out even if I have to make an infielder out of a bullpen catcher," he roared. "I'm gonna tell you this, too! I would use an iron [gun] on any sonovabitch who would sell out this ball club!"[106]

Scowling, Gleason followed his players to the field and took his seat on the bench. To his pleasure, Williams got leadoff man Rath on a pop to Risberg in short left, but then Williams permitted the floodgates to open. Daubert singled to center and moved to second on Groh's single to right. Roush hit another fastball lobbed over the plate for a double over Gandil's head and Daubert scored. Duncan followed with a double to left, driving in two more Reds.

Fourteen pitches by Williams had resulted in four singles and three runs. Gleason stormed toward the mound and signaled for Bill James, but it was too late, for as the *New York Times* said: "The White Sox had folded like an umbrella."[107] Kopf drew a pass from the Sox reliever, and, after Neale fanned, Rariden lined a single to right, driving in the fourth Reds' tally.

Cincinnati got a lone run in the second, but the Sox matched it on Jackson's long home run into the right-field bleachers in the third. The Reds then removed whatever doubts remained among those Comiskey Park faithful still in attendance that they would be the next world's champions by adding another run in the fifth, three in the sixth, and another solo tally in the eighth. With the game safely lost, the Sox burst forth with four runs in their half of the eighth, featuring doubles by Weaver and Jackson and a triple by Gandil, making the final score 10–5 for the Reds. In a fitting, although ironic, final gesture of scorn toward their allegedly invincible foe, Reds players taunted and laughed at the White Sox as they trotted from the field.[108]

Amid the jubilation in the victors' dressing room, Moran boasted: "The Reds are champions of the world, and I am the happiest man in the world tonight. I cannot praise my players too highly. They played remarkable ball, fought every minute to win, and there never was a time when they lost confidence."[109] Pausing a moment, he added, almost defensively: "I want to say the Sox are not quitters. They are a game lot of players. They fought to win, but were outclassed, in my opinion. The Series ended as I thought it would, but I must admit the Sox gave us a scare."[110]

Gleason ranted to reporters immediately after the game. "The Reds beat the greatest team that ever went into a World Series, but it wasn't the real White Sox," he shouted, baring the emotion within his soul. "I tell you those Reds haven't any business beating us! We played worse baseball in all but a couple of games than we played all year. I don't know yet what was the matter. Something was wrong. I don't like the betting odds. I wish no one had ever bet a dollar on the team."[111]

Several hours later, Gleason and Hugh Fullerton visited Comiskey, who was still fuming in his office. "There are seven boys," he stated, "who will never play ball on this team again."[112] Apparently, Comiskey absolved Weaver of blame, a view that was shared by Abe Attell, a gambler who had helped instigate the fix. Attell told Joe Williams of the *New York World-Telegram* in an off-the-record conversation that "one of those players [Weaver] ... didn't have any more to do with throwing that Series than Greta Garbo."[113]

That same night, an inebriated Lefty Williams went to Joe Jackson's suite at the Lexington Hotel and tossed him a dirty envelope. "This is for you, Joe," he slurred. "There's $5,000 in the envelope. It's not all what we were promised, but it's better than getting nothing."[114]

The day after the game baseball writers throughout the nation began to set forth opinions regarding the rumors which had engulfed the Series. Joe Vila, veteran New York scribe, scoffed: "The Reds captured the big title fairly, squarely, and honestly. Fools there were, not baseball men, who tried to create the impression that there was something 'screwy' about the Series, but you'll always run across such skeptics wherever you go. But the integrity of baseball has never been questioned by men who know the inside of the sport."[115] Ralph S. Davis of Pittsburgh chastised the lack of sportsmanship exhibited by Gleason in his post-Series remarks, noting: "Pat Moran showed his baseball genius in the Big Series. He outgeneraled and outguessed Gleason in practically every game that was played, and when it was all over he showed more generous character than did the manager of the losing team. He did not crow as loudly as Gleason cried and whined. The Kid can well take a page from Moran's notebook."[116] James C. O'Leary of Boston was defiant in his columns, stating: "During the fight there were sinister reports that the players on one of the clubs were not trying their best to win — reports which I believe had no foundation in fact. It is incomprehensible why baseball writers should have dignified these reports — lies made out of whole cloth — by printing them and, even for a moment, put a lot of honest ball players under suspicion. It is a shame."[117] Even Oscar C. Reichow of Chicago, who had covered the Chicago Cubs throughout the season for *The Sporting News,* joined the chorus proclaiming the purity of the national pastime, proclaiming: "The White Sox had a host of friends, not only here, but also in every other American League town. Those who had bet on them found it too big a dose to swallow in a sportsmanlike manner and immediately began to holler that the Series was fixed and that $100,000 was divided among seven of the players. How ridiculous! Yet the rumor put a blemish on the honesty of the sport that may be hard to live down."[118]

Courageously standing alone among syndicated columnists was Hugh Fullerton, who, because of his closeness with Gleason and Comiskey, had access to more facts than fellow members of the press. Yet his Chicago newspaper refused to carry his story, and Fullerton was forced to seek a publisher, finally convincing the *New York World* to print his column. "There will be a great deal written and talked about this World Series," he wrote. "There will be a lot of inside stuff that never will be printed, but the truth will remain that the team which was the hardest working, which fought hardest, and which stuck together to the end, won. The team which excelled in mechanical skill, which had the ability, individually, to win, was beaten. They spilled the dope terribly. Almost everything went backward, so much so that an evil-minded person might believe the stories that have been circulating during the Series.... The Reds are not the better club. They are not even the best club in their own league, but they play ball together, and remember that a flivver that keeps running beats a Rolls Royce that is missing on several cylinders. It is not up to me to decide why they did such things. That all probably will come out in the wash. They were licked and licked good and proper, deserved it, and got it."[119]

Using his inside scoop from Comiskey, Fullerton concluded this remarks with two sorrowful predictions: "Yesterday's, in all probability, is the last game that will ever be played in any World Series. If the club owners and those who have the interest of the game at heart have listened during the Series, they will call off the annual inter-league contest. Yesterday's game also means disruption of the Chicago White Sox ball club. There are seven men on the team who will not be there when the gong sounds next spring."[120]

This column, and subsequent ones over the next several months, drew the ire of national baseball publications. *Baseball Magazine* sneered: "If a man really knows so little about baseball that he believes the game is or can be fixed, he should keep his mouth shut when in the presence of intelligent people."[121] Even more vicious and personal was an anti-Semitic editorial penned by J.G. Taylor Spink, publisher of *The Sporting News:* "Because a lot of dirty, long-nosed, thick-lipped, and strong-smelling gamblers butted into the World Series — an American event, by the way — and some of said gentlemen got crossed, stories were peddled that there was something wrong with the way the games were played."[122]

After his angry oath to Fullerton regarding crooked players, Comiskey met with his attorney, Alfred Austrian. The lawyer convinced Comiskey that to fire some of his star players would accomplish nothing positive, as they would simply sign with other teams. Without them, Comiskey's club would be a second-division operation, but with them another pennant was possible. Realizing the logic of the argument, the Old Roman and Austrian devised a plan to appear to be investigating the allegations of corruption while really trying to whitewash them.[123]

To set the scheme into action, Comiskey issued a statement in which he defended the integrity of his players, but also called for an investigation to provide evidence to substantiate the charges made against his team. "There is always some scandal following a big sporting event like the World Series," Comiskey said. "These yarns are manufactured out of whole cloth and grow out of bitterness due to losing wagers. I believe my boys fought the battles of the recent World Series on the level, as they have always done, and I would be the first to want information to the contrary. I would give $20,000 to anyone unearthing any information to that effect."[124]

Immediately those scribes who refused to accept the possibility of a rigged baseball game, innocently applauded Comiskey's carefully contrived stand. Most echoed the sentiment set forth by Oscar Reichow, who wrote: "One does not realize what a blow it was to Charles Comiskey to lose the Series, let alone the falsehood that his men had thrown the games to their opponents. He is certainly on the warpath and has put the matter in the hands of investigators with the thought in mind of ascertaining the originator of the fake. He has offered $10,000 [sic] to any man who can prove that this was done. Baseball has never had a man more honest than the Old Roman, who has always stood for nothing but the cleanest kind of baseball. He has always demanded this in his league and therefore is trying to run to the ground the story that some of his players were paid to lay down."[125]

Fullerton did his utmost, despite earning the wrath of many of his fellow baseball writers, to keep the story alive. Angry that baseball magnates seemed more intent on protecting their investments than delving into the rottenness of the game he so loved, Fullerton wrote: "The Major Leagues, both owners and players, are on trial. Charges of crookedness amongst owners, accusations of cheating, of tampering with each other's teams, of attempting to syndicate and control ballplayers are bandied about openly. Charges that ballplayers are bribed and games are sold out are made without attempts at refutations by men who have made their fortunes in baseball."[126] However, his cries were of no avail, and, by spring, interest in the allegations had melted away like the winter's snow, and all interest was on whether Cleveland or New York could dethrone Comiskey's fabulous squad.

With only Gandil, who had failed to report, missing from the previous season's pennant winners, the Sox remained in the 1920 race, although rumors floated throughout the season that they were still throwing games. Then in September a series of events occurred which rocked baseball, ended the White Sox bid to repeat as league champions, vindicated Fullerton, Lardner, Crusinberry and the others who had tried for so long to speak the truth, and forever changed the famous White Sox squad of 1919 into the infamous "Black Sox."

Reports arose that an attempt had been made to throw a game between the Cubs and Philadelphia Phillies to influence the National League pennant race. With only five games remaining in the regular season, a grand jury convened in Chicago on September 22, 1920 not only to look into this allegation, but also to reexamine the previous year's World Series. Six days later, James C. Isaminger, who covered the Athletics for the *Philadelphia North American,* wrote a blockbuster story in which he related that Billy Maharg, a former boxer, had confessed to the *North American* the previous evening that he and former major league pitcher Bill Burns had instigated the plot to offer $100,000 to eight members of the White Sox to throw the World Series.[127]

On the same day that Isaminger's story appeared, a guilt-ridden Eddie Cicotte went to Comiskey and confessed. "I don't know what you'll think of me," the pitcher said softly, "but I got to tell you how I double-crossed you, Mr. Comiskey. I did double-cross you. I'm a crook, and I got $10,000 for being a crook."[128] Comiskey replied icily: "Don't tell it to me. Tell it to a judge."[129]

Having been indicted, Cicotte had no alternative but to heed Comiskey's admonition. In his two hour and eleven minute testimony before the grand jury Cicotte admitted his role and implicated his co-conspirators, each of whom had been also indicted by the grand jurors. Unable to restrain his tears, Cicotte sobbed: "My God! Think of the children! I never did anything I regretted so much in my life. I would give anything in the world if I could undo my acts in the last World Series. I played a crooked game, and I've lost. I'm here to tell the whole truth. I've lived a thousand years during the last year. I needed the money. I had the wife and kids. I bought a farm. There was a $4,000 mortgage on it. There isn't a mortgage on it now. I paid it off with the crooked money."[130]

Cicotte then elaborated on how the plot was formulated. "The eight of us got together in my room three or four days before the games started," he stated. "Gandil was the master of ceremonies. We talked about throwing the Series. Decided we could get away with it. We agreed to do it. We all talked quite a while about it, I and the seven others. Yes, all of us decided to do our best to throw the games in Cincinnati. Then Gandil and McMullin took us all, one by one, away from the others, and we talked 'turkey.' They asked me my price. I told them $10,000. And I told them that $10,000 was to be paid in advance. 'Cash in advance,' I said. 'Cash in advance, and nothing else.' I told Gandil: 'If you can't trust me, I can't trust you.' I later found $10,000 under my pillow. I don't know who put it there, but it was there. It was my price. I had sold out 'Commy.' I had sold out the other boys, sold them for $10,000 to pay off a mortgage on a farm and for the wife and kids. I am through with baseball. I'm going to lose myself somewhere and never touch another ball.

I feel sorry to have brought this disgrace to my wife and children. I am sorry to have wrecked Mr. Comiskey's chances to win the championship that year. I was the best pitcher in the American League last year up to the time of the World Series. I'd give a million dollars to undo what I've done."[131]

The following day, his head bowed and his face covered by his hands, "Shoeless Joe" Jackson was surrounded by guards as he entered the grand jury room. The star outfielder related how, despite his Series leading .375 average and twelve hits, he had intentionally struck out or hit weak taps at crucial moments and made errant throws to help the Reds get men in scoring position.[132] He also confirmed Cicotte's tale, saying: "Each player dealt separately with Gandil. Gandil, Risberg, and McMullin were the fixers, as far as I know, and Gandil was the leader."[133] Jackson added angrily that Lefty Williams had given him $5,000 but never delivered the remaining $15,000 that he had been promised, and that when he threatened to disclose the fix, Williams, Gandil, and Risberg said: "You poor simp. Go ahead and squawk. Where do you get off if you do? We'll all say that you're a liar, and every honest ballplayer in the world will say you're a liar. You're out of luck. Some of boys were promised a lot more than you and got a lot less."[134]

After testifying for almost two hours, Jackson left the grand jury room smiling, and telling the throng of reporters massed around the Cook County Court House: "I got a big load off my chest. I'm felling better."[135] Asked about his testimony, Jackson retold the highlights, adding "Now Risberg threatens to bump me off if I squawk. That's why I had all the bailiffs with me when I left the grand jury room this afternoon."[136] As he began to walk away, a small boy raced to him and asked: "It ain't true, is it, Joe?" Jackson stared for a moment, nodded his head slowly, and turned away.[137]

Over the following days, Lefty Williams and Happy Felsch followed Jackson into the grand jury room, but Swede Risberg, Fred McMullin, and Buck Weaver refused to testify, choosing instead to post $10,000 bonds and steadfastly maintain their innocence. Chick Gandil simply ignored his subpoena to present himself before the grand jury.[138]

Immediately after Cicotte's testimony, Comiskey sent a terse telegram to Cicotte, Jackson, Gandil, Williams, Risberg, Weaver, Felsch, and utility infielder Fred McMullin, which stated: "You and each of you are hereby notified of your indefinite suspension as a member of the Chicago American League Baseball Club. Your suspension is brought about by information which has just come to me directly involving you and each of you in the baseball scandal now being investigated by the present grand jury of Cook County resulting from the World Series of 1919. If you are innocent of any wrongdoing, you and each of you will be reinstated; if you are guilty, you will be retired from organized baseball for the rest of your lives, if I can accomplish it. Until there is a finality to this investigation, it is due to the public that I take this action even though it costs Chicago the pennant."[139]

Before the grand jury handed down indictments against all eight accused Chicago players in late October, the "Black Sox Scandal" took one more incredible twist. Arnold Rothstein, who had been the silent power behind the entire betting scheme, paid off Abe Attell and Sport Sullivan to flee to Canada and Mexico respectively to prevent them from ever testifying.[140] Then Rothstein went before the grand jury and blamed the fix entirely on Attell, and his story was accepted as fact by the grand jurors. When Attell learned of this, he threatened to return and tell the truth, but when Rothstein sent him $50,000 he changed his mind and remained outside the court's jurisdiction.[141]

Also in October, Major League club owners, having determined that the game needed to reorganize its governing structure, abolished the National Commission and hired federal judge Kenesaw Mountain Landis to be an all-powerful commissioner. To restore the

Some of the accused White Sox players and the counsel pose for photographers before the trial for conspiracy. Standing (left to right), counselors James O'Brien, Max Luster, and two unidentified gentlemen. Seated, Chick Gandil, Lefty Williams, Swede Risberg, Eddie Cicotte, Buck Weaver, Joe Jackson, and counselor Thomas Nash (Chicago Historical Society, SDN-062959).

public's faith in baseball, Landis placed the eight suspended White Sox on the "ineligible list" to prevent them from playing major league baseball until their fate had been determined by a jury.

On June 27, 1921 the trial of the eight players began in Chicago, with Comiskey paying for their legal counsel. The accused had all repudiated their earlier confessions, claiming that they had not been afforded benefit of counsel, and their position was greatly enhanced when their sworn affidavits, as well as their waivers of immunity, were stolen from the State Attorney's office. Their defense was that they had signed contracts obliging them only to play baseball, not necessarily to try to win the games.[142]

On August 2, 1921 the case was turned over to jury, which in less than three hours of deliberation returned with its verdict. All eight Chicago players were acquitted of the charges, and amid rousing cheers from the assembled spectators the judge waved and smiled at the now vindicated White Sox.[143] Happiest of all was Gandil, who shouted over the bedlam: "I guess that'll learn Ban Johnson he can't frame an honest bunch of ballplayers!"[144]

The exonerated Sox celebrated that evening at an Italian restaurant near the courthouse. In the adjoining room was another festive gathering of the twelve jurors who had rendered the decision. The common door between the adjoining rooms was flung open, and the celebration lasted throughout the night, with the players laughing that "Commy" would have to keep his word and reinstate them.[145] Their gloating pleasure would shortlived, however, for at the same time these festivities were at their height, Commissioner Landis was issuing a statement that "regardless of the verdicts of juries, no player who throws a ball game, no player that undertakes or promises to throw a ballgame, no player that sits in conference with a bunch of crooked players and gamblers where the ways and means of throwing a game are discussed and does not promptly tell his club about it, will ever play professional baseball!"[146]

Forty years after the 1919 World Series, Fred Lieb reminisced about that Fall Classic and set forth his perspective on why the scandal occurred. "First," he wrote, "was the greed and avarice that is inherent in so much of the human race. Second, the bad effect of some of the leaders of the clique of otherwise honest players, like the one rotten apple spoiling the entire barrel. Third, the lush money that followed World War I, especially loose money tossed about by underworld characters. Fourth, big league ball players knew that other players were throwing games in early 1919 and 'getting by with it.' Fifth, penurious salaries paid by Charles Comiskey to his great players in 1919."[147] Lieb elaborated on the final, and what he deemed the most important, point, saying: "The major leagues had a bad year in the last war season, 1918, and no one foresaw that the post-war 1919 season would be a boom year. The economical club owners cut down their 1919 schedule to 140 games, and the National League even clipped its player limit from twenty-five to twenty-three. There was a general agreement among club owners to cut salaries to the limit. Cicotte pitched for a reported salary of $5,000 and Jackson, one of the greatest natural hitters of all time, received $6,000. The other implicated players drew considerably less. This did not excuse any player who agreed to the sellout, but it does explain why some of them felt bitter and had larceny in their hearts."[148]

Ironically, perhaps the World Series of 1919 was best summed up in the wisdom expounded by Happy Felsch, the sixth-grade-educated Black Sox outfielder. "I got five thousand dollars," Felsch started at his trial. "I could have got just about that much by being on the level if the Sox had won the Series. And now I'm out of baseball — the only profession I knew anything about — and a lot of gamblers have gotten rich. The joke seems to be on us."[149]

CUBS VS. ATHLETICS, 1929

Unaware of the financial panic that would unravel the prosperity of the Roaring Twenties within a month's time, America's baseball fans eagerly awaited the opening of the 1929 World Series. In keeping with the *Babbitt*-like mentality of the decade, it was appropriate that the two contestants were among the wealthiest teams in major league baseball, and that each had tried diligently to secure through lucrative contract offers the finest athletes available.

Manager Connie Mack's Philadelphia Athletics had undergone a lengthy and painfully slow rebuilding after they had been dismantled for financial reasons by Mack following their humiliating loss to the Boston Braves in the 1914 World Series. The return of the White Elephants, as the A's were affectionately called, to diamond preeminence was culminated in 1929 when Mack's squad compiled a 104–46 record and cruised to an eighteen game margin of victory over the defending world champion New York Yankees.

The Athletics were an awesome, balanced diamond aggregation that boasted hard hitting, superior defense, and solid pitching. Like their sixty-seven-year-old manager, the Athletics were not colorful but exhibited bulldog tenacity. According to Babe Ruth, who was covering the Series as a syndicated columnist, their style was simply to "just grab a mouthful and then hang on."[1] The infield was anchored by slugging first-baseman Jimmie (Double X) Foxx (.354, 33, 118). Joining the Maryland strongman were second-sacker Max Bishop (.232, 3, 36) who led the league with 128 walks, shortstop Joe Boley (.251, 2, 47), and Jimmy Dykes (.327, 13, 79) at third. Behind the plate was Gordon (Mickey) Cochrane (.331, 7, 95). The outfield consisted of, from left to right, Al Simmons (.365, 34, 157), George (Mule) Haas (.313, 16, 82), and Edmund (Bing) Miller (.335, 8, 93). On the mound, the A's were led by second year right-handed curve ball artist George Earnshaw (24–8, 3.29), who led the league in victories, and flame throwing Robert (Lefty) Grove (20–6), who led the league with a 2.81 earned run average and 170 strikeouts. Rounding out the starting staff were erratic southpaw George (Rube) Walberg (18–11, 3.60), Eddie Rommel (12–2, 2.85), Bill Shores (11–6, 3.60), and forty-six year old Jack Quinn (11–9, 3.97), a twenty-nine year veteran of major league ball. Also available for duty was thirty-five-year-old right-handed junkball artist Howard Ehmke (7–2, 3.29), who had pitched only 54⅔ innings before developing arm problems which kept him out of the remainder of the season.

Facing the Athletics was the Chicago Cubs, owned by William Wrigley and piloted by

Cubs team pennant, 1929 (Chicago Historical Society, ICHi-20432)

Joe McCarthy. Wrigley, who since taking over the club in 1916 had spent $2,300,000 to renovate his ball yard, doled out another $400,000 after the 1928 season to purchase the talent necessary to bring a pennant to Chicago's north side team.[2] His efforts proved successful, as the Cubs won the flag with a 98–54 record, finishing 10½ lengths ahead of the Pittsburgh Pirates.

McCarthy's philosophy was, as Babe Ruth noted, "to sock and then sock some more." While the Cub squad was not as balanced as its opponent, it lived up to its pilot's goal, exhibiting awesome batting strength, especially from the right side of the plate, and hitting .303 as a team. Around the infield the Cubs had their only left-handed batter, Charlie Grimm (.298, 10, 91), at first, seven-time batting champion Rogers Hornsby (.380, 39, 149) at second, Elwood (Woody) English (.276, 1, 52) at short, and Norm McMillan (.271, 5, 55) at third. The outfield was equally strong with Riggs Stephenson (.362, 17, 110) in left, Lewis (Hack) Wilson, the league's runs batted in champion (.345, 39, 159) in center, and stolen base king Hazen (Kiki) Cuyler (.360, 15, 102) in right. The only weak spot in the batting order was behind the plate. Regular catcher Charles Leo (Gabby) Hartnett had been relegated to a pinch-hitting role because of a season long sore throwing arm, and thus the backstopping duty had been turned over to light-hitting James (Zack) Taylor (.274, 1, 34) and Miguel (Mike) Gonzalez (.240, 0, 18).

The Cub mound corps represented a balance of experience and youth. Burly, two hundred pound, twenty-six-year-old sophomore hurler Pat Malone (22–10, 3.57), led the National League both in victories and his 166 strikeouts. Two other right-handers, thirty-year-old Charlie Root, in his fourth big league campaign, went 19–6, with an earned run average of 3.47, and seven year veteran Guy Bush, who at thirty-two amassed a record of 18–7, with a 3.66 earned run average. Supporting them were seven year veteran right-hander John (Sheriff) Blake (14–13, 4.29), who led the league by issuing 130 bases on balls, thirty-seven year old righty Hal Carlson (11–5, 5.14), and thirty-seven-year-old southpaw Art Nehf (8–5, 5.59).

During the last week of the regular season, McCarthy expressed pleasure that his foe would be Connie Mack. "Now don't go jumping to conclusions," he quickly added. "I don't mean the American League champions are my idea of a soft touch. They're not at all. I am just thinking back to a dinner given me in Philadelphia by the folks of my home city of Germantown, Pennsylvania back in 1925 after the Cubs had offered me the chance to manage a club in the big leagues. Among the guests was Connie Mack. I was just coming up from Class A ball, a bush league manager, but that didn't make any difference to Mack. He went out of his way to predict a successful venture for me in the National League. He handed out compliments like some of those sluggers of his have been hammering out base hits this year. Later I told him that nothing would please me better than if my first National League flag found me coming back to Philadelphia to play a World Series against his Athletics. Now, here we are."[3]

When asked to verify the incident and give his opinion of his managerial foe, the gentlemanly Mack replied: "I have the greatest respect and admiration for Joe McCarthy. I knew Mr. McCarthy when he was the successful pilot of the Louisville team. You must know that Joe's triumph in the National League reflects credit on Philadelphia, for he was born in Germantown and learned his baseball playing for independent teams on the Philadelphia lots."[4] Asked about the Series in general, Mack said with candor: "I'm not in a position to say anything about the Series. I don't know the Cubs, except for Charlie Grimm, who was with me for a short time in 1916 and 1917. To me, it's just a set of games between two powerful, young teams. I believe it is going to result in baseball at its best. There is sure to be plenty of color in it. To be honest, though, I haven't given it much thought yet. I've been so busy with other things. But I'm going to begin thinking about it soon now."[5]

Reporters then inquired if the A's pilot was going to alter his practice of not announcing his starting pitcher until game day. Mack smiled and said softly: "No, boys. I can say truthfully that right now I don't know, and I don't think that I will know until the Series is about to start. Here is the way I have always argued it: suppose I tell someone he is to pitch and later on conditions compel me to change my mind. That pitcher starts to worry and wonders what happened. I haven't decided even whether it will be a right-hander or a left-hander. All you questioners can keep on guessing, but nobody will know who is going in until fifteen minutes before game time."[6]

Realizing that the taciturn Mack was not going to furnish an abundance of good copy, newspapermen focused on McCarthy. The Cub leader, who seemed to revel in the attention, was more than willing to divulge his game plan. "I like to play for the big inning," he stated candidly, "and I'll gamble on the home run producers on my ball club. Every one of the Cubs takes a life-size cut at the ball and is able to rattle fences. From top to bottom in the batting order there is hitting power, and at least five in the regular line-up are potential home run hitters. We enter into the World Series confidant, but not cocky, about the power our ball club possesses. We just simply do not think the Athletic pitchers will be able to hold us in check for long."[7]

As to the eight straight National League humiliations rendered by the New York Yankees in the preceding two Fall Classics against the Pittsburgh Pirates and St. Louis Cardinals respectively, McCarthy offered no excuses but did make a prediction. "The charge has been made that the last two World Series have been won before the ball games commenced because of the presence of Ruth and Gehrig tossing a scare into the opposition," he admitted, adding hastily: "That is not my charge, understand, but it has been made rather freely. The obvious conclusion is that there is no Ruth or Gehrig in this Series. Anyway, my own thought is that the Cubs do not scare very easily. My club will hit, and hits will win the Series."[8]

Upon arriving in Chicago for the beginning of the Series, Mack teased reporters with hints that George Earnshaw would be his starter in the first game against Charlie Root of the Cubs.[9] Refusing further comment on his hurling choice, the Philadelphia manager announced that he would eschew sending his men to Wrigley Field to become acquainted with the idiosyncrasies of the park. "My boys are very bright boys," he explained, "and they can find their way around the park in no time whatsoever."[10]

On game day, the *Chicago Tribune* editorialized that the upcoming clash was more than merely to decide diamond supremacy; it was to demonstrate the triumph of Chicago's rise to civic glory. "Mr. Wrigley's players have been training intensively in preparation for this Series," the column gushed, "and they will demonstrate that Chicago has a better symphony orchestra than Philadelphia, a bigger jail, more railroads, a cleaner river, and, in all respects, a finer culture."[11]

Even if Chicago could rightfully claim all those superior off-the-field qualities, the one thing it did not possess was the on-the-field acumen of a baseball genius like Mack. At eleven o'clock on the morning of the initial contest, all the Athletics gathered for their regular general pre-game meeting in Mack's suite at the Edgewater Beach Hotel. The conference lasted approximately thirty minutes, and all left except Mack's chief lieutenant Eddie Collins and pitcher Howard Ehmke, who was standing in the middle of the room, with his hat in his hand. Mack inquired: "Is there anything you want to say to me, Howard?"

Ehmke replied solemnly: "I just wanted to ask if you plan to use me in the Series."

"You know what I told you, Howard, after that game against the Yankees when you didn't tell me you had a sore arm and gave up a bases loaded home run to Babe Ruth," the manager responded. "I said that would be the last game you would ever start for us until you came and told me you are ready to pitch."

"Well," Ehmke said softly, "I'm ready to pitch, and I'm ready right now."

Without displaying any emotion, Mack told the pitcher: "All right, Howard. You will pitch today."

"I'll win this game for you, Mr. Mack," Ehmke pledged. "Don't worry."[12]

Years later, Mack revealed that this meeting was nothing more than an elaborate ruse in which not even Collins had been included. "Howard and I sort of put a fast one over on everybody, and an old man likes to enjoy a chuckle at the expense of a younger generation. Only the two of us knew, two weeks ahead of time, that he was going to pitch the opening game," Mack told John P. Carmichael, who was compiling a collection of reminiscences for his book *My Greatest Day in Baseball*. "We were leaving on the final western trip of the regular season when I called Howard up to my office in Philadelphia. 'Now you stay home this trip,' I told him. 'The Cubs are coming in to play the Phillies. Sit up in the stands and watch them. Make your own notes on how they hit. You're pitching the first game but don't tell anybody. I don't want it known.' It was a beautiful game to watch. I don't suppose these old eyes ever strained themselves over any game as much as that one. He pitched off his right hip, real close to his shirt. He kept the ball hidden until just before he let it go. The Cubs never got a good look at it, and, when they did, it was coming out of those shirts in the old bleachers. Howard's lived on that game ever since. So have I."[13]

As Ehmke warmed up along the sidelines, the Athletic players gawked and muttered bitterly. Finally, Al Simmons strode to Mack and asked in a tone of outrage: "Is that fella gonna pitch for us?"

Mack stared at his star outfielder and replied softly: "Why, yes, he is. Isn't it all right with you, Al?"

Simmons swallowed hard and said: "Well, by God, if it's all right with you, Mr. Mack, it's all right with me."[14]

For six innings, the 50,740 spectators jammed into Wrigley Field under an overcast and threatening sky witnessed one of the greatest, and most unlikely, pitching duels in Series history. Grantland Rice watched Ehmke and Root match scoreless frames and wrote that the sluggers of both teams resembled "a class of Indian club swingers giving an exhibition of patting the keen, spicy autumn air."[15]

As the game moved along, Cub batters, who before the contest were eager to face the injury plagued Ehmke, grew frustrated with their futility. Charlie Grimm later recalled that "when we did make contact against old Howard, it sounded like we had hit a wet sponge."[16] When Hack Wilson stomped back to the dugout in the sixth after becoming the fifth straight strikeout victim and the eleventh Cub to fan, a teammate asked Wilson what Ehmke was throwing. "Looks to me like a bean bag," Wilson sneered between curses. Overhearing the exchange, Pat Malone shot back: "Well, why don't one of you guys knock the beans out of it?"[17]

In the top of the seventh, Simmons led off for the A's with a sizzling line drive which Wilson snared off the grass with a diving shoestring effort. The next batter, Jimmie Foxx, who was so strong that one awed opponent stated that "even his sweat has muscles," drove the ball deep over Wilson's head.[18] The center-fielder sped back, leaped, and crashed into the fence, but to no avail. The ball soared into the seats, breaking the scoreless deadlock and giving the Athletics only their third hit off the luckless Root, who subsequently was removed for a pinch-hitter in the bottom of the frame trailing by that lone tally. As Foxx sat on the bench after rounding the bases, Ehmke walked to the man known as "The Beast" and whispered an appreciative, heartfelt "Thanks, Jim."[19]

Mississippi spitball artist Guy Bush retired the visitors without any harm in the eighth, but in the ninth the Cub defense collapsed behind him. After a single by Cochrane, Al Simmons reached first safely when Woody English booted a double play grounder. With runners on first and second, English muffed Foxx's easy roller, filling the bases. Bing Miller then bounced a grounder through the box into center, driving in two insurance tallies.

In the bottom of the ninth the Cubs avoided a shutout only by the grace of a throwing mistake by third-sacker Dykes. Fittingly, with the tying runs on base, pinch-hitter Chuck Tolson struck out, giving Ehmke not only a 3–1 triumph but also a new World Series record of thirteen strikeouts.

Following the final out, the Athletics charged up the dressing room stairs shrieking happily and seeking out the day's hero. "Boy, what a ball game!" screamed Coach Eddie Collins, wrapping Ehmke in a bear hug. "I knew you could do it. You stood their sluggers on their heads."[20] Grizzled Kid Gleason, former manager of the Chicago White Sox now serving as Mack's other coach, playfully kept poking his fist into the pitcher's ribs as he tried to get through his teammates to the showers.[21]

Absent from the raucous scene was Mack, who had departed immediately to his hotel room to rest before meeting the press.[22] When the scribes arrived, the Philadelphia manager patiently consented to answer questions, but prefaced his remarks by asking them: "What is there to say about today's game? The result speaks for itself. Isn't it possible that we simply fooled the Cubs?"[23]

In defeat, the Cubs were sullen, leaving all post-game comments to their manager. "They got the breaks and won. That's all," McCarthy told writers assembled in his clubhouse office. "Ehmke pitched a great game, but not much better than Root though. Ehmke has a submarine delivery you don't see every day. I can't complain about Root's pitching [three hits, five strikeouts, and two bases on balls]. Neither do I feel badly about English's errors. The boy was a bit over-eager. He'll snap out of it."[24]

Asked about his team's chances now that the A's were ahead and had Earnshaw and Grove ready to pitch the next two games, McCarthy demonstrated some of his quick Irish temper. "I can't say that I'm at all dismayed at losing the first game. Losing one ball game doesn't mean losing the Series," he snapped. "Throw out those unearned runs in the ninth inning, and we had the game tied up. The Cubs lost the first one, but they didn't lose much by comparison, in my judgment. They are as good a club as the Athletics, and I look for them to prove themselves a little better when the battle begins again. We'll get them tomorrow."[25]

The following afternoon a throng of nearly 50,000 Chicago faithful paid to see if McCarthy's prophecy would come true. It was a day more fitting for football than baseball. Fans sat huddled in blankets, heavy overcoats, and furs, as a cold wind roared in from Lake Michigan making the stadium flags stand out like billboards.

On the mound for the Cubs was Pat (Blubber) Malone, who, as Westbrook Pegler noted, stood in the center of the diamond and "let fly a fastball like 250 pounds of a determined woman throwing a sugar bowl in an old-fashioned family disagreement."[26] Always cocky and supremely confident of his ability, Malone had boasted before the Series that his fastball would knock the bats out of the Athletics' hands.[27] For two innings, the Cub hurler made good his boast, but in the third he surrendered two singles and a tremendous three-run blast by Jimmy Foxx deep into the temporary bleachers behind the left-field wall. The next inning the Mackmen pushed across another three tallies, and Malone was sent to the showers.

Athletics starter George Earnshaw, who had held the Cubs to two hits while striking out six in four innings, lost some of his concentration in the fifth, and, as Grantland Rice observed, "the Cubs fell on top of his broad, sunburned neck for five hits and three runs, as base hits were popping like machine gun fire."[28] Mack hurriedly brought in Lefty Grove to relieve Earnshaw. The southpaw star escaped the inning without further damage, blanking the Cubs the rest of the way, striking out seven and giving up only three hits. As Rice wrote admiringly: "Grove hasn't any more speed than a rifle ball. He uses more smoke than a pair of burning oil wells. The Cubs couldn't have scored off him in a week."[29] Meanwhile, the Philadelphians tallied three more times, two on a long blast by Al Simmons just inside the right-field foul pole, making the final score a humiliating 9–3.

A grim McCarthy offered no alibis for the loss, but continued to promise better days for his team. "The better ball club won the game. The Athletics simply outclassed the Cubs, and that's all there is to it," he admitted. "It is the proper thing, I suppose," he continued, "to say that we're not licked. This isn't merely the usual statement. I'm on the square with it. The day of rest traveling will give our club a chance to untrack itself. We see no need for losing our nerve over the present outlook. The Cubs have been in tough spots before this and have managed to come through on the bit. They are just as liable to do the same thing in Philadelphia."[30]

Sportswriters did not share McCarthy's optimism. Ed Burns of the *Chicago Tribune* lamented: "Our poor Cubs! Sick at heart and sore of mind and body they are! And extremely disillusioned about their own prowess. It was shocking the way the visitors outclassed our heroes in every phase of the enterprise. It was pitiful the way our once-great warriors folded up in the pinches. It was depressing to compare our pitchers with theirs. Two-thirds of the team appeared punch-drunk before the game was half over. It was ... but let's not get hysterical. Maybe they'll do better."[31] Humorist, and former White Sox pitcher, Nick Altrock noted sarcastically: "You read in all the advance dope how the Cubs would have the edge because Hornsby and Cuyler had so much experience in the World Series before. Well, from the way they've been acting the last two days the only experience they ever got in previous World Series was striking out."[32] In deference to Chicago's gangland reputation, Altrock did offer a backhanded compliment to the Windy City: "Chicago acted fine while the Series was there, considering the circumstances. Not even an umpire was killed. That is a pretty good record for a city where pineapples are more dangerous than toadstools."[33] Of course, the most poetic remark was penned by the legendary Rice, who put the Cubs' collapse into historic perspective. "Some day, before the moon drops from the sky and the world turns back to lava or to dust," he wrote wistfully, "the National League is going to win a World Series ball game — provided the quaint October custom is still carried on. There is such a thing as rubbing it in too roughly, especially when one applies salt and vinegar to the open wounds the lash has made, but if some vital change in the general scenery does not happen in a hurry, the Athletics are going to make it four in a row once more and force the older circuit to step out and prove it is still a major league."[34]

As the "White Elephant Special" carrying the Athletics sped eastward over the rails, Connie Mack sat down beside Earnshaw, who was still smarting from being driven off the mound in the second game. "George," the manager said fatherly, "I'm going to let you pitch again in our next game in Philadelphia. You were pitching too fast when they knocked you out of the box. Take more time between pitches, slow down your rhythm, and you'll beat 'em."[35]

Smarting under the ridicule that they fled Chicago "under cover of false whiskers" to avoid recognition and that the "Series won't go five games unless the Cubs insist on losing that many," the National League contingent of ball players, club magnates, and league officials registered at the Ben Franklin Hotel in downtown Philadelphia.[36] National League President John Heydler, having presided over ten straight World Series losses, was brusque in his dismissal of reporters, but Rogers Hornsby and Joe McCarthy stopped to face the horde of scribes. "I guess we must have looked pretty bad," said the Rajah, who had whiffed four times in the first two games, "but that's done and gone. The breaks couldn't have been worse for us, but our turn can't be far away. We'll get going, and when we do they'll know there is still a lot of fighting to be done before the Series is over."[37] McCarthy echoed his star second-baseman, adding: "This Series is still in the woods, and the big point is that our boys have not lost confidence in themselves. They still believe they are the better team and mean to prove it."[38]

In a private interview with Grantland Rice later that evening, the Cub manager poured out his feelings. "I'll give you the story as I see it," McCarthy said. "That first game might have gone either way. It was nip and tuck, depending on the breaks. We might have won that one just as easily as we lost it. I think you'll agree that at the end of the game the two clubs looked to be evenly matched. It was a great game, and we just missed. In the second game we were outclassed. We looked bad. There is no alibi, and no argument to offer. But that is only one ball game. We've been outplayed and outclassed before in one ball game and came back and looked like another club. I know the odds are against us, but you can tell any part of the world interested in the result that we are still in there fighting and haven't thought about quitting. They beat us in Chicago, but we may surprise them in Philadelphia. Things have happened like that before. Root and Bush are ready whenever I need them. Root pitched great ball, and he is set to do it again. We may be taken, but don't let them figure we are any pushovers."[39]

Balmy Indian Summer temperatures and bright sunshine greeted the capacity crowd of 29,921 paying customers who were escorted to their seats in Shibe Park by one of 246 female ushers, 231 of whom were hired just for the Series. Hundreds of other non-ticket holders paid apartment house owners and residents $5.50 for the privilege of perching on regulation bleachers, fifteen rows deep, which had been constructed on the rooftops of the two-story brick dwellings behind the right-field fence. Bay windows in the upper story apartments served as private box seats for those willing to pay $10 for the additional comfort.[40]

To avoid the necessity for paying a band, the frugal Shibe family, who owned the Athletics, installed an amplifier system atop the right-field wall to broadcast recorded music, marking, as the *New York Times* observed sarcastically, "a new advance in World Series progress."[41] As the tinny, scratchy strains of the national anthem concluded, a moment of silence was observed to pay tribute to the recently deceased former New York Yankee manager Miller Huggins.[42]

The Athletics, who had been exhorted before the game to avoid overconfidence, sent Earnshaw back to the hill to oppose dark-skinned, cadaverous Guy Bush, whose sweeping sidearm pitching motion, according to John Kieran of the *New York Times,* left him "kneeling on the mound like a dervish on a prayer rug."[43] The home team took a 1–0 lead in the fifth, but the next inning, as Grantland Rice wrote, "the Cubs broke from their menagerie cells at last and chased Mack's elephants into the jungle."[44]

As Bush stepped from the dugout to lead off the sixth, McCarthy grabbed the weak hitting hurler, about whom Rice sneered "hadn't hit the size of his cap since last April," and whispered: "See if you can diddle a walk from Earnshaw."[45] Following instructions, Bush, according to John Drebinger of the *New York Times,* "began hopping up and down in the batter's box in the best style of a Mississippi clog dancer."[46] Earnshaw, obviously unnerved by the weird gyrations, threw "the jumping jack" four balls off the plate. After an attempted sacrifice by McMillan resulted in a pop foul to Cochrane, English sent a sharp grounder to Dykes at third, who fumbled the ball for an error. Hornsby shot a single to left, driving in Bush with the tying run. Wilson moved both runners along a base with a grounder to second. Both subsequently scored when Kiki Cuyler, who thus far in the Series had "done little beyond drawing his breath between his teeth and bringing anguish to his friends," smashed a 3–2 pitch through the box, sending the final two runs of the contest across the plate.[47]

A disgusted Mack recapped the afternoon's events succinctly. "It was a tough game to lose, but the Cubs deserved to win," he told writers in the clubhouse runway. "Earnshaw pitched a good game [six hits and ten strikeouts], and so did Guy Bush."[48]

For the Cubs, gaiety reigned. Charlie Grimm, who had left his $450 banjo in Chicago, was playing merrily on one rented for $55 by his teammates.[49] Pausing in his music-making, "Jolly Cholly" shouted: "Hey, when do we get our meal money?" To which Gabby Hartnett replied in his bellowing tenor voice: "You give it all to Bush, Charlie, when you do get it!"[50]

Manager McCarthy was all smiles, slapping backs and congratulating his team. Asked about whether the A's were intentionally trying to rattle Bush as he was preparing to pitch by twice having the public address announcer ask for silence to announce that some individual was to call home immediately because of a death in the family.[51] McCarthy laughed and said: "Well, if they thought they could beat us that way, they're just plain silly."[52] Seeing Hornsby and Cuyler, McCarthy told reporters: "With those two guys coming through with big hits, it meant winning for us. After the slump they had been in, their hitting in the pinches like that changed the whole complexion of things. We now feel we have made the big break in the Series."[53]

Invigorated by their previous day's triumph, the Cubs took the field confident that Root could best ancient Jack Quinn and even the Series. The visitors stunned the sunbathed Columbus Day sellout throng of 29,921 by scoring first on Grimm's two-run homer over the right-field wall in the fourth inning. Then the Chicagoans led off the sixth by lacing four consecutive singles off Quinn and another off Walberg, which, coupled with a sacrifice fly, resulted in five more runs. In the seventh Hornsby tripled to deep center off Eddie Rommel, the third Athletic pitcher, and was sent home on Cuyler's single to left, making the score 8–0 in favor of the Cubs. As Nick Altrock observed cynically: "The Athletics looked so bad they were the golden rod in Connie Mack's hay fever."[54]

In the home half of the seventh, what had been a boring, lopsided game evolved into what Ty Cobb proclaimed to be "the most heart-rending and thrilling battle in World Series history."[55] Simmons opened the frame with a home run onto the roof of the left-field pavilion just inches inside the foul pole. Foxx shot a single to right. Bing Miller banged one to short center, which Hack Wilson lost in the sun. Dykes singled to left, scoring Foxx. Joe Boley slapped another run scoring single to right. Veteran George Burns, pinch-hitting for Rommel, popped to English, but Max Bishop drove a single over Root's head into center, driving home another score.

By this juncture, the two managers had undergone drastic alterations in their thinking. Mack, who had intended to pull all his regulars after the seventh inning, now was thinking of a possible victory. McCarthy, who had been placidly observing a seeming Cub rout, now rushed to the mound to remove Root and bring in former New York Giant southpaw and World Series veteran Art Nehf.

Waiting anxiously at the plate was Mule Haas, who had been a prime target of vicious bench jockeying throughout the Series. Haas met one of Nehf's curves and hit what appeared to be a routine fly to center. Wilson rushed in for the ball, but suddenly hesitated and ducked, blinded by the sun. The ball soared over his head and rolled untouched into the deepest part of the field. By the time it was retrieved, Haas was racing toward home plate for an inside-the-park home run. Jimmy Dykes later recalled the scene: "I was standing in the dugout yelling: 'He's gonna make it! There he goes!' As Mule slid across the plate, I clouted the player next to me across the back and yelled: "We're back in the game, boys!' Only it wasn't a player I hit. It was Connie Mack. I'd never seen him leave his seat during a game before. But here he was, standing up there leaning out of the dugout, watching Haas race to the plate. When I smacked him, I knocked him clear out over the bats in front of the dugout. I was horrified and grabbed Mr. Mack and helped him to his feet. He smiled, reached out, patted me on the arm, and said in that quiet way of his: 'That's all right, Jimmy. Everything's all right. Anything you do right now is all right. Wasn't it wonderful!"[56]

Nehf proceeded to issue a pass to Cochrane, and McCarthy made another long walk to the mound, signaling for Sheriff Blake to stop the Philadelphia scoring tide and protect his club's one-run margin. However, as John Drebinger acidly remarked, "he stemmed it like a man sticking his head in an electric fan."[57] Simmons garnered his second hit of the inning, bouncing a single over McMillan's head at third. Foxx followed suit with his second hit of the frame, a single to center, which drove in Cochrane with the tying run. As the Athletic strongman stood on first, Grimm strolled to the bag and said only partly in jest: "Podner, the next time you come around first-base, I'm going to trip you."[58]

McCarthy, muttering "What can I do?" to himself on the bench, was, as Altrock wrote, "throwing his arm out of joint just waving pitchers off the slab in a parade of wooden soldiers with glass arms."[59] In desperation, he called Pat Malone to the firing line. Malone's first pitch plunked Miller in the ribs, and the bases were loaded. Dykes, also seeking his second safety of the inning, sent a low, hard line drive to left. Riggs Stephenson chased the ball frantically, got both hands on it, and watched helplessly as it slid through his fingers for a double, scoring the ninth and tenth runs of the inning. Malone then fanned Boley and Burns, but the damage, both actual and psychological, had been done. In barely twenty minutes, as John Drebinger observed, the Cub machine, which had been "moving along magnificently and in all its glistening splendor, now lay strewn all over the field, a jangled mess of junk."[60]

With a two-run lead, Mack turned to his ace, Lefty Grove. The fireballing southpaw retired the final six Cub batters, striking out four, preserving the incredible 10–8 Philadelphia victory. At the conclusion of the Chicago collapse, Altrock prophesized: "This World Series has only nine more innings to go, but I don't think Joe [McCarthy] has a pitching staff that can last that long."[61]

The Athletics were stunned by their unlikely victory. Mack, wearing his familiar blue suit, hat in hand, and overcoat folded meticulously over one arm, knocked timidly on the door of the team dressing room. The door swung open, and the players, who rarely saw their manager after a game, suddenly ceased their singing and revelry. "I'd just like to express to you the things I feel," the near septuagenarian Mack said, tears welling up in his eyes, "but I can't. I've never really seen anything like that rally. There is nothing in baseball history to compare with it. It was the greatest display of punch and fighting ability I've ever seen on a ball field. I'll have to let it go at that."[62]

After Mack departed the celebration began anew. Dykes, puffing on a big cigar, said simply: "This Series is all over."[63] Breaking out into laughter, he added: "I sure wish I could bat all the time in the National League. I'd sure lead that circuit. All you have to do against these Cub pitchers is stick your bat out and you get hits."[64] Mickey Cochrane gave praise to the Chicago "bench orators," saying: "They should be in the Kentucky Derby instead of a World Series. They are the best jockeys I ever heard."[65] Told of Cochrane's remarks, Hack Wilson gave forth his only smile of the day, stating: "I'm glad he liked it. They started it, and we say: 'If you want it, we'll give you plenty.' That's what we're doing."[66]

The steady stream of obscenities and invectives did not escape the notice of Commissioner Kenesaw Mountain Landis, who told officials of both clubs: "If the vulgarities and indecent language continues, I'll fine the culprit a full Series share. And if I can't determine who is yelling, I'll fine the manager." When Mack relayed this to his team, Cochrane sneered: "Hell, that's something! After the game we'll serve tea in the clubhouse, girls!"[67]

This reprimand from the Commissioner merely added to the gloom that pervaded the Cub quarters. Hack Wilson, heartbroken and angry, changed his clothes in silence and departed for the hotel. Norm McMillan, who had watched a sure double play ball off the bat of Simmons in that fateful seventh inning bounce over his head for a single, sat in front of his locker, staring blankly, perhaps aware of mutterings by Hornsby that the third-sacker was the game's goat.[68] McCarthy tried to calm his players and absolve Wilson of blame. "The breaks of the game beat us today," he said philosophically, "but we're not whipped in this Series yet by any means. It took the worst breaks I've ever seen. The sun had a lot to do with it. In the seventh the sun shone directly in the eyes of every pitcher I sent out there. It was just going down behind the grandstand. Artie Nehf was almost blinded, and poor Hack was in a terrible fix out there in center-field. Remember, men, you can beat a ball club and even move a ball park, but you can't do either to the sun."[69] Grinning wanly, McCarthy added: "We had good luck against Burns in the seventh, didn't we? Got him out twice. Too bad we had to face those eight other batters in between."[70]

In the lobby of the Ben Franklin, Wilson, who was already being called "Sunny Boy" by critics, met reporters, who asked him for a few words. "I'm the big chump of the Series. I have caught other balls in the sun, and I should have caught those today. I'm a big chump, and nobody is going to tell me different. I just couldn't see the balls. I dropped Dykes' fly in the fifth and put Root in a hole because I was late in locating it. Miller's fly in the seventh was short, and when I got a line on it I was too far back. Haas' ball later in the seventh never was in my vision until it was almost to the ground. I stuck out my bare hand to get it, but it bounced past me for a homer. I was wearing sunglasses, but the sun was so bright that they did me no good."[71]

As Wilson departed, McCarthy joined the lobby assemblage and continued his earlier defense of his beleaguered young outfielder. "You might want to blame Wilson," he said firmly, "but you can't fasten it on him. The poor kid simply lost the ball in the sun, and he didn't put the sun there. Sure, if he had caught Miller's short fly early in the seventh inning, Root would have gotten out with not more than one run against him. Sure, if Hack had caught Haas' fly, which went for a homer, we still would have won. But he didn't catch them because he didn't see them. It wasn't his lack of ability or eyesight, but just bad luck for the National League."[72] In a private conversation with a friend, however, McCarthy expressed his true feelings, sighing: "Sometimes I think nine trained monkeys could do better in a Series than the apes we pay salaries."[73]

Next to Wilson, the most disappointed Chicagoan was William Wrigley. The principle owner of the Cubs was, as Irving Vaughan of the *Chicago Tribune* wrote, "like a man who had built his house of cards and then put it in the path of a big wind."[74] Virtually conceding that his club's chances had disappeared in the bright Philadelphia sunshine, Wrigley tried to put the impact of the World Series into a broader context. "Baseball is a business," he admitted bluntly. "The other National League owners have been hit between the eyes. The National League in 1927 and 1928 suffered Series defeats in four straight games. The league dropped the first two games of the present Series. Then, when it appeared that the Cubs were coming back to regain the league's lost prestige, the sun blinded Wilson. It makes it look as if the American League is far stronger than the National, and that is why the owners in the latter are nettled. In fact, the Cubs, in a full season, probably would whip the Macks easily, but a World Series is not a season."[75]

Most ball players, including Ty Cobb and Babe Ruth, defended Wilson, as did John Kieran, who asked: "What can a fielder do when he loses the ball in the sun? Advertise for it?"[76] However, the Chicago press pilloried the twenty-nine year old outfielder and the entire Cub team. The *Chicago Tribune* printed a parody of "My Old Kentucky Home":

> The sun shone bright in our great Hack Wilson's eyes,
> 'Tis Sunday, the Mackmen are gay.
> The third game's won, and the Cub pitching has gone astray,
> As our Series title fades far away.
> Weep no more, dear Cub fan; O weep no more today,
> For we'll sing one song for the game and fighting Cubs,
> For the record whiffing Cubs far away.[77]

Ed Burns of the same daily moaned: "It remained for our Cubs to furnish the greatest debacle, the most terrific flop, in the history of the World Series, and one of the worst in the history of major league baseball games of all kinds."[78] Honing in on Wilson, Burns noted cruelly: "Tonight Hack has the assurance that he will take his place at the head of World Series goats. But for Hack's blindness the A's couldn't have made more than three runs, if that many. Losing a ball in the sun usually is condoned, but Hack had his warning that his sunglasses were not adequate. He muffed an easy fly in the fifth, which should have caused him to get smokier equipment. But he did not, and, as a result, he and his mates were blown higher out of the water than any other club was ever before."[79]

As no baseball was permitted on the Sabbath in the City of Brotherly Love, the Cubs had an extra day to dwell on the twist of fate that had snatched victory from their grasp in that disastrous seventh inning. As they gathered in the hotel lobby late Monday morning preparatory to leaving for Shibe Park for the fifth game, Root, Grimm, and a few other Cubs decided to go to Wilson's room as a demonstration of friendship and team solidarity. When he opened the door, they patted their teammate on the shoulder, but Wilson backed away and erupted into a towering rage. "You fellows just cut that out and get outta here " he roared to his retreating comrades. "I'm no good and have lost you fellows thousands of dollars. The Cubs ought to send me to a Class B league next year!"[80]

The fifth game was played before another crowd announced as 29,921. Among the spectators was President Herbert Hoover, an avid baseball fan, who was "looking for some excitement to offset the monotony of his official duties."[81] As the Chief Executive, his wife, and members of his cabinet entered the park through a field gate and walked to their gaily decorated boxes along the third-base line behind the Athletics' dugout, the crowd rose and cheered. The President was waving his hat in response when suddenly "some vulgarians besmirched Philadelphia's fair name" by booing and yelling: "Beer! Beer! Beer!" to show their disapproval of the administration's continued support of prohibition.[82] Hoover dismissed the jeers and turned his attention to the canned music coming out of the amplifiers, even asking a where he might purchase a similar system for the White House.[83]

During pre-game practice, Mack ended his lifelong tradition of never entering the dugout once spectators were in the stands by striding over to the Cub dugout to say a few words to McCarthy.[84] He was joined by Mickey Cochrane, who issued a loud invitation to his Chicago detractors: "Hello, sweethearts. We're going to serve tea and cookies in the clubhouse after the game. You girls put on your bib and tucker and come on over and get your share!"[85] Fearing that Landis, who was already ensconced in his box near the Cub dugout, his chin leaning on the rail, had heard the jibe, Mack quickly cautioned his catcher: "Shut your mouth, Mickey! Do you want it to cost us money?"[86]

Rumor had it that Mack intended to start twenty-five year old right-hander Bill Shores against the Cubs' Pat Malone. However, Shores had violated curfew the night before the game and had been arrested for speeding as he was returning to the team hotel.[87] Consequently, Mack turned to his first game hero, Howard Ehmke, to deliver the world championship to Philadelphia.

The teams matched scoreless innings until the fourth, when the Cubs demonstrated some of their reputed offensive prowess. With two out, Cuyler lashed a double over Bishop's head in left-center. Stephenson walked, and Grimm followed with a bloop single into right-center scoring Cuyler. Zack Taylor lined a sharp single to left-center that drove Stephenson across the plate and Ehmke to the showers. Rube Walberg assumed the mound duties for the Mackmen and promptly struck out Malone to end the rally.

Meanwhile, Malone was holding the mighty Athletics at bay, allowing only two hits through eight innings. As the bottom of the ninth opened, even the most faithful Philadelphia rooter thought the Series would move back to Chicago for a sixth battle. The gloom grew deeper as the leadoff man, pinch-hitter Walter French, struck out. Bishop then kept the home crowd's slim hope alive with a line single over third. Then Mule Haas, whom Westbrook Pegler proclaimed to be "the rudest man in the American League," advanced toward the plate, issuing curses toward the Cub dugout.[88]

Malone stared at Haas and fired a high fastball, which, as Grantland Rice observed, was "Haas' favorite dish — he eats 'em cooked or raw."[89] The Athletics' center-fielder walloped the pitch on a line toward right-field. The ball was still rising as it sailed into the stands, high over Cuyler's outstretched glove, for a game tying home run. Coach Eddie

Collins and all the players streamed from the Philadelphia dugout onto the field, pummeling each other, jumping, running, and throwing sweaters, caps, and gloves in the air. Only Mack remained calm, sitting on the bench with his scorecard gripped tightly in his hand, tears filling his eyes at what he later said was a "very helpful hit."[90]

While most attention was centered on the celebration, another scene, this one not so joyful, was occurring between the pitcher's mound and home plate. Malone, fist raised and screaming at catcher Zack Taylor, strode toward home plate. His face beet red, the hurler shouted: "You asked for that one." The contrite backstop replied: "I know it, Pat. But how was I to know he'd hit it that far? We've just got to bear down now, and then win it back in the tenth. You're the one who can do it!"[91] When order was restored, as Rice noted, "the A's bench was a raving and seething mass of ball players, while the Cubs' bench would have made a tomb out of a nightclub."[92]

Malone, still seething, retired Cochrane on a bounder to Hornsby at second, but Simmons pounded a long double off the scoreboard in left-field. McCarthy then ordered an intentional pass to Foxx in order to face Bing Miller.

As the dark-complexioned Miller dug in, Cub bench-jockeys taunted him with his accustomed epithet of "Booker T. Miller! Booker T. Miller!"[93] The nine-year major league veteran calmly watched two fastballs sail across the plate for called strikes and then patiently took two curves for balls. From the on-deck circle, Jimmy Dykes anxiously yelled: "Come on! Hit the damned thing!"[94] Calling time, Miller walked over to Dykes and said softly: "He's gonna throw me a curve, and I'm gonna tear it."[95] What transpired next is best related through the prose of Grantland Rice: "Malone whipped a curve over with everything he had, but something large and round met it squarely in its face. It was Bing Miller's bat. The ball sailed on a line over Hornsby's head toward right-center. Hack Wilson went after it in the manner of a man who would have given a million dollars right there for a motorcycle or an airplane. But he couldn't have caught this drive with either, or a net. It would have gone for a three-base hit, but it was long enough to send Simmons over with the run that gave Connie Mack his fourth World Series, a new record. And it was long enough to lift the President of the United States to his feet again, proving that he's a true fan."[96]

As Simmons stomped on home plate, the Athletics poured out to greet him. Staid Eddie Collins led the celebration, dancing and hurling his sweater coat into the air as he led the team into the clubhouse.[97] In the midst of the hilarity was Mack, throwing his arms around first Haas, then Miller. He then abruptly slipped from the dressing room and ran down the corridor toward his private office in the Shibe Park tower. As he approached his door, three female secretaries burst into the hallway and tried to kiss him, but the elusive Mack escaped their clutches by saying that he was expecting newspapermen shortly. Finally entering the security of his inner sanctum, the exhausted Mack took a sip of water and collapsed on his sofa for a short nap.[98]

Amid the yelling, backslapping, popping of champagne corks, and the blue haze of cigar smoke, Commissioner Landis sought out Cochrane. Finding the burly catcher, Landis put his arm around his shoulder and said: "Hello, sweetheart. I came for my tea and cookies. Will you pour?"[99] Cochrane broke into laughter and asked Landis: "Did you hear me say that?" The Commissioner replied: "Of course, I did. You said it loud enough."[100]

Mule Haas recounted for scribes his game-tying blast. "It looked as big as a watermelon as it came to the plate," he related. "I swung with all my power. I knew the second that the bat met the ball it was a homer, but I lit out for first as fast as my legs could carry me. I think I must have been past first when the ball scaled the screen. Not a Chicago pitcher threw one down my alley all during the Series but that one."[101]

After Mack had composed himself, he met with the press, beginning his comments with an apology for keeping them waiting. "I guess I overdid it," he said shyly. "It was almost too wonderful. Mine is the greatest team in baseball. All season long they have been winning games like the last two for me with desperate rallies, but today I turned mental traitor to them. Mentally, I was on the train to Chicago, wondering who I would pitch in the sixth game when Haas hit that high fast ball over the fence and tied the score. Almost before I could get back into the ballpark, Simmons hit one, then Miller, and the game was over. I had a feeling all along that I shouldn't give up, and now I know that if it hadn't been Haas and Simmons and Miller it would have been someone else. All year they've done that nine out of ten times when we needed a game. I have a remarkable ball club."[102]

Pausing for a drink of water, Mack was assailed by a barrage of questions, mostly about his pitching selections. "You've been wondering all along why Lefty Grove hasn't started a game," he replied. "Now I can tell you that he hasn't been feeling well. Nothing serious, but not feeling well enough to pitch and last nine innings. His pitching fingers have been sore, too. I started Ehmke today because he was anxious to pitch. Anytime Howard says he is anxious to pitch, I'm anxious to have him pitch. When he smiles at me and says he'd like to work, I'll let him do it. He won't fail me often. Today he wasn't quite right."[103]

The ever gracious Mack concluded by heaping praise on his defeated foe. "The Cubs have a great ball club, and I can see easily how they won the National League pennant. They have a fine staff of pitchers, a great infield, a superb outfield, and exceptional catching. We won because we outlucked the Cubs, as well as outplaying them. They were anything but disgraced."[104]

The Cubs may not have been disgraced, but they were seething over their disappointing performance. As Woody English recalled: "It was pretty quiet in the clubhouse. We didn't have too much to say. Everyone was down, real bad."[105] McCarthy, mumbling about "bad breaks," spoke from his heart, with sarcasm intermingling with his anger. "What can I say without violating the rules of the losing manager's union?" he snapped to the assembled writers. "The Athletics are the champions. They took the best we had, and our best wasn't enough. But I'll be damned if I say the best team won. I wish it was ethical for me to say the A's had more luck than I've ever seen in twenty-one years of baseball. I don't mind today's game so much, but I'll never believe what my eyes saw in that bad dream in the fourth game. I want to say, too, that it was grand for Mr. Mack to tell me that he knew he would live to see me win a world championship. I know he will, too."[106]

Expecting that anyone whom had spent a reputed $2,000,000 to win, only to suffer a stunning defeat, would express some bitterness, reporters eagerly awaited Cub owner William Wrigley's comments. However, as Ed Burns of the *Chicago Tribune* noted remorsefully, "Chicago's favorite multimillionaire was far from the picture of a poor soul crying over a broken toy."[107] Addressing the scribes over a post-game snack, Wrigley looked to the future. "We did the best we could, and that wasn't enough. But already we are thinking of next year. We are going to strengthen and fight and stick like everything. You can put the loud pedal on that word 'strengthen.' The Cubs are not going to sit around and figure what might have been in the Series this year. They are going to figure what is needed to prevent a recurrence next year," he proclaimed. "I promised Chicago a pennant, and we all ploughed through disappointments until we got it done. Now I promise Chicago a world championship, and I hope and believe we have gone through all the disappointment required to affect this purpose. I have but one instruction for those two able men, Bill Veeck and Joe McCarthy. It is strengthen for 1930."[108]

In private, however, Wrigley was fuming over McCarthy's handling of the team. The owner was upset that Hack Wilson had led several other Cubs to join him in one of his notorious drinking binges after clinching the pennant, and the World Series debacle simply fortified Wrigley's belief that McCarthy had lost control of the players.[109] Another bone of contention between the owner and his manager was that before the Series, McCarthy had delegated former Cub star shortstop Joe Tinker to scout the Athletics. Tinker subsequently advised that Simmons and Cochrane should be pitched inside, but Hornsby insisted that they be pitched outside. Not knowing that the Rajah was secretly lobbying to replace him as Cub pilot, McCarthy followed his star second-sacker's advice. When Simmons batted .300, with two home runs and five runs batted in, and Cochrane swatted .400 and drew seven bases on balls, Hornsby reassumed the role of innocent by-stander, leaving McCarthy to shoulder criticism for not handling his staff properly.[110]

The split between the owner and manager, while not yet visible to outsiders, was well known by the players, most of whom liked McCarthy more than Hornsby.[111] However, it was Wrigley's team and in the waning days of the 1930 season, in which the Cubs were destined to finish two games behind the St. Louis Cardinals in the pennant race; Hornsby was elevated to the manager's position.

Machiavellian politics aside, the entire Cub squad was touched upon their arrival in Chicago by a cheering crowd of 500 faithful fans who crammed into the train shed at Union Station to meet their heroes. Wrigley and McCarthy stood shoulder to shoulder, the former promising "we'll come back next year," and the latter saying grimly that "the best team didn't win; the best manager won."[112]

As Hack Wilson, whose Series leading .471 batting average had been overlooked by his fielding misfortunes, waddled through the reception line, he shook his head in amazement. "They give me hell with their razzing when I'm going good, but now, when I deserve it, they give me cheers instead," he said. "You can't figure 'em. But I'm still a big chump."[113]

Pat Malone replayed his fatal pitch to Haas for the throng. "I threw Haas a fastball, inside and a bit high," he explained. "I had thrown the same thing to him all day and had fooled him. He just happened to outguess me on this one and away went the ball game. If I had to pitch to him again tomorrow, I would work him the same way."[114]

Every player, including the hypocritical Hornsby, stated that McCarthy had used good judgment in handling his pitchers, and "Jolly Cholly" Grimm left the fans laughing when he informed them that his planned vaudeville act with reserve outfielder Cliff Heathcote had been cancelled. "We were going to play and sing a song," Grimm laughed. "It was 'I'm Flying High, But I've Got a Feeling I'm Falling.' The booking agent thought we'd get hissed off the stage with that, and I guess we would."[115]

The legacy of the 1929 World Series is difficult to assess. From the Philadelphia perspective, it marked the onset of a three year reign by the Athletics, whom Jimmy Dykes later called the greatest ball club in history, as American League champions and two-time world title holders.[116] The victory was deemed so important to Philadelphia's civic pride that Connie Mack became the first sports figure to receive the annual Bok Award for having rendered the greatest service to the city in 1929.[117] For Chicago, it was another faded dream of glory. As local sportswriter Warren Brown observed regarding the Series aftermath: "Everybody in Chicago was mad and kept getting madder. Everybody had something to say—and said it."[118]

For the baseball purist, however, this Fall Classic sent a frighteningly clear message. Bob Wray of the *St. Louis Post-Dispatch* encapsulated this unhappy prophecy for the future of the national pastime in a column entitled simply "The Lost Art."

"The late World Series," Wray observed, "calls attention to the fact that baseball is slipping in one department. In the entire five games, Norman McMillan of the Cubs was the only man to steal a base. This indicates to the old-timer that the baseball of today is 'slipping' sadly. When baseball was young, base stealing was sort of a thermometer which registered the aggressive temperature of a team. The game's changes have brought forth the fact that only major activities count in baseball today. The pilfering of a base is now important only when the final result of the game depends on it. A run more or less is nothing in the life of baseball today. The slogan of baseball today calls for 'bigger and better scores,' not a stolen base once in every other game. Today's fans want to see the home club win and would rather see the victory achieved by mayhem and murder committed against the pitcher, plus plenty of misplays by the opposition. Scientific baseball, as an appeal, has been crowded out by the thrill — which is nothing less than a home run or an extra-base hit."[119]

Wray was correct, as Connie Mack's magnificent offensive machine of 1929, which simply had beaten the hapless Cubs into submission by brute force, altered the face of baseball forever. However, any wringing of hands over the decline of the stolen base was dramatically ended fifteen days after Simmons crossed the plate when the stock market crashed. Ironically and symbolically, perhaps the true legacy of the World Series of 1929 was that, with a burst of unparalleled flamboyant diamond excitement, it temporarily ushered out the nation's "Roaring Twenties" carefree attitude and its belief that money could buy success and happiness — or even a baseball championship of the world.

CUBS VS. YANKEES, 1932

To the pleasure of many baseball writers, especially those in New York, the Yankees ran roughshod over their American League rivals, winning 107 games and finishing thirteen lengths ahead of the three-time defending champion Philadelphia Athletics. These same diamond analysts were taken aback, however, that the New Yorkers' opponent in the fall classic would be neither the defending world champion St. Louis Cardinals nor their neighbors across the Harlem River, the Giants, both of whom had dropped as precipitously as President Herbert Hoover's popularity and ended in a tie for sixth place with identical 72–82 records. Instead, the Senior Circuit would be represented by the Chicago Cubs, whose rather mediocre .584 percentage was one of the lowest for a pennant winner in league history.

Ironically, before the World Series started, there was a promise, albeit slight, that the post-season competition might prove to be spirited because of Chicago's defense and pitching. The Cubs possessed one of the best starting rotations in the National League, headed by Lon (Chew Tobacco) Warneke, whose 22–6 record and 2.37 earned run average led the league in both categories. Joining him were thirty-three-year-old Charlie Root (15–10, 3.58), a veteran of eight big league campaigns, feisty Guy Bush (19–11, 3.20), and steady Pat Malone (15–17, 3.58), with 1931 Series hero spitballer Burleigh Grimes (5–3, 2.81) waiting in the wings. All were right-handers, which led to speculation that southpaw hitters Lou Gehrig, Bill Dickey, and Babe Ruth might use them for batting practice. As Nick Altrock, the former pitcher turned columnist, warned: "The Cubs have a swell pitching staff, but so did the Pirates in 1927. After Ruth got through using the center-field stands for a tennis net, the other Yank sluggers had their turn with practically the same results. The Pirate pitchers took quinine pills for supper. They might not have had malaria, but they sure had the shivers. As far as I have observed, Babe's only weakness is hot dogs, and the Cubs can't pitch him any of those."[1]

Such comments infuriated Chicago's rookie manager and veteran first-baseman Charlie Grimm. "I hear we have no left-handed pitchers," snorted the not-so Jolly Cholly, "but we have right-handers. Yes, we have some right smart right-handers. When you have smart right-handers, what's the use of worrying because you have no left-handers? What do these cuckoos think we won with — hypnotism? People must be daffy to go around saying my Cubs will be whanged around by those Yankees, maybe in four straight."[2]

The New York staff, by contrast, had only one dependable hurler, Charlie (Big Red) Ruffing, a florid, burly, twenty-eight-year-old right-hander, who had gone 18–7 with a 3.09 earned run average in the regular season. Vernon (Lefty) Gomez, despite his 24–7 record, had fallen off badly during the waning weeks of the season finishing with a 4.21 earned run average, which led many writers to believe that the slightly built twenty-three- year-old southpaw's strength had been diminished by the strain of hurling 265 innings. Rounding out the starting mound corps were right-handers George Pipgras (16–9, 4.19), rookie Johnny Allen (17–4, 3.70), and venerable twenty-year veteran Herb Pennock (9–5, 4.59).[3]

On defense the Cubs were deemed by even partisan scribe John Drebinger of the *New York Times* to have an edge in both the infield and outfield. Billy Herman, brilliant second-sacker of the Cubs, was given an advantage over Tony Lazzeri; ex-Yankee Mark Koenig was ranked superior to youthful Frank Crosetti at short; and Woody English and Grimm were granted slight nods over their Yankee counterparts Joe Sewell and Gehrig at third and first respectively. Only behind the plate were the Yankees considered equal defensively, with Dickey placed on a par with the Cubs' Charles (Gabby) Hartnett.[4] Chicago's fly catchers Hazen (Kiki) Cuyler, whom Nick Altrock described as "a bird who can break up a ball game like a parcel post clerk handling a dozen eggs," Riggs (Old Hoss) Stephenson, and Joe Moore admittedly could cover more territory than the New York trio of Earle Combs, (Alabama Arrow) Ben Chapman, and Babe Ruth.[5] In fairness to Combs and Chapman, however, it was the presence of Ruth that cost the outfield respect. At thirty-seven, the Babe had become a distinct liability everywhere except at the plate, although he hardly was the "fat and decrepit old gentleman who knows where his feet are not because he can see them, but because they hurt" portrayed by a *Chicago Tribune* editorial.[6]

Unfortunately for the Cubs, there was more to the game than defense, and in the areas of offense and managerial skill the Yanks had an overwhelming edge. At a casual glance, the Yankee domination at

Hazen (Kiki) Cuyler who was one of the few Cub standouts in the 1932 World Series, batting .278 with a home run (courtesy E. Bruce Kellerman).

the bat was not obvious. Their team batting average of .286 was not significantly higher than the .278 amassed by the Cubs, and Cub regulars Herman, Stephenson, and Koenig had better averages than their Yankee counterparts Lazzeri, Chapman, and Crosetti. The key to Yankee superiority was run production. The American League champions had gone through the entire season without being shut out, which led Altrock to remark that "the Yankees' end of the scoreboard had no more use for zeroes than thermometers in Miami."[7] They came into the Series surpassing the Cubs by 282 runs scored, almost 300 more runs batted in, and more than twice as many home runs. Against this well balanced array of sluggers, Chicago's only hope seemed to rest in following the example of the Cardinals in the 1931 Series and utilize a combination of timely hitting, flawless defense, and clutch pitching to gain victory over a more powerful foe.[8]

Yankee experience was pronounced in the dugout as well as on the field. Joseph Vincent McCarthy rapidly was becoming recognized as one of the premier managers of his time, and his 1932 triumph made him the first pilot ever to win a pennant in each major league. His most significant advantage in the upcoming Series was that he was thoroughly familiar with the Cubs, having taken them from last place in 1926 to a National League crown three years later. Despite this, with four games remaining in the 1930 season and the team locked into a second-place finish, McCarthy was forced to resign rather than be fired by club president William Veeck, who still blamed his manager for failing to defeat the Athletics in the 1929 Series. Among those who had starred for McCarthy during that championship season and remained key players for the 1932 Cubs were Hartnett, Cuyler, Stephenson, Root, Malone, Bush, and Grimm.

Based on the punch of the Yankees and the brains of McCarthy, John Kieran expressed his prediction for the upcoming games in verse:

> Yes, the Cubs were great in Chance's time,
> And the Pirates were rough in Wagner's prime.
> But I'll lay five bucks to a small thin dime,
> There never was a team that came crashing through,
> Like Ruth and the rest of the Yankee crew.[9]

To further undermine the Cubs' chances, turmoil still simmered over the August 2 firing of Manager Rogers Hornsby and the naming of first-baseman Charlie Grimm as his successor. Though inexperienced as a skipper, Grimm took the club into first place, but critics were quick to point out that given the weakness of the league it was entirely possible, as John Drebinger sneered, that "had the batboy been named to replace the deposed Hornsby, the Cubs still might have gone right on to win the flag."[10] While Grimm personally knew little about his American League opponent, he had the benefit of the wisdom of shortstop Mark Koenig, who had been dismissed prematurely by the Yanks for alleged failing eyesight, and Coach Charlie O'Leary, who had held a similar position with the Yankees under Miller Huggins.

Shortly before the Series was to begin the Cubs reopened the managerial wound by refusing to grant a share of their post-season money to Hornsby, saying that he had received his entire $40,000 salary and did not need the extra cash.[11] Furious, Hornsby filed a protest with Commissioner Kenesaw Mountain Landis stating that he was entitled to a share because he had assembled the championship squad and had it in second-place and peaking when he had been removed. "I don't know what the rules on the subject say — I did not read them," Hornsby stated in his protest, adding pointedly, "but I do feel that I deserve a share more than some of those who will receive full portions."[12]

As an added bit of inexplicable foolishness, Cub players voted Koenig only a half-share, even though after joining the team in late August he had played shortstop the final thirty-one games and batted .353. Koenig, who had been praised by Grimm as having made the pennant possible, angrily remarked that it only would have cost each player fifty dollars to have given him a full cut.[13]

The Yankees were insulted by the shabby treatment afforded their former teammate and openly sneered that the Cubs were, in the words of Babe Ruth, "cheapskate, nickel-nursing sonsabitches."[14] To give added weight to their indignation, the Yanks were exceedingly generous, awarding full shares to teammates traded away during the season and to both their original batboy, who had been injured in an automobile accident, and his replacement.[15]

New York fans appeared blasé about the upcoming contest, with most sporting conversation being about the impending heavyweight boxing championship bout between Max Schmeling and Mickey Walker at Madison Square Garden. William E. Brandt of the *New York Times* dismissed the lack of baseball hoopla with a matter-of-fact observation: "The approach of a World Series in any city except New York involves a noticeable crowding of hotels and in the downtown districts an unwanted stir and tension indicative that an event of importance is impending. In New York's immensity ... the hotels absorbed, without the slightest strain, the vanguard of the World Series tourists."[16] Noting the presence of only a solitary man, rather than the customary hundreds, standing in line waiting to purchase bleacher seats, Brandt added warily that "there was, however, a high degree of uncertainty as to how nearly filled the stands would be for the opener."[17]

Chicago, however, was at the other extreme for enthusiasm. Ticket sales boomed, and Internal Revenue agents combed hotel lobbies seeking scalpers who were not paying the tax required on each ticket sold. Government revenue officials also announced that roof sitters, who were charged forty cents to watch the games from housetops across the street from Wrigley Field, would be taxed ten percent.[18]

Not surprisingly, on the eve of the opening contest both managers envisioned taking home the world title. "I have every confidence that our team will give as good an account of itself as any Yankee team ever did in a World Series," McCarthy said with pride over his club's tradition. "We are confident of victory, but I hope not overconfident. They do not belittle the enemy. I know a lot about the Cubs. There isn't a quitter in the line-up. [Yankee owner] Colonel [Jacob] Ruppert wants four straight victories, and I hope he will be gratified. With Ruth ready I am sure the Yankees will not disappoint their fans."[19] The effervescent Jolly Cholly Grimm gushed: "We are going to win. Whether it is five, six, or seven games, I feel that we will win. Generally speaking, I'd say that the Cubs have three assets which the Yankees haven't to such an impressive degree — speed, great fielding, and pitching. You can be sure that every man will break his neck if necessary to win this Series."[20]

Guy Bush, designated as the Cubs' starting twirler, spent the afternoon and evening before the game in his hotel room. "I'm just goin' to take a lot of concentrated rest," the pugnacious right-hander drawled. "Maybe a show would take my mind off the game, but on the other hand I have always found that theatres were not so good for my eyes. So I'm stayin' home tonight. I never pitched an opening game before anywhere, at any time. I hope I can finish it."[21]

Because of inclement weather the Chicagoans took the field for the first game without having had the benefit of any batting or fielding practice at Yankee Stadium.[22] However, no Cub later had the temerity to suggest that was the cause of their humiliating 12–6 trouncing before a disappointingly slim crowd of 41,459. The nearly 30,000 empty seats, most of which were in the bleachers, demonstrated, as John Drebinger noted sadly, "the unpleasant truth that prosperity was still around some unlocated corner" for most depression-ridden New Yorkers."[23]

On the field, events started out with promise for the visitors. Bush, a swarthy, side-whiskered Mississippian whom *Time* magazine described as looking like "a nervous villain in a melodrama," retired the first nine men to face him and held a 2–0 lead, primarily because of a fielding miscue by Ruth. After Herman singled, Woody English cracked a line drive to right. Ruth allowed the ball to elude him, and, while the Babe "trundled after it to the bleachers on shaky legs and slippery footing, looking for all the world like a fat man trying to catch a rabbit," Herman scored and English pulled up at third.[24] After Cuyler fanned, Stephenson singled in a second tally.

In the fourth the Yankees, apparently following McCarthy's pre-game instructions to "take one look at Bush all the way around and then go get him," struck for three runs, including a two-run homer by Gehrig.[25] In the bottom of the sixth "Ruppert's Riflemen" drove across five more runs off Bush and Burleigh Grimes. Bush contributed mightily to his own downfall in that frame by issuing four bases on balls, which led Grantland Rice to observe that the hurler must have decided that "just one lone base on a pass seemed better strategy than the prospect of a violent explosion and a disappearing baseball."[26] Although he surrendered ten hits and all six Chicago runs, Red Ruffing went the distance for the victors, striking out ten Cubs.

Perhaps the most notable feature of the game was the vicious bench jockeying on the part of both clubs. Joe Sewell later recalled that "you never heard such goings on, such yelling and cussing and ripping."[27] For the Yankees, Ruth was the chief tormentor, repeatedly bellowing to the Cubs that they were "cheapskates." In return, the Chicagoans, led by Bush, swore at the Bambino, called him "fat moon-face," and renewed the familiar chant of "nigger" as he came to bat. Refusing to let these attacks on their star go unanswered, the Yanks shouted back, referring to the dark complexioned, dark-haired Bush: "Who are you calling a nigger? Look at your pitcher!"[28]

The Cubs were, as Rice observed, "at their worst" in the initial contest, seemed "plainly shattered," and after "hearing the deep roar of Lou Gehrig's home run a feeling of panic seemed to assail the greater part of the club, especially the pitchers."[29] Despite their farcical play, inept pitching, and failure to hit in the clutch, leaving eleven runners stranded, the Cubs managed to put forth a public display of optimism. Expressing contempt for the New Yorkers, team captain English wrote in his ghosted column: "We were not beaten by an invincible ball club, but through a poorly pitched game and sloppy infield play. On their showing, the Yanks are not a great club. Not nearly as great as the Athletics we met in 1929."[30] Other Cubs kept an enforced silence, as Manager Grimm not only barred reporters from the clubhouse, but also bolted the dressing room door.[31] Emerging later, Grimm would only remark to the gathered scribes: "There's nothing much to say, boys. Mark Koenig hurt his wrist sliding into third, and I am doubtful he will be able to play. If he is out, I plan to put Billy Jurges in his place. But no matter who is in there, you can tell the world that although we got beat today, we'll be in there fighting and that this Series isn't over by a long shot."[32]

In the Yankee dressing room pandemonium reigned. Amid the cheering, actor Bill Robinson, who was a favorite of the New Yorkers, mounted a trunk and started tap-dancing.[33] Ruffing, when asked about his day's performance admitted he was disappointed. "Gee, I would have liked to have gotten thirteen strikeouts and tied the record," he said. "I might have done it, too, if it had been dry. It was pretty hard working out there. My foot kept slipping."[34] Babe Ruth, who had scored three runs and driven in another, said through his cigar smoke that the appendix problems which had plagued him during the season were gone. "I was swinging from it all afternoon," he boomed, adding with a broad grin: "I'm still not strong, you know, not quite full of the old power, but I think I'll show up for the game tomorrow if I don't feel any worse."[35] McCarthy was cornered by Colonel Jacob Ruppert, who reiterated his desire for a four game sweep. "That's a large order, Colonel," McCarthy smiled, 'but we'll sure try. They're a good club, those Cubs, hustlers and fighters, but they didn't get good pitching today and that's the whole story. Bush pitched fine ball until the fourth inning, and then it seemed like he ruined himself trying to pitch too hard to our reputations."[36]

The second contest, played before 50,709 spectators on a crisp, clear autumn afternoon, pitted Chicago's Lon Warneke against Lefty Gomez. As a token of their affection, before the game the Yankee players presented a silver cigar humidor, surmounted on a silver baseball and inscribed with all the names of the team members, to Babe Ruth for playing in his tenth World Series. They also gave McCarthy a silver platter in appreciation for guiding them to the pennant.[37]

As in the opener, the game started out satisfactorily for the Cubs as Herman doubled, moved to second on Crosetti's error, and scored on a sacrifice fly by Stephenson, but then the Yankees' came to bat. John Kieran described the scene in his "Sports of the *Times*" column: "If Caesar was ambitious, then Lonnie Warneke was audacious. He started his mound work by walking Earle Combs and Joey Sewell to get at Babe Ruth. Then he struck out the great Bambino. This is a good trick when it works. When it doesn't, relatives are notified to come around and claim the body."[38] Gehrig and Dickey singled, however, giving the Yanks the lead. The Cubs tied the score in the third, but the came back with two in their half of the frame to recapture the lead, which led Kieran to write: "The Yankee scheme of attack was apparent. Every time the Cubs would get one run, the Yankees would get two. That put the Cubs in a quandary. They didn't know whether to keep scoring or let well enough alone."[39]

For the second consecutive game the Cubs were guilty of tactical miscues. Besides Warneke's surrendering ten hits and four walks in their 5–2 defeat, the National League champions, most notably Gabby Hartnett, committed mental blunders. In the ninth, with his team trailing by three runs, the hefty receiver, one of the slowest of the Bruins, opened the inning with a single down the left-field line and tried vainly to go to second. John Kieran snidely noted that Ben Chapman's throw beat him to the bag by "three city blocks, approximately," while Grantland Rice stated that the distance was "as far as from New York to Buenos Aires."[40] Kieran added whimsically: "What Hartnett would have done with the extra base is a mystery. Perhaps he wanted to take it home as a souvenir."[41]

Because of the Cubs' ineptness the diamond activity lacked excitement. Drebinger observed: "The crowd seemed a trifle resentful that the Yankees made such exceedingly short shrift of the invaders. It doubtless would have preferred to have seen the suspense prolonged past the fourth inning and into the later stages of the game."[42] Rice concurred, but he put the day's events more colorfully than his more serious-minded fellow writer. "The old bear trap, with its clutch of steel, snapped again today, this time upon the other front foot of a struggling and helpless Cub. Now only a small portion of his woolly hide remains in his desperate effort to escape and get a fresh start on home turf. So far the Cubs look to be outclassed by a ball club that carries harder hitting and better pitching. They have seemed to be in a daze through both games, with little of the snap, dash, and hustle they showed on the way to the flag. The Yankees are hard enough to beat without handing them games on silver platters surrounded by watercress and mint."[43] As to the future, both immediate and long range, for opponents of the Bronx Bombers, Rice predicted: "Some sunny day the depression will turn into gay and giddy prosperity. Some day Europe will pay every dime it owes us. Some day no golfer will have another alibi. And some day a National League ball club will roll the Yankees into the gravel ditch and win a game. But until then, in bull markets and bear markets, in times of luxury and in times of want, the Yankees will continue to maul all the National League clubs."[44]

In contrast to the previous day, Grimm opened the dressing room to reporters after the game. Jolly Cholly dismissed his club's poor play, choosing instead to rave over the ten strikeout, one walk performance of Gomez. "One of the greatest pitchers I ever saw!" he proclaimed. "You can talk about Lefty Grove, but that kid showed me more today than Grove did in the World Series I faced him in. Why today he was just as fast as Grove, had a better curve, and what control! I'm satisfied we met a great pitcher and we were beaten. Too much Gomez. That's all there is to it."[45] Hurrying to catch the train to Chicago, Grimm added: "I'm confidant we'll do better at Wrigley Field, and so are the boys. The lights and shadows bothered us here both days, but we know our own park and they'll find us a different outfit there. Charlie Root will work the next game and Pat Malone the fourth."[46] Pressed about his team's chances against the might of the Yankees, the Cub pilot admitted that he may have underestimated his opponent's all-round strength. "We have a club or two in our league that can hit like they do,' he stated. "The Phillies are that way, dangerous every minute. But the difference is that the Phils don't have a couple of pitchers like Ruffing and Gomez. I never saw so many fastballs in all my life."[47]

In the Yankee clubhouse the lean and lanky 6'2" Gomez, who had lost four of his 178 pounds while on the mound, admitted he was pleased with his hurling, even though he had given up nine safeties. "Sure I was nervous," he said as the trainer rubbed his pitching arm. "Who wouldn't be? It was the first time I was ever out there in a World Series. But it didn't last long. After a few minutes I got to liking it, and in the second inning I suddenly got all my stuff. Then I knew I didn't have anything to worry about. It seemed like the further I went, the better I got. Guess I was lucky, though. They weren't swinging where I was pitching."[48]

McCarthy echoed Grimm's praise for Gomez. "Give him all the credit. He pitched one of the sweetest games I ever saw in the World Series. The others did their part, but Lefty made it easy." the Yankee pilot beamed. "Now that they've looked at Ruffing and Gomez, I think I'll give 'em a taste of Pipgras next. After that they ought to be about ready to wrap up."[49]

A somber Babe Ruth, who collected only a single and scored a run, dressed slowly. He was not thinking of his performance, but rather of the gift he had received before the game from his comrades. He kept staring at the humidor, saying: "That was nice of the boys."[50]

As the Yankee special teamed toward Chicago, crowds turned out along the route hoping to catch a glimpse of Ruth and the other New York stars. At Elkhart, Indiana, when the train stopped five minutes to change engines, about fifty young boys climbed aboard, surrounded the Babe, and begged him and other Yanks to sign autographs, which they did with pleasure.[51]

When the train arrived in the Windy City, thousands of spectators greeted the Yankees, and a police motorcycle cordon was required to lead the taxicabs carrying the New Yorkers to their headquarters at the Edgewater Beach Hotel.[52] Another decidedly less cordial assemblage awaited the players outside the lodging site. A double line of hysterical, angry female Cub rooters booed, hissed, and yelled obscenities. As Ruth and his wife Claire approached, several spit on them.[53] Once safely inside the hotel, the Babe was furious. "Say, what do you think of those dames spitting at a guy like that?" he fumed to sportswriter Fred Lieb. "I sure want to get this thing finished up and get outta here."[54]

In an effort to quell the temptation of his players to overreact and try too hard to seek revenge for the hostility shown them, McCarthy gathered his team in the hotel before dinner. "Take it in stride, boys," he cautioned. "we're out here for a couple of ball games. Maybe three. Don't get excited. Just imagine you're down on the South Side getting ready for a series with the White Sox. There isn't any pressure. All we've got to do is go out there and play our regular everyday game."[55]

The next morning several of the Yanks followed McCarthy's advice literally and took advantage of the sunny, warm day to visit the golf pitching green next to the hotel.

They came back smiling and joyous. "It's blowing sixty miles per hour," gushed Lefty Gomez. "I wish I was in there today. I bet I could hit one into those bleachers. Babe and Lou ought to hit a dozen."[56]

In batting practice later that forenoon the two Yankee sluggers proved that the pitcher's prediction might come true as Gehrig smashed seven into the seats and Ruth nine, several of which soared over the four-story high temporary bleachers. Seeing several awed Cubs watching his display, the Babe bellowed good-naturedly: "I'd play for half my salary if I

Wrigley Field during 1932 World Series (Chicago Historical Society, SDN-073624, photograph by *Chicago Daily News).*

could hit in this dump all the time."[57] Ruth then departed to conclude arrangements for his visit the next morning with Lee William Koeppen, a sixteen year old who had been blinded in a bomb explosion in front of a local jurist's home the previous month.[58]

On a warm, clear, windy day the third game, pitting Root against Pipgras, proved to be the most memorable of the Series. The Cubs, inspired by almost 50,000 enthusiastic fans, including Democratic presidential nominee Franklin Delano Roosevelt, furiously battled the Yanks. Ruth put the New Yorkers in front with a prodigious three-run blast in the first inning off Root. As he came around third and passed the Cub dugout he yelled: "You've had your last look at the Stadium, you good-hearted guys. Why I've got more money than all of you!"[59] Then, in the words of veteran Chicago scribe Ed Burns, he "pursed his lips and blew them a salute known as the Bronx cheer."[60] When Ruth took his defensive position in left-field for the last half of the frame, the bleacherites booed loudly. The Bambino responded by pointing to the spot in right-center where his mighty blast had come to rest.[61]

The Yanks picked up another tally in the third on a Gehrig home run, but the Cubs kept clawing their way back. The Bruins scored a run in the first on Kiki Cuyler's double, two more in the third on Cuyler's homer and a double by Grimm, and tied the game in the fourth on a double by Jurges and a single by English. In the fifth, however, Ruth battered the Cubs down and Gehrig knocked them out.

As the Babe stepped to the plate with one out and none on, the crowd tossed lemons at him, while Guy Bush stood on the top step of the Cubs' dugout and began hurling insults, calling Ruth a "fat, old, washed up nigger."[62] Joining Bush in hurling invectives were Pat Malone and Burleigh Grimes, who bellowed "big belly" and "balloon head."[63] Even trainer Andy Lotshaw, who earlier had berated Ruth by yelling "if I had you on my team I'd hitch you to a wagon, you potbelly," chimed in once again.[64] Joe Sewell recalled: "It was just plain brutal. I'd never known there were so many cuss words in the language or so many ways of stringing them together."[65] The Bambino, however, merely grinned and roared: "Wait, you muggs! I'm gonna hit one out of the yard."[66]

Ruth took Root's first offering for a strike and held up one finger toward the jeering Cubs. The second pitch was another called strike, and Bush became so excited that he bounded several feet in front of the dugout. Ruth muttered to Cub catcher Gabby Hartnett that "it only takes one to hit it."[67] The next two pitches missed the strike zone. Ruth then extended his right arm in the direction of Root and pointed. Gehrig, the on-deck hitter, said he heard the Babe yell: "I'm going to knock the next pitch right down your goddamn throat."[68]

Root tossed a changeup curve, low and away, and Ruth belted it 436 feet into the center-field bleachers for one of the longest home runs ever hit in Wrigley Field. As he rounded first-base he laughed and later recalled that he thought to himself "you lucky, lucky bum."[69] Saying something to each Cub infielder as he passed, after touching the plate he clasped his hands over his head like a victorious prizefighter and roared, "Squeeze the Eagle Club!" to the stunned Chicago players in the dugout, much to the delight of candidate Roosevelt, who threw his head back in glee.[70] After serving another home run pitch to Gehrig the shaken Root was lifted, and the Cubs ultimately lost the contest 7–5.

Did Ruth point to the spot where he intended to hit the ball as legend has it? To a man the Cubs vigorously denied it. Charlie Root was vehement, saying: "Ruth did not point at the fence before he swung. If he had made a gesture like that, well, anyone who knows me knows that I would have put one in his ear and knocked him on his ass."[71] Woody English, who was playing third, stated: "He may have been pointing out to right-center, but he wasn't calling his shot. He was just holding up two fingers, suggesting that he had one strike left."[72] Billy Herman concurred, saying: "What Ruth did was hold up his hand to say he had only two strikes on him, that he had another one coming. But he was pointing towards Charlie Root, not toward the center-field bleachers."[73] Grimm was even more emphatic, asserting: "He didn't call his shot. He was shouting at Guy Bush, who was in our dugout. He was yelling: 'You'll be out there tomorrow — so we'll see what you can do with me, you damn tightwad.' As he yelled that to Bush he pointed toward the pitcher's mound."[74] Burleigh Grimes, who later denied he had been involved in the heckling, stated flatly: "He never called it. Forget it."[75] Both Gabby Hartnett and Billy Jurges agreed with their manager, claiming that Ruth simply was pointing toward the Cub dugout.[76]

Yankee players, but not Manager McCarthy, were equally vigorous in their lifelong support of the Babe's alleged feat. Pipgras said: "Yes, sir. He called it. He pointed toward the bleachers and then hit it there. I saw him do it."[77] Joe Sewell was adamant: "I was there. I saw it. I don't care what anybody says. He called it."[78] Ruth pointed with his bat in his right hand to right-field, not center-field. But he definitely called his shot," asserted Gomez.[79] Even Lou Gehrig, never one of the Bambino's biggest boosters during the season, gave grudging admiration to his teammate, asking a reporter: "What do you think of the nerve of that big monkey? Imagine calling his shot and getting away with it."[80]

As for the great man himself, the Babe initially denied calling his homer, telling Chicago writer John Carmichael: "I want to set one thing straight. I didn't exactly point to any spot, like the flagpole. Anyway, I didn't mean to. I just sorta waved at the whole fence, but that was foolish enough. All I wanted to do was give that thing a ride — out of the park — anywhere. No, I didn't point to any spot, but as long as I'd called the first two strikes on myself I hadda go through with it. It was damned foolishness, sure. I just felt like doing it. When I think of what an idiot I'da been if I'd struck out, and I coulda, too, because I was mad — boy, when I think of all the good breaks in my life — that was one of 'em."[81] Moreover, he told his soon-to-be ghostwriter Ford Frick after the game: "Aw, hell! I was just gesturing."[82] Even as late as 1938, when he was coaching for the Dodgers, he told Brooklyn trainer Ed Froelich: "I may be dumb, but I'm not that dumb. I'm going to point to the center-field bleachers with a barracuda like Root out there? On the next pitch, they'd be picking it out of my ear with a pair of tweezers. No!"[83]

How, then, did the legend begin? Joe Williams, sports editor of the *New York World-Telegram* and whose stories were carried by the Scripps-Howard syndicate, was its father, as he was the first writer who witnessed the game to include the "called shot" in his coverage.[84] After the game, Grantland Rice saw Ruth in the clubhouse and said, "Babe, damned if it didn't look like you pointed when you hit the ball."[85] The Babe's face lit up as if inspired, and he muttered, "The hell it did."[86] The seed of the myth was planted, and the Babe reveled in it. Finally, in his 1947 autobiography, he claimed that he actually had planned the performance the night before as revenge for he and his wife being spat upon by the Chicago fans."[87]

However, the question remains of whether the Babe really did "call his shot." Even a long lost home movie of the event offers no answer. The Babe did colorfully signify his intention to hit the ball, and he did. Perhaps that alone should have been enough to become part of the Ruthian mystique, for as Chicago scribe Ed Burns wrote following the contest: "He licked the Chicago ball club, but he left the people laughing when he said good-bye. It was a privilege to be present because it is not likely that the scene will ever be repeated in all its elements. Many a hitter may make two home runs, or possibly three, in World Series play in years to come, but not the way Babe Ruth made these two. Nor will you ever see an artist call his shot before hitting one of the longest drives ever made on the grounds in a World Series game, laughing and mocking the enemy with two strikes gone."[88]

After the game, in the jubilant Yankee clubhouse, Ruth, strolling around naked with a big cigar jammed in his mouth, roared with gusto: "Did Mr. Ruth chase those guys back into the dugout? Mr. Ruth sure did! I guess I showed 'em the old Babe can still hit 'em."[89] Looking as serious as a Sultan of Swat clad only in a cloud of smoke could, he went on: "I told that little kid in the hospital this morning that I was going to hit a home run for him."[90] In his ghosted column the Babe was much more modest about his display of might and that of Gehrig. "Aw, go on now," he purportedly wrote. "The wind was with us, that's all. Anytime they let us hit it into the air, zowie, the wind did the rest."[91]

Tony Lazzeri shouted: "We'll be starting home tomorrow night," and his comrades quickly joined him in chanting the refrain, while Bill Robinson did his ritual post-victory dance.[92] Even the normally cautious McCarthy, sitting with his shirt and shoes off, sensed that the pair of round-trippers by Ruth and Gehrig had broken the hearts of the Cubs and told his players: "Get your bags packed tomorrow morning, fellows. I think we'll be leaving right after the game."[93]

In the home team's quarters Manager Grimm sat down and cried, not because of his team's defeat, but rather because of the cheers his club received as they left the field. "Can you beat that?" he said after regaining his composure. "Don't it make you sick that you can't even win one game for a bunch of folks like that. They ought to throw us in the lake, but listen to 'em. We certainly gave it our all this afternoon. We gave them a battle, but what can you do with fellows like those two big baseball murderers?"[94]

Charlie Root, in relatively good humor considering that he had been rocked for six runs, all as the result of the circuit smashes by Ruth and Gehrig, mused that Ruth had proven he was not human by hitting the pitches he did. "The first one Babe hit," the big right-hander declared, "was a fastball going outside. The second was a change-of-pace going slowly on the outside. If I had to do it all over again I'd throw the same kind of balls to Ruth and Gehrig."[95]

The fourth game, played before another near capacity throng of 49,844 at Wrigley Field, was anti-climactic. Given their premonition of impending doom, many fans thought the events on the field were not as interesting as the unfounded rumor that John McGraw, who had recently stepped down as pilot of the New York Giants, was going to establish a National League franchise in Montreal.[96]

The atmosphere among the players on both teams seemed somewhat indifferent as well, but that was because after the third contest Commissioner Kenesaw Mountain Landis had issued a warning to both squads to refrain from using profanity or every member of the offending club would be fined. Joe Sewell later recalled: "You could have heard a pin drop in our dugout during the game. We sat there like mummies. One thing you didn't do in those days was monkey with Judge Landis."[97]

As with the previous battles, game four started out relatively well for the Cubs, even though starter Guy Bush was lifted after retiring only a single batter and giving up a run on two hits, a walk, and a hit batsman. Warneke put out the Yank rally, and the Cubs came back in their half of the first to score four times off Johnny Allen, three runs coming on a towering home run by reserve outfielder Frank Demaree into the left-field bleachers. In the third, Lazzeri clouted a line drive which barely cleared the right-field bleacher screen for two Yankee runs, making the score 4–3. The Yanks took the lead in the sixth on a two-run double by Gehrig off venerable, thirty-six-year-old southpaw Jakie May, but the Cubs evened the count in the bottom of the frame on a throwing error by Crosetti, one of four New York miscues on the afternoon. In the seventh, however, the Bombers blasted across four tallies, and two innings later sent across another four to make the final count 13–6 for the new world champions. During this final onslaught, dismayed and disillusioned Chicago fans, who had believed for so long in their team, finally gave vent to their pent-up frustrations and mercilessly spewed forth, as Ed Burns noted, "a raspberry serenade the like of which has not been accorded the home team at Wrigley Field in many seasons."[98]

In the Bombers' clubhouse the usually somber Joe McCarthy led the celebration amid the singing of the team's anthem, "The Sidewalks of New York." Surrounded by reporters and his players, he said with obvious emotion: "I'm the happiest man in the world. I figured we could do it. We simply had too much power for them. I am proud of the Yankees. Proud of them as players and as men."[99] Ruth, who had been hit on the right forearm by a Bush fastball in the opening inning, sought out his manager. His arm wrapped in a hot towel to ease the pain and swelling, the Babe clasped McCarthy's hand and boomed: "Boy, what a victory. My hat's off to ya, Mac."[100]

By contrast, the losers dressed in stunned silence. Bush revealed that he had been pitching with an injured finger on his right hand, but he refused to use that as an excuse. "Why tell about these things?" he muttered. "I can take it, and any guy that can't shouldn't be in the business."[101] Grimm, tossing his mitt into his locker, said simply: "That's that."[102] Then he added to no one in particular: "Look at this! I've lost twenty-two pounds since taking over the manager's job. If anyone thinks it has been easy, they can guess again."[103] Turning to look at his downcast players, Grimm realized they needed a boost and yelled: "Hey, we won together and we lost together. It's no disgrace to lose to a ball club like that. Give credit where credit is due. They've got more power than I ever saw before in one place. You fellows gave me all you had. You're damn right you did, and I know it."[104] When queried by writers about his plans, the once again Jolly Cholly lit a cigarette and said: "Well, I'll get out the poles now and go fishing."[105]

Post-mortems of the Series were unanimously unflattering, ranging from the assessment of the *Spalding Baseball Guide* that "it was the tamest Series since 1927, and even less entertaining" to the bitter editorial of the *Chicago Tribune,* which sneered: "If Chicago never wins another championship in either league, it will be too soon. The city wants no more truck with championships. A manager whose young men show any possibility of getting above third place should be fired."[106] John Kieran of the *New York Times* observed cynically, but accurately: "The Yankees flattened the Cubs and left them a mediocre assortment of animal rugs. They simply swaggered away to win in a cake walk. They made the Cubs look like ragged recruits from a very minor league. The Cubs were helpless and looked hopeless. They over-awed and overwhelmed the Cubs. At the close they were hitting everything the Cub pitchers threw towards the plate and stopped running only when they were out of breath. It was a sloppy Series all the way. There were times when the onlookers must have thought that the pitchers of the old type were as extinct as the dodo and the passenger pigeon."[107] Davis J. Walsh of the International News Service summed up the Series with the terse statement: "It was the performance of grown men against children. The Cubs were so bad that their defeat added little to the Yankees' prestige."[108] Grantland Rice used a military analogy to describe the diamond events, writing: "The Cubs never had a chance. Day after day they saw their pitching shot to pieces in each start. One or two sharpshooters might get safely by for a round or two, but the crash of the battle-axes was only delayed until the killing blow finally came off and there was nothing left but debris on the field."[109] *The Sporting News,* summed up the Series by stating simply that "the plight of the Cubs was so bad it verged on collapse."[110]

Not surprisingly, acerbic Westbrook Pegler penned the cruelest analysis: "It will be hard to restore the solemn character of the World Series, which the serious-minded element of the baseball business always loved to refer to as the 'Autumn Blue Ribbon Classic' of the national game, after the happenings which closed out the show in the Cubs' ball yard in Chicago. In four games fraught with fumbles, wild throws, hilarious comedy on the bases, and many other mistakes too subtle for classification in the statistics, the Yanks, playing this burlesque baseball, won with yawning nonchalance and mocking contempt over the Cubs, extending their run of consecutive victories over clubs in the National League to an even dozen since 1927. The problem is this: If the Yankees are a low comedy ball club, which supposedly represents baseball in the highest, and if one of their outfielders [Ruth]—a fat, elderly party who must wear corsets to avoid immodest jiggling—cannot waddle out for fly balls nor stoop for grounders, and if no other ball club in either major league is fit even to challenge them — well, what?"[111]

Such universal criticism aside, in his ghosted column Ruth wrote that it was a great Series, and that he did not think there would be any dispute "in the assertion that the Yankees had a little too much of everything for the Cubs," who were "overmatched." As to his treatment during the games, he said sarcastically: "I enjoyed the Series a lot. The Chicago fans gave me quite a razzing. The Chicago players also handed me quite a bit of joshing. There was great delight in the stands when I fanned, and I got quite a kick out of the home runs in Chicago. But it was in fun, and I know there are no hard feelings on either side. I found the Cubs a fine crowd of fellows, ready to kid, and be kidded, with a smile."[112]

In retrospect, the Series was entertaining because it was so bad. Fourteen errors, eight by the Yankees, dotted the play. The New Yorkers, led by Gehrig's .529, batted .313 as a team and the Cubs a respectable .253 only because the pitching by both staffs was spotty at best. The supposedly superior Chicago mound corps compiled an astounding 9.26 earned run average, while the Yankee hurlers had a less than sparkling 3.25 record.

Yankee boasting notwithstanding, the 1932 squad was not a great team. It was a collection of aging superstars, like Ruth and Pennock, who were appearing in their final World Series, and youngsters, like Gehrig and Gomez, who were on the verge of greatness. The 1932 Bronx Bombers marked the end of the brilliant Yankee dynasty built in the 1920s, but it was not yet composed of all the players who would constitute the next New York juggernaut which in 1936 would begin to dominate baseball once again.

CUBS VS. TIGERS, 1935

Eager to avenge their humiliating 11–0 defeat at the hands of the St. Louis Cardinals in the seventh game of the preceding year's Series, the 1935 Detroit Tigers battled from behind in September to finish with a record of 93–59 and edge out the New York Yankees by three games to retain the American League pennant. Not surprisingly, as they fielded the same lineup as in the previous season, the Tigers remained an awesome offensive machine, leading the Junior Circuit in batting (.290), slugging (.435), runs scored (919), runs batted in (837), and bases on balls received (627). First-baseman Hank Greenberg batted .328 and led the league with 36 home runs and 170 runs batted in. Charlie Gehringer at second-base swatted .330, with 19 homers and 108 runs batted in. Shortstop Billy Rogell (.275, 6, 71) and third-sacker Marv Owen (.263, 2, 71) comprised the left side of the infield. Manager Mickey Cochrane, whose statistics of .319, five home runs, and 47 men driven across the plate were sub-par for him, continued to guide his team from behind the plate. Patrolling the outfield, from left to right, were veterans Goose Goslin (.292, 9, 109), fleet Jo-Jo White (.240, 2, 32), and reliable Pete Fox, who compiled a sparkling .321 average to go with 15 home runs and 73 runs batted in.

On the mound, the Tigers led their league with 87 complete games. Their ace once again was the slight, 150 pound, right-handed curve ball specialist, Tommy Bridges at 21–10, with an earned run average of 3.51 and a league-leading 163 strikeouts. Closely behind was Schoolboy Rowe, whose six shutouts topped the league and complemented his record of 19–13 and 3.68 earned run average. Eldon Auker, whose sparkling 18–7, 3.83 figures placed him among the league's elite hurlers despite being only twenty-four-years-old, and veteran Alvin (General) Crowder, whose claim to fame rested not only with his strong right arm, which delivered a 16–10, 4.26 season, but also in having baseball's sexiest tattoo—a naked woman stretching from his right elbow to shoulder—rounded out the starting corps.[1]

Facing the Tigers were the Chicago Cubs of Manager Charlie (Jolly Cholly) Grimm, whose easy-going manner and good humor led John Drebinger of the *New York Times* to warn that the Tigers should be apprehensive because "they were jostled out of the winner's share of the spoils last year, and might be joshed out of this one by the comical and entertaining Grimm."[2] The Cubs amazed the baseball world by reeling off twenty-one consecutive victories to close the campaign, including a sweep of St. Louis in the season's finale, enabling them to dethrone the Cardinals by a four game margin and finish with a record of 100–54.

While lacking the Tigers' power the Cubs nonetheless were impressive at the plate, lead-ing the Senior Circuit with a .288 average, 847 runs scored, 782 runs batted in, 303 dou-bles, and 404 walks received. The infield consisted of a blend of youth and experience. At first was nineteen-year-old Phil Cavarretta, completing his first full season in the majors, who slugged eight home runs and drove in 82 runs to go with his .275 average. Fifth year second-sacker Billy Herman, a .341 hitter, who led the league with 227 hits and 57 dou-bles, also swatted seven homers and drove in 83 of his mates. Veteran slick-fielding short-stop Billy Jurges batted a weak .241, but contributed a lone home run and 59 runs batted in, while reliable fourth year third-baseman Stan Hack averaged .311 to go with four homers and 64 runs batted in. Behind the plate was rotund, thirteen-year veteran Leo (Gabby) Hart-nett, who batted .344 with 13 home runs and 91 runs batted in. The outfield boasted twenty-three-year-old sophomore sensation Augie Galan (.314, 12, 79) patrolling left, third year man Frank Demaree (.325, 2, 66) was in right, and twelve-year veteran Fred Lindstrom, the former New York Giant third-sacker, who batted .275 with 3 homers and 62 runs bat-ted in, covering center.

The Cub mound corps, which led the league with a 3.26 earned run average, possessed tremendous depth and talent beginning with its two twenty game winners, Bill Lee (20–6, 2.96) and Lon Warneke (20–13, 3.06). Supporting them in the starting rotation were Larry French (17–10, 2.96, with a league topping four shutouts), Tex Carleton (11–8, 3.89), thirteen-year veteran Charlie Root (15–8, 3.09), and Roy Henshaw (13–5, 3.27).

Before the Series opener on October 2, Cochrane, the fiery Tiger skipper whom *Detroit Times* columnist Bob Murphy described as "a human volcano, eternally spouting forth the fumes and flames of inspiration," set forth the reasons why he was certain his club would win the world championship.[3] "My confidence is borne of the realization that this is a team which has improved as much as 25 percent over last year," Iron Mike asserted. "The play-ers are more settled. They have smoother teamwork. We're loosened up. Moreover, we go into this World Series with an added starter. His name is 'Experience.' He wasn't on the club last year, which is one of the reasons the Tigers didn't win the Series. But he is a respected member of the team this year, and a very valuable addition."[4] With evident dis-dain, Cochrane gave a brief synopsis of his opinion of the opposition. "Who have the Cubs got that can break up a game on you?" he asked, and then proceeded to answer his query. "Hartnett, Lindstrom, and Demaree, all right-handed hitters. The others are cream puff hitters. [On the hill] we know Warneke is tough and that he is the man to beat, but Rowe will match everything he's got. The rest of our right-handed staff should give us the edge — maybe in six games."[5]

Nor was Cochrane alone in his assessment of the chances of the National League cham-pions to defeat the Tigers. Davis J. Walsh, baseball writer for the United Press, sneered: "The Cubs, except for Hartnett, are mostly a lot of handkerchief hitters. They don't even blow at the ball. They sniff at it."[6] Veteran New York scribe Bill Corum noted sagely: "'My Boy Charlie' Grimm's fast-footed little bears will not be able to escape the relentless pur-suit of the Tigers' four G-Men — Gordon Cochrane, Greenberg, Gehringer, and Goslin. They are four expert marksmen. Chicago has a pretty fair pitching staff, particularly the part of it that answers to the name of Lonnie (Chew Tobacco) Warneke. But he's no Dizzy Dean. Besides, experience has taught me to be just a little suspicious of any ball team com-ing off a long winning streak. A hot team can go cold on you as quickly as a pretty gal who gets a call from Clark Gable."[7] Staid John Drebinger echoed these sentiments in a more refined manner, writing: "With the experience gained last year, it is difficult to conceive of the Tigers being sidetracked again."[8] Even Dizzy Dean, who so mercilessly ridiculed the

Tigers the previous October, joined on the Bengals' bandwagon, stating flatly: "The Cubs will be lucky to win one game from Detroit. They are in way over their heads."[9]

National League adherents, led by Grimm, quite naturally were more sanguine about retaining the world championship for the Senior Circuit. Jolly Cholly glibly discounted the experience argument by pointing out to writers gathered at the team's headquarters in Detroit's Book-Cadillac Hotel that Freddie Lindstrom had played for the Giants in the 1924 Series, and that he, Hartnett, Demaree, Jurges, Warneke, Root, Hack, and Woody English all had participated in the 1932 post-season classic against the Yankees. Listening to his manager conveniently omit the fact that the Grimm-led Cubs in 1932 were hammered into submission by the Yankees in four straight games, the cherub-faced Gabby Hartnett, grinned broadly and shouted: "And did we ever soak up experience in 1932. Boy, we were simply showered with experience, and we will never forget it!"[10]

After the laughter subsided, Grimm continued his effort to counter the arguments used against his squad, noting that thirty of fifty-seven baseball writers polled by the Associated Press favored the Cubs.[11] "There is no club in baseball that can beat the Cubs the way they are going at present, and that goes for the Tigers, too," Grimm proclaimed. "Sure Gehringer, Greenberg, and Goslin are a dangerous trio. I respect the Tiger team as a whole, but I figure those three are more of a threat than the others. But I have a fine pitching staff, and supporting them will be the best fielding club in the National League. Warneke, one of the best pitchers in the land, will start the opener, and nothing short of kidnapping will make me change. I'm not going to make any rash statement about four straight, but we're going to win and we may wind the Series up in a hurry. I just can't see how the Cubs can lose."[12]

On the eve of the Series, a *Detroit Times* editorial captured the atmosphere of the city and the emotions of its residents: "The president talks about taxation. War threats disturb Europe. The world in general hatches its grist of momentous happenings. But these things are of little interest in Detroit today, for Detroit is possessed with the baseball tremors. Nothing else matters!"[13] At the Tigers' freshly cleaned home, Navin Field, a temporary bleacher section in left-field was being completed.

Charlie Grimm, Babe Ruth, and Mickey Cochrane before the opening game of the 1935 World Series (Chicago Historical Society, SDN-078149, photograph by *Chicago Daily News*).

This new structure, which would reduce the distance from home plate to the wall from 340 feet to a mere 301 feet, was topped by a twenty-foot high fence, which was intended to dissuade fans in what Detroiters dubbed "Vegetableville," from reenacting the produce barrage launched at Joe Medwick in the final game of the previous year's Series.[14]

As the Tigers warmed up before the game, a man approached Cochrane, who was standing near the Tiger dugout, and requested the manager to please autograph a ball for a "little crippled boy." Having heard that request several times before during the season, the Tiger pilot laughed, and said as he signed his name: "Say, aren't there any healthy boys any more. I've given away thousands of baseballs this year, and they were all for 'little crippled boys.'"[15] A touching scene in the Tiger dugout occurred shortly afterward when Tiger players "like a bunch of kids" swarmed upon Babe Ruth, covering the Series with his ghostwriter for a newspaper syndicate. Goose Goslin broke through the mob, carrying a huge photograph of the Bambino. "Autograph this for me, please, Babe," pleaded the future Hall of Famer. "This picture always will stand as a shrine of all that I think a great ball player should be. I mean it. They come and go, Babe, but you will go on forever as the greatest we've ever known."[16] Swallowing hard and trying hold back tears, the Babe signed the picture and embraced Goslin.[17]

During the home team's batting practice, several Cubs sauntered over to the cage to observe the opposing hitters. Phil Cavarretta, a wide-eyed teenager who was admittedly "scared to death" at the prospect of playing in a World Series, watched in awe as Greenberg drove pitch after pitch into the left-field bleachers. He later recalled: "I thought, 'My God, what are we in for?'"[18] Witnessing the same scene, Cub pitchers, doubtlessly "whistling through the graveyard," bravely told reporters: "Aw, he's easy. He can't hit a high one past the infield."[19]

By game time, a throng of 47,391, the largest crowd ever to witness a World Series clash in Detroit, had packed into sun-drenched Navin Field to see Schoolboy Rowe square off in the opening tilt against his fellow Arkansan Lon Warneke to determine, as John Kieran of the *New York Times* wrote, "who's who in the baseball zoo."[20]

In the top of the first, Galan poked a low drive over second. Rogell dove for the ball but merely deflected it into short center. As John Drebinger vividly described, Rogell quickly "jumped to his feet and looked frantically about him like a man who had just discovered he has lost his wallet. Charlie Gehringer, standing a few feet away, seemed to be at a loss as to what to do, so he did nothing," and Galan wound up on second with a double.[21] Billy Herman tapped a roller to Rowe, who fired the ball past Greenberg for an error, allowing Galan to score. After Lindstrom's sacrifice, Hartnett singled to right, sending Herman across the plate. Rowe then steadied himself and pitched shutout ball until the ninth, when Demaree smashed a long solo home run into the left-field bleachers, making the final score a 3–0 Cub victory.

Two aspects of the clash stood out. First was Warneke's dominating pitching. "Chew Tobacco," who, as Bill Corum raved, had his "hook breaking like a leading lady's heart in the second act," stifled the Bengals on four hits.[22] The second feature was the savageness of the bench jockeying by the Cubs, whom Greenberg described as "a bunch of SOBs."[23] Before the Series Grimm had promised: "We're going to give the Tigers all we have all the time, and that goes for the good old jockeying, too. We're not going to let them start pushing us around."[24] Herman "Flea" Clifton, the slightly built Tiger substitute infielder, recalled: "Anything they thought could get you riled up, they'd try. They'd talk about your mother, your father, your sister. Like when I walked out there. What was that little tune that the Cubs sang to me?

'Pappy's in the poorhouse,
Sister's in jail.
Momma's on the front porch,
Pussy for sale.'"[25]

Like the Cardinals in 1934, the Cubs' primary target for the most vicious verbal assault was Greenberg, because, as Grimm stated pointedly, "Do you heckle a substitute or a star?"[26] However, given the treatment of Clifton and other lesser players, perhaps the Cubs thought every Tiger was a star. Grimm doubtless adopted this tactic with ferocity as a result of being advised before the Series by Dizzy Dean "to keep riding Greenberg from the bench and he won't give you much trouble."[27] Thus, beginning in the first inning, Cub jockeys, led by Jurges, Herman, Demaree, and reserve catcher Walter Stephenson, taunted the Tiger first-baseman with ethnic slurs, calling him a "Jew bastard," "Jew son of a bitch," and "Kike." When Jurges shrieked "Throw him a pork chop. He won't touch it!" plate umpire George Moriarty took action. The burly former football star strode over to the Cub bench and warned Grimm: "No ball player could call me the names you did to him and get away with it. If I hear any more such profanity I'll chase all five of you off the bench, with you leading the parade!"[28]

In the riotous Cub dressing room, Grimm and his team claimed Moriarty had overreacted. Amid the laughter and playful roughhousing, Grimm admitted that his men "had said some things that were not very nice," while Jurges complained, "It's just ribbing each other. What the hell!"[29] Stephenson joked innocently: "All I said was, 'You big so and so, why in so and so don't you learn to handle your big feet.' Then the Umpire raised hell with me."[30]

The overriding emotion, however, was exultation. One Cub sneered, "Them ain't Mickey's tigers, them's Mickey's mouses," while Gabby Hartnett added derisively, "They must be better hitters than they showed today."[31] Grimm was bubbling with gleeful pride. "You guys are all gentlemuns," he shouted. "Great big gentlemuns. Helluva home run, Frankie. Nice going everybody. You guys are all gentlemuns! We've got to take three more. I don't know if it'll be the next three, but we'll certainly win three of the remaining six contests."[32]

Finally calming down, Grimm singled out Warneke as the day's hero. " Warneke pitched a beautiful game. Why those Tigers practically had their bats knocked right out of their hands," the Cubs' skipper gloated. "I regard Warneke as the greatest right-handed pitcher the National League has seen since Grover Alexander. And I've seen 'em all."[33] Turning his attention to Rowe, Grimm confessed: "I didn't realize this boy Rowe was such a great pitcher. I thought he'd have one of those leaning back deliveries. Instead he shot them right from the shoulder, and, boy, how he could shoot 'em."[34]

Warneke, grinning broadly, explained what the victory meant to him in practical terms. "It feels pretty darn nice," he drawled. "Every guy would like to win a Series game. I don't care about it being a shutout. Why, shucks, I'd just as soon it'd been a 25–24 score, so long as we won. The main thing is that we won. It means more money and everything. That's all I care about — winning. It means we get more bucks."[35]

Rowe, who had been the first Tiger to enter the clubhouse, fired his glove into his locker and then sat dejectedly, with his head in his hands contemplating his eight strikeout, no walk, seven-hit losing performance. When teammates attempted to console him by yelling, "Touch luck, big boy!" Rowe sneered: "Hell, that's all I've been hearing all season! I just failed 'em, that's all."[36]

Among the other Tigers there was a stunned sensation, not so much by their loss as by the mound wizardry of Warneke. "Whew!" sighed Cochrane as he slumped in his dressing room office wire cage. ""Did you ever see such pitching? You'll go a long time until you see better pitching than that which Warneke tossed at us this afternoon. I hope we don't have to look at anything better than we did out there today. He had the greatest assortment of stuff we've looked at this season. Early in the game his curve was breaking nicely. Then, when his curve failed, he switched to a puzzling fastball. And how he pitched! We just couldn't do anything. When you hold our gang like that, you're pitching, and my hat's off to Warneke."[37]

Asked about the epithets he endured, Greenberg, always a gentleman, said softly: "It's all in the game. Why squawk about it now? I was a sucker to let them get my goat. The Cubs should be fined, however."[38] Later that evening, the big first-sacker, who had been called before Commissioner Landis after the game, told reporters: "Landis got on me like a district attorney," demanding a full account on what the Cubs had said and Moriarty's reply.[39] Exhibiting his customary dignity and sportsmanship, Greenberg refused to offer any details on the former and regarding the latter, said only: "I did not overhear any part of the argument between Moriarty and the players."[40]

Yankee manager Joe McCarthy tried to lift the spirits of the American League champions, telling them optimistically: "The first game doesn't mean a thing. You still have the Series in the bag. Sure Lon Warneke did one of the sweetest jobs of pitching I've ever seen, but that doesn't mean a thing. I know you have the stuff, and I'd bet my bottom dollar on it."[41]

Despite the great mound work, the initial battle was played poorly, especially by Detroit. John Drebinger stated the obvious, writing that the Tigers "never recovered from the unexpected development of the first inning."[42] Bill Corum was more pointed, stating derisively: "I knew before the first inning was over there was something vaguely reminiscent about the play of the Tigers. I once saw a ball game on the Fourth of July between the Booneville Very Boues and the American Beauty All Star Girls (four of whom were men), and while I'm inclined to doubt the four males were Goslin, Gehringer, Rogell, and Greenberg working their way up to the major leagues, that's what the Tigers reminded me of in the first inning. They covered a world of ground sitting down. The Cubs, of course, shouldn't win four straight, and won't unless the Bengals continue to tighten up like the tenor string on a bull fiddle. So I must go on liking the Tigers a little longer. If they stop behaving like a nervous debutante who flowers haven't arrived they'll win."[43]

The second clash was battled before 46,742 spectators huddled in blankets, bed quilts, scarves, gloves, fur coats, and heavy Ulsters to ward off the effects of temperatures in the mid- forties and a strong north wind that whipped snow flurries into a lively dance across the field.[44] Longtime baseball scribes claimed it was the coldest day for a Series game since these same two teams battled in 1907 amid a snowstorm, and wondered aloud if the announced temperature was above or below zero.[45] John Kieran wrote that the climate was more conducive for a "Byrd expedition than a ball game."[46] During pre-game drills, Cochrane asked plaintively to no one in particular: "What are we playing today, baseball or Nanook of the North? We better get hot today or we'll freeze to death."[47] Cub players huddled around a bonfire built in front of their dugout and sympathized with Lindstrom, who moaned about trying to play the outfield in the gale-like wind: "All a guy can catch out there today is double pneumonia."[48] Despite the abominable conditions, the game was not postponed because, as John Kieran mused: "Commissioner Landis came out of his igloo and ordered the campaign to proceed relentlessly. He was afraid if they halted at all, the two teams would be frozen up or snowed in for the winter."[49]

Taking the hill for Detroit was Tommy Bridges. Opposing him was a surprise starter, the antiquated Charlie Root, who had won fifteen games and begged Grimm for a chance to atone for his dismal performance (0–1, 10.38 earned run average) in the 1932 World Series. Grimm acquiesced, but as Damon Runyon observed: "Sentimental gestures are very nice in love, but not in war or baseball."[50] Hearing that Root would start, Babe Ruth, resplendent in a brown suit and tie and overcoat with a white carnation, sat in the press box next to his ghost-writer Bill Slocum and blurted that Root would not last an inning.[51]

Taking their manager's admonition to "get hot" to heart, Jo-Jo White led off the first inning with a single to left and scored on Cochrane's long double to right-center. Gehringer drove Cochrane in with a single to center. Greenberg then drove Root to an early shower by lofting a long home run into the left-field stands, giving the

Larry French and Phil Cavaretta trying to keep warm before second game of 1935 World Series (Chicago Historical Society, ICHi-35199, photograph by Wide World).

home team a 4–0 lead. This onslaught prompted John Kieran to note acerbically, "As they say in vaudeville, Root opened and closed in one," while Damon Runyon likened the Tiger blitzkrieg to the world situation, saying, "The Tigers took Charlie like the Italians figure to take Ethiopia."[52]

The Tigers added three runs off reliever Roy Henshaw in the fourth and another solo tally off Fabian Kowalik in the seventh, making Tommy Bridges, who spun a masterful six-hitter, an easy 8–3 victor. The result validated the wisdom of Grantland Rice's observation that after the first inning "the smart move would have been to call off the game, award it to the Tigers, and possibly choke off some ten thousand cases of pneumonia."[53]

In the losers' locker room, the always upbeat Grimm let out a whoop and exhorted his players: "That's the way to get beat. Get the hell kicked out of you and have it over with. Hell, you guys looked better losing than those guys did winning. You're still big gentle-muns. We're just as happy over here as they are over there."[54] Still smiling, the Cub pilot said sarcastically to reporters: "You notice that we didn't use cuss words to Greenberg today. We got on him in the most polite manner possible. We spoke real nice to him. We even called him Henry Benjamin so the umpires wouldn't be shocked. Yes sir, we were so nice we got him to fumble and commit two errors, and that means we'll win the Series at home."[55] Pointing to his players, Grimm exclaimed in a shrill yell: "Yes sir, my boys, you won the Series today when you got the Greenberg goat. We'll keep that goat and feed him the best tin cans we've got in Chicago."[56]

Picking up on their manager's confidence in his victory strategy, Cub players chimed in with enthusiastic vocal support. Lindstrom bellowed: "Yes, sir, we'll have Greenberg on our side from now on!" and Stan Hack shrieked: "He's listening to us all the time. We've got him going. That's why he fumbled those balls."[57]

Becoming momentarily serious over his club's first defeat since September 4, Grimm told newsmen: "Look, they just beat us that's all. We took a good licking. We took it early, and we took it often. Bridges looked swell in there. He had a lot of stuff on the ball, and he took good care of us. Charlie Root had a world of stuff, too, but they swung their bats where he threw the ball. He just couldn't get loose in that ice-covered hurricane. That Greenberg home run was a home run anywhere. White's hit in the first was a lucky one, as was Mike's, but, hell, somebody's got to have the luck. We had it yesterday, and the Tigers had it today. We knew we had to lose sometime, and we don't feel bad about it. All we looked for here was an even break. I've still got Bill Lee and Warneke ready, and we are now back home for three days."[58]

In their clubhouse, the Tigers were jubilant. Cochrane slammed his mitt and chest protector down on the floor of his office cage and shouted: "I knew they couldn't keep us down forever. We've been hitting hard all year, and I knew sooner or later we'd bust out. When we're hitting we're a tough club to beat, and the Cubs will find that out. Watch us go from here on. I figured Tommy would do it. He had plenty of stuff, despite the cold weather, and he would have shown those Cubs some pitching if he'd been forced to. But he eased up after getting that lead. It will be Auker in the opener in Chicago, and the Cubs will look at something they've never seen before when he starts shooting that underhanded delivery at them."[59] Standing within earshot of Cochrane's remarks, Auker blurted: "I'm ready for those birds right now. I never felt better in my life. I wish it was game time tomorrow right now."[60]

Attention then turned to the verbal assault emanating from the Tiger dugout, aimed at Grimm, who was acting as third-base coach. Asked about Grimm's complaint to Umpire Moriarty that Tiger coaches Heinie Schuble and Del Baker, along with outfielder Gerald Walker and pitcher Alvin Crowder were abusing him, Crowder feigned surprise and replied to the writers: "Why, I didn't have the least idea that he'd take exception to anything I said. I was just stating facts, the same as I always do, only I might have been making 'em a little louder. First I said to Mr. Grimm that I wondered how his little old Cubs ever won the National League flag — or I guess I called it a pennant — and then I called over to him about his pitchers. I was fair. They have good enough pitchers. Then I spoke to him about his fielders. There are some nice fellas on that club — some not so good as others — so I dwelt on the latter. Then I come around to his hitters, and boy I poured it on him. And, by the way I was talking, Mr. Grimm knew I wasn't making occasional observations. Why all I did was point out to Mr. Grimm that he didn't have any power. So I told him we'd take three out of the next four games. Oh, I added a little bit to it, but that was the gist. Why even Moriarty told him: 'Aw, what the hell, Charlie. They ain't botherin' you. They ain't cussin' you. They ain't swearing at you. They're gentlemanly about it. They're just havin' a good time.'"[61] Judge Landis, however, called in Moriarty, Grimm, and several players after the game, and after listening to their account, dismissed Crowder's version of the incident, telling reporters: "In my time in this world I have always prided myself on a command

Chicago Mayor Edward Kelly and Postmaster General James Farley greet Gabby Hartnett the third game of the world Series at Wrigley Field, October 4, 1935 (Chicago Historical Society, SDN-078146, photograph by *Chicago Daily News*).

of lurid expressions. I must confess that I learned from those young men some versions of the language even I didn't know existed."[62]

Bridges, smoking a cigarette and sipping scotch, maintained his usual quiet demeanor.[63] "The boys sure were hitting," he said softly, "and I didn't have to do much pitching out there with a seven run lead. I had a fine hook today. My only trouble was in controlling it in the latter part of the game. My biggest problem was keeping my hands moistened. Without moisture the ball gets away from you."[64]

The day's only sour note for the Bengals was a wrist injury suffered by Greenberg. In the seventh inning, he was hit by a pitched ball from Kowalik. The next batter, Pete Fox, singled to right and, when Demaree lobbed the ball toward second, Greenberg raced for the plate. The cut-off man, Billy Herman, fired the ball to Hartnett, who, as he blocked the plate for the tag, fell on the on-charging runner. Greenberg's left wrist curled up against his body and snapped. In an effort to conceal the extent of the damage, which x-rays later showed to be a multiple fracture, Greenberg finished the game in excruciating pain, his wrist beginning to swell to twice its normal size.[65] Cochrane dismissed questions about his star's injury, lying to reporters by saying only: "I feel it is only of minor consequence, and I am relieved it is not his throwing arm. He'll be all right tomorrow."[66]

The following afternoon under a clear autumn sky and a balmy gentle breeze that barely rippled the banners flying over Wrigley Field in Chicago, Tiger starter Eldon Auker prepared to face the Cubs' Bill Lee. Two hours and twenty-seven minutes later, the smaller than anticipated crowd of 45,532 had witnessed what Babe Ruth claimed was "one of the greatest games ever in a World Series, filled with exciting rallies, brilliant catches, turmoil with umpires, ninth inning scoring, and overtime."[67] Even the usually restrained John Drebinger was swept up by the drama, writing: "Rarely has World Series competition provided a more wildly exciting battle than that which unfolded itself today, with heroes made and unmade so fast the altercations could scarcely be followed by the naked eye."[68]

The Cubs, paced by Frank Demaree's home run into the right-field bleachers, took a 3–0 lead before the Tigers struck back with a lone run in the sixth on a run-scoring triple by Fox and erupted for another four tallies in the eighth, driving Lee from the mound and forcing Grimm to utilize Warneke in relief. Tiger reliever Schoolboy Rowe could not hold the 5–3 lead, as he was rapped for three hits and a sacrifice fly, which enabled the Cubs to knot the score at five-all and send the game into extra innings.

After a scoreless tenth, Rogell opened the eleventh with a single past third, and was forced at second by Owen. After Rowe fanned for the second out, Jo-Jo White's single to center drove Owen home with what proved to be the winning run.

Like the earlier contests, this one was marred by feuds with umpires and vicious bench jockeying. Tiger third-base coach Del Baker was ejected by National League arbiter Ernie

Charlie Gehringer (left) and Hank Greenberg (right) during 1935 World Series (courtesy State Archives of Michigan).

Quigley for protesting too vociferously the umpire calling Pete Fox out on Hartnett's pick-off throw at third that nipped a potential Tiger rally in the sixth. In the home half of the same fame, Moriarty of the American League ruled that Cochrane's heave had cut down Cavarretta's attempted steal of second. This revived the previous day's animosities between Moriarty and the Cubs. In response to raucous jibes from the Cub bench, Moriarty, in the words of John Kieran, "stalked over to the enemy trench like Mussolini advancing on Chicago's Addis Ababa. There were some remarkably ferocious gestures and a fine flow of oratory, but unfortunately no one was hit."[69] Moriarty, while restraining his normal penchant for physical confrontation, gave the heave-ho to Manager Grimm, and in the next inning he made more room on the Cub bench by ousting reserves Woody English and Tuck Stainback.

In the dressing quarters following the game, Grimm, who revealed that he had violated rules by continuing to manage his team after his ejection by standing in the clubhouse runway and giving orders through a hole he had punched in the door to the dugout, was livid with rage.[70] "To squawk about an umpire in a losing game is never a graceful thing," fumed not-so-jolly Cholly. "The Tigers won a great game, and we've got to come back tomorrow whether we like Moriarty or not. I cannot keep from saying, however, that in all my years in baseball I never heard an umpire abuse members of a ball team with the language Moriarty used to Herman, to Jurges, to English, and to me, and then to the entire bench. I thought I had a right to make a protest on his calling out Cavarretta on an attempted steal at second-base. I swear that I did not use profane or abusive language, and everybody in the ballpark knows I didn't lay hands on Moriarty. The first thing I knew I was being showered with not only profane, but the most obscene, language I ever had to take from anybody. Moriarty has imagined himself in sole charge of the show ever since he came over to the bench in the Detroit opener and warned us against doing any bench jockeying that might hurt Hank Greenberg. He's been bossing not only [Umpire Bill] McGowen of the American League, but the National League umpires, Quigley and [Dolly] Stark, like they were little boys. If a manager can't go out and make a decent kick, what the hell is the game coming to!"[71]

Pausing just long enough to catch his breath, Grimm resumed his tirade. "I don't advance the chasing of Woody and George Stainback as an alibi, but if they hadn't been chased I certainly could have used them to advantage after we tied the score on Rowe in the ninth. I still insist there was nothing strong enough in their language to merit their being run out of the park regardless of the Moriarty position."[72]

Supporting Grimm's assertions were the Cub players, National League President Ford C. Frick, who had been sitting in a box seat near the Cub dugout, and *Chicago Tribune* correspondent Ed Burns. Coach John "Red" Corriden snorted: "Moriarty was guilty of antagonizing and demoralizing our ball club."[73] Coach Roy Johnson added that Moriarty had made "improper reflections on our ancestry."[74] Stainback explained earnestly: "My only response to Moriarty's obscenities was to suggest to the former Tiger manager and player that he take his hands out of his pockets and bear down."[75] Frick, who had spent the previous two years as Babe Ruth's ghostwriter, added with transparent mock innocence: "Moriarty used blasphemous language in talking to the Cubs' bench. Undoubtedly there were a lot of hot words exchanged on both sides. In at least one instance I overheard the word 'meathead' directed at Moriarty."[76] Burns, writing a column intended to incite the Cub faithful to come out to the park, verbally sneered: "The Cubs think Moriarty is a bully. They hiss on whatever claims he may have for gentlemanly and sportsmanlike conduct on the field. He cursed and ranted at the Cubs, who beefed at his showing of the day. They did not claim, however, that he at any time deliberately tried to favor the Tigers, a team for which he played third-base for eight years [1909–1916] and which he managed in 1927 and 1928."[77] For obvious reasons, however, Burns neglected to mention that Moriarty spent his first two years in the major leagues, 1903 and 1904, as a Chicago Cub.

That evening, Commissioner Landis ordered Moriarty and the aggrieved Cubs to testify in a closed meeting at his office the next morning. Reporters who eavesdropped outside the door primarily could hear little more than muffled voices, but once they clearly heard Billy Herman state emphatically: "Judge, I never cursed an umpire in my entire career. I will make an affidavit on it."[78] On another occasion, Moriarty was heard to bellow defiantly to the Chicago players: "I can lick the whole Cub team. If you fellows start anything today, I'll take care of all of you!"[79]

After the heated fifty-five minute conference concluded, Landis announced that he would make no judgment until the Series ended, but he instructed Cub President Philip Wrigley to silence his players for the remainder of the games.[80] Ultimately, the Commissioner imposed penalties of $200 each on Moriarty, Grimm, Jurges, Herman, and English, the heaviest fines ever levied in a World Series to that date. Grimm later recalled with pride: "It's on the record that I paid the fines against English, Jurges, and Herman. Moriarty was a tough gent."[81]

Meanwhile, the Tigers were elated at their come-from-behind victory. Sitting exhausted in front of his locker and sipping a bottle of soda pop, Manager Mickey Cochrane met the press. "What a battle it was! They threw everything they had at us, and it wasn't enough. I wonder how Grimm feels now, after he has seen his pitching staff battered up? What's left to throw tomorrow? He used Warneke and French, two of his best bets, today and wound up on the wrong end," the Tiger skipper said with a smile. "We've got the old General, and he's just as apt to go out and stand the Cubs on their ears tomorrow — and we're in a position to throw Bridges right back at them in game five. That ought to be enough to win."[82]

Asked about the rowdiness of the play, Iron Mike grinned. "It was a battle out there. It was the toughest World Series game I've ever been in. The boys asked and gave no quarter. There were so many things going on out there I don't remember what happened when Umpire Moriarty chased Grimm and the others out of the game," he said innocently. "I don't know why Umpire Quigley should have chased our coach, Del Baker, though. Why, Baker didn't even swear at him. He just grabbed Quigley by the arm."[83]

Game four was played under gray, wintry skies, with a biting wind blowing in off Lake Michigan, which lowered temperatures to the upper forties. During fielding drills, the players put on an animated display for the early arrivals in the near capacity throng of 49,350, but as James P. Dawson of the *New York Times* observed: "They had no alternative. It was either move fast or freeze."[84] Garbed as though they were at a late season football game, fans kept their blood warm by constantly jeering Moriarty throughout the contest.[85]

Watching the Cubs take batting practice, Alvin Crowder, the thirty-six-year-old veteran who was in his third consecutive World Series and scheduled to be Detroit's starting hurler, was asked by a writer: "How does this Chicago club look to you?" The sad-faced pitcher replied: "Well, I'll tell you. I'm not talking right now for publication, but those boys out there kind of interest me. They look like nice free swingers, and they seem to like to hit at first balls. I like boys like that. I usually find that those nice enthusiastic free swingers ain't too hard to fool. No, sir, I wouldn't be surprised if I go out there and sort of fool some of those Chicago batters."[86]

Despite surrendering a towering home run into the right-field stands in the second inning to Hartnett, Crowder baffled the Cubs on three hits throughout the first eight innings, before settling for a five-hit, five strikeout 2–1 victory over Tex Carleton. His slow curves and deliberate delivery kept the Cub batters constantly off balance. The "General" was so nonchalant that he even reenacted the Yankee's Lefty Gomez' famous stalling tactic of standing on the mound watching an airplane lazily circle Wrigley Field.[87]

Crowder, who sat between innings in the dugout wrapped from head to foot in a long brown overcoat to keep warm, also was instrumental in both the Tiger runs.[88] In the third inning, he led off with a single to right and scored what was then the tying run on Gehringer's double into deep left-center. In the sixth, with two out Flea Clifton, inserted into the line-up at third so that Owen could replace the ailing Greenberg at first-base, lofted a high fly to Galan in left. The Cub outfielder, running up the slope toward the wall, lost his balance, the ball trickled off his gloved fingers, and Clifton loped all the way to third-base on the error. Crowder followed and tapped a soft, one-hop liner to Jurges for what should have been the final out, but the Cub shortstop took his eyes off the ball. The sphere skipped into short left, permitting Clifton to score what proved to be the winning run.

Jubilation reigned in the Tiger dressing room, with cries of "It's all over but the shouting" and "Try and stop us from winning the Series now" filling the air.[89] Crowder was hoisted on the shoulders of Schoolboy Rowe and substitute backstop Ray Hayworth. "Here's the guy who did it!" they shouted. "Here's the guy who did it!. He showed those Cubs they weren't so hot."[90]

Slumped in his office chair and drinking his familiar post-game bottle of soda, Cochrane lauded his pitcher. "The old General pitched one of the greatest World Series games I ever saw," he proclaimed to reporters and a radio audience. "He pitched smart baseball, always cool, and never upset no matter what happened. Why, in the ninth inning when I walked out to him after the Cubs got men on first and second with one out, I asked him if his arm was tired, and he answered: 'Hell, no! I'll get 'em, Mike. I'll get 'em.' And that's just what he did. He got Stan Hack to hit into a double play — and what a double play! Rogell stopping a smash, making a perfect throw to Gehringer, who made a perfect pivot and throw to first. The General just curved 'em to death. He didn't give those guys anything good to hit. He's just a smart old guy who knows how to use his stuff. I just don't see how the Cubs can stop us now. Our pitching staff is in much better shape than that of the Cubs."[91]

The Tiger pilot singled out Flea Clifton for praise as well. "That Clifton," he said admiringly of the twenty-five-year-old substitute third-sacker, "I never saw anything like him. Golly, what a courageous kid he is. Do you realize that he was the difference between victory and defeat in this game? If he had cracked, we would have sunk. But he's more than stood up. He's the biggest star of this Series. Even if Greenberg returns, Clifton stays in. I could not take a game guy like that out of our line-up."[92]

In the losers' quarters, the peppery Grimm tried to rally his troops after their heartbreaking defeat. "We're still in the Series," he yelled. "It takes four to win. You played great ball, fellows. Line drives at 'em all day. You're still a great ball club. We're not licked yet."[93]

Offering the horde of sportswriters slices of a seventy-five pound cake donated to the club by a local café, Grimm continued. "I'll throw Warneke at 'em tomorrow," he said between bites of cake. "He'll pull them right back where they belong. You can't deny Crowder pitched a great game. He deserves a lot of credit. Carleton pitched a great game, too, but the breaks went to the Tigers. Breaks usually decide ball games. It was a tough one that either side could win with just one break. When it came, it went their way. But it isn't over yet. We'll get 'em. I know my Cubs."[94]

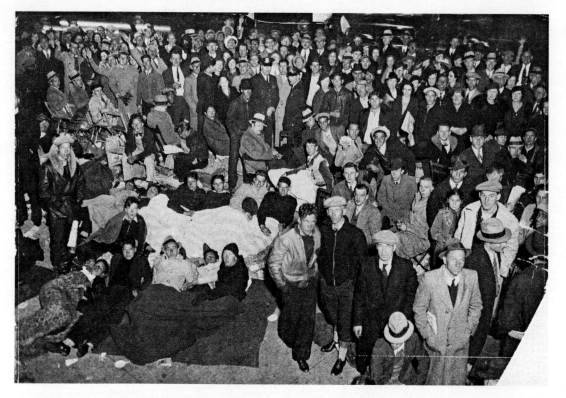

Fans waiting outside Wrigley Field to purchase tickets, 1935 World Series (Chicago Historical Society, ICHi-38989).

The day's goats, Galan and Jurges, offered no excuses for their errors, which cost their club the win. "It just popped out of my hand," Galan said remorsefully. "I can't explain it."[95] Jurges was equally contrite, admitting: "I was careless, I guess. The chance was too easy."[96]

Asked about his teammates' misplays, Carleton was gracious. "Just one of those things," he said. "That was a spinner Jurges missed. He looked up for a second, and when he looked down again the ball wasn't where he thought it was. I shouldn't have thrown Crowder the ball I did."[97] Brightening, the hurler raised his voice so all could hear and urged the other players to keep their heads high, reminding them: "Heck, guys, we won twenty-one straight. We ought to be able to take three straight now!"[98]

The fifth game of the Series, and the final home game for the Cubs, was played under near perfect autumn weather, with a bright sun making the chilly temperature bearable. Another near capacity crowd of 49,237 Chicago faithful passed through the turnstiles, as John Drebinger sagely observed, "hoping for the best, but fearing the worst."[99] On the mound for Detroit was Rowe, who was seeking to atone for his defeat in the opener. Facing him for the Cubs was fellow Arkansas right-hander Lon Warneke, whose masterful four-hit shutout had bested the Schoolboy in that contest.

The desperate Cubs got off to a 2–0 lead in the third inning when reserve outfielder Chuck Klein, once one of the most feared sluggers in the National League, momentarily recaptured the form of his youth and followed Billy Herman's triple with a blast deep into the right-field bleachers. The home team added another tally on an error by Owen and a double by Herman to earn an easy 3–1 victory for Warneke, who pitched six innings of three-hit ball before retiring with a sore right shoulder.

Grimm was elated by his club's clutch performance. "We're going back to Detroit, aren't we?" he roared over the locker room bedlam. "Nice going everybody. Nice hitting, Chuck Klein. We've got to win the next two in Detroit, and we're going to do it. It's French tomorrow, and we'll bring 'em right down to the seventh game and take 'em the way the Cards did last year."[100]

Later, sitting in his office, Grimm addressed writers and broadcasters. "In spite of everything, our Cubs are still in this World Series," he stated with satisfaction. "They'll never be able to shout 'Schoolboy Rowe' at us again. We've beaten him twice in this Series, and we're proud of that because he's a great pitcher. But the greatest pitcher this Series has seen is Lon Warneke. He wouldn't quit out there. I had to order him out, though every pitch from the third inning on was causing him pain. He didn't even say a word about it, but Gabby Hartnett found out. Even then, Warneke wanted to go on, but Lon Warneke's arm is worth more to me than all the World Series that will ever be played."[101]

The ailing hurler, stretched out on the rubbing table with a heat lamp glaring on his right shoulder, still had his huge wad of chewing tobacco in his cheek as he spoke to reporters. "I didn't tell Charlie that I was through because I wanted to win," he drawled. "I felt it hurting in the third when I pitched to Rowe, but the pain didn't get tough until the sixth. Then every throw pained my shoulder. Hartnett asked me what was wrong, and when I told him he signaled to have them warm up some relief. Until the shoulder went out, I had a lot of stuff. I'll be all right in a day or two, I expect."[102]

During the contest, Cub players had resumed their verbal vituperations of home plate Umpire Moriarty when he initially called a strike on Gehringer, who led off the ninth, but then reversed himself. On the next pitch, Gehringer singled past third and ultimately crossed the plate with the Tigers' lone run. Hartnett had kept a steady stream of mild criticism against Moriarty throughout the game, but he erupted when Gehringer scored, bellowing in Moriarty's face: "It's a well known fact that you're the lousiest umpire in the world!"[103] Subsequently, in the midst of the hi-jinx in the Cub locker room, Billy Jurges assembled the writers and, with an unsuccessful attempt at solemnity, informed them: "There's a scandal in this World Series! Moriarty isn't on the Detroit club's eligibility list!"[104]

Cochrane and his team, doubtless reliving in their minds how the world championship had eluded them the previous year after holding a two-game margin on the Cardinals, were desolated by the game's outcome. The Tiger manager sat in the subdued dressing room and, after consoling Rowe, told writers and radiomen: "The Cubs are a tough bunch to beat. Make no mistake about that. But we still have them on the run. They're in a tough spot. Seldom does a team come through with three straight victories to win a Series. I don't believe they will either. They haven't the pitching, for one thing. We've seen the last of Warneke. I'll pitch Bridges tomorrow, and then it will be over. We'll beat them in the sixth game. There will be no seventh."[105]

In a mid-July like setting, a record Detroit throng of 48,420 paid customers jammed into Navin Field in hopes of witnessing that city's first modern world's baseball championship. As Cochrane had promised, the Bengals pinned their hopes on "Tennessee Tommy" Bridges, the 150 pound right-handed mound artist whom Bill Corum observed did not look strong enough "to break an overripe egg against a concrete wall, but who could fog a fastball through there with the best of 'em."[106] For the Cubs, survival rested with seven-year veteran southpaw Larry French, whom the Cubs had acquired from Pittsburgh during the off-season. As French, who had lost the third game in relief, strode to the mound to start the game, a confidant Jolly Cholly tossed him the ball and wisecracked the admonition: "This is a nice Series, Larry. You keep it going."[107]

Detroit jumped to a 1–0 advantage in the first inning on singles by Cochrane and Gehringer and a run-scoring double to left by Pete Fox. The battling Bruins, however, drew even in the third on singles by Jurges, French, and Herman. Detroit regained a one-run margin in the fourth on singles by Gee Walker, Billy Rogell, and a ground out by Bridges. In the fifth, however, Billy Herman stroked a two-run shot over the left-field screen to give the visitors a 3–2 lead. Cochrane's squad knotted the seesaw contest in the sixth on Rogell's ground-rule double to left and Owen's single to the same field. The tense struggle remained deadlocked at three-all until the ninth.

In the top of the final frame, Stan Hack, who was having a sub-par Series with only four hits, opened with a tremendous blast over Gee Walker's head in center for a triple. Bridges proceeded to hitch up his trousers and struck out Billy Jurges, bringing French to the plate. Grimm, who thought all his remaining pitchers were "pretty well used up or ineffective," let his starter stay in the game and bat.[108] Vainly waiting in anticipation of the squeeze bunt sign, French, who had batted a mere .141 during the season, took two called strikes from plate umpire Ernest Quigley before tapping a weak grounder to Bridges, who looked Hack back to third before tossing to first to retire French.[109]

Augie Galan, a .160 hitter in the Series, strode gamely to the plate, but was induced by Bridges to fly softly to Goslin in left to end the threat. Billy Herman, sitting on the bench, later recalled: "When I think back to that Series all I can see is Hack standing on third-base waiting for someone to drive him in. Seems to me now he stood there for hours and hours."[110]

The home half of the ninth started inauspiciously with French fanning Flea Clifton. The crowd roared as Cochrane lined a single off Herman's glove. With everyone in the stands on their feet and screaming exhortations, Gehringer lashed the ball straight at first-baseman Cavarretta, who later explained what occurred: "More in self-protection than anything else, I threw up my gloved hand. The ball tore right on through, and I was just about able to stop it with my bare hand. If I had knocked it down with my glove I could have gone to second with it and forced Cochrane. But the ball had really stung my bare hand, and I didn't want to risk a throw to second. I was afraid it might wind up in left-field. So I took the sure way out and stepped on first, but that got Cochrane to second."[111]

That brought to the plate veteran Goose Goslin, who, like Crowder, was in his third consecutive Series and thrived on pressure situations. Grimm elected to pitch to Goslin rather than walk him intentionally to get to Pete Fox, who was the Tigers' leading hitter in the Series. As Goslin approached the plate, he turned to blue-suited Umpire Quigley and confidently predicted: "Ernie, if they pitch that ball over this plate, you can go take that money suit off."[112]

Goslin was jammed by French's first pitch, but he got enough of the bat on the ball to send it looping over Herman's head. As Herman recalled sadly: "I ran out for it. Billy Jurges ran out for it. Frank Demaree came in from center for it. But nobody could quite catch up to it, and it just dropped onto the grass in center-field and Cochrane scored. Damn, that was so frustrating, running after the ball that's got the World Series riding on it, knowing that you're not going to catch it, and knowing that you're not going to miss it by much. It just drops onto the grass and breaks your heart."[113] Cavarretta, who saw Cochrane jump on home plate, cut off the relay and walked dejectedly to the dugout. Criticized for not letting the throw go through to Hartnett, the youthful first-baseman retorted: "The game was already over. They could have shot it in from the outfield with a rifle and there was still no way."[114] Cavarretta glumly echoed Herman's thoughts, adding: "But you can't imagine how frustrating it was to see that ball bloop up into the air and know it wasn't going to be caught."[115]

With Goslin's hit, as Grantland Rice waxed poetically: "The Leaning Tower can now crumble and find its level with the Pisan plain. The Hanging Garden can grow up in weeds. After waiting forty-eight years, the Detroit Tigers are at last champions of the world."[116]

The Cubs' clubhouse was funereal except for Grimm, who was exhorting his men to lift their heads high in defeat. "I'm proud of you all," he proclaimed with evident sincerity. "We'll get 'em next time. It was the breaks that beat us in three tough, close games. We got beat by a good ball club. There's no disgrace in that. There isn't a game of the six that I'm ashamed of. You were wonderful kids. We did our best, so what the hell! We're still National League champions, and that's more than anybody expected. We're not world champions, but nobody can say we were badly beaten. It just wasn't in the books for us to win, so forget it and have a good time during the winter! Keep those chins up!"[117]

Spying French sitting on a stool in front of his locker, his head in his hands, sobbing, Grimm went to console him. Extending his hand to his manager, French whispered, "I'm awful sorry, Charlie."[118] "Sorry for what?" Grimm replied. "You've got nothing to be sorry about. You pitched a damn swell game and got beat. I don't believe you ever pitched a better game in your life. You couldn't overcome the breaks, that's all. Go in the shower and get ready to go home."[119]

Gabby Hartnett, the jovial rotund receiver, helped to lighten the mood as well by becoming the first major league player to go on radio naked, as he answered questions standing in the middle of the dressing room wearing nothing but a shaving mug in his hand.[120] "I ought to be arrested for talking to so many people this way," Gabby cracked to his radio listeners. Asked what kind of a pitch Goslin hit, the catcher snorted: "He hit a $50,000 pitch — the lucky stiff!"[121] Hartnett quickly added with pride: "We got beat by a good ball club, and they beat a good one!"[122] Herman, with a towel surrounding his midriff, left the showers spitting water and expletives about Moriarty. Grabbing the microphone from Hartnett, the peppery second-baseman blurted: "Folks, we got beat by a great ball club, but I want you to know that a better ball club got beat!"[123]

Among the Tigers, raucous celebration reigned supreme. Although physically drained and slumped in his chair in his wire-mesh office cage, Cochrane could not contain his elation. "What a thrill! What a game to win! What a heart Bridges has! What a money player Goslin is! I'm the happiest guy in the world!" Iron Mike said, his words spewing forth like machine gun bursts. "I've had many big moments in my life, none to equal the thrill of crossing the plate with the winning run. Boy, that was great! I thought I would never get there. That Bridges! What a thrill he gave me. That little guy has the heart of a lion. It looked bad when Hack tripled to start the ninth, as Tommy didn't have as much stuff as he had the other day. Then he started pitching. He pitched six of the greatest curves I ever caught to retire the side. They were sweethearts. What a pitcher! What a heart! Just 150 pounds of guts and courage, that's what he is. Why, the little guy never flinched. He bore down in there and pitched his very heart up for the Cubs to hit at. Yes, sir, we're the champions, but it will be a long time before you see a greater exhibition of pitching in the clutch."[124] As an afterthought, he urged National League President Ford Frick, who had come to congratulate the Tigers, to "please give Charlie Grimm and his gang all the credit in the world; they fought us like a bunch of bulldogs all the way."[125]

Media representatives inquiring about his clutch hit mobbed Goslin. "What were you thinking when you went up there in the ninth?" someone shouted. "About the difference between a winning player's share and a losing player's share," Goslin stated frankly, "and particularly about how badly I personally needed that difference."[126]

Bridges, who had not witnessed the game-winning blow because he was having a cigarette in the runway to the clubhouse, told writers that he had not been fearful during the Cubs' last inning threat.[127] "When Hack banged out that three-bagger in the ninth," Bridges said softy, "I realized it wasn't a sweet spot. But all you can do is pitch when it's your pitching day. I wasn't scared, but I had a funny little feeling. It's the feeling I usually have in the first inning of a ball game. It's sort of a dry feeling in your throat and a kind of shuddery feeling all over you. It only lasts a couple of minutes. Then you settle down."[128]

For the city of Detroit, the Series was an economic godsend, with almost $2,000,000 worth of business coming to the Motor City. Moreover, civic leaders predicted that additional tourism would result because Detroit could lay claim to not only the world baseball champions, but also world heavyweight boxing champion Joe Louis and world motorboat racing champion Gar Wood, all of whom would promote the city and its products.[129]

As a World Series, the 1935 classic received mixed reviews. Predictably, baseball officials lavished praise on the games, with Commissioner Landis, American League President Will Harridge, and his National League counterpart, Ford Frick, all anointing it as "the grandest World Series ever played."[130] Arch Ward of the *Chicago Tribune* wrote: "It was a great Series, well played, and interesting. From our viewpoint, it would have been a greater Series, better played, and more interesting if the Cubs had won, but that is local partisanship."[131] Even cynical Chicago sportswriter Warren Brown was moved to offer a backhanded compliment, claiming that only the animosity of the players made the games worthwhile: "It was a bitter Series, make no mistake about that. It was bitterly fought by both sides, with the pressure high at all times. This was a brute strength Series, and the strength seemed to be with the Tigers."[132]

However, there were vocal critics as well. Parsimonious Tiger owner Frank Navin, who had purchased the team from William Yawkey in 1907 and thrice endured post season failures, sourly set forth the downside of the victory he had waited so long to achieve. The grim-visaged, bespectacled Navin stunned reporters expecting a victory oration, by issuing a warning to his players not to expect salary increases for the upcoming season. "Our profits amount to very little," he said with the dour expression of a wealthy man viewing the tax collector approaching his door. "It is great to sit here and know we have a ball team of world champions—I've been waiting thirty years for this—but don't overlook the fact that there is grief attached to it."[133] Navin was spared enduring lengthy grief, however, as the following month he fell from his horse during a pleasure ride and died from the injuries incurred shortly afterward.[134]

Other critics leveled their barbs at the players' personal behavior and diamond abilities. Unlike Warren Brown, John Kieran viewed the Series negatively primarily because of the conduct of the Chicagoans, telling his readers: "There were times during the recent World Series when an onlooker might have been puzzled as to whether it was Chicago versus Detroit or the Cubs versus Umpire Moriarty for the big baseball title. There is something wrong in an athletic program when a referee, judge, or umpire comes even close to being a prominent figure in the general firing, if not the final score. There is always a lot of loud and loose language flowing out of rival dugouts in any hot baseball series. Perhaps that is one little matter the presidents of the two leagues and Judge Landis might take a hand in suppressing. It is no credit to baseball."[135] Damon Runyon offered another critical observation, noting: "The pitching on both sides, except in spots, was scarcely big league, and the thinking was strictly Class B. The final game was exciting for spectators, but it wasn't big time baseball. However, it saved the Series from going into baseball history as one of the dullest on record."[136]

Such profound and weighty praise and/or criticism placed on the outcome of these baseball games, belies the fact that the World Series, no matter how exciting or poorly played, is but a momentary diversion from the great issues of the times. Given the continuing world economic crisis and a rising threat to peace caused by Italian Dictator Benito Mussolini's military thrust into Ethiopia, perhaps the World Series of 1935 was best put in perspective by Havey J. Boyle, sports editor of the *Pittsburgh Post-Gazette,* who wrote: "It is well that our troubles are so slight that our joy can be so intense over a base hit by Goose Goslin. How different, I thought, was this from the scenes you see of other peoples yelling and shouting for some dictator who wants them to go out and have their eyes shot out, who wants mothers to cry over bloody and lifeless messes that once were their sons, and whose aim is to stay in power regardless of what misery they bring. The Tiger victory was good not only for baseball, but good for the country. Anyone liking this country as she stands today will always support and encourage this game of baseball, which so innocently and cleanly appeals to so many thousands."[137]

CUBS VS. YANKEES, 1938

After the New York Yankees clinched their third successive American League crown, during the victory celebration Manager Joe McCarthy raised his glass in a toast and thundered to the assembled writers, players, and club officials: "Boys, this is the greatest ball club I ever managed. I might say that this is the greatest club in the history of baseball."[1] While this might have seemed like normal managerial boasting, no less an authority than the Philadelphia Athletics' venerable pilot Connie Mack concurred, stating: "I've been in the major leagues since 1886, and there has never been anything like these Yankees."[2]

Whether or not this assessment was correct, there could be no doubt that the Bronx Bombers of 1938 were a formidable squad. Coasting through September, the Yankees won 99 games and finished 9½ lengths ahead of the second-place Boston Red Sox, thereby demonstrating once again the truth of New York sportswriter Tom Meany's observation that the American League was the sporting world's version of "Snow White and the Seven Dwarfs."[3]

The Yankees were an extremely well balanced club, which John Drebinger of the *New York Times* claimed functioned as a unit better than any in baseball history.[4] Offensively they boasted tremendous power. The infield consisted of veteran Lou Gehrig (.295, 29, 114) at first, twenty-three-year-old rookie second-sacker Joe Gordon (.255, 25, 97), shortstop Frankie Crosetti (.263, 9, 55), and third-baseman Red Rolfe (.311, 10, 80), with Bill Dickey (.313, 27, 115) behind the plate. From left to right, the outfield was patrolled by George Selkirk (.254, 10, 62), Joe DiMaggio (.324, 32, 140), and Tommy Henrich (.270, 22, 91). All were solid, if not spectacular, defensively and, led by Crosetti's 27 pilfers, the starting lineup combined for 81 stolen bases. On the mound, the Bomber staff combined for a 3.91 earned run average, led by starters Red Ruffing (21–7, 3.32), Lefty Gomez (18–12, 3.35), Monte Pearson (16–7, 3.97), and Spurgeon (Spud) Chandler (14–5, 4.03), and reliever "Fordham Johnny" Murphy (8–2, 4.25).

In the National League, the Chicago Cubs continued their pattern dating back to 1929 of winning the pennant every third year. As the season progressed, it seemed no club was able to assert itself. The defending champion New York Giants dropped from the race in mid-summer when injuries felled pitching ace Carl Hubbell and shortstop Dick Bartell. Pittsburgh, which had led the league on Labor Day by seven games, collapsed in the stretch, as did the Cincinnati Reds. Meanwhile, the Cubs, a nondescript outfit that had stumbled along all year in fourth place, suddenly caught fire in September, winning nineteen of twenty-two games. On September 28, when Gabby Hartnett clouted his famous "homer in the gloamin'" against the league leading Pirates, the Cubs moved past the Buccaneers into first place and finished the season with a 89–63 mark.

Before the World Series began, veteran *Chicago Tribune* baseball expert Irving Vaughan compared the Cubs to the Yankees position by position and concluded that it was "not difficult to figure why the American Leaguers should be the top-heavy favorites."[5] The infield, consisting from third to first of Stan Hack (.320, 4, 67), Billy Jurges (.245, 1, 47), Billy Herman (.277, 1, 56), and James (Ripper) Collins (.267, 13, 61), and catcher/manager Gabby Hartnett (.274, 10, 59), was no match for their Yankee counterparts either in offense, defense, or speed. The outfield of Frank Demaree (.273, 8, 62) in left, Joe Marty (.243, 7, 35), and converted first-sacker Phil Cavarretta (.239, 1, 28) in right were equally inferior to their American League counterparts. On the mound, the Cubs were led by starters Bill Lee (22–9, 2.66), erratic Clay Bryant (19–11, 3.10), Larry French (10–19, 3.81), and Tex Carleton (10–9, 5.41). Ironically, Dizzy Dean (7–1, 1.81), the sore-armed right-hander who had been purchased by the Cubs from the St. Louis Cardinals for $185,000, was considered to have the best chance of stopping the New Yorkers because his slow balls might get the Yanks off stride. Therefore, Vaughan concluded, "nothing could be said in favor of the Cubs' batting ability" and, other than Lee and Bryant, the pitching staff "might prove embarrassing against a club of even ordinary batting strength."[6]

Not only Vaughan ridiculed the weakness of the Cub hurlers. On the night before the Series opened, National League President Ford Frick approached a group of New York writers gathered at press headquarters in Chicago's Congress Hotel. Veteran scribe Frank Graham inquired how Frick's rheumatic arm was feeling. Frick replied innocently, "Great. I can go three innings." "Well," chuckled Graham, "that's more than Hartnett's pitchers will be able to."[7]

In New York, Drebinger did a similar analysis, but, unlike Vaughan, he did not totally eliminate the possibility of an upset. The Chicagoans, he reasoned, had a chance "simply because of the manner in which they won their pennant, and because baseball is a game in which the psychological factor and sheer playing talents are singularly interwoven. Such teams are almost impossible to figure. It was just such a fever that gripped the Cards in 1934, sweeping them past the Giants in the final two days and into a world championship."[8] Drebinger predicted that the Series would be decided by the first two games. "If the New York steamroller flattens Lee and Bryant," he said, "all will be over in four. But if Gabby can crowd just a little more steam into his already overtaxed boilers, a repetition of the sensational seven game Series of 1934 between the Cardinals and Tigers may not at all be impossible."[9]

To compound these deficiencies on the diamond, the Cubs created a poor off-field image by repeating their penchant for what Babe Ruth had called "nickel-nursing." On July 20, Manager Charlie Grimm was fired, even though his club had moved within 5½ games of first, and was replaced by catcher Gabby Hartnett. Unfortunately, Chicago players voted not to grant their former pilot a portion of their post-season money, just as an earlier Cub team had done to deposed skipper Rogers Hornsby in 1932 when, ironically, he had been replaced by Grimm. Players cited Grimm's refusal to congratulate them for clinching the pennant as the reason for snubbing "Jolly Cholly," but most observers seconded Ed Burns of the *Chicago Tribune* who stated the boys simply decided "they needed the dough more than Charlie."[10]

Owner Philip K. Wrigley expressed surprise at the action, stating "it was a trifle short-sighted on the part of the boys."[11] He refused to intercede on Grimm's behalf, however, saying share distribution was "strictly up to the players to decide."[12] As if to defend himself from any hint of collusion, Wrigley indignantly added: "Grimm has done very well financially. The Cubs not only paid him for his time as manager, but also to the end of the year."[13]

Grimm graciously tried to remain above the controversy. "There is no place for an ex-manager in the Series' pool or around the clubhouse," he explained. "I was all for them throughout the season and still am. I said that I wouldn't go to the park except to pick up my stuff. That it wouldn't help the team or Gabby to have me sitting in the grandstand. It's too bad they misunderstood, but I just figured the clubhouse wasn't the place for me."[14]

The former skipper immediately was hired by Chicago radio station WBBM to broadcast Cub and White Sox games. Before the Series began, however, Commissioner Kenesaw Mountain Landis ruled him out of the booth because of his "recent connection with the National League."[15] After Landis rejected appeals on his behalf from National League President Ford Frick and his American League counterpart William Harridge, Grimm departed for his home in St. Louis.[16]

Despite the prophecies of impending doom, Chicago was swept up in World Series frenzy. More than 300,000 cheering fans greeted the Cubs as they participated in a half-mile parade ending at City Hall. A blizzard of confetti rained upon the players as The Windy City put on its biggest public display of affection "since the soldiers came back from the World War."[17] Basking in the emotional outpouring of affection, the always jovial Hartnett proclaimed loudly: "Hell, this is swell!"[18]

Visitors from across the nation teemed into Chicago to attend the opening games of the fall classic and spent an estimated $1,000,000 in hotels, nightclubs, restaurants, and shops, bringing temporary economic relief to businesses still reeling from the depression.[19] Scalpers were asking $40–$50 for single reserved seat tickets for which they had paid $16.50 for a three-game strip, and more than 2,000 fans engaged in a sidewalk vigil the night before the first game in hopes of purchasing $1.10 bleacher seats when the gates opened at 9:30 the next morning.[20] High school youngsters dickered to sell their places in line for $2, other enterprising youths sold boxes to serve as chairs to those in line, and dozens of hucksters peddled hot dogs, ice cream, soda pop, and "Champion Cubs" pennants.[21] Nearly 10,000 curious spectators arrived to watch this scene and stare at those waiting for tickets, which elicited a profound observation from a prospective ticket-buyer resting in a steamer chair: "Yes, I suppose it does seem silly that we're here, but it's not as pointless as all those folks standing around gawking at us as though we are freaks in a sideshow."[22]

As the two teams engaged in their final workouts, each manager was supremely confident. McCarthy exhibited none of his usual reserve, telling reporters he anticipated capturing the prize that had eluded Connie Mack in 1931—winning a third consecutive world championship. "I said the day we clinched the pennant that this club was the best I had ever managed or ever saw," he reminded newsmen. "I'm still holding to that opinion and so I can see only one result. The boys are all in fine shape. The only doubtful one is Spud Chandler, who is having trouble with his right elbow. But our other pitchers are ready, and the hitters figure to break out in an explosive manner. I'm sorry my old friend Gabby Hartnett will have to take it, but we'll be out to clinch the Series as short and snappy as we can."[23]

The florid-faced, thirty-eight year old Hartnett, accompanied by Ford Frick, met reporters as the Cubs left the field after a grueling practice. "We'll win the Series," the Cub leader boldly predicted. "We have the kind of pitching that will fool those Yankee sluggers, and we'll do some slugging ourselves. Sure the Yankees are a wonderful team. They're positively marvelous, and Joe McCarthy in the years he managed the Cubs was my best friend.

He still is, but I'm afraid he's in for an awful jolt when this Series is over."[24] Turning to the league president, Hartnett said earnestly: "I don't promise you a victory, but I will promise you that this will be one of the fightin'est clubs you will ever have seen in a World Series. Win or lose, those Yankees will know they've been in a fight."[25]

A capacity crowd of 43,642, bundled in fur coats and steamer robes to ward off the effects of a gale force north wind, jammed Wrigley Field for the initial battle. Outside the park hundreds of disappointed ticket-seekers gathered on rooftops and balconies of adjacent buildings to catch a glimpse of the diamond action.[26]

Before the pre-game ceremonies, Frick dropped by the Cubs' clubhouse to offer a brief pep talk. He urged them not to believe the myth of Yankee invincibility and reminded the National League champions that the Yankees were an aging club, with Gehrig, Ruffing, Dickey, Selkirk, and Rolfe all in their thirties. "They've let down in September, and it'll be difficult for them to get back," he said, brimming with what he hoped would be contagious optimism. "Play as you did all through August and September, and you can beat them."[27]

By the second inning, the hopes of the Cub faithful were dimmed and the yells of encouragement diminished, as the Yankees tallied two runs on a walk, two singles, and an error by Herman to take at 2–0 lead over the Cubs' ace right-hander Bill Lee. The home team regained a run in the third, but the Yankees matched it in the sixth, making the final score 3–1 in favor of the American Leaguers. The game was completely void of drama and suspense, and one blasé observer wrote: "It was more like a big fellow, very sure of himself, pushing a plucky little fellow around, almost at will—although doing it very humanely."[28]

The Chicagoans managed nine hits off Ruffing, but as "Bugs" Baer noted, "like the hobo cooking waffles over a candle, they couldn't make two at the same time."[29] Observing that the big New York right-hander was aided throughout the game by snappy fielding behind him, Baer said that "the Yanks saved Ruffing like he was a pawn ticket for their only overcoat," and added generously that "outside of the final score the two teams were as well matched as Mrs. Astor's pearls."[30]

In the losers' clubhouse, the Cubs, though defeated, exuded confidence. "The Yanks didn't beat us," shouted Hartnett to the assembled reporters, who were more numerous than normal because McCarthy had closed the Yankee clubhouse to writers. "That kid Crosetti out there at short beat us. He was all over the place. You couldn't get a thing past him. He cut down Hack trying to score the tying run in the third and was in on a couple of double plays. He really played a helluva game."[31] His face tomato red, Hartnett continued his tirade. "What the hell," he screamed. "Those guys had better look better tomorrow than they did today or we'll mop up the field with them. They were just lucky, that's all. They got three cheap runs. A base on balls and an infield boot gave them a couple of runs. They won on three unearned runs in my book. We should have won 1–0."[32] Pausing long enough to light a big black cigar, he pointed a finger at the scribes and said sternly: "Get this, you guys. We'll battle them silly tomorrow. They're more scared than we are."[33]

The Cub pilot then strode into his office and dropped into his chair. Suddenly he rose, muttering to himself: "Oh, I have an announcement to make. I gotta make this one myself." Lumbering into the dressing room, he bellowed: "Dean goes tomorrow!"[34]

As writers rushed to Dean's cubicle, they heard him say to the manager: "I'll flatten 'em, Leo."[35] Turning his attention to the assembled gathering, the former Cardinal ace, exhibiting some of his former braggadocio, said hoarsely: "I said as soon as we captured the National League pennant that me and Bill Lee and Clay Bryant would win the world championship. Me and my brother Paul won it in 1934 with two games apiece, and I lost a game. Bill lost a tough one today, but there's still time for him to take two just like I did in 1934 when there wasn't any travel dates for resting like there is in this Series."[36]

Tony Lazzeri, the thirty-four-year-old veteran who had been released by the Yanks after the 1937 and signed by the Cubs to steady their infield, seconded Billy Herman's claim that the Yankees were "just a lot of lucky stiffs," and also asserted that his old mates were engaged in sign stealing.[37] Although no one in the Cub camp took his charge seriously, as such larceny was not practiced commonly in the National League, it was true.[38] Earle Combs, coaching at third for the Bombers, pilfered Hartnett's signs throughout the game and transmitted them to the batters. For Lee's curve he cupped his hands and yelled, "there it is," "be ready," or gave forth a shrill whistle. For a fastball he used a short phrase built around the word "come," such as "come on, kid" or "here it comes."[39]

A slightly less than capacity crowd of 42,103 disheartened fans paid to see if, as Charles P. Ward of the *Detroit Free Press* wrote, "a tired old guy with a creaky arm, a stout heart, and a canny pitching brain" could keep the Cubs in contention for the world championship.[40] Facing the colorful ex-Cardinal was the Yankees' Lefty Gomez, an erratic, irrepressible southpaw known by his teammates as "El Goofy." This mound match-up prompted John Kieran of the *New York Times* to ponder if the commissioner should have "called on the four Marx Brothers to umpire the game."[41]

Before the game, Old Diz, now a "glum shadow of his once gay and defiant self," spoke with Grantland Rice about his chances.[42] Chilled, even through his warm-up jacket, by the northeast wind that made the temperature seem twenty degrees lower than its actual fifty-three, Dean said: "This kind of weather gets me down. I don't like playin' none in the winter, but I'll chunk 'em in my overcoat if I have to. Goddamn, it's cold."[43] Asked about the condition of his arm, Dean replied, flashing his famous smile: "Well, it's still hangin' on, and maybe it ain't what it used to be — but what is? I only wish I had that ol' fog ball a mine workin' like it used to work, but I guess you can't have everything."[44]

Gabby Hartnett and Dizzy Dean during the national anthem before game two of the 1938 World Series (Chicago Historical Society, ICHi38988).

For seven innings Dizzy's $185,000 sore arm held the mighty Yankees to two runs. He started by tossing them his "mush ball," which Kieran noted, "can be caught by the teeth without any damage to a man's dental equipment."[45] As the game progressed, Dean continued to throw pitches "as soft as a sofa cushion and as big as a watermelon," and when the Yankees did hit the ball "it sounded as though they had kicked a bundle of wet wash."[46] Joe Williams, legendary columnist for the *New York World-Telegram,* wrote of the scene: "First it was astounding, next incredible, then just plain annoying to see Dean take one Yankee hitter after another and make a first class sap out of him."[47] Williams added Dean's slow stuff was keeping the vaunted Bomber sluggers "more off balance than a country store-keeper's books."[48]

Equally annoying to the Yankees was that Dean exhibited some of the old cockiness for which he had become notorious in his glory days. In the fourth inning Old Diz lined a single to left. Standing on first, he turned and shouted to the Yankee dugout: "Why don't you great sluggers get out your press clippin's and read how great you are?"[49] He then led off the seventh with his second hit, a single to right, and taunted the Yankee bench by thumbing his nose at them. Gomez, however, had the last laugh by picking Diz off the bag.[50]

Through seven frames, Dean had faced only twenty-four batters and was nursing a 3–2 lead. Selkirk opened the Yankee eighth with a single to right but was forced at second by Gordon. The next batter was Crosetti. Dean ran the count to 2–2 and thought he had fanned him on the next pitch, but "The Crow" checked his swing on a slow curve barely off the corner of the plate. Crosetti drilled the next offering into the teeth of the wind. Left-fielder Carl Reynolds watched helplessly as the ball dropped into the bleachers for a two-run homer that gave the Yankees a 4–3 lead. As Crosetti rounded third, the heartbroken Dean yelled: "You wouldn't a got a loud foul off me two years ago, Frankie. You'da never done that if I'da had my fastball." Crosetti responded honestly, yelling: "Damned if you ain't right, Diz."[51]

In the ninth, Dean made what Hartnett called his only bad pitch of the day, a fastball, letter-high, to DiMaggio, who crushed the ball over the left-field wall onto Waveland Avenue for a two-run homer.[52] As Hartnett walked toward the mound signaling for Larry French in the bullpen, Dean stood on the mound "drinking in his last draught of glory."[53] The emotional moment that followed was captured by Henry McLemore of the United Press: "Dizzy Dean shuffled down baseball's last mile today. From the sunshine that bathed the pitching mound at Wrigley Field he walked into the shadows of the dugout and on through the green door that leads to the showers. It isn't a very big door. It isn't very high, because the shoulders of the men who pass through it are always weighted and sagging with disappointment. Let it be said that Dizzy Dean walked it gloriously. He went out just as he had come into the big leagues years ago—proud, swaggering, courageous, and unwilling to yield an inch until a better man made him yield it. For every step he took the customers, appreciative of his courage, thundered a salute. Their cheers came up from the steel stands like the roar of an angry surf to break about Dizzy's head like long combers on a tropical reef. Not a man, woman, or child in the big field was seated when the Arkansas boy, with a heart as big as any watermelon he picked as a youngster, ducked his head under the roof of the dugout and — with a tip of his blue cap — disappeared from sight."[54]

Having witnessed a seemingly certain victory stunningly turned into a 6–3 loss, the Cub players trooped into their clubhouse in funereal silence. Dean sat by his locker, his shoulders hunched, as his mates walked by, their expressions paying silent homage. Larry French placed an arm around Dean, and young Phil Cavarretta wrapped his arms around the legendary hurler and said softly: "Pitched a great game, Diz. Sorry we couldn't help you out."[55]

"I just throwed myself out," Dean explained. "I gave them all I had, but it wasn't good enough. My arm started hurtin' in the second. It felt like the bone was stickin' out of the flesh after the sixth inning. They're the luckiest bunch of ball players I ever pitched against. It was my toughest defeat. Until Crosetti walloped that pitch I was sure I could make it. That boy crossed me up. With the count 2–2 I tried to get him to bite on a dinky curve, just a little outside. But though I put the ball just exactly where Gabby and I wanted it to go, he let it go by. Then, when I had to put it in there, he whacked it. But those things happen. You can't help it."[56]

Hartnett, trying to conceal his disappointment, not only lauded Dean, but also bravely encouraged his players. "Diz was in there with nerve and heart," the Cubs' skipper told everyone within earshot. "What a pitcher he'll make next year if his arm responds to treatment through the winter. Say! DiMaggio really hit the hell out of that ball, didn't he? Boy, that was a blow! But never mind. We're not through yet. We're still looking for our first break. We'll still get them."[57] While his words elicited the usual positive responses, most Cub players doubtless secretly agreed with the comment of "Bugs" Baer that they were "deader than fish on a plate," even though the Yanks had afforded them "more chances than a matrimonial agency."[58]

The Yankee dressing room was pandemonium. Yelling and resounding backslaps intermingled with the off-key strains of "East Side, West Side," as the Bombers celebrated their triumph. Gehrig, who was beginning to feel the initial effects of the amyotrophic lateral sclerosis that would claim his life less than three years later, sat quietly next to DiMaggio, each puffing on cigarettes and conversing softly.[59] The usually stoic McCarthy bounded throughout the room offering praise to everyone, especially Dean. "Dean had plenty of heart in there, boys," he shouted, pausing to hug Crosetti. "You can't take that way from him. His arm may be gone, but he was a puzzle to us for seven innings. He pitched a great game until the Yankee power finally found its range. Once we got it — oh, boy! What a team! It was just boom, boom, boom, and then it was over. It was quite a thrill seeing him out there. Diz is different than any pitcher we looked at all season, and even a rank minor leaguer, if he had a funny pitch, could give the best club in baseball a tough time of it for a little while. That was our trouble with Ol' Diz. But we caught up with him."[60]

A reporter interrupted, asking if the Yankee boss was insinuating that Dean was a minor leaguer. "Anything but," McCarthy insisted. "He's got the greatest heart in baseball, and that's no reflection on any other player in the game. I never saw anything like Diz. They tell me he has to have his arm massaged between innings."[61]

The happy-go-lucky Gomez, who gave up nine hits and a walk in seven innings, was pleased with his sixth consecutive post-season victory without a loss. "I didn't pitch a good game," he admitted, "and I was lucky to win. My fast ball wasn't breaking, especially in those early innings."[62] Spying McCarthy, he went over and thanked him for his patience in letting him, as Baer observed, "last longer than a bum's socks."[63] McCarthy dismissed his modest hurler with a wave, saying: "Aw, go on, Lefty. You were great."[64]

The Series moved to New York for the third game, and a relatively sparse crowd of 55,236 turned out in perfect baseball weather to witness Monte Pearson duel with lanky right-handed fireballer Clay Bryant. For four innings it was, as John Kieran said, "as quiet as a night at the North Pole," and "a man who had the forethought to bring along a good book would have been the envy of his neighbors."[65] Perhaps trying to emulate the unexpected early success of Dean, Bryant surprisingly tantalized the free swinging Bombers with an assortment of slow curves. Damon Runyan noted: "He threw a sort of hara-kiri ball. It was a slow thing, and you cannot see how a pitcher can fail to commit pitching suicide throwing it at Joe McCarthy's window breakers."[66]

In the fifth the excitement began. Stan Hack slashed a double, his sixth hit of the Series, off the left-field fence. Herman fanned, but Gordon booted an easy grounder by Cavarretta, and the visitors had runners on the corners. Joe Marty slapped a vicious grounder to Rolfe at third, who fired to Gordon to begin what looked like a sure double play. Gordon took the throw, touched the bag, and fired the ball toward first. However, Umpire Charlie Moran, a former football player and coach of Center College's "Praying Colonels," gave, according to Kieran, "a gallant, but painful, imitation of a man trying to catch a thrown ball with his teeth."[67] While Hack scampered across the plate, players and trainers from both teams rushed into the field to aid Moran, who was oozing blood from his lips. A shaken Gordon later recounted the incident: "I didn't stop to look before wheeling and throwing—I hadn't time. Then I heard the crack as the ball hit Moran in the face, and I saw blood dripping from his mouth. It made me feel funny for a time, but Moran reassured me when he stepped over and shook my hand. I'm awfully sorry it happened, but Moran sure can take it. He never even went down."[68] After a ten minute delay, the game resumed with the Cubs having a 1–0 lead.

In their half of the fifth, Gordon knocked a homer into the left-field stands for the first hit off Bryant, tying the score. From then on, Bryant was "like a milk bottle on a fence rail—all ready to be knocked off."[69] Pearson singled, Crosetti drew a pass, and Rolfe singled in the go-ahead run for the Yanks.

The following frame, the Cubs were, as Baer stated cruelly, "beaten like the whites of eggs in a bakery shop."[70] DiMaggio and Gehrig singled to lead off the inning. Dickey popped out, but Selkirk walked to fill the sacks. Gordon then drove in two more runners with a sharp single to left. Bryant was then removed in favor of thirteen-year veteran right-hander Jack Russell, who retired the side.

Larry French took the mound for the Cubs in the seventh and retired the side in order, but in the eighth Dickey launched a towering drive into the right-field grandstand. French's next pitch was high and hard, barely hitting George Selkirk's bat before it would have beaned him. The ball rolled in front of the plate, and Hartnett fired to first retiring the batter. Selkirk stalked toward the mound and had to be restrained by the umpires, thereby depriving the Cubs, as Kieran jibed, of their only "chance to get a decision over the Yankees."[71] Neither club tallied again, and the Cubs went down for a third straight time 5–2, as Pearson completed a five-hit, nine strikeout performance in which he was "never in more trouble than a sand flea in the Sahara."[72]

Humiliated beyond their worst fears, the Cubs were so enraged after the game that Hartnett barred New York reporters from the locker room for nearly half an hour so his players could vent their emotions in private.[73] Once the door was opened, newsmen were treated to snarling accusations. French asserted that he had not been trying to hit Selkirk and shifted the blame on Earle Combs, charging: "Combs has been stealing our signals and calling our pitches right along, so I thought I'd cross him up. He just called the wrong ball to Selkirk."[74] Jack Russell boldly snarled: "They can't beat us four straight. They couldn't do that even to the St. Louis Browns!"[75]

Hartnett alone tried to show poise, singing merrily in the shower and later announcing sweeping changes in his line-up. "I'm not hitting and neither is Carl Reynolds, so tomorrow Ken O'Dea is going to do the catching and Frank Demaree is going to play left," the manager proclaimed. "If this doesn't help, nothing will."[76] Hartnett added forthrightly: "We're down, but we're not out. You're never out in this game until the last putout is made. The situation looks hopeless, I'll admit, but there's always a chance, and we'll see if we can't take it tomorrow."[77]

The Yankees, by contrast, were in a frenzy of elation. They had parlayed seven hits into five runs, which, as Baer said admiringly, was like "squeezing grape juice out of lemons" and wasting "less than a lady shaking the table cloth into the bread pudding."[78] The humorist added prophetically: "The Yanks haven't got the Series yet, but they sure have torn the cellophane off."[79]

"What is there to say?" grinned McCarthy, amused at Gehrig and DiMaggio engaging in noisy horseplay with their mates. "I think it was a great game to watch. The boys did a little hitting. We had plenty of good pitching. We had everything, including great defensive plays. And they were stopped. I'll throw Ruffing at them tomorrow. We want to get it over with as quickly as possible."[80] Asked whom he would use in the fifth game, McCarthy replied in amazement: "What the hell are you talking about—a fifth game?"[81]

Earle Combs, told about French's remarks regarding theft of signs, roared with glee: "Why Frenchie is crazy to make a crack like that. You don't have to steal signals with the poor stuff he's got!"[82] Selkirk commented on the incident defiantly: "French used some hard words in telling me I wasn't going to hit a homer off him, and I simply told him I'd slap him down and started right at him to make good. I wasn't looking for it, but if he was, he was going to get it."[83]

Ed Barrow, Yankee business manager, when asked if a Yankee sweep would be good for baseball, replied indignantly: "Of course, we'll try to make it four straight. What is more, we'll strengthen the Yankees during the off-season if we can. The theory of baseball, as I always understood it, is to put the best possible team on the field that we can. If the champions of the other league can't beat us, what can we do about it? No one can suggest that we deliberately weaken ourselves. It seems to be that it is up to the others to find a way of stopping us."[84]

During the drills before the fourth game, McCarthy was sitting in the Yankee dugout, vigorously chewing a brand of chewing gum not manufactured by Cubs' owner Philip Wrigley, and speaking casually to reporters. "Some people think we should have won four straight last fall," he said, adding with determination: "Well, I'll not give them any chance to talk this year. Every man on the club is out to make four straight."[85]

For two hours and eleven minutes, the 59,847 Yankee partisans watched their heroes methodically devastate six Cub hurlers, giving Ruffing an easy 8–3 victory to clinch McCarthy's third straight world championship. The Yankees, "like a band of executioners, knew that they had a job to do, and they got it over with as quickly as possible."[86] Starter Bill Lee, who Kieran aptly noted, "enjoyed the same sort of support Czechoslovakia received in another recent crisis," surrendered three Yankee runs.[87] Charlie Root gave up one in his three inning stint, Vance Page permitted two more, and Tex Carleton the final pair. Only Dean and French escaped the Yankee barrage, but they combined for only two-thirds of an inning.

Late in the game, the public address announcer intoned to the fans who joyously were littering the field with scorecards: "Please refrain from throwing paper on the field in justice to the Cubs." Sitting in the press box, Eddie Zeltner of the *New York Daily Mirror* sneered: "In justice to the Cubs the Yankees should have stopped throwing Ruffing."[88]

After the game, McCarthy, who took personal pride in gaining the honor of being the first manager to win three consecutive World Series by defeating the club that had fired him eight years earlier, was supremely happy both for himself and his team. "One of the great things about this club," he said with pride, "is that we had no particularly outstanding star, no player that stood out far above the others. We just had a good club, from the top of the line-up to the bottom, and everybody was hustling every minute. They all did a helluva job."[89]

Pressed by reporters and radio announcers for more comments, the Yankee pilot seemed at a loss for words. "What more can I say?" he responded. "The best club won. We're the greatest ball club ever assembled. I firmly believe this. We had everything and outclassed the Cubs at every turn."[90]

Seeing his old friend and catcher pushing through the crowd to offer congratulations, he added with obvious sincerity: "The only regrettable part of it is that a grand guy like Gabby Hartnett should be the victim."[91] The Cub pilot threw his arm around McCarthy's shoulders, saying: "A better guy in the world couldn't have won it." McCarthy smiled and replied: "Thanks, Leo. But I'm still sorry it had to be you."[92]

Amid the strains of "East Side, West Side" and "For He's a Jolly Good Fellow," Barrow was telephoning Yankee owner Jacob Ruppert. The terminally ill Colonel, who had missed his first World Series since taking sole control of the team in 1923, was reported by Barrow to be overjoyed at the club fulfilling his desire for a sweep of the Cubs.[93] Commissioner Landis breezed in only long enough to mutter to Barrow: "The same old thing. A grand Series. A wonderful victory for a wonderful team."[94]

American League President Will Harridge laughingly denied he was growing weary of the monotony of congratulating winning Yankee teams. "So long as it's our league, it's all right," he assured reporters. "The Yanks were the best team and they won as they should. It was a grand, great Series."[95] Asked if New York's dominance was a threat to baseball, especially in other American League cities, he turned serious and stated firmly: "They talk of the Yankee menace, but a club isn't such a menace when it draws a million fans at home and another million on the road. All we ask is to close the gap between the first and second place clubs. Perhaps the National League has more reason to fear that Yankee menace than we."[96]

Among the exultation was a tragic portent of the future. Lou Gehrig sat wearily in a corner away from the tumult, smoking a cigarette and reflecting on his sub-par .286 average with no runs batted in. "I had a lousy Series," he admitted, adding: "But I think I'll do fine in 1939 — this was just a bad year for me."[97]

Among the Cubs there was much grumbling and bitterness. Billy Herman spoke for most of his mates when he shouted: "They didn't beat us. We beat ourselves. It was a swell Christmas gift. We were terrible. We gave them every damn game. Look each game over. Look at the blunders we made. It was awful. We simply gave it to them!"[98]

Hartnett, Dean, and Ripper Collins disagreed with their fiery field leader. The Cub manager stated the obvious: "The better club won. We tried, but we didn't have it. Not by a long shot."[99] Dean reluctantly conceded that the 1938 Yankees would have defeated his old Cardinal squads, but added: "They never would have beaten us in four straight though."[100] It was the light-hearted Collins, however, who best summed up what really had happened in the Series by wisecracking: "We came, we saw, and now we go home. It's lucky we didn't get hurt!"[101]

Despite his public show of good sportsmanship, Hartnett was fuming over the humiliating display by his team. On the train back to Chicago, he stormed into the club car and screamed at players sitting around a poker table. "Look at yourselves," he bellowed, his face becoming more crimson than its normal florid hue. "You call yourselves ballplayers? You guys were terrible! To let those people beat you four in a row! A lot of you people will not be on this ball club next year. I'm going to try to make some deals, get rid of some of you people. A lot of you are not going to be here next year."[102] Phil Cavarretta later recalled: "We thought he was coming in to build our spirits. This bawling out was tough to take."[103]

The worst aspect of the Series was that, Herman's beliefs to the contrary, it was so lopsided that it brought universal scorn upon the Cubs. John Kieran wrote that the "Cubs had about as much chance with that Yankee gang as Little Red Riding Hood's grandma had when the Big Bad Wolf dropped in for lunch."[104] He added, however, that the Series proved baseball was honest because "if the Cubs had won a game from the Yankees there might have been loud cries of 'fake' and a demand for a federal investigation."[105] Al Schacht, the former Washington Senator pitcher turned diamond comedian, was even more cruel, recalling his earlier comment: "If the Cubs win a game in this Series they should be given a saliva test."[106] *Time* magazine sneered that the Yankees "made the Cubs look as though they would have felt more at home in the Three-I League."[107] John Drebinger of the *New York Times* said simply "it was, in truth, as one-sided a struggle as any Series has ever provided."[108]

Nor were the Cubs spared by their hometown scribes. Ed Burns of the *Chicago Tribune* lambasted the locals for exceeding "all previous flopperoos in the sad series of engagements from which they have just barely escaped alive."[109] His scathing indictment concluded: "The Cubs are the most spectacular home stretch drivers in baseball, but they ought to stay out of all post-season games. A good team might have made a good series against the Yankees, but they were pathetic. They did little that any team from the Class D Evangeline League couldn't have done. If Joe McCarthy hated Gabby Hartnett and had asked his boys to mutilate the Cubs as a matter of revenge, there is no telling what might have happened. But the homicide squad unquestionably would have had plenty of work."[110]

In fairness to the Chicago contingent, what the World Series of 1938 truly demonstrated was the strength of the Yankee franchise. As John Drebinger wrote admiringly: "By an amazing system of organization, the Yanks have built themselves into their present great structure, under conditions wholly permissible. And there is little the seven remaining battered clubs in the American League or the routed National League pennant winners can do about the matter."[111] *The Sporting News* echoed this belief in a sarcastic editorial lampooning the whining of other teams against the might of the world champions: "In considering the question 'how to stop the Yankees?' other major league owners seemingly have only two alternatives—to built up to the champion's strength or to curtail their power by deadening the ball or limiting hits into short field stands to doubles and triples instead of home runs. Any suggestion that the Yankees might be deliberately weakened to aid other clubs represents truly wishful thinking."[112] While it seemed true that, as an awed Chicago fan gasped, "Them guys simply ain't human," or that as one wag stated, "If Hitler wants to prove how tough his Nazis are he should play the Yankees," *The Sporting News* offered hope to the other fifteen major league franchises.[113] "It must be remembered," the "Bible of Baseball" assured followers of the national pastime, "that even supermen are human, and that the longest reign must eventually come to an end. When that time occurs—and fate has a way of unexpectedly intervening—the club that is best prepared to move into the place so long occupied by the Yankees, and the rewards to the newcomer, will be all the greater for having dethroned the mightiest champion of them all."[114] Unfortunately for Cub fans, that honor would not fall to their team.

CUBS VS. TIGERS, 1945

The 1945 American League pennant race was one of the greatest, and most unusual, in league history. The Washington Senators, who were expected by virtually every baseball analyst, as well as their owner, Clark Griffith, to repeat their role as doormats, fashioned an amazing 87–67 campaign. Unfortunately, Griffith, always wanting to pocket extra revenue and never entertaining a thought that his team would challenge for the title, had consented to enough double-headers throughout the season so that the Senators completed their schedule a week ahead of the rest of the league, thereby making Griffith Stadium available to be leased to the Washington Redskins professional football team for the beginning of that squad's regular season. Thus, the Senators were forced to sit helplessly listening to radio broadcasts to learn how their only challengers, the Detroit Tigers, would do in their final four contests.

Going into the last day of the season, the Tigers entered rain-drenched St. Louis for a double-header with the defending champion St. Louis Browns needing only a split to assure the championship. If the Browns swept the twin bill, however, the Senators would be the pennant winners by a half-game. With the Bengals trailing 3–2 in the top of the ninth, Captain Hank Greenberg, who had been discharged from the military on June 14 and resumed playing on July 1, demonstrated that his tour of duty had not diminished his diamond skills by lofting a towering fly into the left-field stands for a grand slam home run, giving the Tigers the flag with an 88–65 mark, the lowest winning percentage (.575) in league history. While Detroit acclaimed this heroic blast, Washington players, who had a reputation for taunting Greenberg with anti-Semitic jibes, grumbled: "Goddamn that dirty Jew bastard, he beat us again."[1]

Manager Steve O'Neill's team without question was the weakest American League representative in the history of the World Series to that date. Irving Vaughan of the *Chicago Tribune* labeled them a "war-born outfit, hence not up to what it took to win pennants in the pre-war days."[2] Arthur Daley of the *New York Times,* doubtless still smarting that the Yankees were not in the Fall Classic, sneered: "The Tigers are frisky ancients who will set an Olympic record for antiquity when they take the field."[3] Even the partisan *Detroit News* grudgingly concurred with those assessments, but added defensively: "This Tiger club of ours is like the child who is not less beloved for being in a lot of trouble. No one calls it a classic nine by older standards, yet it has broken the Detroit record for attendance in a season."[4]

Undeniably the Tigers were a trifle long in the tooth. The infield consisted of three players listed as thirty-two-years-old: slugging first-sacker Rudy York, whose .264 average was bolstered by 18 home runs and 87 runs batted in, league Most Valuable Player Eddie Mayo, a second-baseman who hit .285, with 10 homers and 54 runs driven across the plate, and Jimmy Outlaw (.271, 0, 34) manning third. Shortstop James (Skeeter) Webb, who claimed to be thirty-three years of age but was really two years older, made Outlaw look like Ty Cobb by comparison, hitting a miniscule .199, with no homers and a paltry 21 runs batted in. Thirty-six-year-old catcher Paul Richards batted .256, with 3 round-trippers and 32 runs driven in. The outfield was even more aged, comprising of forty-year-old Roger (Doc) Cramer (.275, 6, 58) trying to cover center, flanked by thirty-four-year-old Greenberg (.311, 13, 60) in left and Roy Cullenbine (.277, 18, 93), a mere babe at thirty, lodged in right. However, as Arthur Daley sagely observed, some of those "ages were akin to what football folk describe as 'program weights' and therefore should be accepted with a generous portion of salt."[5]

The mound corps was considerably more youthful and amassed a sterling 2.99 earned run average, while leading the Junior Circuit in strikeouts (588), saves (16), and shutouts (19). Twenty-four-year-old "Prince Hal" Newhouser, whom Rogers Hornsby, one of the most highly regarded hitters of all time, labeled "one of the greatest pitchers in the last twenty years," followed up his spectacular 1944 season [29–9, 2.22] with another impressive record of 25–9, leading the league in victories, complete games (29), innings pitched (313), strikeouts (212), shutouts (8) and earned run average (1.81).[6] Complementing him in the starting rotation were thirty-year-old Dizzy Trout (18–15, 3.14), thirty-four-year-old Al Benton (13–8, 2.02), and twenty-six-year old, 5'7" Frank (Stubby) Overmire (9–9, 3.88).

The Tigers were also bolstered by the addition of Virgil (Fire) Trucks, who had been discharged from the navy just seven days before the World Series was to begin. The baby-faced twenty-six-year-old right-hander, who had a tiger tattooed on his muscular pitching arm, was lauded by O'Neill as being "faster than Bobby Feller" and the possessor of the finest curve ball he had seen all season.[7]

Following their 1938 pennant-winning campaign, the Cubs had nose-dived into the National League's second-division, finishing fourth in 1939 and fifth in 1940 and 1943, with sixth place seasons in 1941 and 1942. In 1944, the Chicago squad inched up into the fourth spot, but was a staggering thirty games behind the champion St. Louis Cardinals. Thus it was earth-shaking diamond news when the Cubs, led by Charlie Grimm, who took the reins from Jimmie Wilson in May to begin his second tour of duty as the club's manager, compiled a 98–56 mark to nose out the defending world champion St. Louis Cardinals by three games. Like their opponents, the Bruins hardly were a picture of youthful vigor. Stan Hack (.323, 2, 43), a fourteen-year veteran at age thirty-six anchored the infield at third, while shortstop Roy Hughes (.261, 0, 8) and second-sacker Don Johnson (.302, 2, 58) were both thirty-two. First-baseman Phil Cavarretta, still a youthful twenty-nine, led the Senior Circuit with a .355 average to go with 6 home runs and 97 runs batted in. Behind the plate was thirty-year-old Mickey Livingston (.254, 2, 23). In the outfield the Cubs were relatively youthful for a wartime team with thirty-year-old Bill (Swish) Nicholson (.243, 13, 88) stationed in right, rifle-armed twenty-four-year-old sensation Andy Pafko (.298, 12, 110) patrolling center, and twenty-seven-year-old Harry (Peanuts) Lowrey (.283, 7, 89) covering left.

The strength of the "Grimmlins," as the Cubs were affectionately dubbed in honor of their popular banjo-strumming pilot, was pitching, as the moundsmen led their league with eighty-six complete games and a team earned run average of 2.98. Even veteran baseball scribe and fierce Tiger loyalist H.G. Salsinger of the *Detroit News* grudgingly admitted on the eve of the Series: "While the Chicago Cubs have no pitcher as good as Harold Newhouser, they have five pitchers who, on form, are better than anyone else on the Detroit staff."[8] The ace of the Bruins was twenty-seven-year-old right-hander Hank Wyse (22–10, 2.68), who was joined in the starting rotation by thirty-six-year-old Claude Passeau (17–9, 2.46), Paul Derringer (16–11, 3.45), and Ray Prim (13–8, 2.40), both thirty-eight years of age, and twenty-nine year-old Hank Borowy (11–2, 2.13), who had been acquired in midseason from the New York Yankees for $100,000. Available for relief duty were Paul Erickson (7–4, 3.32) and Bob Chipman (4–5, 3.50), both of whom were in their late twenties, and thirty-nine-year-old Hy Vandenberg (7–3, 3.49).

When the National League champions and their wives arrived in Detroit for the Series opening games, they discovered that the Tiger management, citing lack of adequate hotel accommodations, had booked them aboard two passenger steamers moored in the Detroit River. Not realizing they were the butt of a joke, some of the Chicagoans expressed outrage, with one angry player telling writers: "We don't ask for much, but you'd think after winning a pennant we'd at least be able to sleep in a regular hotel."[9] Hank Wyse recalled: "Phil Cavarretta and his wife, my wife and I, Peanuts Lowrey and his wife, we didn't stay on that boat. The room was a big as a small bathroom, couldn't even get our bags in there. My wife didn't like it. Good Christ, I thought it would be fun. Cavarretta called me and said, 'Let's get out of here. Let's go. We're not gonna stay in this tub.' He got hold of [traveling secretary] Bob Lewis and told him, 'If we don't get a hotel room, we ain't gonna play.'"[10] Lewis quickly discovered that the Tigers had reserved rooms at for them at the Book-Cadillac Hotel, the Detroit Leland, the Statler, and the Fort Shelby, but even after they were comfortably ensconced in their official quarters the players failed to appreciate immediately their humorous welcome to the Motor City.[11] By the end of the evening, however, the victimized athletes were laughing and referring to themselves as the "Yacht Club Boys."[12] As the two teams took batting and fielding practice the day prior to the opening game at Briggs Stadium, which glistened under a new $30,000 coat of green paint, the temperature hovered in the upper forties and snow flurries swirled in the breeze.[13] Affable Steve O'Neill, a broad smile brightening his round face, met with reporters. "My club is ready," he began predictably. "The boys are in shape physically and mentally. I feel confident we have the pitching and the hitting to beat the Cubs. Newhouser, Overmire, and Trucks will be my three starters for the local games. I'll save Paul Trout for the first game in Chicago."[14] Asked if he was planning to have Newhouser make three starts, O'Neill started to reply but was interrupted by Eddie Mayo. "What do you mean three times?" the infielder yelled. "How can we use Hal three times when we're going to take those Cubs four straight?"[15]

Paul Richards, returning from a chat with Cub reserve catcher Dewey Williams, whom he described as "one of my pups when I was managing the Atlanta Crackers a few years back," echoed the confidence of his manager and teammate.[16] "We will beat the Cubs sure as I am a Waxahachie, Texas newspaperman," he assured his listeners, "because when you've got the pitching variety and talent that we've got, you're a mighty tough customer."[17]

Grimm strolled out to watch the Tigers practice. Roy Cullenbine, the switch-hitting outfielder, spied the Chicago pilot and began lofting drives into the right-field stands. After seeing him hit what seemed to be "a thousand in there," Grimm, running his fingers through his graying brown hair, bellowed to the Tigers: "Hey! Does that Cullenbine think he is amusing me, or is he going to do all your batting?"[18]

Joking with writers later in the clubhouse, Grimm, perhaps remembering the 1935

World Series, strove mightily to refrain from making a flat prediction of victory. "We'll play a game every day," he said with a smile, "and we'll try to win it. Beyond that I do not care to go."[19] Then casting aside his uncharacteristic restraint," "Jolly Cholly" gushed: "I know my boys can beat the Tigers. I don't think it will be a walkover, but I think we'll finish it in six games."[20]

Starting hurler Borowy savored his role. "I always like to face clubs I can beat," he told reporters in a matter-of-fact manner. "I think you'll find that I've beaten this club pretty often. I've won eleven and lost three against Detroit."[21]

Suddenly all the writers' attention was diverted as Dizzy Trout barged into the room. Beaming, the Tiger pitcher acted as a one-man welcoming committee, shaking hands and patting his opponents on their backs.[22] Taken aback by the brashness of the Dizzy Dean imitator, the disconcerted Cubs ended the press conference and headed for the showers.[23]

After eight consecutive days of rain and spurts of snow, the weather for the initial contest was, according to a local scribe, "as near perfect as any fan has any right to demand in this latitude in this time of the year."[24] As the 54,637 fans crowded toward their seats, a forty-five piece band played, beginning its concert appropriately with "It Ain't Gonna Rain No More" and concluded with the crowd lustily harmonizing in "Take Me Out to the Ball Game."[25]

Before throwing the ceremonial first pitch to Tiger catcher Paul Richards, baseball's

Crowds gathering outside Briggs Stadium for opening game of 1945 World Series (courtesy State Archives of Michigan).

new commissioner, United States Senator Albert B. "Happy" Chandler of Kentucky, addressed fans both in attendance and listening to the game via national and international radio broadcasts. After conveying the regrets of President Harry S Truman, an avid baseball devotee, for not being able to attend any of the games because of his post-war administrative obligations, the Commissioner said solemnly: "No matter who wins the Series, the people are the winners. This is one of the things we fought a war for. Giving us our first World Series in peacetime in four years."[26]

Once the contest started, Tiger faithful received an unexpected jolt as Newhouser was greeted rudely by the visitors. After retiring leadoff man Stan Hack, Johnson singled, stole second, and after Lowrey flied out, moved to third on Cavarretta's infield single. Johnson scored on a passed ball that bounded far from Richards, and Cavarretta raced all the way to third. Pafko was given an intentional pass, and Nicholson tripled off the right-field wall, driving home both runners. Livingston singled Nicholson across the plate but was caught attempting to steal second, ending the threat, but not until the Cubs had presented Borowy a 4–0 cushion.

After retiring the side in order in the second, "Prince Hal" was pummeled from the hill in the third. Johnson led off with a double over the aged Cramer's head in center, moved to third on a sacrifice, and scored on Cavarretta's single to center. Pafko drove in another tally with a double to left-center, which got past Cramer's outstretched glove. Livingston's single drove in a third Cub run and brought O'Neill to the mound to invite Newhouser to take an early shower and turn the ball over to Al Benton. On Benton's first offering, the over-eager Cubs once again ran themselves out of an inning when Livingston was thrown out trying to pilfer second. However, by that time the Cubs had so dramatically demonstrated their obvious superiority in every aspect of the afternoon's battle that a press box wag wisecracked snidely: "Only an atomic bomb can save the Tigers."[27]

Jim Tobin relieved Benton to begin the fifth and, after holding the Cubs scoreless for two innings, was rocked in the seventh for a home run by Cavarretta. Pafko followed with a single to center, stole second, moved to third on a passed ball, and scored the Cubs' ninth and final run on a single by Nicholson. Meanwhile, Borowy was spinning a masterful six-hit shutout, striking out four and issuing five passes.

In the Chicago dressing room post-game celebration, the forty-eight-year-old Grimm had a grin from ear-to-ear and was whistling with boyish enthusiasm. Embracing his former Pittsburgh teammate, legendary shortstop Walter (Rabbit) Maranville, Grimm shouted: "Well, we did it! It's a nice cold day to get nine runs, isn't it?"[28] Plopping onto a stool, still shivering from the frigid temperature, the Chicago manager answered reporters' questions about his team's triumph. "The break for us came when Cavarretta beat out that hit to Mayo in the second after Johnson's steal. After that it was easy. Newhouser was in the hole several times, and we just hit every time he got his fastball over — and how our boys love that fastball!" he raved, adding diplomatically: "Nevertheless, Newhouser's a helluva pitcher, boys. Don't take that away from him."[29]

Borowy, the slim Fordham University graduate who had lamented before the game that he was less effective in cold weather, told reporters: "I couldn't stay warm. For five innings, I just couldn't seem to get my arm loose. After that I felt warmer, but I didn't stay warm, and my arm was never loose. It was a great game to win though. The boys sure pounded that ball, didn't they?"[30]

The Cub hurler then singled out sixty-five-year-old trainer Andy Lotshaw as the real hero of the day. Between innings Lotshaw soaked bricks in hot water and then placed one on the pitcher's arm and another under his feet for warmth as Borowy huddled on the bench while his mates were at bat.[31] Anticipating another cold day, Lotshaw, with his upper and lower dentures safely stuffed in his hip pocket, joyously screamed in the dressing quarters: "Where are them bricks? Get me them bricks! I'll need 'em tomorrow!"[32]

The Tigers stormed into their clubhouse with fire in their eyes. Newhouser sat on a stool in front of his locker in a state of disbelief. Circling like vultures armed with microphones and note pads, the media representatives began shouting questions at the Tiger ace. Newhouser rose and addressed them with unexpected, and refreshing, candor. "I feel terrible. I simply didn't know how to pitch to them," he confessed. "They're all new to me. You can't throw to those guys simply from advice. All I knew about them was from what others told me. You can't necessarily expect to handcuff a fellow with a low fastball just because another pitcher tells you he did it once. You gotta pitch against 'em to know. I thought I had plenty of stuff and my control was all right, too. If I had gotten past the first inning, things would have been different, but Johnson stealing second was one of those things that started them off and there was no stopping them."[33] His dejection turning to determination, he added: "After looking at those hitters, I'll be a lot better pitcher against the Cubs the next time. The next time I'll get away to a good start, and I'll beat those Cubs yet. I'm not that bad!"[34]

Paul Richards, the genial and usually sure-handed backstop who suffered the indignity of permitting two passed balls and a like number of stolen bases, shouldered much of the blame for the defeat. Most of all, he resented Johnson's steal of second. "He never should have got away with that," Richards said glumly, sitting in front of his locker peeling off his socks. "Shucks, he had no start on me. I would have caught him had I made a good throw. There were three times we could have gotten off the hook in the first inning, and if we had it would have been a different ball game. There was that stolen base, that scratch hit by Cavarretta because Mayo underestimated his speed and was playing too deep, and Nicholson's triple which just eluded Cullenbine's grasp. But, shucks, we didn't guarantee we'd beat 'em in four games.[35]

O'Neill, respected for his down-to-earth approach to baseball, made no effort to offer a profound excuse for his team's shellacking. "There is nothing much you can say about a 9–0 beating,' he conceded, forcing a weak smile through the cloud of smoke from his cigar as he sat in his tiny wire cage office. "They just clubbed us plenty. They deserved to win, and they had the class today. They hit the ball with men on bases, and we didn't. That's the answer."[36] Running his hand over his graying black hair, the fifty-four-year-old former catcher added the timeworn philosophical observation of a manager whose team has just been trounced: "It's better than losing by one though. When you blow a close one you sit up all night going over one play or another that might have changed the result. You blame yourself for not doing this or not doing that. You curse a bad break here and there. Sometimes it haunts you for days. But when you blow 9–0 you just write it off as one of those things."[37]

O'Neill's spirits rose and he burst into laughter when "Deacon Bill" McKechnie, manager of the Cincinnati Reds, who had been patsies for the Cubs throughout the National League season, entered the room and put his arm around the Tiger skipper's shoulders. McKechnie whispered loudly, in mock confidentiality: "Cheer up, Steve. You've only lost one game to those guys. They beat us twenty-one times."[38]

Returning to his suite in the Detroit Leland Hotel, O'Neill was heartened further by reading the observations of two of his fellow American League pilots. Joe McCarthy of the Yankees warned New York scribe Dan Daniel: "Don't quit on Detroit. It will win the Series. It will win because it has Virgil Trucks, and it will win with Greenberg."[39] The astute eighty-two-year-old manager of the Philadelphia Athletics, Connie Mack, dismissed the final score and chose instead to analyze the game hurled by Borowy. "I don't think Borowy pitched a good game," declared the American League patriarch. "He was in trouble the first six innings and only superlative fielding saved him. I still have faith in the Tigers."[40]

Many sportswriters, however, did not share in such sanguine prospects for the Detroiters. Bob Murphy of the *Detroit Times* bitterly described the day's fiasco in his column. "Too much speed. Too much hitting. Too much ball club," he groused. "That about explains why the men of Jolly Cholly Grimm made our Tigers about as limp as a 'tiger rag.' Certainly no team ever looked worse in a World Series game. This I can say without fear of contradiction. Detroit will *not* get worse. You saw them scrape the bottom of the barrel in the opener. If the men of Steve O'Neill didn't get all the bad baseball out of their systems in that game, then we really are in for something and you can start for your favorite duck hunting blind."[41] H.G. Salsinger echoed his intra-city rival, noting: "Compared with the Cubs, the Tigers are slow, sluggish, and often slovenly in running the bases. They are satisfied with one base, while the Cubs take two. The Tigers, not infrequently, reduce two-base hits to singles, while the Cubs stretch singles into two-baggers."[42]

The cruelest analysis came from acerbic syndicated columnist Bill Corum, who said that the Tigers "run up and down like wooden horses on a slow merry-go-round."[43] Noting the Bengals' age and erratic play, Corum wrote cynically: "The Tigers looked to me like tigers with five legs, which is one too many according to the wild animal books. One of which legs was forever getting in the way. If the Tigers had been any slower Washington would have to turn the clocks back to wait for them. The Tigers looked as if they were playing in sticky molasses against Brother Grimm's spirited Grimmlins. Like when Rudy York, who practically would have hit the tower of the Empire State Building with a shot to start the sixth inning and finally wound up on first base in as magnificent a burst of speed as we've seen since Man O' War retired. That smash went 365 feet to deep left-center, which means by simple arithmetic that if Rudy could have hit one 730 feet he would have gotten to second. This being the Motor City, I guess that York must have been waiting for the new cars to come rolling off the line. Right now, Stephen O'Neill had better be lookin' around for a new clutch and high-speed forward for his Tiger bandwagon. It can stand a 'souping up.'"[44]

The second game, played under a cloudless sky with a sixty-degree temperature, pitted two pitchers boasting American Indian heritage, Hank Wyse and Virgil Trucks, the latter having been on the mound for only six innings of major league ball in the past two seasons because of military service. Though outwardly festive, the crowd of 53,636 had, as John Drebinger of the *New York Times* noted, "an ominous feeling that the Cubs would repeat their performance of the previous afternoon."[45]

For three innings the contest was scoreless, but sloppy Tiger fielding gave the visitors the lead in the fourth. With one out, Cavarretta looped a soft liner to right-center, which neither Cramer nor Cullenbine made an effort to catch. Seeing this nonchalance, Cavarretta turned what should have been an out into an easy double. "Swish" Nicholson's single to right brought Cavarretta home with the initial run of the contest.

With two out in the fifth, the hometown heroes finally demonstrated the offensive power for which they were known during the regular season. Light-hitting shortstop Skeeter Webb singled to left after two were out. Inexplicably, this seemed to rattle Wyse, who proceeded to walk Mayo on four straight pitches. Cramer followed with a line shot over third, driving in the Tigers' first run of the Series and sending Mayo to third. As Hank Greenberg left the on-deck circle, Jim Tobin raced from the dugout and intercepted the big slugger.

Tobin, who had spent his entire career with Pittsburgh and Boston in the National League before coming to Detroit in mid-season, whispered to Greenberg that Wyse always threw curve balls in situations similar to this.[46]

Wyse, who before the game had confided to Chicago writers that "I think I know how to pitch to Hank," tossed up a hanging curve, high and inside, which Greenberg walloped 365 feet into the lower left-field stands, giving the Detroiters a three-run lead.[47] Watching Mayo, Cramer, and Greenberg parade around the bases, John Drebinger wrote: "It mattered not how slow-footed the Bengals were at this particular moment. They could have walked backwards and still made it."[48] Trucks blanked the Cubs the rest of the way, making the final score 4–1 and prompting one press box wit to state that his headline would read: "Poetic Victory — Virgil and Homer."[49]

In the jubilant Detroit clubhouse, writers mobbed Greenberg and Trucks. After posing hugging his pitcher, Greenberg was unusually talkative. "If I said I got a thrill out of that home run, it would be an understatement, but this ain't my biggest day in baseball, boys," he said with a broad smile. "That will come after we win three more games. I hope all you guys are back calling on me tomorrow."[50] Remembering all the criticism heaped upon the squad after the previous day's debacle, he added, with a tinge of sarcasm: "We wanna make a Series out of it. Maybe it'll be a good Series after all."[51]

Trucks, who fulfilled his pre-game pledge that "this is one ball game I'm gonna win," was overjoyed.[52] "It hardly seemed possible that in a World Series box score you'd see 'winning pitcher — Trucks.' It's my first full game since last June when I was pitching for a navy team in Guam," he said in his heavy Alabama drawl. "Gosh, I still wake up at six in the mornin' and I just waits for someone to shake me outta the sack. I felt strong all the way through, and I was bearin' down too much to get nervous. In fact, I'm ready to go out there at 'em again right now. I was relyin' on control all the time, tryin' to get the ball exactly where Paul gave the target. But it was Hank's home run that did it. After that I had no worries. It's the one time that the army helped the navy!"[53] This wisecrack led Arch Ward of the *Chicago Tribune* to remark that the "Cubs are not the first strong team to learn you can't whip Uncle Sam's army and navy or the men who have made them the greatest fighting forces the world has known."[54]

Richards muscled his way through the writers to embrace his batterymate. Then he lightheartedly explained why Trucks deserved so much praise. "Say, he doesn't even know the names of some of his teammates yet because he hasn't been back long enough to get acquainted," Richards said admiringly. "Another fellow in his spot would hesitate about taking such an important job, but he said, 'Give me the ball.' That's just plain courage."[55]

The Cubs dressed quietly in their somber quarters. Wyse was downcast, lamenting bitterly: "The pitch Greenberg hit wasn't even over the plate. I expected him to let it go past, but instead he knocked me out of a chance to win my first World Series game."[56] Stan Hack, despite getting three hits in as many times at bat, said that Trucks was simply too good. "He was awfully fast," Hack said, shaking his head. "Just as fast as Bob Feller when I looked at him. He just didn't give us any good balls to hit."[57]

Grimm tried to remain jovial, bellowing to his men: "Tomorrow's another day, just like yesterday. Today's only today."[58] The Cub pilot then tossed a bouquet to Trucks. "From where I stood on the third-base coaching line, I thought he was faster than any pitcher we faced in the regular season. It's the fastest stuff I've watched all year. He had good stuff all the way, and he didn't miss that plate often, did he? When you go up against pitching like that — well, you just have to wait for another day."[59]

Trainer Andy Lotshaw, the self-appointed team spokesman, issued the day's best quote.

"We'll still beat them guys easy," blurted the near septuagenarian. "You can hear their bones creak when they run to first. Hell, they're all older than I am!"[60]

As the perfect ending for his not-so-perfect day, Grimm was berated in the lobby of his hotel by several players' wives about the poor seats they had in Briggs Stadium. Making the best of a situation over which he had no control, Grimm tried to laugh the crisis away, telling eavesdropping scribes: "One of the wives told me that during the game a man came by in an airplane and asked her the score. She yelled back, 'Fly a little lower, mister, find out for yourself, and then let me know. You at least can go below the clouds. I can't.'"[61]

Later that evening at a party honoring Grantland Rice, the dean of Detroit sportswriters, E.A. Batchelor, who had been covering baseball in the city for nearly four decades, was asked to comment on the current World Series. "It's a freak Series, and don't be surprised if there isn't a freak ending," he predicted. "In this Series, it is Steve O'Neill's son-in-law, Skeeter Webb, who is among the top Tiger hitters. Whoever heard of a relative coming through anytime? But here's a relative, supposedly the weakest Tiger of all, setting the pace. Don't be surprised if tomorrow Stubby Overmire goes out and pitches a no-hitter or a perfect game. He'll toss the soft stuff at the Cubs and they'll probably think he's still taking his practice pitches and refuse to take their bats off their shoulders. Yes, by all means, this Series has got to have a freak ending, what with the Tigers hitting doubles and getting singles and the Cubs hitting singles and getting doubles."[62]

The third game was also played in Detroit because federal travel regulations limited the major leagues to just one change of locations.[63] Included in the 55,500 spectators jammed into Briggs Stadium to watch Claude Passeau match curves with Overmire were nearly nine hundred wounded American soldiers who were patients at Percy Jones Hospital in Battle Creek. The GIs had been promised seats, but it was learned the day before the game that, through an error, none had been reserved. The *Detroit News* and its radio affiliate WWJ put out the appeal: "Who will give up their seats for the ball game so that a wounded veteran can see it?"[64] The response was overwhelming, with most donors stating a similar refrain: "I've got a boy in the service, and I couldn't enjoy the game if I knew that some wounded veteran could use my seat."[65] By mid-morning of game day so many tickets had been turned in that wounded servicemen from hospitals in the Detroit area also could attend.[66] Even Commissioner Chandler's wife donated her ticket and those of her two daughters so that three amputees could view the contest from the Commissioner's box.[67]

During the warm-ups, the diminutive Overmire posed for photographers next to massive, 6'1", 220 pound Rudy York. Spying the duo, Cub coach Red Smith hollered good-naturedly: "Who's that with you, Rudy? Your little son?"[68] Across the diamond, Passeau, a lanky Mississippi right-hander who owned 640 acres on which he grew tung nuts, from which high-grade oil was manufactured, was talking happily about the cool, damp, overcast weather. "I sure like this," the most prosperous businessman in the major leagues drawled to Arthur Daley of the *New York Times*. "I pitched at least ten games in weather like this and did pretty well."[69]

Once the contest began, Batchelor's prophecy seemed to be coming true, but for the wrong pitcher. For the second consecutive afternoon, both combatants entered the fourth in a scoreless deadlock. Leading off that frame, Lowrey doubled off the left-field wall for only the second safety off Overmire. Cavarretta laid down a bunt, and, although Lowrey would have been an easy out at third, Overmire, perhaps overly worried about the Cubs' highly touted speed, opted to toss to first to retire the batter.[70] Pafko drew a pass, and a Texas League single by Nicholson drove in Lowrey and advanced Pafko to second. After Livingston was retired, Roy Hughes dropped another bloop hit over short, sending Pafko across the plate. The Cubs added another tally in the seventh off Al Benton on Passeau's sacrifice fly, making the score 3–0.

Meanwhile, Passeau, keeping the Tiger hitters off balance by constantly tugging at his cap, hitching up his pants, rubbing his hand on his shirt front, and juggling the ball in his glove, spun a mound masterpiece, permitting the Bengals only a lone hit, a second inning single by York.[71] What made this World Series one-hitter, previously accomplished only by Ed Reulbach of the Cubs, all the more astonishing was that Passeau's career had seemed threatened before the season when he had to undergo surgery to remove calcium chips from his pitching elbow.

In the raucous Cub locker room, Grimm led the cheers, singing: "Mr. Chips, Mr. Chips, chips in his elbow, what a ball game he pitched."[72] Embracing the thin, almost frail-looking twirler, whose uniform number thirteen defied superstition, in a bearhug, Grimm cut loose with a shrill two-fingered whistle that reverberated through the room. "Every time Passeau rattles his right elbow it sounds like china in a dish boiler," Jolly Cholly joked. "But what a game he pitched. A one-hitter, wow! He looked marvelous. I was saving him. He hadn't pitched since September 26, and that [eight-day] rest prepared him for the supreme test. We beat 'em thanks to those two dipsy-doodlers by Nicholson and Hughes. Just a couple of cuties. Both of those hits together wouldn't have made the fence, but they did the trick. Boys, we're on our way."[73]

Passeau was characteristically quiet in his moment of glory, showing reporters his swollen, inflamed, knotted elbow. "That knot didn't bother me at all," he said softly. "That stuff the trainers rubbed on it had it heated all afternoon and kinda hot. I threw a lot of forkballs at 'em, and they didn't do much with 'em. I never knew I had a one-hit game. I only wanted to win, and I'm tickled I did it the way I did. I had good control out there all afternoon and felt fine. York hit a fastball that time he singled. I was trying to shoot one past him. Of course, the best thing I had out there was fast outfielders making all those plays behind me."[74] Asked about the charge that he threw a spitball, Passeau shrugged, and replied innocently: "Aw, the Tigers kept hollerin' at me, 'Get him a bucket of water,' but I couldn't throw a spitter even if it was legal. That's just the way my fastball acts— it sails or sinks six inches to a foot."[75]

"Hey, boys, you won't get much more out of Passeau," shouted reserve infielder Billy Schuster, sitting at the adjoining locker. "Right now he's used up about a week's worth of conversation."[76]

In the Tigers' lair, the Detroit batsmen sat in stunned silence after being horse-collared for the second times in three home games, while losing pitcher Overmire was disconsolate. "It's tough to lose on those kind of hits," he said bitterly. "That big Nicholson caught an outside curve on the end of the bat. He just got a teeny piece of it for a blooper that just escaped Skeeter. That was the one that hurt me. I was out of the inning otherwise. That hit of Hughes was a slider just off his fist. This was my big chance, and I'll probably never get into another World Series. It's gonna be hard to forget about those two cheap hits."[77]

O'Neill patted Overmire on the back before meeting the press. "It was too much Passeau, that's all," the Tiger manager said grimly. "He pitched a marvelous game. He had swell control. His slider worked nicely, and he was fast. They got a couple of bloop hits and that decided it. But don't forget that Frankie pitched a good ball game today, too. It was a tough one for him to lose, but when you get only one hit, and a single at that, you can't have much to say."[78] Hearing one of his players sneer that Passeau "didn't have nothin' but a fastball," O'Neill turned and silenced the grouser, yelling: "From where I stood on the third-base coaching line it looked as if he did all right with just the fastball."[79]

Paul Richards, ever the optimist, attempted to put the humiliating performance into perspective. "Had we won today, would that have won the Series for us?" he asked rhetorically. "Of course it wouldn't. They won, but they haven't got the Series. Not by a long shot. We'll get 'em tomorrow."[80]

On that upbeat note, the Tigers joined the Cubs on the teams' special train to Chicago to conclude the Series. Before the fourth contest, amid festivities replete with marching bands and scantily clad drum majorettes, movie actress June Haver bolted from the stands, rushed onto the field, and planted a kiss on the cheek of Manager Grimm and then on that of bashful Hank Borowy.[81] Peering at the scene from his press box perch, serious-minded Arch Ward pondered over such a lack of propriety in the national pastime's greatest spectacle. "It was good clean fun and all that," he conceded, "but we wonder what would happen if Grimm and Borowy dashed onto a set at Twentieth Century Fox studio and reversed the procedure?"[82]

The 42,923 fans were also delighted at the spectacle of local tavern owner Billy Sianis parading a goat around the stands and into the box seat section of Wrigley Field. He had purchased a ticket for the animal, which wore a blanket on which was pinned a sign reading "We've got Detroit's goat."[83] Much to the displeasure of the spectators, ticket or not, stadium authorities refused to permit the goat to remain at the game or to be admitted in the future, and amid a shower of booing, Sianis and his goat were escorted out of Wrigley Field.[84]

As had become the fashion in the two preceding contests, the rival hurlers, Dizzy Trout for the Tigers and the Cubs' Ray Prim, permitted no scoring for the first three frames, which were played under dark, threatening skies. In the fourth, however, both the sun and the Tigers broke through. The visitors bunched a walk and four hits to drive four runs across the plate and Prim to an early shower. That cushion was more than sufficient for Trout, who was seeking to gain a measure of revenge for when, as a teenager, the Cubs had rejected him in his bid to become their batting practice pitcher.[85] The "quaint Hoosier of a few million words," as Ed Burns of the *Chicago Tribune* depicted Trout, cruised to an easy 4–1 victory and fulfilled his pre-game pledge to his teammates that "if you give me four runs, I'll win in a breeze."[86]

The Detroit right-hander kept the Cub batters off balance with unusual deliberation, interrupting play several times either to knock mud off his spikes or wipe perspiration from his eyeglasses.[87] However, as John Drebinger aptly noted: "If there were times when Dizzy seemed to have difficulty seeing the Cubs, the National Leaguers seemed unable to see Trout scarcely any of the time, and, as they had no spectacles of their own to wipe, they just groped their way hopelessly to the end."[88] In fact, Dizzy was so leisurely between pitches that it reminded veteran scribes of the 1935 Series, between the same two teams, when Tiger hurler Alvin Crowder stood on a mound several minutes watching an airplane lazily circle the field.[89]

To cap off his six-strikeout, five-hit performance, which would have been a shutout had York not made a wild throw in the sixth inning which permitted an unearned run to score, the irrepressible Trout raced to the plate after the final out to shake hands first with batterymate Richards and then home plate arbiter Jocko Conlan, complimenting the later for calling "a swell game."[90] Emulating the antics of Dizzy Dean, Trout tipped his cap to the crowd, chatted with folks in the front row boxes, and even extended his hand to several non-receptive Cub players before leaving the field.[91]

Upon reaching the dressing room, Trout's gloating continued unabated. "I guess we showed 'em something," he shouted to reporters. "What's that they've been sayin' about ol' Diz not havin' his stuff anymore. He had plenty out there today! I threw my 'atom ball' today. You know. You just throw it at 'em and they can't to a thing with it. Now don't start laughin' when I say this, but I was thinkin' out there. I was disappointed though. Some bird in Detroit offered a dozen nylon stockings to any Tiger hittin' a home run. I told my wife, 'Honey, every time I get to bat I'll take one full swing for you, the fence, and the nylons. After that you'll be on your own.' No luck, and it looks as if ol' Diz won't get another chance to swing."[92]

Pausing long enough to finish his bottle of beer and kiss a baseball for a photographer, Trout resumed his oration. "It was a particular thrill for me to win this one in my second World Series start. Last time in a World Series I got to the third inning in 1940 when the Cincinnati club knocked me out," he babbled excitedly. "Today, however, it was different. They never bothered me. I had good stuff and was strong all the way. The Cubs are a good club though. I don't think they're as tough as the Yankees, but they have power. The big thing is that we beat 'em. Now we'll beat 'em in the Series, too. Just wait and see!"[93]

"Nice work fellas," roared O'Neill, trying to be heard over his pitcher's yapping. "Looks as if we've got 'em now. Let's go out and finish it."[94] Turning to reporters, he added confidently: "We've got the edge 'cause I've got my two best pitchers ready for 'em. It's TNT from here on. Trout beat 'em today, and now the Cubs must be doing some serious thinking about facing Newhouser and Trucks in a row. They are the two best pitchers I know of."[95]

As usual, Grimm assumed his cheerleader role. "Up and at 'em, men," he urged as he entered the clubhouse, pausing to frown at the good luck horseshoe of yellow flowers sent to the Cubs from the manager's Elks Club in Washington, Missouri. "Hang in there. It will be Borowy and more base hits tomorrow."[96] Moving to his stool to start disrobing, Grimm offered reporters his analysis of the game. "Trout was very good. He was fast, at least fast enough to beat us, but our pitching wasn't so bad either. If we had got some hits, we would've been all right. The other fellows just played good ball. You can't take that away from them. I still think it will be a six-game Series, and I think we'll win."[97]

Equally gracious was Prim, who forthrightly explained his early exit. "The trouble was that they were hitting 'em where nobody wasn't," he said in his folksy manner. "The Tigers were supposed to hit, and I was supposed to keep 'em from hitting. They did, and I didn't."[98]

The fifth contest, which pitted Newhouser against Borowy, was played before 43,463 spectators basking under sunny skies and enjoying a warm, stiff breeze blowing out toward center-field. During pre-game drills, Dizzy Trout was holding court in the Tiger dugout. "There's nothin to it," the pop-off artist told writers in his rapid-fire fashion. "Newhouser will win today, Trucks tomorrow, and we're all on our way home. We're a cinch."[99]

Although the score was tied 1–1 after five frames, the contest devolved into a diamond comedy. Bill Corum, whose cynicism was exceeded only by his acerbic wit, captured the essence of the tragic-comedy, writing: "Baseball hasn't produced anything as funny since the delightful Brooklyn Dodgers of Uncle Robbie's [Wilbert Robinson] time [1914–1931], when players read the funnies on the bench between innings and hummingbirds flew from beneath their caps when they doffed them to the crowd. This was a ball game that had everything, most of it unbelievable. Outfielders and infielders on both teams stood around in small groups discussing something, possibly high taxes or the scarcity of sugar, while pop flies dropped down into their serious, and no doubt fascinating, discussions, like the bride's bouquet at a society weeding."[100] Nor was Corum alone in his opinion. Frank Graham, another New York scribe, grumbled. "It was the fat men against the tall men in a game of picnic baseball. It was the worst game ever played, " while his Gotham counterpart, Joe Williams, headlined his story: "Newhouser Wins Double-header; Beats Cubs and Tigers."[101] Among writers only Chicago's Warren Brown was not grumbling. He was smugly reminding his fellow press box denizens of his pre-Series prediction that, "I don't think either team can win it."[102]

The laughter first arose when the Tigers hammered Borowy from the mound in the sixth with four straight hits. As the dejected hurler strode to the dugout, the loudspeaker blared the ironic emergency announcement: "Will Coroner Al Brodie call his office at once."[103] Another of the most the laughable occurrences was in the ninth inning when Andy Pafko, the normally gifted Cub flyhawk, who had robbed both Cramer and Greenberg with one-handed stabs of long drives in the third, raced after a blast off the bat of Roy Cullenbine. He crashed into the center-field wall and began groping through the lush ivy covering the barrier so frantically that, as Arthur Daley recounted, "no one would have been surprised had he emerged with a rabbit in his hand."[104] Meanwhile, the umpires stopped Cullenbine at second-base, because Wrigley Field ground rules stated that any ball entwined in the foliage was a ground rule double. Later, Pafko denied, with a sly smile and wink, allegations from writers that he actually placed the ball in the greenery knowing that he could not otherwise prevent Cullenbine from reaching third."[105]

Not to be outdone, Cullenbine and Cramer staged an Alphonse and Gaston routine in the bottom half of the same inning, with each calling for the other to grab a soft fly off the bat of Cavarretta before it dropped untouched for a two-base hit. After the game, they sheepishly explained that each had shouted "all right," thinking that it meant it was "all right" for the other to catch the ball.[106]

Nor was the frivolity limited to the defense. On the base paths both teams mimicked the Keystone Kops. Watching both Eddie Mayo and Hank Greenberg sprawling trying to round first, Arthur Daley noted that "the more suspicious folks wonder if some conniving Cub follower had scattered banana peels there."[107] After the game, Greenberg, who had twisted an ankle in his fall, insisted: "There's a soft spot around first, and you sort of sink when you hit it."[108] Hearing his big outfielder's alibi, O'Neill countered: "Yup, and the Cubs know where that spot happens to be, but we don't."[109]

For the Cubs, Mickey Livingston first drew groans and then laughter from the crowd when he hit a seventh inning drive down the right-field line. Rather than starting to run, the Cub backstop just stood at the plate waiting for the umpire to rule whether the ball was fair or foul. Had it not eluded the bumbling Cullenbine and bounced into the seats for a ground rule double, Livingston could have been thrown out at first.[110]

As a result of such antics, the players were subjected to derision by sportswriters, few of whom seemed to care that with their 8–4 triumph the Tigers had grabbed a one-game lead in the Series. While this reaction could be expected by scribes from New York, who always derided teams not named New York or Brooklyn, and Chicago, who could try to use poor-play as excuse for defeat, some of the harshest words were penned by abashed Detroiters. Bob Murphy's column in the *Detroit Times* moaned: "This World Series clambake of 1945 undoubtedly is producing the worst baseball the annual series has ever known. There are a lot of people in the nation, including such theatrical promoters as Billy Rose and Mike Todd, who think the Tigers and Cubs might have a longer run on Broadway than *Tobacco Road* or *Oklahoma.* They are much funnier than Bob Hope. Lew Fonseca will shoot 20,000 feet of film on this Series for his American League picture. It should be funnier than the old Max Sennett comedies."[111] The more serious-minded H.G. Salsinger merely sneered: "This has looked like the finals of a shop league."[112]

With no believable rebuttal possible, players and managers of both teams agreed with the writers. O'Neill candidly told the assembled media: "It was a sloppy sort of game, and we won even though we looked bad. The big thing was that we finally got to hitting' that Chicago pitching. With luck, Newhouser could have had a two-hit shutout."[113] Grimm, who should have realized it was not going to be his day when Rudy York's liner near the Cub dugout in batting practice smashed Roy Hughes' ankle and forced him out of line-up, said only: "We got the hell kicked out of us. It was just boom, boom, boom — that's all. We'll still beat 'em, but I see now it'll take seven games."[114]

The Cubs' hope to stay alive in the Series rested with Passeau, who was matched against Trucks on a blustery, cloudy day with temperatures hovering in the upper forties. Those among the 41,708 who shivered through what turned into a twelve inning, three hour twenty-eight minute battle witnessed another entertaining, but inept, exhibition, labeled by Ed Burns of the *Chicago Tribune* as "tragedy and farce."[115]

The Cubs tallied four runs in the fifth, aided by York's pratfall trying to field a bunt, Trucks playing dropsy with another bunt, and Richards letting a throw from the outfield sail past him, to take a 4–1 advantage and drive Trucks from the mound. They added another run in the sixth when the slow-footed Greenberg failed to snare a soft fly which dropped in front of him for a double, and another two runs in the seventh on two walks and a pair of doubles. However, the Cubs lost Passeau in the sixth when a drive through the box by Jimmy Outlaw tore the nail off the middle finger of Passeau's pitching hand. He continued, but gave up a run in that frame and two more in the next before retiring in favor of Hank Wyse.

With the Chicago ace removed, the Tigers rallied for four runs in the eighth, the final two coming on a prodigious 400 foot home run over the left-field wall by Greenberg, tying the score at eight-all. Although the Detroiters were elated, unbeknownst to them they had lost the game an inning earlier because of the most famous base running blunder in Series history. Charlie Hostetler, a forty-year-old reserve outfielder who was pinch-hitting for Webb, led off the seventh with a slow roller which Hack fumbled at third for an error. After a ground out moved the runner to second, Roger Cramer rifled a shot to left. The subsequent events were described vividly by J. Roy Stockton of the *St. Louis Post-Dispatch*: "At the crack of the Cramer bat on that single, Hostetler was off with the wind. Not exactly with the grace of a gazelle, but certainly off. Charlie made it to third, but as he rounded the bag his right foot caught in his left pant pocket or vice versa. He started to fall and followed through. Nobody ever fell more earnestly. He hit both knees and was flat on his tummy. Someone remarked that the Tigers weren't so hot to their right or left, but they certainly knew how to go on their stomachs. Before Charlie could use the proper leverage to regain a standing position he was tagged out. If Hostetler would have scored and everything subsequently happened as it did, the Tigers would have won the game 8–7 and been champions of the world. Of course, if Aunt Mehitabel had a long beard, a moustache, and had been named Cyrus, she would have been your Uncle Cy."[116] Years later, Cramer recalled the incident bitterly: "Yeah, Hostetler was on the team. He cost us the game. He shouldn't have been in there. He couldn't play."[117]

In the bottom of the twelfth, with pinch-runner Bill Schuster on second and two out, Hack lined a Dizzy Trout fastball to left for an apparent single, which would have advanced Schuster to third. As Greenberg knelt to field the ball, it hit the a sprinkler head, took a crazy hop three feet over his shoulder, and Schuster crossed the plate with the winning run and giving Borowy, who had pitched four scoreless innings in relief, his second World Series triumph.

This play had yet another zany twist. Greenberg was charged with an error, but following the game virtually every Detroit player and sportswriter present berated official scorers Ed Burns, H.G. Salsinger, and Martin Haley in the press room at the Palmer House to intercede on Greenberg's behalf. Five hours after the battle ceased the scorers reconsidered and ruled, as Ed Burns snidely wrote, that "Greenberg, the great Greenberg had not erred" and that the batter, Stan Hack, should be credited with a double and run batted in.[118] Informed of the change by United Press writer Walter Byers, Greenberg smiled and relayed a message to his advocates, which said: "Thanks a lot, fellows. I appreciate it."[119]

The Cubs were ecstatic over their victory. "It was the screwiest game I've ever seen," admitted Grimm in the raucous locker room, "and I hope I never have to suffer through another like it as long as I'm manager. It reminded me of the 1929 World Series when the A's exploded with a ten-run inning. Jimmy Foxx went by me three times at first-base, and I told him I'd trip him if he came around there one more time."[120] Slapping his boisterous players on their backs, the pilot continued happily: "Let me take out my store teeth so I can talk louder. It's wonderful, just wonderful. How about Borowy? With seven and one-half hours of rest he went in and put it in there. Boy, that's working. He's my boy! What a beautiful way to win it! What a beautiful hop! No ball ever took such a beautiful hop!"[121]

Passeau, displaying his injured, bloody digit to writers, said he wanted to stay on the mound "but couldn't grip the ball."[122] When informed that the Tigers had revived their assertion that he was throwing a spitball, Passeau laughed and replied cryptically: "Well, they'll never catch me."[123]

In the glum Tiger dressing room Manager O'Neill summed up the feelings of his squad. "It was a tough one to lose," he said quietly. "We should have won it in regulation time. We had plenty of chances, but nothing went right. We made a lot of bad plays, and we did a lot of bad base running. There'll be no workout tomorrow. I think a day off will do the fellas more good. I'll pitch Newhouser next. I don't know who they'll pitch. They just about ran out of pitchers taking this game, but they don't have a pitcher that is ready to match Newhouser. I think Grimm will just pick one and pray."[124]

The fifth and sixth games verified the fears of baseball purists that they were witnessing a parody of what should have been the Fall Classic, and, with the realization that "there might never be another like it until the next world war," they awaited with trepidation the final act of the show.[125] Of course, like all attempts at entertaining the masses, this theatre on the diamond received mixed reviews. One of the choreographers, Detroit General Manager Jack Zeller, while chagrined by the awkward performances by his actors, noted that the houses were packed and beamed: "You've got to admit that the people love it."[126] Stockton, the St. Louis outside observer, penned a bittersweet column, stating: "They're a little short of ball players in this fourth World Series since Pearl Harbor, but they're long on excitement. There couldn't be more thrills if the Little Potatoes-Hard-to-Peel were playing the Cherokee Street Young Businessmen's Association in a winner-take-all ball game. Baseball is a great game, and ball players or not, you can't beat this annual October show. The ball players, when they come back, may make baseball a little better, but they can't furnish you any more thrills than these wartime performers have furnished. May the worst team win."[127] Chicago's Arch Ward offered a similar backhanded compliment in his critique, saying: "The first six games have been replete with brilliant outfield catches, flashes of pitching excellence, amateurish base running, and some of the sloppiest fielding ever perpetrated before a World Series crowd."[128] John Drebinger bared his stodgy New York aloofness at what seemed to pass for entertainment in the Midwest, writing: "Even the oldest of observers are frank to confess they have never witnessed such a profusion of sparkling plays and glaring blunders, spiced by incredible stumbling on the base paths, as the present classic has unfolded."[129] Perhaps, however, the most insightful evaluation came from two actors who had performed in earlier productions of the Fall Classic — Frankie Frisch, the veteran All Star second-baseman and manager, and his old Gas House Gang nemesis Dizzy Dean. Sitting in the press box, Frisch guffawed, "I wouldn't have missed this Series for a million bucks, Diz!" Dean replied, "Brother, you ain't kidding."[130]

A crowd of 41,590 mostly partisan Cub fans poured through the turnstiles to view the deciding battle, and those unable to get into Wrigley Field could, for $7.50, watch from the third floor apartments behind the right-field wall.[131] One enterprising unemployed resident in the tenement accommodated twenty fans in his bedroom, serving them free coffee.[132]

The twenty-four-year-old Newhouser, whom Stockton dubbed "a relative spring chicken among the oldsters in Detroit uniforms," was coming back after only two days' rest to face Borowy, who was pitching his third game in four days.[133] Standing near his dugout, "Prince Hal" accurately forecast what was to transpire, telling reporters: "I'm gonna be all right, but I can't for the life of me figure how Borowy can hold up. We'll have him out of there in a hurry."[134]

Hank Greenberg sat huddled in the dugout wearing a jacket and gloves trying to keep warm on yet another cold and overcast afternoon. A young writer approached him and inquired inanely if he thought the Series would end with the seventh game. The gentle Tiger giant replied courteously, saying with a grin: "I doubt it. That would be too commonplace."[135]

In actuality, Greenberg's placid demeanor belied a serious injury. His wrist, which he had jammed trying to stroke an outside pitch to right in the final inning of the preceding game, was swollen so badly that he could not grip a bat properly. Ten minutes before game time, Greenberg took O'Neill aside, telling him, "I think for the good of the team I better not play today. I can't throw. I can't hit. With all that it means to the rest of the players, I think I should get out of the line-up."[136] Concerned about the psychological effect Greenberg's absence might have on his team's morale, the manager convinced his star to play, but Greenberg consented only after O'Neill pledged to take him out "if anything goes wrong."[137]

Across the field, the Cubs were grumbling vociferously about Grimm's choice of Borowy. After warming the tired-armed hurler up along the sideline, reserve catcher Dewey Williams warned reserve shortstop Len Merullo and Phil Cavarretta: "He just don't have it. If he pitches, there goes our money."[138] Furious, Hank Wyse added: "Grimm ain't pitchin' the pitchers right. He should use Paul Erickson or Hy Vandenberg."[139] Hearing of this potential insurrection, Grimm gathered his players and snapped: "Hank's a hot pitcher, and he's our best. I have confidence in him."[140]

Unfortunately, the game itself was anti-climactic. The first three Tiger batters — Webb, Mayo, and Cramer — all singled, giving Detroit a 1–0 lead and sending Borowy to an exceedingly quick shower. Knowing that Borowy's weary wing could not last, Dewey Williams took it upon himself to warm up Vandenberg. To his amazement, Grimm inexplicably ordered Derringer to get ready.[141] "Oom Paul" was summoned to the mound, and, as Williams graphically recounted, "promptly got the shit kicked out of him," giving up three more runs, one being set up by a surprise bunt by Greenberg and another as the result of a bases loaded walk.[142]

The Chicagoans touched Newhouser for single runs in the first, fourth, and ninth, while Detroit added a run in the second, another in the seventh, and two in the eighth, providing

Newhouser a 9–3 world championship triumph. In the uproarious Tiger locker room, the boyish hurler, being drenched with champagne and beer, was overjoyed with his less than scintillating ten-hit, ten strikeout performance. "I felt great out there all the time," he kept reiterating to newspapermen and radio broadcasters. "I never felt tired. I felt about the same as always, except that my back hurt some. Nothing could have stopped me though. This is gonna be the greatest memory of my life. Nothing in the world will ever dull this game in my mind. It just couldn't be done."[143]

Near his locker, Greenberg was regaling the media with boasts about his acting ability. Revealing his injury, the Tiger idol laughed: "It was the best bluffing job I ever hope to put through in my lifetime. I didn't want the Cubs to know anything was wrong with my wrist."[144]

In reality, this entire Greenberg episode was in keeping with the comedic aspects of the Series. If the Cubs, as they purported, had no inkling of the Bengal's injury it was because they had not read the early edition of the *Chicago Tribune* and not as a result of Greenberg's cloak and dagger subterfuge. Ed Burns of the *Tribune* headlined his story "Bruised Wrist May Cramp Greenberg's Style Today." In it Burns informed his readers: "Hank Greenberg, the Detroit Tigers' slugging left-fielder, will go into today's game against the Cubs with a bruised right wrist, which may impair his batting swing he said last night."[145]

Hearing Greenberg yell "We won this for Steve O'Neill—a guy who never second-guessed a ball player and always understood our every position," the big Irish skipper grew emotional.[146] "This is a great thrill for me," he said, almost in a whisper. "I've been in baseball for thirty-six years. I've played in the minors and majors. I've managed in the big time and the small time. But this is the first time I've ever had the pleasure of leading a world champion. My boys did that for me. I tell you it's a great feeling—a great thrill."[147] Flashing his broad smile, he admitted: "As far as baseball goes, it wasn't much of a Series, but it must have been great for the fans. They saw everything, including a lot of things we managers never like to see."[148]

The losers were sullen and felt betrayed by their manager. Cavarretta and Merullo both sneered that they would always believe that they had the better team.[149] Wyse was more to the point, growling to anyone who would listen: "It was Grimm's fault. He didn't pitch the pitchers right."[150]

Grimm was disappointed, but neither downcast nor defensive, as he met the media. "Well, I ain't gonna hang myself,' he joked when asked what he was going to do now that the season was over.[151] Casting a glance toward Borowy, who was sitting and sobbing, Grimm grew serious. "You gave it a good try, Hank," he yelled consolingly. "Hey, it's too late now. We were beaten by a good ball club, but not a better ball club than I have. Just good pitching beat us. I'll always think we would have won if Passeau hadn't hurt his finger. But these guys are still champs in my book. They gave it everything they had. I knew Borowy didn't have a lot when he warmed up, but I wanted to give him a try. I thought maybe he'd get by until he warmed up to the job. I feel bad. Losers always do. But losing the Series can't take away the fact that we unseated the mighty Cardinals."[152]

Post-Series analyses ran the emotional gamut from ridicule to sentimentality. Not unexpectedly, New York journalists, whose world centered around their teams, were the most severe critics. Arthur Daley sneered: "The 1945 World Series moved into the record books as one of the most grotesque, funniest, and incredible post-season affairs that our national pastime has ever had. Practically everything happened, except that no fielder was hit on the noggin by a fly ball. The Tigers were playing their positions from memory—and some of them didn't remember much, at that. Thank heavens no one was kilt [*sic*], but podnuh there was a couple of mighty close calls."[153] John Drebinger wrote sourly: "To those who suffered through the tense, nerve-wracking moments of the seven games, it doubtless will be all right if there is never another like it. It was a Series in which all the conditions of war that had lowered the standard of play during the past four years seemed to reach their peak. There were blunders that one would scarcely expect to see in a picnic game. Outfielders, especially the creaking oldsters of the Tigers had on their battlefronts, stumbled all over themselves as pop flies dropped between them, and they fell flat on their faces as they tried to circle the bases. The Tigers won only because, in addition to their inherent ability to belt a long ball, they had an ace pitcher in Hal Newhouser."[154]

Malcolm "Iffy the Dopester" Bingay of the *Detroit Free Press* concurred with his eastern press brethren regarding the quality of play, but he also saw a positive side to the Series. "Neither team missed a mistake that could possibly be made," he admitted. "The only reason they didn't throw to more wrong bases was that there was only three to throw at. But our brave Tigers outsmarted them pesky Cubs. We let 'em play dumber baseball than we did. It was one of them kind of Series where I never could tell whether it was great pitching or just bad hitting. They couldn't hit, they couldn't bunt, they couldn't field, they couldn't throw, and they couldn't run bases, on either side, according to Hoyle. All I can say is that the lads fought every minute of play. They gave everything they had and for that reason nobody should shoot the piano player."[155]

Bingay was joined in his praise of effort over raw ability by editorials in both of the other two Detroit daily newspapers. The *Detroit Times* editorialized: "After all, what are real champions? They are those who accept the challenge and ask no odds. They are those who take the breaks as they come and rise above the bad ones. They are those who battle undismayed against setback after setback. Especially they are those who prove their mettle in the ultimate crisis. That's the kind of champions the Detroit Tigers are this year. In these disturbed days, they might well serve as an inspiration to the rest of us. The thought of quitting was never in them. We might, all of us, remember that."[156] The *Detroit News* echoed this theme, noting: "The fact remains that there is a strange, almost mystical, connection between Detroit's fortunes in the world of sport and the state of the local mind and morale. In the dark days of the pre-war depression, Detroit's comeback curiously coincided with the sudden eruption of a whole galaxy of athletes who made this the 'City of Champions.' Again this fall, when a mass neurosis settled on us and the whole town seemed gripped by a home front battle fatigue in which energies went limp, tempers shortened, and all reason fled, the athletes came through. We needed a miracle, and this the Tigers— bless them — have provided. For a couple of weeks they gave us something on which all hearts were set. About this the learned *Washington Post* said: 'It is precisely because it makes no great difference to the future of civilization or to the prospect of an enduring peace whether the Tigers or the Cubs win that these contests are socially so valuable. They offer us a sort of catharsis for the tensions of our prejudices and our fears.'"[157]

Syndicated columnist Bill Corum, known for his biting wit, could not resist the temptation to ridicule the Series, but even he could not fail to comment on its social and economic significance. "The new title holders have a great future, but it's all behind them," he quipped. "As much as they wanted at times to hate the thought of it all, the Tigers finally backed into the championship like a lady driver tearing off both fenders backing into the wrong garage. It may be that two worse teams than these will meet for the baseball championship of the world during World War III, but I'm already laying plans to miss that one."[158] As though confessing, he added: "Half of this is half kidding, of course, but the other half tells the story. The great majority of the fans seemed to like the Series. They filled practically ever seat in both parks, fair weather and foul, for all seven games. I think it is only fair to say that baseball as a whole not only reaped a rich financial harvest from the Series, but also gained in public favor. After all, only a super optimist gibes at the infirmities of age. In some families they have walking canes handed down from generation to generation."[159]

Of the tens of thousand of words penned on this World Series, those of J. Roy Stockton provided the most balanced and insightful epitaph to the 1945 baseball season. "It was an interesting Series because it went down to the last ditch, and you couldn't tell until the last day who was going to win. But it probably was the most poorly played title series in the history of the game. The final game undoubtedly ended an era in baseball — the era of World War II baseball. A game played by over-aged veterans, inexperienced youngsters, and minor league players enjoying a brief whirl in big league uniforms. Probably by next fall many of the good ball players will be back. Certainly the baseball will be better. Perhaps the next World Series and others in the future will be contests of great skill and great speed played by outstanding physical specimens. But this was a good show and fine thrilling entertainment, regardless of who wears the uniforms. The Series attracted 333,457 persons, more than ever paid to see any other title competition on the diamond. The receipts also set a new record. So what does it matter that flies were lost in the sun, if infielders threw to the wrong base, and if runners fell down carrying important runs? It was wartime baseball on its way out."[160]

Despite Stockton's remarks about the miscues not mattering in the Series for the nation at large, they did matter for the Cubs and their fans. The loss was a bitter pill to swallow, but it would choked them had they known that this less-than-classic performance would mark the Cubs final appearance in a post-season game for the remainder of the twentieth century and into the twenty-first.

WHITE SOX VS. DODGERS, 1959

The 1959 baseball season was filled with surprises in both leagues. In the Senior Circuit, the San Francisco Giants squandered a seemingly certain trip to the World Series by dropping seven of their final eight games and slipped to third place. Meanwhile, the defending two-time league champion Milwaukee Braves and the amazing Los Angeles Dodgers, who had finished seventh the preceding year, slipped by the Giants and ended in a first place tie with identical records of 86–66, necessitating a best-of-three game playoff series.

On a drab, rainy overcast afternoon in Milwaukee, the Dodgers, behind Larry Sherry's 7⅔rds innings of four-hit shutout relief work, captured a 3–2 victory before 18,297 shivering spectators. The teams then flew to Los Angeles for a game the following afternoon. Under sunny skies and a temperature in the upper eighties, an unexpectedly meager crowd of 36,853 rattled around in the vast Coliseum to see if their adopted heroes could bring a major league pennant to the City of Angels in only its second major league season. In a sloppily played, four error contest, in which the aces of both teams— the Dodgers' Don Drysdale and the Braves' Lew Burdette — looked like minor leaguers, the Dodgers outlasted Milwaukee by a score of 6–5 to end the playoff and claim their third league crown in five years.

In Brooklyn, where the hatred was still red-hot towards Dodger owner Walter O'Malley for hijacking their Beloved Bums to the West Coast solely to enter a more lucrative market for his product, residents cursed the good fortune of the architect of their displeasure. One of the Flatbush faithful muttered: "With Walter O'Malley's luck, the Dodgers couldn't miss. He'll get richer because of the playoff. Then the Bums will make O'Malley still wealthier in the World Series. He's Midas with a California suntan."[1] Hearing this, Arthur Daley of the *New York Times* remarked: "Even if the cynicism is removed from the statement, the facts are essentially correct. The president of the Los Angeles Dodgers is so lucky that if he fell into a mud hole he'd emerge with a gold watch in his hand."[2]

The National League champions were, as veteran New York writer Red Smith put it, "a curious mixture of age and youth, seasoned survivors of the Dodgers' days in Brooklyn and rookies known only by vague rumor a few months ago."[3] In fact, Manager Walter Alston, who had guided the Dodgers to their first world championship in 1955 in a seven game series with the New York Yankees, performed what many considered to be managerial magic in lifting his 1959 squad to the pennant. However, critics sneered that the secret to Alston's success was not prestidigitation, but rather the cavernous Los Angeles Coliseum, the Dodgers' temporary home until the new park at Chevez Ravine could be completed. The Coliseum was a football stadium, with a seating capacity of more than 92,000. To convert the huge bowl into a baseball park, strange field dimensions were established, which made the field "lop-sided, knock-kneed, pigeon toed, and cross-eyed."[4] Along the right-field foul line, the stands were 300' from home plate, but the fence sharply jutted out to 375' in right-center and 400' to straightaway center. Most unusual, however, was what cynics dubbed "O'Malley's Chinese Wall"—a 42' high wire mesh screen beginning at the left-field foul pole only 251' from home plate and running from the foul line to the 320' sign in left-center. Unlike the "Green Monster" in Boston's Fenway Park, which was painted solid green, the open fence of the Coliseum presented a difficult background for batters and fielders alike, and even a smiling Alston was forced to admit that his team had an advantage over those visiting the Coliseum because "we are used to the screen."[5]

Leading the Dodgers to their unexpected pennant was thirty-three year old slugger Edwin (Duke) Snider (.308, 23, 88), a veteran of thirteen seasons who held the then National League record for World Series home runs and runs batted in with ten and twenty-four respectively. Flanking Snider at various times were twenty-four-year-old Don Demeter (.256, 18, 70), twenty-one-year-old Ron Fairly (.238, 4, 23), and twenty-eight-year old Chuck Essegian (.304, 1, 5), none of whom had more than three years experience in the major leagues, and the more experienced twenty-nine-year-old, bushy-browed Wally Moon (.302, 19, 74), thirty-one-year-old Eldon (Rip) Repulski (.255, 2, 14), and thirty-seven-year-old Carl Furillo (.290, 0, 13). Anchoring the infield was another former darling of Brooklyn, thirty-five-year-old first-baseman Gil Hodges, who, like Snider and Furillo, was participating in his seventh World Series. Rounding out the infield were second-sacker Charlie Neal (.287, 19, 83), rookie shortstop Maury Wills (.260, 0, 7), and eight-year veteran Jim (Junior) Gilliam (.282, 3, 34) at third. Behind the plate were third-year receivers John Roseboro (.232, 10, 38) and Joe Pignatano (.237, 1, 11), along with rookie Norm Sherry (.333, 0, 2).

The Los Angeles mound corps, like the position players, was a skillful blending of past and future greatness. Southpaw Johnny Podres (14–9, 4.11), the hero of the 1955 World Series, Roger Craig (11–5, 2.06), Clem Labine (5–10, 3.93, and Carl Erskine (0–3, 7.71) were a poignant reminder of the Brooklyn era, while erratic fireballer Sandy Koufax (8–6, 4.05), Don Drysdale (17–13, 3.46 with four shutouts, which tied him with teammate Roger Craig for the league lead), Stan Williams (5–5, 3.97), Danny McDevitt (10–8, 3.97), and relief ace Larry Sherry (7–2, 2.19) represented the Dodgers' hopes for a new diamond dynasty.

The Chicago White Sox, managed by Senor Al Lopez, who had led the Cleveland Indians to a league championship in 1954, compiled a 94–60 record to stun the American League by finishing five games ahead of Cleveland and fifteen lengths in front of the defending champion New York Yankees. In bringing Chicago its first American League title in forty years, the White Sox, as Arthur Daley observed, went "back to baseball's Neanderthal Age, playing the dead ball style in this jackrabbit era."[6] With a team batting average of only .250 and a mere ninety-seven home runs, fifty-one fewer than the Dodgers, the "Go-Go Sox," as they became known, won with speed, defense, and pitching. Offensively, as Daley noted with admiration, the Sox "regarded a walk, a stolen base, a wild pitch, and a sacrifice bunt as a rousing rally."[7] Around the infield, the Chicagoans entered the Series with thirteen-year veteran National League slugger Ted Kluszewski, a late-season acquisition from the Pittsburgh Pirates who hit .297 with two homers and ten runs batted in for the Sox, at first, another thirteen-year veteran, diminutive Nellie Fox (.306, 2, 70) patrolled second, slick-fielding shortstop Luis Aparicio led the major leagues with fifty-six stolen bases to accompany his .257 average, six round-trippers, and fifty-one runs batted in, and twelve-year veteran Billy Goodman (.250, 1, 28) shared third-base duties with twenty-nine-year-old John (Bubba) Phillips (.264, 5, 40). The team's only reliable source of power came from thirteen-year veteran catcher Sherman Lollar (.265, 22, 84).

Unfortunately for the Sox, their outfield was even less potent than their inner defense in delivering extra-base blows. Left-fielder Al Smith (.237, 16, 55) was the biggest threat, but he was a defensive liability. Although center-fielder Jim Landis (.272, 5, 60), right-fielder "Jungle Jim" Rivera (.220, 4, 19), and rookie reserve flycatcher Jim McAnany (.276, 0, 27) were gifted glove artists, they posed little threat at the plate.

The heart of the Sox was its mound corps, led by thirty-nine-year-old Early Wynn (22–10, 3.17) and twenty-six-year-old Bob Shaw (18–6, 2.69). Joining these right-handers in the starting rotation were fellow righties Dick Donovan (9–10, 3.66) and Barry Latman (8–5, 3.75), and veteran southpaw Billy Pierce (14–15, 3.62). Heading the bullpen were a pair of right-handed aces, thirteen-year veteran Gerry Staley (8–5, 2.24, 14 saves) and Omar (Turk) Lown (9–2, 2.89, and a league-leading fifteen saves).

Because the team plane did not arrive in Chicago until 4:24 a.m., Manager Walter Alston announced that his weary players would forego their workout, even though it would be their only chance before the opening game to learn about the lights, shadows, and winds that made Comiskey Park a tricky place in which to play. Explaining his decision to his coaches and scouts, Alston said with a wry grin: "I grant you that all that is important, but I think it's even more important that our fellows stay awake out there."[8]

Conversely, the White Sox, who clinched their pennant on September 22, were "spouting vim, vigor, and vitality" as they went through their brisk morning drill.[9] Asked if he thought he could run on Roseboro, whom Alston praised as possessing as quick and accurate an arm as any catcher he had ever managed, Luis Aparicio replied: "If I get the jump, I'm gonna go."[10] Not wishing to disparage Roseboro, he added quickly: "They stop me sometimes in the American League. It can be done."[11]

The eve of the Series provided off field gossip, as a long simmering feud between Chicago owner and president Bill Veeck and his Milwaukee Braves counterpart, Lou Perini, reached headline status. Seeking revenge for Perini's refusal to grant him any complimentary seats at the 1958 World Series games in Milwaukee on the grounds that his purchase of the controlling interest in the White Sox from Mrs. Dorothy Comiskey Rigney had not yet been finalized, Veeck refused Perini's request for extra seats for the Milwaukee contingent at the opening contest. Questioned about his alleged violation of protocol among owners, an angry Veeck, referring to the years following the sale of his interest in the St. Louis Browns, replied: "Nobody gave me anything when I was out of baseball. Particularly Perini. In fact, he took my twelve seats away from me last year. I had a promise of twelve from the Braves in August, and I still had twelve in September. Then at Series time I was told I had none. Not two, not one, but none. Mr. Perini needed my twelve for himself. OK. Now this is the day of reckoning. I'm doing what Mr. Perini wishes he could do this October. I'm taking care of my fans first."[12]

Veeck, known for his marketing skills and flaunting of baseball tradition, was at his best for the opening championship contest. Jump Jackson's Dixieland Band entertained fans as it wended its way through the stands, and each of the more than 20,000 female fans received a red rose as she entered the stadium, which Veeck had ordered not to be draped with the customary interior bunting.[13] Veeck instead had the stadium's exterior adorned with flags and hanging baskets of flowers, explaining that the club was proud of Comiskey

Park's interior beauty and wanted fans across the nation watching on television to see the park as it was during the regular season.[14] The club president also ordered the team to replace its red and white striped black stockings with white stockings with red and black stripes, and had Urban Faber and Ray Schalk, the battery that clinched the Sox's last world championship in 1917, participate in the ceremonial first pitch.[15] Faber, known for his spitball, drew a good-natured roar from the crowd of 48,013 as he pretended to "load up" the ball for a moist delivery.[16]

The only glitch in the day's proceedings for the home team came as recording artist Tony Martin began to sing the national anthem and the flag stuck at half-staff on the 100' center field pole.[17] By day's end even that seemed an appropriate gesture to welcome the visiting Dodgers, who suffered a humiliating 11–0 rout, equaling the record for the most lopsided Series defeat set by the 1934 Detroit Tigers in losing to the St. Louis Cardinals.

The demise of the "Hollywood contingent" on the pleasantly cool, sunny afternoon was reviewed movie-style, by Arthur Daley of the *New York Times:* "The hard-hitting, swift-moving, tobacco-chewing desperadoes from the Loop came a rootin' and a tootin' into town. They shot up the place, wrecked all the furniture in the First Chance Saloon and terrified all the strangers from Los Angeles. Then these badmen evaded the posse and safely made it to their hideout in the canyon without ever being apprehended. The Angelenos never knew what hit them. The raid caught them unprepared, and they never did get their six-guns out of the holsters. The lone departure from the normal hoss opera script was that the tall-in-the-saddle guys were led by an Injun, a real mean hombre named Early Wynn. The redman — at least he's part Indian —claims that he comes from the same tribe as Pocahontas, but he interceded for no palefaces today. He mowed them down implacably."[18]

Because of limited space in the clubhouses, post-game interviews were held in three locales— the White Sox dressing room, the Dodger dressing room, and the Bards' Room, where local sportswriters traditionally gathered.[19] Lopez and his players, while pleased with the game results, were gracious to their foes. Claiming his first World Series triumph after suffering four straight defeats at the hands of the New York Giants in 1954 as the manager of the Cleveland Indians, Lopez spoke for his team when he stated: "It was a good game. It was a bad day for Los Angeles. Any club can have a bad day."[20] Veeck, congratulating his players, joked: "In the third inning, when we scored seven runs, I almost left. I thought I was in the wrong park!"[21]

In the Dodger dressing quarters the atmosphere was more upbeat than downcast. Veteran utility infielder Don Zimmer shouted: "If you think we feel bad, how do you think the Braves feel? Boys, the Go-Go Sox are dead. They've got no chance."[22] After echoing Zimmer's cry, Duke Snider, who two errors in the third inning helped the Sox tally seven times, was smirking as if "he had been caught stealing watermelons."[23] "If we'd lost 2–1, we'd eat our hearts out," Snider said, "but 11–0! Hell, we just got beat, and the best thing to do is grin and bear it."[24] Leaning back in his chair, the jovial flycatcher reflected on his record setting errors: "Shucks, I've got lots of records— most Series strikeouts and eight strikeouts in a five-game Series."[25]

Alston, whom one reporter described as being "as relaxed as spaghetti" after the loss, said with a weak smile: "I hated to see the ball club look so bad. They beat our brains out, but we're not that bad. You know we're a better team than this! We've done it the hard way all year, and there is no reason why we won't come back. You know, everyone told me about how fast the White Sox were, but they didn't tell me about all that power."[26]

The always ebullient Johnny Podres, who was scheduled to pitch the following day, was asked if he had learned anything about the White Sox. "Only that they're high ball hitters. so I'll try to keep the ball down," he replied.[27] Becoming serious, Podres made a prediction for reporters. "I have no idea how many games this thing will go," he stated, "but I know we're gonna win it. Sure we got skunked today, but I really think our club should be more relaxed right now than we've been all season. We won the big ones to get here, and I don't see why we can't win 'em now. I know this ball club of ours is gonna score some runs, and the Sox aren't gonna get eleven every day."[28]

The morning of the second game brought a steady rainfall, which led to a hurried conference between Commissioner Ford Frick and chief umpires Bill Summers of the American League and Frank Dascoli of the National. After calling the weather bureau, Summers proclaimed sourly: "They say there is no rain at the airport, but we're not playin' at the airport!"[29] However, the skies cleared and an hour before game time another perfect sunny day greeted the 47,368 spectators who jammed into Comiskey Park in hopes of witnessing a repeat performance of the previous day's thrashing of the National League champions.

Before the game began, two items held the attention of press box denizens. First was a report written by J.G. Taylor Spink in *The Sporting News,* which had been denied by Calvin Griffith, owner and president of the Washington Senators, that he was moving his team to Minneapolis before the 1960 season.[30] Second was how Veeck had obtained a special dispensation from Archbishop Meyer of Chicago permitting meat to be eaten at the ballpark by all Roman Catholic personnel, including players, umpires, officials, fans, and sportswriters attending Friday's game.[31]

Yet another unfortunate event marked the singing of the national anthem. While the flag was raised flawlessly for the second game, vocalist Nat "King" Cole, the second of Veeck's advertised "Parade of Stars" brought in to sing the "Star Spangled Banner," not only was off key several times, but also forgot the lyrics, blaring out: "o'er the land and o'er the sea and the home of the brave."[32]

The Sox scored two runs off Podres in the first, but the Dodgers tallied once in the fifth and three more times in the seventh of starter Bob Shaw to take a 4–2 lead. In the home half of the eighth, Kluszewski led off with a single and went to second on Lollar's infield single off Gilliam's chest. Reserve first-baseman Earl Torgeson was inserted as a pinch-runner for the slow-footed Kluszewski before Al Smith entered the batter's box. Then came what many believe was the turning point of the Series. Smith lined a two-bagger into deep left-center. Torgeson scored easily, but Lollar, whom Arthur Daley noted was "no express, but strictly a local, with as much speed as a glacier" was thrown out at home by twenty feet on a perfect relay by shortstop Maury Wills.[33] Reliever Larry Sherry assured his teammates as he took the mound: "Don't worry, the big kid will beat them for you," and then fulfilled his boast by fanning pinch-hitter Billy Goodman and inducing Jim Rivera to end the inning by fouling out to Roseboro.[34] The Sox went down in order in the ninth, giving the Dodgers a hard-fought 4–3 victory.

The victorious Dodgers exuded a brash cockiness after tying the Series. Coach Charlie Dressen, asked about the Lollar incident, sneered: "Looks like they put in a runner for the wrong man," and pitcher Clem Labine jibed: "Go-Go Sox? They look like the Slow-Slow Sox."[35] Charlie Neal, the 156 pound second-sacker who belted a pair of homers, wondered aloud how Shaw "ever won eighteen games"[36] Zimmer bellowed: "When you play teams like the Braves, Giants, and Pirates all year, this team don't scare ya!"[37] Gilliam chimed in: "And the Cubs, too," implying that the Sox would be no better than the sixth best team in the Senior Circuit.[38] Winning hurler Podres added: "They're definitely not as good as the Giants and Braves. They sure don't have their power."[39]

Reserve backstop Joe Pignatano fumed at the Sox for another reason, angrily telling

Charley Neal's seventh inning home run in the second game of 1959 World Series in Comiskey Park. Note NBC television camera (Chicago Historical Society, ICHi-22605, photograph by Alfred A. Novick).

reporters: "We're gonna beat 'em in five, just so we don't have to come back here. They gave our wives lousy tickets. The whole club is teed off about it. Our wives are stuck way out in the right-field corner where they have to crane their necks to see around girders."[40] Labine, eavesdropping on the catcher's tirade, added: "Their wives are gonna sit under the center-field clock in the Coliseum — and Bill Veeck, too!"[41] Alston, absent-mindedly dressing in front of his locker, casually concurred with his team's assessment of the Sox. Suddenly, he broke out laughing and said: "You think I'm not nervous. Looka here. I put on two different socks this morning. You can bet I'll wear the same two tomorrow!"[42]

Lopez slowly entered the Bards' Room to face the press, knowing the Lollar play would be foremost in every writer's mind. "Lollar hesitated before he reached second," he explained to the initial query. "He thought Al Smith's deep ball might be caught. That ruined the timing on the play. There was a 3–2 count on Smith, so Lollar and Earl Torgeson were off with the pitch. [Third-base Coach] Tony Cuccinello was watching the ball and figured Lollar was going to score. With his eyes on the ball, Tony didn't see that Lollar had hesitated, so he kept waving Lollar on. He figured that Lollar would score behind Torgeson, and that on the throw to the plate Smith would move to third with the winning run. I can't criticize Tony. It was the right play. Tony played it to win, as we've played it all year. It just didn't work."[43]

A somber Cuccinello assumed all the blame for the decision. "Yes, I waved Lollar in all the way," he said to radio interviewers in the Chicago dressing room. "At first I didn't think the Dodgers had a chance to get him. After all, even though Lollar is slow, he was running with the pitch. I kept yelling: Go! Go! But after I had given Sherm the go sign I realized things were not going so well. If I figured the relay was gonna be done so well I wouldn't have sent him in. Maybe it would have been different if Lollar hadn't stopped on his way to third. Looking back on the play, I can't say I would do it the same way all over again. It was my fault."[44]

Later that evening, what *The Sporting News* labeled the "largest sports airlift in history" occurred when United Airlines flew four charted DC-7 and three DC-6 aircraft carrying 410 players, officials, wives, and newsmen from Midway Airport on a six hour thirty minute flight to Los Angeles. Commissioner Frick and his chief aide, Charlie Segar, flew to the coast in a charted private jet, because as Frick explained: "We're in a hurry to get out there to make sure everything is in order for the third game."[45]

Los Angeles was in a state of baseball mania as it prepared for its initial World Series. Before the contest, everyone seemed intent on nothing but the Series. Groundskeepers at the Coliseum were toiling frantically to get the field back into perfect shape after the Southern California-Ohio State football game on Saturday afternoon; crooner Frank Sinatra gushed: "The World Series is a jazzy deal, Daddy-O"; and the local Red Cross chapter issued a light-hearted list of recommendations entitled "The Care and Welfare of Dodger Fans During a World Series."[46] Its helpful hints included:
"For men:

  • Control your temper. White Sox fans hit back.
  • Don't flail about during moments of exultation. You may hit another Dodger fan.
  • During dropped third strikes or White Sox grand slam homers lower your head quickly between your knees to avoid fainting.
  • Be sure your mouth is empty during cheering. Those in front of you will appreciate it.
  • Sit among your own kind. If you sit among the enemy, you spend half your time planning to slug the guy yapping at Drysdale.
  • Watch those hot dogs. Chomped-on fingers taste O.K., but they don't feel so good.

"For women:

  • Don't wear high heels. It will be easier on your escort's instep if you are given to frenzied behavior.
  • Leave your hat home. If you must wear one, make it a beret or a beanie. It's much easier and safer to tear off and throw in moments of frustration.
  • Don't cheer too enthusiastically if you are encased in one of those whalebone things. If shapeliness is important, try the flexible kind. Strangling your emotions isn't healthy.
  • Don't apply makeup during those moments when those sitting around you are reaching for foul balls, unless your lipstick happens to be the tasty kind and digestible."[47]

Arriving at the Coliseum, most members of the White Sox stood and stared at the makeshift left-field 40' screen wall that loomed a mere 250' from home plate. Billy Pierce winced and stated: "It's so close it almost chokes ya to death."[48] Dick Donovan was more philosophic, saying: "I honestly can't say it doesn't bother me, but you've got to be a positive thinker. I'd bunch my three outfielders to the right and let Lu Aparicio also play left-field. Does anyone ever make an out here?"[49] Al Smith was more concerned by the background caused by the center-field seats than by the screen. "Man, it's gonna be rough hittin' out of those white shirts," moaned Smith. "And, boy, that mound looks awful close. Drysdale will look like he's steppin' in your face."[50]

Lopez and Ted Kluszewski joined the conversation. "Big Klu," who had played in the Coliseum during his stint with the Pirates, issued a warning. "You have a tendency to shoot at it," he observed, "but I'm telling our right-handed hitters that they are better off to forget about it and just hit the same as usual."[51] Lopez seconded his first-baseman, adding: "You have to stay natural. You can't let this thing get you. A batter would be foolish to change his style because of it."[52] Flashing a broad grin, Lopez chuckled: "Everyone says we're a club with a powder puff punch. Maybe this is just the type of field made to order for us."[53]

Under a blistering Southern California sun, a Series record 92,394 spectators packed into the Coliseum to view Dick Donovan square off against flame-throwing Don Drysdale. During the pre-game ceremonies John Riatt sang the national anthem flawlessly and former Dodger outfielder Zack Wheat, recently elected into baseball's Hall of Fame, threw out the ceremonial first pitch. In the stands Lou Perini got his revenge as Dodger Vice President Buzzy Bavasi gave Veeck a reasonably good seat, but the remaining ninety-nine tickets allocated to the Sox entourage were, according to Bavasi, "about as close to the field as the foothills of the San Bernadino Mountains."[54]

For six innings the contest was scoreless, with Donovan permitting only one hit and Drysdale nine. In the seventh, Donovan wilted under the blazing sun and 100 degree temperature. With one out, Neal got what Dodger fans referred to as a "screen-o," bouncing a single of the left-field barrier. After Moon sacrificed Neal to second, Norm Larker and Gil Hodges drew bases on balls, and Lopez removed Donovan in favor of Gerry Staley. Carl Furillo pinch-hit for Don Demeter and bounced a single past Aparicio that scored two runs. Each team tallied a run in the eighth, making the final score 3–1 for the Dodgers and giving Larry Sherry, who hurled the final two innings, his second consecutive save.

Meeting the media after the game, Alston refused to talk about the victory until he had denied the report that he had called the White Sox "a bunch of second-raters" or that he thought "three or four teams in the National League were better than the White Sox." Flashing a rare display of temper, Alston, puffing furiously on a cigarette, stated: "I most emphatically deny ever making any statements even faintly resembling those. I'd have to be stupid to say that about a team that beat us 11–0. In all my years in the big leagues I've never talked about any other club, and it would be silly to start now."[55] Regaining his composure, Alston admitted that he selected Furillo to pinch-hit be he "wanted a man who doesn't strike out" and that the Dodgers were lucky to win because "if the ball Furillo hit hadn't taken a bad hop, Aparicio would have had it."[56]

In the losers' dressing room, Lopez held court for the media. "I still think we have a helluva chance to win the Series," he said with a weary smile. "We haven't done anything easy this year, and it looks like it's going to be the same in the Coliseum. "I'm not going to make any alibi about the weather or playing conditions. The weather was no worse than that we played in much of the year, and the playing conditions were the same for both clubs. The big trouble was that the Dodgers hit when it counted and we didn't."[57] Asked about the game winning hit, Lopez offered a mild rebuke against his shortstop. "Had he reached for the ball with his gloved hand instead of with both hands, Lu would have had a much better chance to adjust and at least knock the ball down."[58]

Losing hurler Donovan, known for his quick temper and New England terseness, was puffing on a cigar while dressing. Asked if the heat had gotten to him, he replied: "No, the

Dodgers got to me. They got to me good."[59] Another reporter inquired what Donovan had been throwing. The hurler replied with a wink: "Sliders, fastballs, and a change-of-pace. When the ump wasn't looking, I loaded 'em good with spit."[60] In reply to a query about the screen, Donovan joked: "Listen, if I was manager of the Los Angeles club I'd get eight baseball players and an ape. Even an ape could play left-field in this park."[61]

Told that his good-natured behavior was a surprise, as he had been expected to be sulking, Donovan flicked ashes from his cigar and said sarcastically: "Blow my stack? Naw, I'm a nice guy. I love to be a good loser. When I'm beaten, I say what's the difference? And if anyone thinks I mean all this baloney, he's nuts!"[62] Donning his blue suit jacket, the pitcher departed, yelling over his shoulders to reporters: "You can give the rest of your questions to Staley. Staley always finishes up for Donovan."[63]

The fourth contest, played before a new record throng of 92,650, was a rematch between Wynn and Craig. In the third frame, the Sox unraveled, as after Wynn had retired the first two batters the Dodgers combined five hits and two errors to claim a 4–0 lead. "The team that scrounged and scrimped and never gave anything away all season," wrote a stunned Arthur Daley, "suddenly became as wildly extravagant as a big shot executive with an unlimited expense account."[64]

The Sox always appeared ready to overtake the Dodgers and finally tied the score in the seventh with a four-run rally off Craig, highlighted by a three-run homer by Lollar. However, in the bottom of the eighth, Gil Hodges lofted a towering fly over the left-field screen off Staley, giving the home team and reliever Sherry a 5–4 triumph. Arthur Daley likened the game's conclusion to a horror movie, writing: "Like a monster that emerged alive from one of those Hollywood horror movies The Thing gave shudders and thrills today. The Thing is a grotesque screen at the left-field end of the misshapen ball field laid out in the Coliseum. It has been terrifying pitchers since the Dodgers moved to this Never-Never-Land from Brooklyn. It frightened Roger Craig in the seventh inning. Then it gave Gerry Staley the screaming-meemies in the eighth."[65]

David Condon of the *Chicago Tribune* poignantly reviewed the game as being more like a sad novel of unfulfilled dreams. "The bell tolls with an ominous echo this mournful night. It tolls with the somber suggestion that the 1959 World Series will be finished here tomorrow. It tolls for Chicago's Cinderella team in spiked slippers. That costly smash by Gil Hodges pushed the Sox to the verge of midnight. They know it. They know that nightfall, too, may find their championship hopes entombed within the gray walls of the mammoth Coliseum. They await a fateful tomorrow. But each hears the bell tolling. Each is apprehensive that he hears a requiem. There is the hollow realization that the Go-Go Sox may be gone."[66]

Despite the gloomy scenario set forth by Condon and others, inside the Chicago clubhouse there was no despair, only anger and a promise of going back home for a sixth game. Al Smith slumped on the dressing room bench, wiping his smog-reddened eyes, and muttered disgustedly: "Hodges' run was an easy out anywhere but here. It landed ten rows behind the 320' sign. I watched it all the way, but I couldn't do anything about it."[67] Sitting on a trunk, Lopez, his right elbow resting on a stack of towels, was exhausted, but he still managed a smile and gave the assembled media both a prediction and a history lesson, saying softly: "We're going to take this Series back to Chicago. We still have a helluva chance. The Dodgers are a good team, but not that good. We've been doing a cliffhanging act all season. It takes four games to win the World Series, and they haven't won the fourth one yet. Sometimes that's the hardest one. Don't forget last year's Milwaukee-Yankee Series. The Braves were ahead three games to one, just like the Dodgers are now. You know what happened — the Yankees came back to win the Series."[68]

As the Dodgers trooped into their dressing room, Alston held up three fingers and pointed to a sign on the chalkboard that read: "One to go-go-go!"[69] The players, however, were so careful to avoid any premature celebration that one writer said they reminded him of "mourners passing before a beloved brother's bier."[70] Asked about the lack of emotion, Alston noted: "They know that it isn't over yet. When they win it — if they do — you'll hear one helluva racket."[71]

As they took the field for batting and fielding drills before the fifth game, the Chicagoans sported a new look. At the suggestion of trainer Eddie Froelich the customary black stockings with red and white stripes returned. "Eddie thought it would change our luck," Lopez explained, "and I'm for anything to do that. We'd go barefoot if it would help."[72]

Lopez met the media during practice and tried to explain the reasons for his club's disappointing California performance. "We are a defensive club with good pitching and speed," he began. "The Coliseum robs us of these good points. It isn't the short fence that hurts because of balls hit against it or over it. Where that short left-field handicaps us is that we can't run. You can't go from first to third, and you can't even score from second on a clean hit. Those are things we have been able to do all season to score because we can't overpower anybody. When we come into the Coliseum that is taken away from us. Therefore, our speed doesn't do us any good. Insofar as fielding is concerned, you can't make those outstanding plays because you can't see the ball. On top of that, the infield surface is treacherous."[73]

Standing nearby, team captain Nellie Fox interrupted to add the players' perspective. "We can't forget the conditions are the same for both clubs," Fox said, his famous chaw of tobacco firmly lodged in his cheek. "But there is one difference. The Dodgers have played in this park — pardon — stadium for two years. They have had a chance to adjust themselves to the conditions, at least to some extent. Certainly they know how to play the left-field fence, and they know how to play this tricky infield that is the worst in the big leagues. The grass is heavy matted stuff used for football. The ball is slowed up by it, and then it hits the skin part, which is hard and fast as lightning. Ground balls can take sudden skipping hops, and you can't gauge the speed as they come off the grass and onto the hard ground. That's really what happened on that grounder by Furillo that hopped over Aparicio's glove."[74]

Hearing Fox's comments, Paul Richards erupted in laughter. "The way they're playing," the Baltimore Oriole manager cracked, "they wouldn't have been able to win even in Yellowstone Park."[75]

For the third consecutive afternoon a new attendance record was established as 92,706 sweltering fans wedged into the mammoth bowl demonstrating, as Arthur Daley noted with remorse, "that they would walk barefooted on live coals to root for the Dodgers — Flatbush never had such crusading fervor."[76] Among the throng was Ty Cobb, who was collecting autographs on three baseballs for his grandchildren.[77] Absent again, however, was Joe DiMaggio, who had viewed the opening game in the Coliseum from a box seat. The "Yankee Clipper" had decided to watch the remaining games on television in his hotel room, explaining: "I can't follow the ball in that place after it leaves the bat. It's no fun. I don't envy those players trying to see it in that white shirt background."[78]

Commissioner Frick was also coming under attack for scheduling games to begin at 1 o'clock, during the hottest part of the day. Not only was the Coliseum field baked into adobe-like concrete, but also more than sixty spectators had had to be treated for heat prostration in the opening game.[79] As David Condon accurately observed: "Health was endangered because the television sponsors wanted early afternoon starts; the sponsors dared not have the World Series, with its great audience, cut into the lush evening program hours. If playing the World Series in the Coliseum is any yardstick, baseball has become much more of a business than a sport. Maybe that's the way the ball is bouncing these days."[80]

Once the game began, Sandy Koufax and Bob Shaw engaged in a tense pitching duel. In the fourth, the Sox took a one-run lead off Koufax, and entering the home half of the seventh Shaw, who had wriggled out of precarious situations in the third, fourth, and fifth innings by forcing the Dodgers to leave runners on the bases, maintained his slender lead. Then, in the seventh, with one out, Chuck Essegian drew a pass and Don Zimmer was inserted as a pinch runner. Pinch-hitter Duke Snider forced Zimmer at second, and Johnny Podres was inserted as a pinch runner for the gimpy-kneed Snider. Gilliam singled off the screen, sending Podres to second. Lopez, whose "mental generator was giving off sparks," moved Al Smith from right to left and inserted Rivera into right for defensive purposes.[81] After Shaw wild pitched both runners ahead a base, Charlie Neal drove a shot toward the gap in right-center, but Rivera, flashing the speed that Smith did not possess, made a spectacular catch only eight feet from the wall to preserve the lead.

The following inning, the Dodgers launched yet another assault. Wally Moon led off the frame with a drive to center that Landis lost in the sun. After Larker flied out to right, Hodges singled to center and took second on Landis' futile throw to cut down the lead runner.

With men on second and third with one out, a managerial chess match ensued. Alston sent up Ron Fairly, a left-handed batter, to pinch-hit for Demeter. Lopez countered by bringing in southpaw Billy Pierce. Alston responded by lifting Fairly for right-handed slugger Rip Repulski, who was given an intentional pass to load the bases. Alston called upon Furillo to deliver in the clutch again. Lopez strode to the mound and waved for Donovan. Tossing the New Englander the ball, Lopez admonished: "Get it over, and keep it low!"[82] Donovan induced Furillo to pop to third, and Zimmer to loft a soft fly to left to end the threat. Donovan then retired the Dodgers in the ninth to preserve Shaw's 1–0 victory and send the Series back to Chicago.

In the subdued Los Angeles dressing quarters, still filled with cases of champagne and television cameras in place to capture the joy of the anticipated crowning of new world champions, a youthful reporter commented to Alston: "Hey, Walt. I notice the 'One to go-go-go' sign is still up." Alston looked at the writer quizzically and replied: "Sure. That still stands."[83] Asked about Lopez' maneuvering, Alston smiled and said with candor: "I'll give Al a helluva lot of credit for bringing in Rivera. He made the right move at the right time. However, in the eighth it all worked out the way I wanted it to, with Furillo up and the bases loaded. I can't think of anybody I'd rather have up there at a time like that. He just missed his pitch."[84]

Lopez, beaming for the first time in days, held the locker room door open, urging reporters: "Come right in, fellas. Remember I told you that if we won this one we'd take the World Series. We're gonna win this thing!"[85] First to be surrounded by the correspondents and camera crews was Donovan, who merrily bantered with them. "How do I feel? I won't be able to stop smiling for three days. I wish I could in all honesty say I was completely calm, but I've never been in a spot exactly like that. I wasn't exactly whistling 'Yankee Doodle.' What was I throwing? Mostly fastballs and sliders, and, of course, a couple of spitters."[86] Erupting with laughter, he added: "I was just kidding about the spitters. Why should I tell the Dodgers what I throw? Let 'em find out for themselves."[87]

Asked if he could have made the catch in right like Rivera did, Al Smith smiled and shook his head thoughtfully. "I really don't know," he said, his eyes twinkling. "There is a lot to getting the jump on the ball and things like that. Let's just say I'm glad we didn't have to find out."[88]

On the flight back to Chicago, Barry Latman vocally proclaimed his displeasure regarding Lopez' pronouncement that Wynn would start game six, instead of Latman. Lopez spoke to his young hurler and explained: "If I start you and we lose, I get second-guessed. If I start Wynn and lose, no one will say a word."[89] To reporters, Lopez justified his decision in less self-serving terms, saying: "I've always said that in a game I had to win, Early would be my pitcher, and we never needed one more than this one."[90]

Shortly after arriving in Chicago, Wynn verbally lambasted the Los Angeles press and the Coliseum. "Those bush league reporters made us look like a lousy club just because we've had some bad experiences in that circus grounds they call a ballpark out there," the burly hurler snarled to the assembled media members and Sox fans. "They've been saying we ought to try to get into a third major league. They come around to interview you. Then you'd look in the paper the next day, and you couldn't recognize what you had said. One guy asked me so many silly questions I wondered if he had ever been in a ballpark before. I told him to go sit in the stands and give me his typewriter; I'd write his story for him. The Dodgers are a real good ball club. It's a shame to make them play in that place, much less decide a World Series. Maybe we ought to finish in Soldiers' Field. I'm not taking anything away from the Dodgers. Their guys don't like playing in that place either, even though they've had a chance to get used to the hardship. Well, now we're back in a real ballpark, and I think everybody's happy about it."[91]

Under sunny skies and pleasant temperatures, 47,653 patrons pushed through the gates intent on seeing the White Sox capture the Series tying game. During Chicago's batting practice, the early arrivals were treated to some unexpected entertainment when Mrs. Antoinette Greene jumped from the box seats in right-field and began to run the bases. She rounded first, slid into second, regained her feet and slid into third with two police-women, Mary Scannell and Francine Grannon, in pursuit, amid laughter and applause from the Go-Go Sox players. Mrs. Greene might have completed her trip and escaped had she not heeded the pleas of photographers to slide into third once again. This enabled the police to seize her and escort her from the field to be charged with disorderly conduct. Asked why she made her dash, Mrs. Greene gushed: "I just got so excited I couldn't contain myself. I wanted to see how fast I could run the bases."[92]

Unfortunately, the unfulfilled trip around the sacks was an omen for the Sox, as they, too, failed to complete their quest. In the third inning, Duke Snider rocked Wynn for a two-run homer, and in the following frame they battered Wynn and Donovan for six more runs, giving Johnny Podres an 8–0 lead. Podres, however, fell victim to his own emotions in the bottom of the fourth and was removed in favor of Larry Sherry, who completed the contest. Podres later explained what occurred: "Early Wynn knocked down a few of our guys, and they started grumbling on the bench for me to 'knock somebody on their ass.' So in the bottom of the fourth I figured it was a good time. I had a man out, nobody on base, and an 8–0 lead. Jim Landis was the batter. I wanted to push him back a little bit. So I threw one. It was a good brush-back pitch, high and inside. The problem was, Landis had decided to bunt, and damn if he didn't go right into the ball. The thing sailed up and got him right in the head. When he went down I started shaking. Hitting him like that shook me up so bad I lost my composure. I walked the next guy, grooved one to Kluszewski which he hit into the right-field stands. Then I walked the next guy. The next guy who walked was Walter Alston and the one after him was me."[93]

Another fourth inning Dodger casualty was Coach Charlie Dressen, who became the first participant in a World Series game since Washington outfielder Heinie Manush in 1933 to be ejected by an umpire for misconduct.[94] Dressen had been verbally assailing not only Sox players, but also plate umpire Dascoli for his calls on balls and strikes. While Dascoli ignored the profanities hurled by Dressen, second-base umpire Ed Hurley did not, and warned Dressen to be quiet. When Dressen screamed that Hurley should "shut up," the American League arbiter gave him the thumb. The fiery coach raced toward Hurley, raised his arm as though preparing to throw a punch, and had to be restrained by Alston. For his actions and language, which were both seen and heard by Commissioner Frick, the Dodger coach was fined $200 "for profanity" and $100 "for showboating tactics" after he was ejected.[95]

The 9–3 final score was not indicative of the thrashing received by the local team. Erudite Red Smith of New York, one of the greatest literary writers of sports since Grantland Rice, placed the sixth game into perspective as part of Chicago's frontier heritage: "The settlers fought to the last man, but Fort Dearborn lies in smoking ruins tonight, every defender dead and scalped. Everybody but Mrs. O'Leary's cow got into the act today when a howling pack of savages from the West, cutting, shooting, and burning, breached Comiskey Park's tall green stockade and laid waste to the championship dream which American League baseball fans here had clutched to their bosoms through forty barren years. Not since the fire of '71 had inhabitants of this trading post seen such a disaster. By the start of the eighth inning, women and children were fleeing for the exits, but there was no escape. Charlie Dressen, savage sub-chief of the merciless crew, was waiting in ambush to pick them off as they fled, having been excused from the Dodgers' dugout by the umpires. It was the sort of thing ordinarily forbidden on Chicago's South Side except in the stockyards themselves."[96]

Even the weather seemed symbolic, as though "the far-thinking and dramatic Bill Veeck had ordered it."[97] Arthur Daley wrote of the day: "The sun beamed down cheerfully at the start of the game. By the time it was over even Chicago's sky had donned mourning of dark black. In the last half of the ninth, the tears, sprinkles of rain, came. The beloved White Sox had lost in the World Series."[98] The meteorological analogy was carried further by Red Smith, who observed: "An instant after the final putout, a great, bright rainbow arched across the sky, ostensibly corny. It flamed on the dark and dismal horizon of the East, but the light that painted its coarsely garish hues came from the West. Ah, Hollywood."[99]

In the tiny, hot, antiquated visitors' dressing room along the west wall of Comiskey Park the Dodgers began the victory celebration that would later move to a Chicago hotel and finally back to Los Angeles. Dodger veterans of the 1955 championship took the triumph more or less in stride, but the younger players poured beer over one another's heads, leading a scribe to remark ruefully: "What a waste."[100] Alston, after smiling at Zimmer's repeated chants of "So the Coliseum got 'em," greeted Lopez and White Sox Vice President Charles Comiskey, who offered their congratulations.[101] The soft-spoken Alston then told reporters: "This victory seems bigger to me right now than the 1955 championship over New York in seven games. This was a better team effort. It was the hardest working team I've ever had. I can't single out any player as our key man, but I'll say I've never seen a kid so young as good as Larry Sherry."[102] Dressen shouted: "We beat 'em at their own game. We out-ran 'em, out-pitched 'em, out-fielded 'em, and Lord knows we sure out-hit 'em. We just played better."[103] Veteran Carl Furillo offered the most profound explanation of why the Dodgers were the new world champions, saying: "We won because we had the will and the heart. Their criticism of our ballpark made us all the more determined, and every man put out something extra."[104]

Meeting the media, Lopez tried to mask his obvious sadness at losing his second World Series in six years. "It was just one of those bad days for us," he lamented. "We never had a chance. They were hitting the ball solid. Wynn had all his stuff, and he sure did a good job. As someone said: 'you can't win 'em all,' but I sure would have liked to have won this one."[105]

The Sox skipper then encapsulated why his team was defeated. "The Dodgers played good ball, real good ball, and Alston did a helluva job of managing," he stated. "They had momentum carried over from their regular season closing series. We hurt ourselves mainly because we couldn't hit with men on the bases in the games at Los Angeles. And our defense was bad in the games there, too. But that's not an excuse. The Coliseum is as fair for one club as another. Larry Sherry, their relief pitcher, and Charlie Neal both did great jobs. Sherry was the decisive factor, though."[106]

Veeck was his usual candid self, confessing: "We didn't have the same chance as the Dodgers. We got licked by the one thing we didn't have in common: power. It would have been the same outcome if all the games had been played here or in Los Angeles. We didn't have the same opportunity to win. The Dodgers were the better club."[107]

Wynn, biting his lip in a vain effort to control his emotions, assumed full blame for the day's debacle. After apologizing to Lopez and club Vice President Charles Comiskey, the veteran hurler said simply: "I goofed it up good. I was trying to baffle 'em, and it didn't work. I thought I had pretty good stuff, and I wasn't tired. There were no effects from only having two day's rest or anything. Then Snider got hold of a high, outside fastball and gave it a ride. It was just a bad job."[108]

Jim Landis, whose initial reaction to the day's event was that he was "glad to be alive" after being beaned, later reflected: "The Dodgers were more of a veteran club with Snider, Hodges, and Furillo. They may have been on the downside, but they had been there many times before. I know this seems like a lousy reason, but our composure wasn't as good as theirs, and in a Series with 90,000 people watching, veterans can make a difference."[109]

Whatever the reason, one thing was indisputable: the Go-Go-Go White Sox had become the "Going-Going-Gone" White Sox."[110] Oliver Kuechle of the *Milwaukee Journal* was accurate in his harsh assessment that the White Sox "went hunting an elephant with a bean blower and wound up just where such hunters usually wind up. The 'go-go-go' Sox were a happy figment of publicity and the champions of a very ordinary American League."[111] Til Ferdenzi of the *New York Journal-American* wrote that the Series was "artistically an undistinguished event in the history of baseball" and that it should be referred to as the Sherry Series because without him the Dodgers would have been "the White Sox in Los Angeles livery."[112] Lou Smith of the *Cincinnati Enquirer* assessed the Series well, stating that "the better of two mediocre teams won."[113] Joe Williams of the *New York World Telegram & Sun* seconded Veeck's analysis, writing: "The Dodgers deserved to win. They had the pitching and the punch, and P&P will always constitute the meat and potatoes of a winning baseball menu."[114]

Ironically, the only overt display of emotion over the result of the Series came from the jilted former Dodger fans in Brooklyn and those in the Dodgers' new home in the West. Embittered Brooklynites cursed Dodger owner Walter O'Malley and screamed abuse at their former heroes, telling New York interviewers: "They stink! They're lousy bums! They're lousy! They don't deserve the pennant or the World Series."[115] Happy Angelenos, however, joyfully held up newspapers with the headline "Dodgers Wash Out Sox!" and repeated the joke: "Why are the White Sox going to change their name to the White Nylons? Because nylons get more runs!"[116]

The 1959 World Series conjured up no memories of illustrious contests of the past. It was, as Jimmy Cannon of the *New York Journal-American* noted, "as bland as an ulcer diet."[117] Yet it was noteworthy. More than 42,000,000 people watched the games daily on NBC television, a total 3½ times the number of fans who had attended the modern World Series since its inception in 1903.[118] It was the first World Series in which a Morse code operator was not on duty in the press box, as teleprinting machines were utilized.[119] It not only smashed attendance records, but it resulted in baseball's first half-million dollar gate, as receipts from the first game in Los Angeles totaled $549,071.76, and afforded a record winner's share of $11,231.18 per man.[120] Perhaps, however, it was Jimmy Powers of the *New York Daily News* who best put the 1959 World Series into perspective: "One has to admit this was a terrific Series. Not so much for the classic purity of play, which was woefully absent, but from the standpoint of color, drama, backdrop, and historic first appearance under the subtropical palmettos of California."[121]

WHITE SOX VS. ASTROS, 2005

Before the 2005 season, at least one major baseball publication predicted a fourth place finish for the White Sox in the five team American League Central Division and the odds of winning the World Series were 22–1.[1] Manager Ozzie Guillen's team, however, confounded the experts by getting off to a fast start, fighting off a late season rush by the Cleveland Indians, and winning the Central Division by a six game margin over the Tribe, finishing with a record of 99–63. The Sox then swept the defending world champion Boston Red Sox in the American League Divisional Series and suffered only a single defeat at the hands of the Los Angeles Angels of Anaheim in the American League Championship Series to capture the pennant and send the Sox to the World Series for the first time in forty-six years. As a team, the Sox rated only twelfth in batting, with a .262 average, but, like the 1959 Go-Go Sox, they were known for their clutch hitting and ability to come from behind to win close games by manufacturing runs. According to outfielder Aaron Rowand the Sox motto was "don't score more than we have to," and the Sox proved this by having a record of 35–19 in one-run games.[2] From third to first, the infield consisted of Joe Crede (.252, 22, 62), Juan Uribe (.252, 16, 71), Tadahito Iguchi (.278, 15, 71), and Paul Konerko (.283, 40, 100). Scott Podsednik (.290, 0, 25), who led the team with 59 stolen bases, in left, Aaron Rowand (.270, 13, 69) patrolling center, and Jermaine Dye (.274, 31, 86) in right made up the outfield. A.J. Pierzynski (.257, 18, 56) was the first-string catcher, and Carl Everett (.251, 23, 87) served as the regular designated hitter.

The bulwark of the Sox success was the pitching staff, led by starters Mark Buehrle (16–8, 3.12), Freddie Garcia (14–8, 3.87), Jon Garland (18–10, 3.30), and Jose Contreras (15–7, 3.61). The bullpen was anchored by Dustin Hermanson (2–4, 2.04 34 saves), Cliff Politte (7–1, 2.00, 1 save), Damasco Marte (3–4, 3.77, 4 saves), Bobby Jenks (1–1, 2.75, 6 saves), and Shingo Takarsu (1–2, 5.97, 8 saves).

The National League champion Houston Astros overcame a 15–30 start to win the wild card berth, with a record of 89–73. Manager Phil Garner's squad then defeated the National League East Division champion Atlanta Braves in the National League Division Series and the Central Division champion St. Louis Cardinals to claim their first league championship in their 44-year history. Like their World Series opponents, the Astros were viewed as longshots for postseason play, generally picked to finish no higher than third and a 20–1 pick to win the world championship.[3] This led Chicago's Guillen to predict: "I think it's going to be a real attractive and weird World Series because you've got two teams that aren't supposed to be there. You're not going to see the big name franchises. I think it's just good for baseball, these two franchises that that have never been there — one the first time ever, the other people forget when was the last time."[4]

Mirroring the Sox, the Astros were a good hitting team, which relied on pitching for success. The infield was anchored by eighteen-year-veteran Craig Biggio (.264, 26, 69) at second, surrounded by shortstop Adam Everett (.248, 11, 54), Morgan Ensberg (.283, 36, 101) at third, and first baseman Mike Lamb (.236, 12, 53). The outfield was manned by Chris Burke (.250, 5, 26) in left, Willy Taveras (.291, 3, 29) in center, and sometime first-sacker Lance Berkman (.293, 24, 82) in right. Brad Ausmus (.258, 3, 47) was behind the plate.

The heart of the Astros' strength was its mound corps, anchored by starters Roy Oswalt (20–12, 2.94), Andy Pettitte (17–9, 2.39), Roger Clemens (13–8, 1.87), Wandy Rodriguez (10–10, 5.53), and Brandon Backe (10–8, 4.76). The relievers were headed by Brad Lidge (4–4, 2.29, 42 saves) and Dan Wheeler (2–3, 2.21, 3 saves).

On the eve of the Series, the press paid more attention to the ethnic make-up of the Sox, the Cub-Sox division in Chicago, and the differences between Chicago and Houston than on the upcoming diamond classic. The *Chicago Sun-Times* dubbed the 6–5 favorite Sox "Team Diversity" because it was represented by not only players, coaches, and trainers from the United States, but also Japan, Venezuela, Cuba, Puerto Rico, Korea, Dominican Republic, and the Netherlands.[5] Guillen added: "They get along because they have to. They're going to spend a lot of time together. No matter what country, what color, what religion, what you believe, we have a team.... They might not hang out together on the street, but when they're in the ballpark, they have to fight for one together for one reason, the Chicago White Sox."[6] A *Chicago Tribune* editorial echoed this sentiment asserting proudly that while there was not a native Chicagoan on the Sox, they were "a team of spirit, determination and diversity that reflects its city. A century ago the Cubs had a poetic-sounding double play combination of Tinker to Evers to Chance. Today's Sox have Uribe to Iguchi to Konerko. It doesn't roll off the tongue, but it sure sounds like the Chicago of today."[7]

The intra-city Chicago rivalry manifested itself, sometimes bitterly. A "Voice of the People" letter to the *Chicago Tribune* stated succinctly: "On the North Side, it has always been 'boo-hoo, that mean billy goat won't let us win the World Series ... it's not our fault, we're cursed ... wahhhhhh!' What a bunch of babies. On the South Side, we don't need to hide behind a curse. We take our lumps, make no excuses, claim no curses and show up and root for our team, win or lose.... The South Side has always been tougher, and always comes out on top. Remember what happened on St. Valentine's Day in 1929? That was a little dispute between Al Capone's South Siders and Bugs Moran's North Side gang. Guess who won? That's right the South Side. So take that curse baloney and stuff it."[8] In another *Tribune* article, Brian Hiatt, likening the Cubs and Sox to two homely sisters, wrote wistfully: "This year the Sox have a date for the prom. Cub fans don't and haven't in the last 60 years. Not only is our acne-scarred, mouthy, bratty little sister going to the prom, she just might be crowned queen. We're so happy for you, Sox fans. Now excuse me, I'm going upstairs to my room to pout."[9] Even Illinois Governor Rod Blagojevich, a devoted Cub loyalist was enmeshed in the rivalry. After saying he wanted the Sox to win, he added that he would not wear a Sox cap. "You love your team, and I love the Cubs. I think it would be wrong for me, now that the White Sox are going to the World Series, to put their hat on," the Governor explained, adding diplomatically: "I wish, and I'll be very frank here and I would say this to Mayor [Richard J.] Daley's face, I wish the World Series were going to be on the North Side of the city and not on the South Side of the city, if I had my druthers. But since it's not on the North Side of the city, I'm delighted that it's on the South Side of Chicago."[10] Many Cub fans were not as generous as the Governor, as *Time* reported that a poll showed 36 percent of Cub fans would be rooting for Houston.[11]

A *Tribune* staff writer said the Series would be the "City of Big Shoulders meets Space City, USA" and that the "White Sox are named after an actual object. The Astros, formerly called the Colt 45s, were named in 1965 for Houston's new NASA Space Center. Or perhaps it is a nod to the Jetsons' dog."[12] Another noted that U.S. Cellular Field, or "New Comiskey" as many Sox fans still referred to it, sounded better than Houston's Minute Maid Park, known affectionately as "The Juice Box," adding: "Minute Maid Park sounds like the name of a horse track. I know they were renamed the Astros because of the space program being headquartered in Houston, but why isn't it Tang Field?"[13] A *Tribune writer* observed cynically that in Houston, "a city with a huge inferiority complex, wrapped inside an identity crisis, surrounded by low self-esteem," the Museum of Natural Science featured an exhibit called: "Diana: A Celebration," displaying "such rare scientific specimens as '28 stunning designer dresses' once worn by the late Princess of Wales."[14] He further noted that the lead sentence on the city's website stated: "The heat. The humidity. The hurricanes. The flying cockroaches. The mosquitoes. The traffic. The construction. The sprawl. The refineries. Houston. It's worth it," and that the city deserved its signature phrase: "Houston — we've got a problem."[15]

Meeting with reporters before the initial contest, Guillen, dubbed by Sox faithful as "The Wizard of Oz," playfully stated, "I'm not the best manager, but I am the best looking."[16] Becoming serious, Guillen reminisced about his baseball hero, Chico Carrasquel, who had played shortstop for the White Sox from 1950–1955, and had died in May, 2005. Guillen said wistfully of his fellow Venezuelan: "He never was a selfish guy. He never was jealous about anything. He was just happy with what he had. The way the White Sox helped him and the way he felt proud to be a Sox. Sometimes you feel guilty about winning before someone else does. That's how I feel about Chico. You know, I have two pictures of Chico hanging in my office. I don't have a picture of my parents."[17] He smiled and added: "He'd better be looking down on us. I'm going to come to him and say, 'Just put your hands on us and we'll see what happens.'"[18]

For the Astros, the pre-Series intrigue for the Series centered on oft-injured Jeff Bagwell, a fifteen-veteran of 2,150 games for the Houston franchise. Despite being limited to thirty-nine games because of shoulder problems, Bagwell was the spiritual leader of the team and hoped to be used as a designated hitter during the games played in Chicago. However, he added that Manager Garner's decision had to be based on what was best for gaining victory, saying somberly: "It has to be about the team. It can't be about me. It would be a great story if I can DH. It has to be for the right reasons. It can't be because I played here for so long. That wouldn't be fair to these guys. We have a bunch of kids that love to play baseball. They work hard at it. That's refreshing to see in this day and age. It's not about money. It's about loving to play. It gives you a little rejuvenation."[19] Mike Lamb stated bluntly: "He [Bagwell] should be the designated hitter. That's pretty simple. If it means less playing time for me, so be it." Brad Ausmus summed it up simply, saying: "I think the guys in this clubhouse would be disappointed if Bagwell wasn't in the lineup."[20] Garner, amid criticism that his heart was dictating to his head, started Bagwell.

The Series opened in Chicago, which one writer said "was as restless as a toddler in an art museum," on Saturday, October 22, with Jay Mariotti of the *Chicago Sun-Times* noting in Grantland Rice style the significance of the event. "When Chicago hosts a World

Series, it stands to reason that the Great Lake will become a tropical forest, the aldermen will scrub themselves with detergent, and Oprah [Winfrey] will morph into a waif," he wrote. "But the pie has fallen from the sky, crazily enough, crashing onto the South Side like a lost meteor and ready to unfold in dramatic splendor."[21]

Following the ceremonial first pitch by 71-year-old Luis Aparicio, the base-stealing hero of the 1959 White Sox, who was accompanied to the mound by other 1959 Sox players Billy Pierce, Jim Rivera, Jim Landis, and Bob Shaw, and a flawless rendition of the national anthem by Josh Groban, a crowd of 41,206 settled in on a chilly (53 degree), drizzly, windy evening to watch Jose Contreras face Astros ace Roger Clemens.

Despite surrendering an early 405' center-field home run blast to Mike Lamb, Contreras, whom Julia Keller of the *Chicago Tribune* described as having "a face like a Founding Father, a brooding, thoughtful visage that belongs on a stamp or a coin as much as on a baseball card," fooled the Astros "as if he were serving up complicated words in a spelling bee."[22]

Meanwhile, the 43-year-old Clemens, the oldest pitcher to start a World Series game since Grover Cleveland Alexander in 1926, showing the effects of a lingering hamstring strain, surrendered a 383' home run to Jermaine Dye, whom a writer noted in classic style hit the ball "with the matter-of-fact efficiency of a guy finishing up some paperwork at the office."[23] Clemens limped from the game the game trailing 3–1 after throwing 54 pitches in a "two inning eyesore," looking, as Jay Mariotti noted, "every hour of his 43 years, 2 months, and 18 days on earth."[24] Another observer noted that the Sox "treated the Hall of Fame bound 43-year-old like a shopworn relic from an old-timers' game."[25] Suddenly the game had become anti-climactic, as Julia Keller admitted, because "there was no one to hate, no aging legend to fear and resent and secretly revere. Just an opposing team."[26]

The Astros tied the score in the third, but in the fourth Joe Crede, as Keller vividly described, swung his bat "like it was a broom and his momma had told him to sweep the porch because his pretty cousin was coming over," and launched a long home run off reliever Wandy Rodriguez, giving the Sox a 4–3 lead.

In the visitors' eighth, Willy Taveras rapped his second double of the game and drove Contreras from the mound in favor of Neil Cotts. Berkman drilled a single to left, which was hit too hard for Taveras to score. Chris Burke entered the game as a pinch runner for Berkman. Cotts then fanned Morgan Ensberg on a 94-mile-per-hour fastball and Mike Lamb on a 90-mile-per-hour fastball. With Jeff Bagwell coming to the plate, Guillen raced to the mound, his arms spread three-feet wide at the waist, looking as a reporter recounted, like a man "sharing with the crowd the size of the last fish he caught."[27] To Chicago fans, however, this was Guillen's trademark gesture to bring in his "big boy," 24-year-old Bobby Jenks, whom Jay Mariotti dubbed "Mr. Tons of Fun," the 6'3", 270 pound right-handed flame-throwing reliever.[28] The crowd cheered Jenks, as Rick Morrissey of the *Chicago Tribune* noted, "as if he had just lowered taxes."[29]

With Bagwell poised to assume the storybook hero's role, Jenks reached back and fired two straight 99-mile-per-hour fastballs. The next three pitches were clocked at 100–miles-per-hour, and the overpowered Bagwell struck out swinging. Jenks then proceeded to strike out the side in the ninth to preserve a 5–3 victory for Contreras.

In the victors' clubhouse, there were expressions of pleasure, but not wild jubilation. As A.J. Pierzynski explained: "It means nothing. If it was our fourth win, it would mean something."[30] Asked about Guillen's manner of signaling for him to enter a game, Jenks grinned and replied diplomatically: "I think it's pretty funny, calling the big guy in. He does a lot of things out of humor. He doesn't mean anything by it, and I take it with a smile."[31] Jenks said of his clutch strikeout of Bagwell: "Looking at the scouting reports, I knew he chases fastballs outside the zone, so that was what I was trying to do. My strength against his weakness."[32] Guillen summarized the contest as "a good Chicago baseball game," but he bemoaned that his team "should have scored a little bit more."[33] The Sox manager then praised his squad's efforts against Clemens, saying: "He's the best pitcher ever in the history of baseball. When you make him leave in the second inning, no matter what you bring in from the bullpen, it's not going to be better than him."[34]

The Astros were downcast but not despondent over their defeat, with Brad Ausmus stating: "It's not a best of one series. It certainly isn't anything we don't think we can't overcome."[35] Lance Berkman was dismissive that the Astros went 2-for-11 with runners in scoring position, noting dryly: "It's the way we play baseball. We're not the least bit concerned about that. We know that we're going to give ourselves a chance to score runs, and sometimes we get it done and sometimes we don't. I don't think tonight was about our inability to get guys in, but their bullpen making quality pitches when they had to. The story of the game is the times we had guys on and hit balls hard and they made great defensive plays."[36] Mike Lamb echoed this sentiment, saying defensively: "Obviously, we need to do a better job, but we've struggled with that all year and we're in the World Series. I don't think it's time to panic. We haven't panicked all season, so why start now? It's not like Cotts and Jenks have invisible pitches. I don't think we got absolutely fooled."[37] Morgan Ensberg, who led the team in runs batted in during the season, was less philosophic, and blamed himself for the defeat, stating: "You can't strike out with a man on third and no outs. You have to put the ball in play. I didn't do that in the eighth. I blew it."[38] Bagwell said of his inability to get the game-tying hit off Jenks: "Easier said than done. It's not like the guy is throwing soft-toss to me. If I see that pitch 250 times, I'm still not going to hit it. It's hard in those situations. I loved the opportunity, and I wish I had the at-bat over again, but that's just not the way it is."[39] Manager Garner snorted the obvious: "What hurt was, we struck out for five of the last six outs. That's what hurt us."[40] Pitching coach Jim Hickey spoke of the courage of Clemens and the psychological impact of his early departure, saying: "He wanted to give us another couple innings, so we wouldn't burn up the bullpen in the first game. That's Roger for you. But we decided the best thing to do was shut him down. I don't know [if Clemens' exit lifted the spirits of the White Sox], but you'd rather see a rookie, I suppose, than Roger Clemens."[41]

The following evening, 41,402 spectators braved temperatures in the lower 40s, a 10 mile per hour wind, and a steady rain to witness Mark Buehrle face Andy Pettitte in a battle of southpaw aces. The Sox took an early 2–1 lead primarily because of poor fielding by third-sacker Ensberg, who had hit a home run in the second to give the Astros a 1–0 margin, who gave what a *Houston Chronicle* writer described as a futile "*ole* wave" at Rowand's grounder, and left-fielder Chris Burke misplayed a lazy fly by Pierzynski into a another single, and after Crede blooped a single to right, Biggio dropped a pop fly to left to let in the second Sox tally.[42] However, Lance Berkman's sacrifice fly in the third tied the game and his two-run double in the fifth gave the Astros a 4–2 lead entering the seventh inning. In that frame, Garner elected to remove Pettitte, who had allowed eight hits and thrown 98 pitches, and bring in right-hander Dan Wheeler, who subsequently was removed after surrendering a hit, a walk, and hitting Jermaine Dye with a pitch that the Astros claimed hit Dye's bat, not his arm. With the bases loaded, two out, and Paul Konerko at the plate, Garner summoned in reliever Chad Qualls, whom a Chicago writer noted "had been advertised as being tough as trigonometry."[43] Konerko promptly blasted the first pitch over the left-field fence for the first ever Sox Series grand slam and only the eighteenth in Series history, giving Chicago a 6–4 lead.

Buehrle was replaced by Cotts to begin the eighth, and Cotts gave way to Jenks after Houston got two runners on after two were out. Jenks got the final out in the eighth, but with two out and two on in the ninth, pinch hitter Jose Vizcaino singled to short left. Podsednik raced in and heaved a weak two-hop throw to home, which was, in the words of Thomas Boswell of the *Washington Post,* "so lame that the slender White Sox speedster almost could have run the ball to the plate faster."[44] With the game tied, Guillen trotted to the mound to take the ball from Jenks. Pierzynski consoled the distraught hurler by saying, "We'll come back. Don't worry."[45] The Sox escaped the inning without further damage.

In the ninth, fate afford Podsednik a chance to redeem himself, and he seized the opportunity by lifting a 2–1 fastball from ace reliever Brad "Lights Out" Lidge 408' into right-center for his first home run of the year, giving the Sox a hard-fought 7–6 victory. In the Sox dressing room, Pierzynski revealed that during batting practice Podsednik had predicted he would hit a home run.[46] Podsednik quickly added that he was no Babe Ruth, admitting: "I didn't call the shot. No one in the ballpark expected me to hit a home run. That was just fun conversation. But it came at a good time, didn't it?"[47] Konerko said sheepishly: "I'm yesterday's news because of Podsednik."[48] Referring to the birth of his first child earlier in the week, the Sox slugger beamed, and said: "Not too many times are you going to hit a grand slam in a World Series game and have it the second-best thing that happened to you in a week."[49] Jenks spoke of Vizcaino's hit, explaining: "I made a good pitch. The guy was brought in just to face me, left on right. It was a good pitch down and away. He just got enough of it to get it over. We won. That's all that matters."[50] Dye, when asked about the controversial decision on being hit by a pitch, was candid. "It didn't hit me," he confessed. "I turned and he [Umpire Jeff Nelson] told me it hit me. When an umpire tells you to go to first base, you go to first base. I'm not going to tell him I fouled it off."[51] Guillen summarized his feelings simply: "This team made me mad for seven innings. Then, all of a sudden, they made me smile in the ninth."[52]

Houston players were angry that they lost and placed themselves in what Steve Campbell of the *Houston Chronicle* called "a blindfold-and-cigarette predicament," but they looked forward to playing in their home park where they had a major league best record of 53–28.[53] Lidge said of his gopher ball to Podsednik: "I didn't want to fall behind in the count 3–1 and have a chance of him getting on base. I wanted to throw him a strike. It probably got too much of the plate. Obviously, it did. My thinking is, he's not a home run hitter, and I don't want him to be on the bases where he's a threat. You have to put it behind you. These things happen."[54] Manager Garner, visibly angry, snorted: "Clearly, everything they're doing right now is right. They can't do anything wrong. I'm confident we can come back. I'm not comfortable. I'm upset."[55]

During the travel day, Guillen announced that his designated hitter, Carl Everett, would not be used as a position player in the National League park, where the designated hitter was not permitted. Asked if he had told Everett why he was being benched, the Sox manager replied with typical candor: "He should know. I don't like to talk to the players about what I'm going to do because that's what the manager controls. It's not because you don't respect the player. I'm the manager, you're the player. When I put you in, you'll play. If not, and you want to know why, come to me and ask me about it. You might not want to hear what I have to say. Everett has to have a clue about why he's not playing. He's not going to play in front of Podsednik, Rowand, and Dye. I hope he's smart enough to understand that. I'm the manager, and you have to go by my rules."[56]

To further energize Houston emotions, it was revealed that a Chicago fan allegedly harassed and struck Patty Biggio, wife of the Astros second baseman, during the second game. Craig Biggio related the story to a *Houston Chronicle* reporter: "He slapped her and ran. She ran after him. My brother-in-law ended up putting him against the wall. That's pretty sorry. You don't slap a New Jersey girl and get away with it."[57] Brad Ausmus related that his wife, Liz, had been the recipient of lewd gestures and vulgar taunts from Chicago fans, adding: "If I was from Chicago, I'd be embarrassed by the way the Astros' families were treated by the White Sox fans."[58] Garner stated: "The word was that the guy had been gouging her a little bit, pulling her hair, and just doing some stupid things, things that are just not necessary. Cheer and be as loud as you want to be and whatever else, but don't do that."[59] Morgan Ensberg tried to twist the incident into a demonstration of cultural differences between the North and South, writing in his column: "I think there is something to be said about people from Texas. People from the South have a lot of respect for others. Things are different here. There are good people all over the world. There are good people in Chicago, but I think the fans in our city pull hard for us and don't wish ill will on the other team. You get things like this that I think throw a really dark shadow on the city, because you're not talking about fair play. You're talking about bush. That's bush league."[60] Although the Biggios refused to press charges, Sox skipper Guillen offered to resolve the incident himself, saying: "The guy who did it, he should be brought to Biggio, he's the one that can hopefully get him back. I wish she would have grabbed something and broken his head. If that happened to my family, it would have been a big problem. I told the police, 'Don't put him in jail. Bring him to me in the dugout.'"[61]

Houston players were further aggravated by Commissioner Bud Selig's ruling, based on a desire for popular television shots from an advertising blimp, that the retractable dome on Minute Maid Park had to remain open, thereby minimizing the noise generated by the fans. Third baseman Morgan Ensberg, writing for the *Houston Chronicle,* bemoaned the decision, whining: "The roof is one of our advantages. We've earned the right to have at least a little of a home-field advantage."[62] Mike Downey of the *Chicago Tribune* countered by writing sarcastically: "The gall, making a team play a game of baseball outdoors!"[63] Downey even suggested new lyrics for "Deep in the Heart of Texas," which was sung during the seventh-inning stretch at the Juice Box: "A roof at night (clap, clap), stops Sox of White (clap, clap) deep in the heart of Texas."[64]

The third contest, played under a partly cloudy sky and temperatures in the lower 60s, pitted Jon Garland against Roy Oswalt. Following a rendition of the national anthem featuring Wynona Judd and Michael McDonald, the Astros thrilled the 42,848 fans by getting off to a 1–0 lead on a double by Biggio and a single by Berkman. They extended the lead to 3–0 in the third on a single by Adam Everett, a sacrifice by Oswalt, a run scoring single by Biggio, and another run scoring single by Ensberg. Houston added another tally in the fourth on a solo home run to left-field by Jason Lane.

In the fifth, however, the Sox pushed five runs across the plate to take the lead. Crede led off the frame with a home run, Uribe and Podsednik singled, and Iguchi's single to center scored Uribe. Dye singled home Podsednik, and Pierzynski's double to center cleaned the bases, giving the Sox a 5–4 advantage.

Although Oswalt threw 46 pitches in the fifth, he remained on the mound until the eighth when Dan Wheeler took the hill. For the Sox, Cliff Politte relieved Garland in the eighth. Politte retired the first two batters before giving a pass to Ensberg. Guillen, who wanted southpaw Neil Cotts to face left-handed batter Mike Lamb, then lifted Politte. After giving a walk to Lamb, Cotts was removed in favor of Dustin Hermanson, who surrendered a run scoring double down the left-field line to Jason Lane, evening the score at 5-all. The score remained tied until the 14th inning when reserve infielder, and former Astro, Geoff Blum lined a two-run home run to right-field off Ezequiel Astacio, giving the Sox a 7–5 lead. The record-setting 5 hour, 41 minute contest ended with the Astros submissively going down in the home half of the inning. John P. Lopez of the *Houston Chronicle* noted sadly: "Everything the Astros have done so well [in the regular season], all the nuggets of gold found in the strangest of places, began to dry up and blow away like tumbleweed" leaving the remaining faithful in Minute Maid Park feeling "desolate and quiet and resigned."[65] More cruelly, the *New York Times* stated: "It's a good thing the retractable roof at Minute Maid Park wasn't closed, as the Astros wanted it to be. Workers would have had to fumigate the place before the Astros and White Sox could have played [the fourth game]."[66]

Knowing that no team had ever come back from a 3–0 deficit to win a World Series, Garner, having thrown a chair down a tunnel after the loss in a temper tantrum that a New York writer said "would have made Billy Martin blush," still fumed over his team leaving thirteen runners on base in the last eight innings, saying brusquely: "I'm really ticked off. I don't like to lose. That's some pretty poor hitting, absolutely rotten hitting. We had our chances. It's amazing. I don't know how you win a ballgame when you can't hit the ball. We managed to stay in the ballgame, but we might have played 40 innings and it didn't look like we were going to manage to get a runner across. It's embarrassing to play like this in our hometown. We had some chances, but we didn't even hit the ball hard."[67]

Analyzing the game from another perspective, Rick Morrissey of the *Chicago Tribune* said that the Astros' minds were not on the game, writing that "If a UFO had crashed into centerfield, the Astros wouldn't have been any more distracted than they already were. The trouble was roof-in-mouth disease. They spent way too much time talking about the controversy."[68] Richard Justice of the *Houston Chronicle* expressed the similar thought in trying to explain the rare home field defeat. "Maybe they were distracted. Maybe they let that silly argument about the roof get in their heads," he mused. "If they did, shame on them."[69]

Following the ceremonial first pitch by Juan Marichal, the fourth game turned into a classic pitching duel between Freddie Garcia of the Sox and Brandon Backe of Houston, with each hurling shutout ball for seven innings. In the eighth the Sox finally broke through. Pinch hitter Willie Harris singled to left and took second on Podsednik's sacrifice bunt. Carl Everett moved Harris to third on a groundout to second, and Harris touched the plate on Jermaine Dye's bouncing ball that trickled through the center of the diamond for a single. With a 1–0 lead Guillen removed the tiring Garcia and brought in Cliff Politte and then Neal Cotts to pitch the eighth. Juan Uribe snuffed out a potential tying run with two out in that frame by making a backhand stab of a broken-bat roller to short off the bat of Lamb and just barely throwing out the runner at first. Uribe's dramatics led one writer to marvel: "Uribe is not a shortstop. He's a heart-stop."[70]

First game hero and second game goat Bobby Jenks took the mound in the ninth and was greeted by Jason Lane with a bloop single into center that dropped between Rowand and Uribe. Ausmus sacrificed Lane to second. Chris Burke popped a foul fly into the crowd along the third-base line, but Uribe leaned far into the hostile fans and made a spectacular, potentially game-saving, catch. The next batter, Orlando Palmeiro, bounced a high-hopper over Jenks' head for what seemed to be a certain infield hit, but Uribe charged the ball and fired it to first to barely beat the on-rushing runner to the bag and give the Sox their first world championship in eighty-eight years. Fittingly, the famine was broken on the 139th birthday of Kid Gleason, the manager of the 1919 White Sox.

In the solemnity of the losers' dressing quarters, Phil Garner made the perfunctory gracious statement of the losing manager, saying: "The bottom line is they did a pretty good job of pitching against us. I congratulate the Chicago White Sox. They played well all year, and they deserve to be called world champions."[71] Brad Lidge, the losing hurler who went 0–2 with a 4.90 earned run average in his three Series appearances, was less generous, sneering that Dye's game winning single was a " twelve hopper," and stating defensively: "I finished pretty good the last two outings. I don't feel I ended on a bad note. You win and lose as a team, and the fact we lost today I'll remember more than the individual things. We congratulated each other. No one's hanging their head."[72] Craig Biggio, who batted a mere .222 in the Series, blamed fate, not poor hitting [the Astros batted .203 for the Series] for the Sox victory, saying philosophically: "It was just little things here and there that they were able to come out on top. I believe in destiny and fate, and it was more their destiny to win this Series than it was ours."[73]

Houston writers were not as congratulatory toward the Sox as they were denigrating to the Astros. Typical was an article for the *Houston Chronicle* by Fran Blinebury entitled "Astros' offense lays one big egg." Blinebury wrote: "It's been 88 years since the Chicago White Sox last won a World Series. It only seems that long since the Astros last scored a run. The White Sox finally exorcised the ghost of Shoeless Joe Jackson. Now the Astros will be haunted by the demons of Hitless Morgan Ensberg, Batless Brad Ausmus, and Punchless Adam Everett."[74] Richard Justice writing for the same newspaper noted: "The Astros needed one lousy hit. Yet the magic they found during the regular season, the magic they'd had in the first two rounds of the playoffs, was gone for good."[75] A similar, but gentler, sentiment was expressed by the *Chronicle*'s John P. Lopez, who opined: "The Chicago White Sox proved to be everything the Astros were but better. [The Sox] played better defense, ran smarter on the basepaths, were more daring and more complete. It was an awful ending. But it was, finally, a taste."[76]

In the jubilant Sox clubhouse, as one writer ruefully reported, "perfectly good champagne was wasted."[77] Guillen gushed: "For the first time in my life, for those last two innings my heart was pounding like crazy. I was so excited, I said, 'Wow, this moment is going to happen. A lot of people have been waiting for this moment and it's going to come true.'"[78] Later, he explained why he lingered in the dugout after the final out, saying: "A lot of people thought because of the way I am I was going to jump around like one of my players. I have to respect the Astros' team. I have to respect the Astros' management. I was so glad for my players, jumping back and forth. It was amazing to see, like little kids jumping back and forth."[79]

Carl Everett trumpeted the call of Chicago supremacy, yelling: "We're no longer the second team in Chicago. It's all South Side. South Side is No.1. North Side, you're behind us now."[80] A.J. Pierzynski, drenched in champagne, shouted: "They called us chokers. Now they can call us champions. They can call us whatever they want, but they had better call us champions."[81] Series Most Valuable Player Jermaine Dye, who batted .438, and Sox owner Jerry Reinsdorff remained low key during the celebration, the former describing his game winning at-bat as "sticking with the game plan of going up there, looking for a slider and just not trying to do too much with it," and the latter saying simply: "When you go 88 years, it's time."[82]

What made the White Sox triumph all the more sweet was that in an era of high salaried free agents, the Sox were, as Bill Madden of the *New York Daily News* pointed out, "a collection of rejects, misfits and outcasts bonding together in defiance of all those who have disparaged and discarded them."[83] While concurring that the Sox were a lower payroll club because of their means of talent acquisition, General Manager Ken Williams was quick to note that although 22 of the 25 players on the Sox World Series roster came from other organizations, that did not reflect the minor league talent level of the Sox, saying: "I don't want anyone to get the idea that we don't value our scouting and player development system. The fact is, we've used our farm system to make a lot of the deals to put this club together."[84] Perhaps, the most important message of the White Sox triumph was set forth by Chicago Mayor Richard Daley, who asserted there was a "life lesson" in the South Side victory. "No one looked at the White Sox," he stated. "The press discounted them — 'It's just a fluke' and 'They're going to collapse, they are going to fall down. Nothing is going to happen.' But you never give up. You don't give up to criticism; you don't give up to lack of acknowledgment by other people. You just move along. And that's what they did. This team moved along."[85] For North Side fans, the greatest lesson was perhaps that now that the "Curse of the Bambino" has ended and the sins of the Black Sox have been atoned, perhaps in 2006 the spirit of forgiveness will remove the "Billy Goat Curse" and the Cubs could face the defending champion White Sox in a centennial rematch of the 1906 World Series.

NOTES

Chapter 1— 1906

1. Peter Golenbock, *Wrigleyville* (New York: St. Martin's Press, 1996), p. 102.

2. *Ibid*. Taft was the half-brother of future President and Supreme Court Chief Justice William Howard Taft.

3. *Ibid*.

4. *Ibid*, pp. 103–104, 111.

5. *Ibid*, p. 119. In actuality, the number of short to second to first twin killings engineered during the Cub glory years of 1906–1909 was quite small: eight in 1906, seven in 1907, eight in 1908, and six in 1909, for a total of twenty-nine. If the second to short to first double plays are included, the total rises only to fifty-four. The reason Adams penned "Baseball's Sad Lexicon" in 1910 was to offer a tribute to the number of double plays the Cub infield perpetrated against his beloved Giants in the 1908 season. The verse read:

These are the saddest of possible words:
'Tinkers to Evers to Chance,'
Trio of bear cubs, and fleeter than birds,
'Tinker to Evers to Chance.'
Ruthlessly pricking our gonfalon bubble,
Making a Giant hit into a double–
Words that are weighty with nothing but trouble:
'Tinker to Evers to Chance.'

6. *Ibid*, p. 120.

7. Frederick G. Lieb, *The Story of the World Series* (New York: G.P. Putnam's Sons, 1965), pp. 44–45.

8. Golenbock, *Wrigleyville*, p. 121.

9. Joe S. Jackson, "Extreme Calm Marks Eve of Championship Struggle," *Detroit Free Press*, October 9, 1906.

10. Ralph S. Davis, "Cubs are Modest," *The Sporting News*, October 13, 1906; Golenbock, *Wrigleyville*, 124.

11. Charles Dryden, "Dryden's Story of Sox Triumph," *Chicago Tribune*, October 10, 1906.

12. *Ibid*.

13. *Ibid*.

14. I.E. (Sy) Sanborn, "Sox Gain Victory in First Big Game," *Chicago Tribune*, October 10, 1906.

15. *Ibid*.

16. Joe Vila, "Superbas' Stars," *The Sporting News*, October 27, 1906.

17. *Ibid*.

18. Sanborn, "Sox Gain Victory in First Big Game," *Chicago Tribune*, October 10, 1906.

19. *Ibid*.

20. "Notes on the Side and Comment on the Game," *Chicago Tribune*, October 10, 1906.

21. *Ibid*.

22. *Ibid*.

23. *Ibid*.

24. Charles Dryden, "Sad Slaughter of the Sox," *Chicago Tribune*, October 11, 1906.

25. Lieb, *The Story of the World Series*, p. 46.

26. Dryden, "Sad Slaughter of the Sox," *Chicago Tribune*, October 11, 1906.

27. *Ibid*.

28. I.E. (Sy) Sanborn, "Nationals Win 7–1 Second Game," *Chicago Tribune*, October 11, 1906.

29. Lieb, *The Story of the World Series*, p. 47.

30. *Ibid*.

31. Charles Dryden, "Beaten by a Nose," *Chicago Tribune*, October 12, 1906.

32. *Ibid*.

33. I.E. (Sy) Sanborn, ""Rohe and Walsh Win for the Sox," *Chicago Tribune*, October 12, 1906.

34. Dryden, "Beaten by a Nose," *Chicago Tribune*, October 12, 1906.

35. Sanborn, "Rohe and Walsh Win for the Sox," *Chicago Tribune*, October 12, 1906.

36. Dryden, "Beaten by a Nose," *Chicago Tribune*, October 12, 1906.

37. Lieb, *The Story of the World Series*, p. 48.

38. Joe S. Jackson, "Rohe Hero of Sox," *Detroit Free Press*, October 12, 1906. Despite his heroics, Rohe played for the White Sox only one more year, batting .213. He was released after the 1907 season and never played another game in the major leagues.

39. Dryden, "Beaten by a Nose," *Chicago Tribune*, October 12, 1906.

40. "Americans in Lead for World's Honors," *New York Times*, October 12, 1906.

41. Sanborn, "Rohe and Walsh Win for the Sox," *Chicago Tribune*, October 12, 1906.

42. *Ibid*.

43. *Ibid*.

44. Charles Dryden, "Back to the Coop With Hoodoo Hen," *Chicago Tribune*, October 13, 1906.

45. Lieb, *The Story of the World Series*, pp. 48–49; Golenbock, *Wrigleyville*, p. 123.

46. "Players Will Divide $33,400," *Chicago Tribune*, October 13, 1906.

47. Charles Dryden, "Sox Sight the Blankets," *Chicago Tribune*, October 14, 1906.

48. I.E. (Sy) Sanborn, "Sox Bat Heavily, Beat Spuds 8–6," *Chicago Tribune*, October 14, 1906.

49. Joe S. Jackson, "Sox Win With Stick," *Detroit Free Press*, October 14, 1906.

50. Sanborn, "Sox Bat Heavily, Beat Spuds 8–6," *Chicago Tribune*, October 14, 1906.

51. *Ibid.*

52. *Ibid.*

53. *Ibid.*

54. Jackson, "Sox Win With Stick," *Detroit Free Press*, October 14, 1906.

55. Dryden, "Sox Sight the Blankets," *Chicago Tribune*, October 14, 1906.

56. Sanborn, "Sox Bat Heavily, Beat Spuds 8–6," *Chicago Tribune*, October 14, 1906.

57. Charles Dryden, "Swift Kick Beats Spuds," *Chicago Tribune*, October 15, 1906.

58. Lieb, *The Story of the World Series*, p. 49.

59. *Ibid.*

60. I.E. (Sy) Sanborn, "White Sox Flag, Beat Cubs 8–3," *Chicago Tribune*, October 15, 1906.

61. Dryden, "Swift Kick Beats Spuds," *Chicago Tribune*, October 15, 1906.

62. I.E. Sanborn, "Deserved to Win," *The Sporting News*, October 20, 1906.

63. Lieb, *The Story of the World Series*, p. 51.

64. "Frantic Rooters Crowd Onto Field," *Chicago Tribune*, October 15, 1906; "World's Championship Goes to Americans," *New York Times*, October 15, 1906.

65. "Frantic Rooters Crowd Onto Field," *Chicago Tribune*, October 15, 1906.

66. *Ibid.*

67. *Ibid.*

68. *Ibid*; "Doings in the Windy City," *Detroit Free Press*, October 15, 1906.

69. Joe S. Jackson, "White Sox Conquerors," *Detroit Free Press*, October 15, 1906.

70. "Doings in the Windy City," *Detroit Free Press*, October 15, 1906.

71. "Sox Humble Cubs," *The Sporting News*, October 20, 1906.

72. "Doings in the Windy City," *Detroit Free Press*, October 15, 1906.

73. *Ibid.*

74. "Sox Humble Cubs," *The Sporting News*, October 20, 1906.

75. "Fairly Won, Says Chance," *Chicago Tribune*, October 15, 1906.

76. *Ibid*; Jim C. Hamilton, "Reverse of Dope," *The Sporting News*, October 20, 1906.

77. Joe S. Jackson, "Game That They Play, Not Men Who Play It, Decides World Title," *Detroit Free Press*, October 16, 1906. Murphy added to the pool $2,777.49 that was owed players as their share of receipts from exhibition games played since July 29, the date from which players and the club divided profits equally. He also gave each player a gift of $100, bring each players total share to almost $700, but that paled in comparison's to the $1,945.29 received by each White Sox. Adding to the grief of some Cub players was the knowledge that they had wagered more on the outcome than they had received as the loser's share. "Sox Humble Cubs," *The*

Sporting News, October 20, 1906; Golenbock, *Wrigleyville*, p. 123.

78. "Fairly Won, Says Chance," *Chicago Tribune*, October 15, 1906.

79. Vila, "Superbas' Stars," *The Sporting News*, October 27, 1906.

80. "Fairly Won, Says Chance," *Chicago Tribune*, October 15, 1906.

81. "Fans Frantic in Streets," *Chicago Tribune*, October 15, 1906; "Notes and Comments on the Game," *Chicago Tribune*, October 15, 1906.

82. "Fine Fob Chains for Sox," *The Sporting News*, November 3, 1906.

83. *Ibid.*

84. *Ibid.*

85. I.E. Sanborn, "Unjust to Chance," *The Sporting News*, October 27, 1906; Golenbock, *Wrigleyville*, p. 100.

86. W.M. Rankin, "Fast and Clever," *The Sporting News*, October 27, 1906.

87. "Editorial," *The Sporting News*, October 27, 1906.

88. W.M. Rankin, "Season Too Long," *The Sporting News*, October 27, 1906.

89. Joseph M. Cummings, "Picked White Sox," *The Sporting News*, October 20, 1906.

90. Golenbock, *Wrigleyville*, p. 123.

Chapter 2 — 1907

1. Golenbock, *Wrigleyville*, p. 124.

2. "Sox Manager Says Tigers Will Win," *Detroit Free Press*, October 6, 1907.

3. Peter Williams (ed.), *The Joe Williams Reader* (Chapel Hill: Algonquin Books, 1989), p. 6. The self-imposed silence continued throughout the 1908 season and World Series as well.

4. As in 1906, Chance refused to use Lundgren in the Series, claiming that he was not a cold weather pitcher.

5. I.E. Sanborn, "Much Excitement," *The Sporting News*, October 10, 1907.

6. Joe Vila, "Their Best Asset," *The Sporting News*, October 10, 1907.

7. Richard Bak, *A Place for Summer* (Detroit: Wayne State University Press, 1998), p. 88.

8. Lee Allen, *The World Series* (New York: G.P. Putnam's Sons, 1969), p. 62.

9. "Baseball Championship," *New York Times*, October 7, 1907; I.E. (Sy) Sanborn, "Way Cleared for Diamond Battles," *Chicago Tribune*, October 8, 1907. Jennings' cry was a shortened form of "Here we are!"

10. Malcolm W. Bingay, *Detroit Is My Own Home Town* (New York: Bobbs-Merrill Company, 1946), pp. 168–169; Lieb, p. 54; Ernie Harwell, *Diamond Gems* (Ann Arbor: Momentum Books, 1991), p.p. 156–157. Bingay covered sports for many years for the *Detroit Free Press*, writing in a Damon Runyon style under the name of "Iffy the Dopester."

11. Bingay, *Detroit Is My Own Home Town*, p. 170.

12. Harwell, *Diamond Gems*, p. 158.

13. W.G. Merrill, "Honesty of the Game," *The Sporting News*, October 24, 1907.

14. Al Stump, *Cobb* (Chapel Hill: Algonquin Books, 1996), p. 157.

15. *Ibid.*

16. Charles Dryden, "Fandom in the Corridors," *Chicago Tribune*, October 8, 1907.

17. *Ibid*; Sanborn, "Way Cleared for Diamond Battles," *Chicago Tribune*,October 8, 1907.

18. Sanborn, "Way Cleared for Diamond Battles," *Chicago Tribune*, October 8, 1907.

19. *Ibid*.

20. *Ibid*.

21. "Poets Hard at Work," *Detroit Free Press*, October 8, 1907.

22. "Tigers and Cubs Fight to a Draw," *New York Times*, October 9, 1907.

23. Charles Dryden, "Tigers and Cubs in Drawn Battle," *Chicago Tribune*, October 9, 1907.

24. *Ibid*.

25. I.E. (Sy) Sanborn, "First Game Goes Twelve Innings to Tie," *Chicago Tribune*, October 9, 1907.

26. Bingay, *Detroit Is My Own Home Town*, p. 171.

27. Charles C. Alexander, *Ty Cobb* (New York: Oxford University Press, 1984), p. 61.

28. Cobb, *My Life in Baseball* (Lincoln: University of Nebraska Press, 1993; reprint of 1961 Doubleday edition), p. 74.

29. *Ibid*, p. 24.

30. I.E. (Sy) Sanborn, "Notes of the Series," *Chicago Tribune*, October 9, 1907; H.E.K., "In the Wake of the Base Hit, An Error," *Chicago Tribune*, October 9, 1907.

31. Lieb, *The Story of the World Series*, pp. 54–55.

32. *Ibid*. The decision was based on the hard, scrappy play exhibited by both teams.

33. Joe S. Jackson, "National Commission Compels Cubs to Wear Their Old Uniforms," *Detroit Free Press*, October 10, 1907.

34. *Ibid*; Dryden, "Tigers and Cubs in Drawn Battle," *Chicago Tribune*, October 9, 1907.

35. Sanborn, "Notes of the Series," *Chicago Tribune*, October 9, 1907.

36. Joe S. Jackson, "Tie Game Aids Players in Financial Way," *Detroit Free Press*, October 9, 1907; Golenbock, *Wrigleyville*, p. 126.

37. Joe S. Jackson, "Jennings Says Defeat Will Make Tiges Fight Harder," *Detroit Free Press*, October 10, 1907.

38. I.E. (Sy) Sanborn, "Another Victory Won by the Cubs," *Chicago Tribune*, October 11, 1907.

39. *Ibid*.

40. "New Song for Tigers," *Detroit Free Press*, October 11, 1907.

41. Ty Cobb, p. 74.

42. Charles Dryden, "Cubs' Slugging Beats Detroit," *Chicago Tribune*, October 11, 1907.

43. *Ibid*.

44. *Ibid*.

45. *Ibid*.

46. *Ibid*.

47. "Cubs Tame Tigers," *The Sporting News*, October 17, 1907.

48. "We Never Quit, Says Hughie," *Detroit Free Press*, October 11, 1907.

49. H.E.K. (Hugh E. Keogh), "In the Wake of the News," *Chicago Tribune*, October 8, 1907. In 1887 Detroit, then in the National League, defeated St. Louis of the American Association eleven wins to four.

50. I.E. (Sy) Sanborn, "Cubs Win Again by Great Play," *Chicago Tribune*, October 12, 1907.

51. Charles Dryden, "Tigers Bearded in Their Lair," *Chicago Tribune*, October 12, 1907. No home runs were hit by either team in the Series.

52. "Editorial," *The Sporting News*, October 10, 1907. The leading advocates for dropping Detroit from the league and replacing it with Buffalo, New York were located in Cleveland, which sought to eliminate its near-by competitor.

53. *Ibid*.

54. Sanborn, "Cubs Win Again by Great Play," *Chicago Tribune*, October 12, 1907; Joe Falls, *The Detroit Tigers* (New York: Walker and Co., 1989), p. 20.

55. Falls, *The Detroit Tigers*, pp. 20–23. The "wildcat stands" remained through 1910 after which club owner Frank Navin, who had purchased half interest in the club from Yawkey after the 1907 World Series, bought the property on National Avenue and razed the stands. John McCollister, *The Tigers and Their Den* (Addox Publishing Group, 1999), p. 35.

56. *Ibid*; "World Championship Notes," *New York Times*, October 12, 1907.

57. "World Championship Notes," *New York Times*, October 12, 1907; Dryden, "Tigers Bearded in Their Lair," *Chicago Tribune*, October 12, 1907.

58. Golenbock, *Wrigleyville*, p.p. 126–127.

59. Lieb, *The Story of the World Series*, p. 52.

60. Dryden, "Tigers Bearded in Their Lair," *Chicago Tribune*, October 12, 1907; Sanborn, "Cubs Win Again by Great Play," *Chicago Tribune*, October 12, 1907.

61. Sanborn, "Cubs Win Again by Great Play," *Chicago Tribune*, October 12, 1907.

62. Golenbock, *Wrigleyville*, p. 127. The so-called "press box" at Bennett Park was, in the words of Harry P. Edwards of the *Cleveland Plain Dealer*, an "outrage." Newsmen had to climb a forty-foot ladder to the roof of the first-base pavilion and sit without any shelter from wind, rain, sun, snow, or pigeons. Edwards concluded his tirade by saying: "My only regret is that Secretary Navin of the Detroit club could not be forced to sit upon that perch for about two weeks straight." ("Ideal Ball Team," *The Sporting News*, October 17, 1907). As a consequence, Joe S. Jackson, the hard-drinking sports editor of the *Detroit Free Press* organized the Baseball Writers Association before the 1908 World Series.

63. Golenbock, *Wrigleyville*, p. 127; Lieb, *The Story of the World Series*, p. 56.

64. I.E. (Sy) Sanborn, "World's Pennant Stays in Chicago," *Chicago Tribune*, October 13, 1907.

65. *Ibid*.

66. Charles Dryden, "E-e-yah and A-las for Tigers," *Chicago Tribune*, October 13, 1907. Murphy had been so confident of victory in 1906 that prior to the Series he had designed and ordered expensive, bejeweled cuff links for his players as a gift.

67. *Ibid*.

68. *Ibid*; Sanborn, "World's Pennant Stays in Chicago," *Chicago Tribune*, October 13, 1907.

69. Lieb, *The Story of the World Series*, p. 57; "Late News," *The Sporting News*, October 17, 1907.

70. "Late News," *The Sporting News*, October 17, 1907.

71. Lieb, *The Story of the World Series*, p. 57.

72. *Ibid*.

73. Golenbock, *Wrigleyville*, p. 128.

74. Joseph L. Reichler, *The World Series* (New York: Simon and Schuster, 1978), p. 103.

75. Joe Vila, "Hat's Off to the Cubs," *The Sporting News*, October 17, 1907; Stump, *Cobb*, p. 157; Daniel Okrent and Harris Lewine, *The Ultimate Baseball Book* (Boston: Houghton-Mifflin, 1988), p. 64.

76. Cobb, *My Life in Baseball*, p. 79.

77. "Fairly Beaten," *Chicago Tribune*, October 13, 1907.

78. *Ibid*.

79. Vila, "Hat's Off to Cubs," *The Sporting News*, October 17, 1907.

80. "Fairly Beaten," *Chicago Tribune*, October 13, 1907.

81. "Milking the Detroit Baseball Public," *Detroit Free Press*, October 13, 1907.

82. W.M. Rankin, "Season Too Long," *The Sporting News*, October 20, 1906.

83. Hamilton J. Hamilton, "Year's Best Team," *The Sporting News*, October 14, 1907.

Chapter 3 — 1908

1. Lowell Reidenbaugh, *Baseball's 25 Greatest Pennant Races* (St. Louis: *The Sporting News*, 1987), pp. 24–25. Years later, McGinnity confided to veteran writer Fred Lieb that Cub pitcher Floyd Kroh had tossed in a new ball to Evers from the Cub bench, and that was the one Evers used to tag the bag for the force out. "I can swear on a stack of bibles," the Giants' pitcher told Lieb, "that Evers never touched his base with the ball that had been in play." Frederick G. Lieb, *The Baseball Story* (New York: G.P. Putnam's Sons, 1950), 179.

2. Reidenbaugh, *Baseball's 25 Greatest Pennant Races*, p. 25.

3. *Ibid*. An excellent source for the 1908 National League campaign is G.H. Fleming, *The Unforgettable Season* (New York: Fireside, 1981).

4. Lieb, *The Baseball Story*, p. 180.

5. *Ibid*.

6. "Brush Will Not Go To Court," *Chicago Tribune*, October 10, 1908.

7. Golenbock, *Wrigleyville*, p. 150.

8. *Ibid*.

9. "Jennings Hears From McGraw," *Chicago Tribune*, October 10, 1908.

10. Golenbock, *Wrigleyville*, p. 151.

11. Lieb, *The Baseball Story*, pp. 180–181.

12. "Cubs and Tigers Ready for Battle," *New York Times*, October 10, 1908.

13. *Ibid*; "Rival Managers Confident," *Chicago Tribune*, October 10, 1908.

14. "Well, We Like Cub Meat, Too," *Detroit Free Press*, October 9, 1908.

15. Horace S. Fogel, "Tigers' Weakness," *The Sporting News*, October 22, 1908.

16. Lieb, *The Story of the World Series*, pp. 57–58.

17. "Rival Managers Confident," *Chicago Tribune*, October 10, 1908.

18. "Editorial Notes," *Chicago Tribune*, October 10, 1908.

19. I.E. Sanborn, "Cubs in the Lead in World Series," *Chicago Tribune*, October 11, 1908.

20. *Ibid*.

21. *Ibid*.

22. Golenbock, *Wrigleyville*, p. 151.

23. "Statements of the Leaders," *Chicago Tribune*, October 11, 1908.

24. *Ibid*.

25. *Ibid*.

26. "Cubs Earn a Victory Over Detroit on a Muddy Field," *New York Times*, October 11, 1908.

27. Fogel, "Tigers' Weakness," *The Sporting News*, October 22, 1908.

28. Will B. Wreford, "Crowd at Opening Game Disappoints," *Detroit Free Press*, October 11, 1908.

29. Golenbock, *Wrigleyville*, p. 151; Lieb, *The Story of the World Series*, p. 59. Murphy was investigated by the National Commission, but, even though he was reprimanded for his pricing practices, no proof of collusion with scalpers was unearthed. Included in the crowd were Miss Ina Eloise Young of the *Trinidad* (Colorado)*Chronicle-News*, the only female sports editor in the United States, and fourteen field photographers.

30. I.E. Sanborn, "Homer by Tinker Gives Cubs Game," *Chicago Tribune*, October 12, 1908.

31. Lieb, *The Story of the World Series*, p. 59.

32. Sanborn, "Homer by Tinker Gives Cubs Game," *Chicago Tribune*, October 12, 1908.

33. "Statements by the Leaders," *Chicago Tribune*, October 12, 1908.

34. *Ibid*.

35. "Tribute to Tinker," *Chicago Tribune*, October 12, 1908.

36. HEK, ""In the Wake of the Second Blow Administered by Cubs," *Chicago Tribune*, October 12, 1908.

37. "Statements by Leaders," *Chicago Tribune*, October 12, 1908.

38. *Ibid*.

39. I.E. Sanborn, "Jennings Talks About Game," *Chicago Tribune*, October 12, 1908.

40. "Tigers Pull Cubs Down to Defeat," *New York Times*, October 13, 1908.

41. Lieb, *The Baseball Story*, p. 182; Lieb, *The History of the World Series*, p. 61.

42. "Victory of Tigers Gingers Up Loyal Fans in Detroit," *Chicago Tribune*, October 13, 1908.

43. I.E. Sanborn, "Cubs Lose Game; Tigers Win 8–3," *Chicago Tribune*, October 13, 1908.

44. "Tigers Pull Cubs Down to Defeat," *New York Times*, October 13, 1908.

45. Sanborn, "Cubs Lose Game; Tigers Win 8–3," *Chicago Tribune*, October 13, 1908.

46. Stump, *Cobb*, p. 165.

47. *Ibid*.

48. *Ibid*.

49. *Ibid*., 166.

50. Lieb, *The Story of the World Series*, p. 60.

51. "Come On, You Tigers!" *Detroit Free Press*, October 13, 1908.

52. HEK, "In the Wake of Blow Number Three Landed by the Cubs," *Chicago Tribune*, October 14, 1908.

53. "Notes of the Game," *Chicago Tribune*, October 13, 1908.

54. HEK, "In the Wake of Blow Number Three Landed by the Cubs," *Chicago Tribune*, October 14, 1908.

55. "Miner Brown Stops Detroit Sluggers," *New York Times*, October 14, 1908.

56. Lieb, *The Story of the World Series*, p. 60.

57. I.E. Sanborn, "Cubs Supreme in Baseball World," *Chicago Tribune*, October 15, 1908.

58. Golenbock, *Wrigleyville*, p. 153.

59. "Statements of the Leaders," *Chicago Tribune*, October 15, 1908.

60. Will B. Wreford, "Tiges Now Only Wait Melon Cutting," *Detroit Free Press*, October 15, 1908.

61. "Editorial," *Chicago Tribune*, October 15, 1908.

62. HEK, "In the Wake of the Final Blow," *Chicago Tribune*, October 15, 1908.

63. Sanborn, "Cubs Supreme in Baseball World," *Chicago Tribune*, October 15, 1908; I.E. Sanborn, "Only One Regret," *The Sporting News*, October 22, 1908.

64. "Tiger Fans Analyze Series and Concede Cubs the Palm," *Chicago Tribune*, October 15, 1908.

65. "Keep Their Title," *The Sporting News*, October 22, 1908; Joe S. Jackson, "Trying to Forget," *The Sporting News*, October 22, 1908.

66. Lieb, *The Story of the World Series*, p. 61.

67. "Baseball Writers Organize," *New York Times*, October 15, 1908.

68. "Hail to the Champions!" *Detroit Free Press*, October 15, 1908.

Chapter 4 — 1910

1. Artie Hofman, "Sure Cubs Will Win," *Chicago Tribune*, October 16, 1910.

2. Fielder Jones, "Sees Even Fight," *Chicago Tribune*, October 16, 1910.

3. While in college, Collins surreptitiously had played professional baseball, including one season for Mack, under the assumed name of "Eddie Sullivan." Joseph Gies and Robert H. Shoemaker, *Stars of the Series* (New York: Thomas Y. Crowell, 1964), p. 36.

4. Lieb, *The Baseball Story*, p. 188.

5. Jones, "Sees Even Fight," *Chicago Tribune*, October 16, 1910.

6. Ring Lardner, "Big Mob Greets Chance's Stars," *Chicago Tribune*, October 17, 1910.

7. Fielder Jones, "Cubs Show Nerve on Eve of Battle," *Chicago Tribune*, October 17, 1910.

8. Hofman, "Sure Cubs Will Win," *Chicago Tribune*, October 16, 1910; Artie Hofman, "Champs Fit for Fight of Lives," *Chicago Tribune*, October 17, 1910. In his October 17 article, Hofman's exuberance got the better of him when he declared that he would not trade either Jimmy Sheckard or Frank Schulte for Ty Cobb.

9. "Views From Rival Camps Before Battle," *Chicago Tribune*, October 17, 1910.

10. *Ibid.*

11. *Ibid.*

12. *Ibid.*

13. "Scribes Use Knees for Desks," *Chicago Tribune*, October 18, 1910.

14. "Scalpers Do Big Business," *Chicago Tribune*, October 18, 1910.

15. "Game is Late in Starting," *Chicago Tribune*, October 18, 1910.

16. Gies and Shoemaker, *Stars of the Series*, p. 36; Gene Schoor, *The History of the World Series* (New York: William Morrow and Company, 1990), p. 36.

17. E.A. Batchelor, "Bender's Great Hurling Beats Cubs in Opener," *Detroit Free Press*, October 18, 1910; "Athletics Take First World Series Game," *New York Times*, October 18, 1910. The *Times*, obviously peeved by the absence of a New York team in the World Series, gave equal coverage to the New York Giants–New York Yankee series for the "World Championship of Manhattan" and lifted virtually all of its World Series coverage verbatim from *Chicago Tribune* accounts written by I.E. Sanborn and Fielder Jones.

18. Batchelor, "Bender's Great Hurling Beats Cubs in Opener," *Detroit Free Press*, October 18, 1910.

19. "Views From Rival Camps After Battle," *Chicago Tribune*, October 18, 1910.

20. *Ibid*; "Mack Lauds Bender," *The Sporting News*, October 20, 1910.

21. "Views From Rival Camps After Battle," *Chicago Tribune*, October 18, 1910.

22. *Ibid.*

23. *Ibid*; "Chance Sensed Trouble," *The Sporting News*, October 20, 1910.

24. Artie Hofman, "Cubs Not Gloomy After One Defeat," *Chicago Tribune*, October 18, 1910.

25. *Ibid.*

26. "Cubs in Traffic Accident," *Chicago Tribune*, October 19, 1910.

27. H.E.K., "Even Up Series Here," *Chicago Tribune*, October 19, 1910; Doc White, "Macks Outclass Cubs," *Chicago Tribune*, October 19, 1910.

28. White, "Macks Outclass Cubs," *Chicago Tribune*, October 19, 1910. For a detailed account of the tarnished batting race see Alexander, *Ty Cobb*, pp. 95–96.

29. Ty Cobb, "Game Most Spectacular Played in Big Series," *Detroit Free Press*, October 19, 1910.

30. E.A. Batchelor, "Athletics Get Six Runs in Seventh and Win 9–3," *Detroit Free Press*, October 19, 1910.

31. Jim Nasium, "Backtrailing Baseball," *The Sporting News*, October 20, 1910.

32. Batchelor, "Athletics Get Six Runs in Seventh and Win 9–3," *Detroit Free Press*, October 19, 1910.

33. "Statements by Rivals After Second Contest," *Chicago Tribune*, October 19, 1910.

34. *Ibid*; "Mack Sees Victory," *The Sporting News*, October 27, 1920.

35. "Statements by Rivals After Second Contest," *Chicago Tribune*, October 19, 1910.

36. *Ibid.*

37. *Ibid.*

38. Artie Hofman, "Games in Chicago to Turn the Tide," *Chicago Tribune*, October 19, 1910.

39. *Ibid.*

40. Ralph S. Davis, "Favored Mackmen," *The Sporting News*, October 27, 1910.

41. Schoor, *The History of the World Series*, p. 38.

42. I.E. Sanborn, "Fans Greet Cubs in Arrival Home," *Chicago Tribune*, October 20, 1910.

43. "Crepe Placed on Door of the Cubs' Office," *Chicago Tribune*, October 20, 1910.

44. I.E. Sanborn, "Athletics Drive Cub Pitchers Out," *Chicago Tribune*, October 21, 1910. Cub outfielders admitted after the game that the drive was a home run. Fielder Jones, "Macks Superior at Every Point," *Chicago Tribune*, October 21, 1910.

45. E.A. Batchelor, "Cubs Take Their Worst Defeat From Athletics," *Detroit Free Press*, October 21, 1910.

46. *Ibid*; I.E. Sanborn, "Athletics Drive Cub Pitchers Out," *Chicago Tribune*, October 21, 1910.

47. Batchelor, "Cubs Take Their Worst Defeat From Athletics," *Detroit Free Press*, October 21, 1910.

48. Sanborn, "Athletics Drive Cub Pitchers Out," *Chicago Tribune*, October 21, 1910.

49. James Hart, "Youth is Cubs' Nemesis," *Chicago Tribune*, October 21, 1910. Hart was referring to Chance and Steinfeldt, both thirty-three, thirty-four-year-old Mordecai Brown, and thirty-five-year-old Johnny Kling.

50. H.E.K., "Spurious 'Salve' Only Kind Left," *Chicago Tribune*, October 21, 1910.

51. *Ibid.*

52. Overall, who owned shares of California gold mines, made a brief, ineffective comeback for the Cubs in 1913 going 4–5, with a 3.31 earned run average and then retired permanently.

53. "Views From Rival Camps After Battle," *Chicago Tribune*, October 21, 1910.

54. *Ibid.*

55. *Ibid.*

56. *Ibid.*

57. "Loaded Cigar for Morgan," *Chicago Tribune*, October 21, 1910.

58. I.E. Sanborn, "It is Seldom That a Funeral is Postponed Because of Mean Weather," *Chicago Tribune*, October 22, 1910; "Editorial," *Detroit Free Press*, October 22, 1910.

59. Harvey Woodruff, "Are Cub Fans Willing to be Known to World as Quitters?" *Chicago Tribune*, October 22, 1910.

60. Ring Lardner, "Cole Cubs' Hope in Today's Game," *Chicago Tribune*, October 22, 1910.

61. "New Balls in World Series?" *Chicago Tribune*, October 22, 1910.

62. *Ibid.*

63. *Ibid.*

64. Lieb, *The Baseball Story*, p. 188. With Shibe in on the "secret," it is a safe assumption that Mack and his players were given the information and thus had an advantage over the Cubs.

65. "Statements From Rival Camps," *Chicago Tribune*, October 23, 1910; I.E. Sanborn, "Cubs 'Come Back' to Win in the Tenth," *Chicago Tribune*, October 23, 1910.

66. "Statements From Rival Camps," *Chicago Tribune*, October 23, 1910.

67. *Ibid.*

68. Artie Hofman, "Cubs Show Class in Fourth Game," *Chicago Tribune*, October 23, 1910.

69. Schoor, *The History of the World Series*, p. 39.

70. *Ibid.*

71. Joseph Durso, *Baseball and the American Dream* (St. Louis: The Sporting News, 1986), p. 98.

72. E. Sanborn, "Athletics Win World Series," *Chicago Tribune*, October 24, 1910.

73. *Ibid.*

74. "Tear Souvenirs From Macks," *Chicago Tribune*, October 24, 1910.

75. "Statements From Rival Camps," *Chicago Tribune*, October 24, 1910.

76. *Ibid*; E.A. Batchelor, "Players Share in Sunday Gate Instead of Saturday," *Detroit Free Press*, October 24, 1910.

77. "Statements From Rival Camps," *Chicago Tribune*, October 24, 1910.

78. Artie Hofman, "Beaten Fairly," *Chicago Tribune*, October 24, 1910.

79. Christy Mathewson, *Pitching in a Pinch* (New York: Stein & Day, 1977), p. 141; "Believe Mackmen Wise to Signals," *Chicago Tribune*, October 25, 1910.

80. Mathewson, *Pitching in a Pinch*, p. 141.

81. *Ibid.*, pp. 141–142.

82. Batchelor, "Players Share in Sunday Gate Instead of Saturday," *Detroit Free Press*, October 24, 1910.

83. *Ibid*; "Statements From Rival Camps," *Chicago Tribune*, October 24, 1910.

84. *Ibid.*

85. "Two Ton Elephant for Mack," *Chicago Tribune*, October 27, 1910.

86. E.A. Batchelor, "Ineffective Pitching Killed Cub Chances, *Detroit Free Press*, October 25, 1910.

87. James A. Hart, "Scoffers Again Cub Fans," *Chicago Tribune*, October 23, 1910.

88. "Another World Series," *The Sporting News*, October 27, 1910.

89. *Ibid.*

Chapter 5 — 1917

1. Rowland was a Class C league pilot when Comiskey hired him to manage the White Sox in 1915, replacing Jim "Nixey" Callahan. He earned his nickname because of his penchant for wearing cream colored trousers and a matching jacket. Schoor, *The History of the World Series*, p. 72.

2. Harvey Frommer, *Shoeless Joe and Ragtime Baseball* (Dallas: Taylor Publishing Co., 1992), p. 76.

3. Allen, *The World Series*, p. 85. Cicotte was 13–12, with a 3.02 earned run average in 1915.

4. James Crusinberry, "Analyze Cicotte's Delivery," *Chicago Tribune*, October 6, 1917.

5. John Carmichael, "The Chicago White Sox" in Ed Fitzgerald (ed.), *The American League* (New York: Grosset & Dunlap, 1955), p. 43; E.A. Batchelor, "Cicotte Choice of Rowland to Pitch," *Detroit Free Press*, October 6, 1917.

6. I.E. Sanborn, "White Sox Versus Giants," *Chicago Tribune*, October 1, 1917.

7. "Cicotte and Psychology," *New York Times*, October 18, 1917.

8. Crusinberry, "Analyze Cicotte's Delivery," *Chicago Tribune*, October 6, 1917.

9. Frommer, *Shoeless Joe and Ragtime Baseball,*" p. 77.

10. Charles C. Alexander, *John McGraw* (New York: Viking Press, 1988), p. 196.

11. "Do Fans of Old and John McGraw Agree?" *The Sporting News*, October 18, 1917.

12. Alexander, *John McGraw*, p. 197.

13. Schoor, *The History of the World Series*, p. 73.

14. I.E. Sanborn, "White Sox Versus Giants," *Chicago Tribune*, October 3, 1917.

15. *Ibid.*

16. *Ibid.*

17. *Ibid.*

18. I.E. Sanborn, "World Series an Even Bet, With Many 'Ifs," *Chicago Tribune*, October 4, 1917.

19. "Before the Battle," *Chicago Tribune*, October 6, 1917.

20. "Schupp May Start Giants to Victory," *New York Times*, October 6, 1917. The clutch power hitting of Frank Baker of the Athletics in 1911, Hank Gowdy of the Boston Braves in 1914, Harry Hooper of the Red Sox in 1915, and Duffy Lewis of the Red Sox in 1916 led their teams to world championships.

21. "Before the Battle," *Chicago Tribune*, October 6, 1917.

22. *Ibid.*

23. "Giants in Chicago for the Series," *New York Times*, October 5, 1917. Doubtless much of the Sox confidence was a result of witnessing the Cubs defeat the Giants 9–5 in a sloppily played exhibition two day's before the Series' opener. The contest, which McGraw insisted on having to keep his players from becoming rusty, was at Wrigley Field because Comiskey refused to permit his rain-soaked park to be used, despite Rowland's earlier pledge to McGraw that he could practice there any time. "I'll call my players off," Rowland had informed the Giant management. "There will be no repetition of the 1914 Series when George Stallings, manager of the Boston club, raised a protest because of the alleged turndown he received from Manager Mack over the use of the Athletics' field for practice." "Conquering Sox Get Home," *New York Times*," October 4, 1917.

24. "McGraw Boosts Liberty Loan," *Chicago Tribune*, October 1, 1917.

25. "Series Money to Loan," *New York Times*, October 2, 1917; "Commy Realizes on Investment," *Detroit Free Press*, October 7, 1917. The October 2 issue of the *Times* also noted that National Baseball Commission Chairman Garry Herrmann previously had recommended that all proceeds received by the National Commission from the World Series, club owners, and players, after expenses were paid, should be invested in the second issue of Liberty Bonds.

26. Frommer, *Shoeless Joe and Ragtime Baseball*, p. 77; Noel Hynd, *The Giants of the Polo Grounds* (Dallas: Taylor Publishing, 1995), p. 204. The Giants retained their regular season garb of white or gray with purple trimming, but they did sport new autumn brown sweater jackets. "Chicago in Gala Array," *New York Times*, October 7, 1917.

27. "World Series Notes," *Chicago Tribune*, October 8, 1917.

28. Batchelor, "Cicotte Choice of Rowland to Pitch," *Detroit Free Press*, October 6, 1917; "Fans Line Up in Rain," *New York Times*, October 6, 1917.

29. Batchelor, "Cicotte Choice of Rowland to Pitch," *Detroit Free Press*, October 6, 1917.

30. E.A. Batchelor, "White Sox Beat Giants in First Game for Title," *Detroit Free Press*, October 7, 1917; "Home Run Hit Defeats Giants as Series Opens," *New York Times*, October 7, 1917; "Chicago in Gala Array," *New York Times*, October 7, 1917.

31. Batchelor, "White Sox Beat Giants in First Game for Title," *Detroit Free Press*, October 7, 1917; "World Series Notes," *Chicago Tribune*, October 7, 1917.

32. "Chicago in Gala Array," *New York Times*, October 7, 1917.

33. "Bonnet or Game," *Chicago Tribune*, October 7, 1917.

34. "Home Run Hit Defeats Giants as Series Opens," *New York Times*, October 7, 1917.

35. Batchelor, "White Sox Beat Giants in First Game for Title," *Detroit Free Press*, October 7, 1917.

36. *Ibid.*

37. Jack Lait, "O. Henry Clan Weeps and Cheers as 'Hap' Swats," *Chicago Tribune*, October 7, 1917.

38. "Here are Views on Mr. Cicotte," *Chicago Tribune*, October 7, 1917.

39. E.A. Batchelor, "Giants Still Confident," *Detroit Free Press*, October 7, 1917.

40. *Ibid.*

41. James Crusinberry, "Sox in Front," *Chicago Tribune*, October 7, 1917.

42. *Ibid.*

43. "20,000 Fans Would Hang Weatherman," *New York Times*, October 10, 1917.

44. "White Sox Rout Hopes of Giants in Second Game," *New York Times*, October 8, 1917.

45. *Ibid.*

46. *Ibid.*

47. *Ibid.*; "Still in Fight," *Chicago Tribune*, October 8, 1917.

48. "Faber Explains His Classic Bone," *The Sporting News*, October 18, 1917; Stephen D. Boren, "Blunders on the Base Paths Part of World Series Lore," *Baseball Digest*," October, 1991, pp. 23–24.

49. "Faber Explains His Classic Bone," *The Sporting News*, October 18, 1917.

50. "What Faber Said," *Chicago Tribune*, October 9, 1917.

51. "Faber Explains His Classic Bone," *The Sporting News*, October 18, 1917.

52. *Ibid.*

53. James Crusinberry, "Four Straight," *Chicago Tribune*, October 8, 1917; "Commy Quits Game After Big Fourth," *Chicago Tribune*, October 8, 1917.

54. "Commy Quits Game After Big Fourth," *Chicago Tribune*, October 8, 1917.

55. Crusinberry, "Four Straight," *Chicago Tribune*, October 8, 1917.

56. "White Sox Rout Hopes of Giants in Second Game," *New York Times*, October 8, 1917.

57. *Ibid.*; Ralph S. Davis, ""Fallacy of Doping a Series is Shown," *The Sporting News*, October 18, 1917.

58. "Giants Still in the Fight," *New York Times*, October 9, 1917; "White Sox Rout Hopes of Giants in Second Game, *New York Times*, October 8, 1917.

59. "Giants Still in the Fight," *New York Times*, October 9, 1917.

60. *Ibid.*

61. "Royal Welcome for Giants," *New York Times*, October 11, 1917.

62. Hynd, *The Giants of the Polo Grounds*, p. 205.

63. "Liberty Bonds for Fans," *New York Times*, October 9, 1917.

64. "20,000 Fans Would Hang Weatherman," *New York Times*, October 10, 1917; Hynd, *The Giants of the Polo Grounds*, p. 205; "Benton Masters Sox and Giants Get Third Game," *New York Times*, October 11, 1917.

65. "20,000 Fans Would Hang Weatherman," *New York Times*, October 10, 1917; "World Series Notes," *Chicago Tribune*, October 11, 1917; "Royal Welcome for Giants," *New York Times*, October 11, 1917; Hynd, *The Giants of the Polo Grounds*, p. 205.

66. "Royal Welcome for Giants," *New York Times*, October 11, 1917; E.A. Batchelor, "Two Home Runs by Benny Kauff Wreck Chicago's Chances," *Detroit Free Press*, October 12, 1917.

67. "Benton Masters Sox and Giants Get Third Game," *New York Times*, October 11, 1917.

68. *Ibid.*

69. "James Crusinberry, "Welcome Home," *Chicago Tribune*, October 11, 1917.

70. *Ibid.*

71. *Ibid.*

72. Batchelor, "Two Home Runs by Benny Kauff Wreck Chicago's Chances," *Detroit Free Press*, October 12, 1917.

73. *Ibid.*; "Kauff Got His Hits,"*Chicago Tribune*, October 12, 1917.

74. "Kauff's Homers Win for Giants and Tie Series," *New York Times*, October 12, 1917; Batchelor, "Two Home Runs by Benny Kauff Wreck Chicago's Chances," *Detroit Free Press*, October 12, 1917. By poling his drive over the short 257' right-field barrier Kauff joined Pat Dougherty of the 1903 Red Sox and Harry Hooper of the 1915 Red Sox as the only players to hit two home runs in a World Series game.

75. "Kauff's Homers Win for Giants and Tie Series," *New York Times*, October 12, 1917.

76. "Batchelor, "Two Home Runs by Benny Kauff Wreck Chicago's Chances," *Detroit Free Press*, October 12, 1917.

77. E.A. Batchelor, "Snowstorm Hits Chicago on Eve of Fifth Game," *Detroit Free Press*, October 13, 1917.

78. "Kauff's Homers Win for Giants and Tie Series," *New York Times*, October 12, 1917.

79. "World Series Notes," *Chicago Tribune*, October 12, 1917.

80. "Statements," *Chicago Tribune*, October 12, 1917.

81. I.E. Sanborn, "Fighting Mood to Rescue Sox or Giants Win," *Chicago Tribune*, October 13, 1917.

82. *Ibid.*

83. "Sox Smash Way to Late Victory in Fifth Contest," *New York Times*, October 14, 1917.

84. *Ibid.*

85. *Ibid.*; E.A. Batchelor, "Game Snatched From Outstretched Arms of Enemy," *Detroit Free Press*, October 14, 1917; James Crusinberry, "Fans Go Wild, Even Players Dance in Glee," *Chicago Tribune*, October 14, 1917.

86. Crusinberry, "Fans Go Wild, Even Players Dance in Glee," *Chicago Tribune*, October 14, 1917.

87. Batchelor, "Game Snatched From Outstretched Arms of Enemy," *Detroit Free Press*, October 14, 1917.

88. "Sox Smash Way to Late Victory in Fifth Contest," *New York Times*, October 14, 1917.

89. Walter Trumbull, "All Dependent on One Pitch," *Chicago Tribune*, October 14, 1917.

90. Schoor, *The History of the World Series*, p. 75; Lieb, *The Baseball Story*, p. 212.

91. *Ibid.*

92. Alexander, *John McGraw*, p. 202.

93. "Giants Confident of Downing the Sox," *New York Times*, October 15, 1917; Frank Graham, *McGraw of the Giants* (New York: G.P. Putnam's Sons, 1944), p. 107.

94. James Crusinberry, "Gotham at Train to Welcome Sox With Mailed Fist," *Chicago Tribune*, October 15, 1917; William G. Weart, "Unfair Tactics Stir White Sox to Life," *The Sporting News*, October 18, 1917.

95. Crusinberry, "Gotham at Train to Welcome Sox With Mailed Fist," *Chicago Tribune*, October 15, 1917.

96. "It's Easy Now," *Chicago Tribune*, October 14, 1917.

97. *Ibid.*

98. Trumbull, "All Dependent on One Pitch," *Chicago Tribune*, October 14, 1917.

99. George S. Robbins, "Chicago Mad With Joy Over Victory of Rowland's Team," *The Sporting News*, October 18, 1917.

100. I.E. Sanborn, "Sox Win World Title, 4–2," *Chicago Tribune*, October 16, 1917.

101. "Zim's Race With Collins Cost Capt. Herzog $1,700," *Chicago Tribune*, October 17, 1917.

102. E.A. Batchelor, "National Leaguers Blow Sky High," *Detroit Free Press*, October 16, 1917.

103. "White Sox Take World Title in Torrid Finish," *New York Times*, October 16, 1917.

104. "Sanborn, "Sox Win World Title, 4–2," *Chicago Tribune*, October 16, 1917.

105. *Ibid.*

106. Rowland deeply resented being called "busher." He told *Chicago Tribune* writer Harvey Woodruff in 1915: "I am a bush leaguer. It is no disgrace. But if you call me a bush leaguer at the end of 1916 after I have served a year, I may regard it as a reflection." Harvey Woodruff, "'Bush League' Manager Cops World Title," *Chicago Tribune*, October 16, 1917; Hynd, *The Giants of the Polo Grounds*, p. 208; Joseph Durso, *Baseball and the American Dream* (St. Louis: The Sporting News, 1986), p. 122.

107. "White Sox Take World Title in Torrid Finish," *New York Times*, October 16, 1917.

108. "Statements," *Chicago Tribune*," October 16, 1917.

109. *Ibid.*

110. *Ibid.*

111. *Ibid.*

112. Schoor, *The History of the World Series*, p. 76.

113. *Ibid.*; Hynd, *The Giants of the Polo Grounds*, pp. 207–208; Alexander, *John McGraw*, p. 202. After hearing Zimmerman's statement, and knowing that the Giant third-sacker was not known for his intelligence, Klem quipped: "I was afraid he would." Hynd, *The Giants of the Polo Grounds*, p. 207.

114. Graham, *McGraw of the Giants*, p. 107; Frank Graham, "The New York Giants," in Ed Fitzgerald (ed.), *The National League* (New York: Grosset & Dunlap, 1955), p. 230; Hynd, *The Giants of the Polo Grounds*, p.p. 207–208.

115. Hynd, *The Giants of the Polo Grounds*, p. 207; "White Sox Down Giants Again," *New York Times*, October 17, 1917.

116. "Evidence Clears Zimmerman of Charge of Pulling Bone," *The Sporting News*, October 25, 1917.

117. *Ibid.*

118. *Ibid.*

119. Ralph S. Davis, "McGraw Still After Mamaux," *The Sporting News*, October 25, 1917.

120. *Ibid.*

121. "Evidence Clears Zimmerman of Charge of Pulling Bone," *The Sporting News*, October 25, 1917.

122. John Alcock, "Bands to Welcome Champs Back Home at Station Today," *Chicago Tribune*, October 17, 1917. Comiskey never would have thought it possible that this would be the last world championship banner captured by the White Sox in the twentieth century.

123. I.E. Sanborn, "Both Managers Go Wrong," *Chicago Tribune*, October 17, 1917.

124. "Analyzing the Series," *The Sporting News*, October 18, 1917.

Chapter 6 — 1918

1. Golenbock, *Wrigleyville*, pp. 160–161.

2. *Ibid*, pp. 160, 163.

3. *Ibid*, p. 163.

4. *Ibid*, pp. 166–167.

5. *Ibid*, p. 172.

6. Schoor, *The History of the World Series*, pp. 77–78.

7. Harry Bullion, "Pitchers in Doubt on Eve of Struggle for Baseball Title," *Detroit Free Press*, September 4, 1918.

8. Paul J. Zingg, *Harry Hooper* (Urbana: University of Illinois Press, 1993), p. 167; "Cub Boss Sends Thanks to Sox," *Chicago Tribune*, September 15, 1918.

9. "Cubs are Favored in the World Series," *New York Times*, September 1, 1918.

10. Robert W. Creamer, *Babe: The Legend Comes to Life* (New York: Simon and Schuster, 1974), p. 175.

11. *Ibid.*

12. I.E. Sanborn, "Lone Run in Fourth Enough for Ruth to Best Vaughn," *Chicago Tribune*, September 6, 1918.

13. Creamer, *Babe: The Legend Comes to Life*, p. 173; Ken Smith, *Baseball's Hall of Fame* (New York: Grosset and Dunlap, 1952), p. 115; George Herman Ruth, *Babe Ruth's Own Book of Baseball* (Lincoln: University of Nebraska Press, 1992), pp. 34–35. When Ruth wrote this book in 1928 he was so mad at Yankee business manager Ed Barrow that he purposefully claimed Bill Carrigan, not Barrow, was manager of the 1918 Red Sox.

14. "One Run Gives Red Sox First Game," *New York Times*, September 6, 1918.

15. Creamer, *Babe: The Legend Comes to Life*, p. 175; Smith, *Baseball's Hall of Fame*, p. 115.

16. James Crusinberry, "All Primed to Yell, But Precise Hurling Gives Fans No Chance," *Chicago Tribune*, September 6, 1918.

17. *Ibid*; "One Run Gives Red Sox First Game," *New York Times*, September 6, 1918.

18. "One Run Gives Red Sox First Game," *New York Times*, September 6, 1918.

19. *Ibid.*

20. Creamer, *Babe: The Legend Comes to Life*, p. 177.

21. "Cubs' Task Now Easier," *New York Times*, September 7, 1918.

22. Harry Bullion, "Series is Evened by Raid on Bush in Second Inning," *Detroit Free Press*, September 7, 1918.

23. James Crusinberry, "Triumph of Cubs Accompanied by Thud of Players in Scrap," *Chicago Tribune*, September 7, 1918.

24. "Red Sox Check Rally in Ninth," *New York Times*, September 8, 1918.

25. *Ibid.*

26. "Players in World Series Uneasy Over Meager Receipts," *New York Times*, September 9, 1918.

27. "Jim Vaughn Blames Himself for Defeat," *Chicago Tribune*, September 8, 1918.

28. Creamer, *Babe: The Legend Comes to Life*, pp. 175–176; "Players to Protest to Commission on Reduction of Purse," *Chicago Tribune*, September 9, 1918.

29. Creamer, *Babe: The Legend Comes to Life*, p. 176.

30. Harry Bullion, "Nothing Bulky About World Series Receipts," *Detroit Free Press*, September 9, 1918.

31. "Wild Toss Gives Red Sox Victory," *New York Times*, September 10, 1918.

32. Eugene C. Murdock, *Ban Johnson* (Westport: Greenwood Press, 1982), p. 165; Creamer, *Babe: The Legend Comes to Life*, pp. 178–179.

33. Schoor, *The History of the World Series*, p. 80; Creamer, *Babe: The Legend Comes to Life*, p. 179.

34. Harry Bullion, "Players Strike for More Cash; Will Not Get It," *Detroit Free Press*, September 11, 1918; "Here's Comish's Rule on Split," *Chicago Tribune*, September 11, 1918.

35. Bullion, "Players Strike for More Cash; Will Not get It," *Detroit Free Press*, September 11, 1918.

36. I.E. Sanborn, "Vaughn Finally Subdues Red Sox With Five Hits," *Chicago Tribune*, September 11, 1918.

37. Creamer, *Babe: The Legend Comes to Life*, p. 180.

38. *Ibid*; Zingg, *Harry Hooper*, p. 170.

39. Creamer, *Babe: The Legend Comes to Life*, p. 180; Zingg, *Harry Hooper*, pp. 170–171; Murdock, *Ban Johnson*, p. 165.

40. Zingg, *Harry Hooper*, p. 171.

41. *Ibid*; Creamer, *Babe: The Legend Comes to Life*, p. 180.

42. *Ibid.*

43. *Ibid*, p. 181.

44. *Ibid.*

45. "Vaughn Mows Down Red Sox," *New York Times*, September 11, 1918; "Red Sox Beat Cubs in Close, But Not Exciting, Battle," *New York Times*, September 12, 1918.

46. "World Series Notes," *Chicago Tribune*, September 12, 1918; "Wrangle Over Money Retards Game Hour; Means Series' Knell," *Chicago Tribune*, September 11, 1918.

47. Sanborn, "Vaughn Finally Subdues Red Sox With Five Hits," *Chicago Tribune*, September 11, 1918.

48. Thomas S. Rice, "Scribbled by Scribes," *The Sporting News*, September 12, 1918.

49. "Red Sox Beat Cubs in Close, But Not Exciting, Battle," *New York Times*, September 12, 1918.

50. *Ibid.*

51. *Ibid.*

52. "The Last Say," *Chicago Tribune*, September 12, 1918; Schoor, *The History of the World Series*, p. 80.

53. "The Last Say," *Chicago Tribune*, September 12, 1918.

54. "Players Childlike in Their Little Ways," *The Sporting News*, September 19, 1918.

55. "Red Sox Players Each Draw $1,108," *Chicago Tribune*, September 13, 1918; I.E. Sanborn, "Cubs 'Divvy' Money So Pals in Service Receive Share Each," *Chicago Tribune*, September 13, 1918; Zingg, *Harry Hooper*, p. 175. If it was not the "Curse of the Bambino" that has caused Boston to lose every World Series since Babe Ruth was traded to the Yankees, perhaps it was the "Curse of the Banned Emblems." To lift this hex, in 1993, the Red Sox organization requested the Commissioner's Office to strike medals for the families of the 1918 world champions. However, no action was taken. "Curses!" *The Sporting News*, August 30, 1993.

56. Harry Bullion, "National Game Goes Out Shy of Respect Due It," *Detroit Free Press*, September 13, 1918.

Chapter 7 — 1919

1. Frommer, *Shoeless Joe and Ragtime Baseball*, p. 86.

2. *Ibid*, p. 91. Moran managed the Reds for four more seasons before dying in March, 1924 on the eve of spring training.

3. *Ibid*, p. 101.

4. Donald Honig, *Baseball America* (New York: Galahad, 1985), p. 108.

5. Frommer, *Shoeless Joe and Ragtime Baseball*, p. 97.

6. Murdock, *Ban Johnson*, p. 185; Schoor, *The History of the World Series*, p. 81.

7. Schoor, *The History of the World Series*, p. 81.

8. Murdock, *Ban Johnson*, p. 185; Frommer, *Shoeless Joe and Ragtime Baseball*, p. 93.

9. Dan Daniel, "Over the Fence," *The Sporting News*, October 5, 1939.

10. "Redland Field is Ready for Opener," *New York Times*, October 1, 1919.

11. "Reds Rout White Sox in Opening Game of Series," *New York Times*, October 2, 1919.

12. "Sousa Leads Band at Redland Field," *New York Times*, October 2, 1919; "Gossip of the First Game," *The Sporting News*, October 9, 1919.

13. "Sousa Leads Band at Redland Field," *New York Times*, October 2, 1919.

14. Murdock, *Ban Johnson*, p. 187.

15. Eliot Asinof, *Eight Men Out* (New York: Henry Holt, 1963), p. 53.

16. Jerome Holtzman, *No Cheering in the Press Box* (New York: Henry Holt, 1995), p. 155.

17. *Ibid.*

18. Asinof, *Eight Men Out*, p. 59.

19. "Gossip of the First Game," *The Sporting News*, October 9, 1919.

20. Joe S. Jackson, "Sidelights on the Game," *Detroit Free Press*, October 2, 1919.

21. Charles Fountain, *Sportswriter: The Life and Times of Grantland Rice* (New York: Oxford University Press, 1993), p. 174.

22. Gies and Shoemaker, *Stars of the Series*, p. 57.

23. Frommer, *Shoeless Joe and Ragtime Baseball*, p. 101; Schoor, *The History of the World Series*, p. 82; Asinof, *Eight Men Out*, p. 68.

24. "Reds Rout White Sox in Opening Game of Series," *New York Times*, October 2, 1919.

25. Fountain, *Sportswriter: The Life and Times of Grantland Rice*, p. 174.

26. "Reds Rout White Sox in Opening Game of Series," *New York Times*, October 2, 1919.

27. Schoor, *The History of the World Series*, p. 82.

28. *Ibid.*

29. "Statements of Rival Managers," *Detroit Free Press*, October 2, 1919.

30. James Crusinberry, "Defeat to Spur Gleason's Team to Real Fighting," *Chicago Tribune*, October 2, 1919.

31. *Ibid.*

32. Asinof, *Eight Men Out*, p. 72.

33. *Ibid.*

34. Jonathan Yardley, *Ring* (New York: Random House, 1977), p. 214; Frommer, *Shoeless Joe and Ragtime Baseball*, p. 106.

35. Joseph L. Reichler (ed.), *The World Series* (New York: Simon and Schuster, 1975), p. 147.

36. "Reds Rout White Sox in Opening Game of Series," *New York Times*, October 2, 1919; John Mosedale, *The Greatest of Them All* (New York: Dial Press, 1974), p. 12. In later years, Ruether admitted: "What hurt me was the disclosure they were merely fooling around. It's hard to believe. I thought I had worked a tight game." Mosedale, *The Greatest of Them All*, p. 12.

37. "Statements of Rival Managers," *Detroit Free Press*, October 2, 1919.

38. Asinof, *Eight Men Out*, pp. 73–74.

39. Frommer, *Shoeless Joe and Ragtime Baseball*, p. 103; Lieb, *The Baseball Story*, pp. 218–219.

40. Frommer, *Shoeless Joe and Ragtime Baseball*, p. 103.

41. *Ibid.*, pp. 103–104; Lieb, *The Baseball Story*, p. 219; Murdock, *Ban Johnson*, p. 189.

42. Frommer, *Shoeless Joe and Ragtime Baseball*, p. 104; Asinof, *Eight Men Out*, p. 83.

43. "White Sox Again Defeated by Reds," *New York Times*, October 3, 1919.

44. Harry Bullion, "Williams Wild, Reds Win 4–2," *Detroit Free Press*, October 3, 1919.

45. Fountain, *Sportswriter: The Life and Times of Grantland Rice*, p. 175.

46. "White Sox Again Defeated by Reds," *New York Times*, October 3, 1919.

47. Asinof, *Eight Men Out*, p. 89; Frommer, *Shoeless Joe and Ragtime Baseball*, p. 105.

48. Asinof, *Eight Men Out*, p. 89; Frommer, *Shoeless Joe and Ragtime Baseball*, p. 105.

49. *Ibid*; Asinof, *Eight Men Out*, p. 89. Although there was a rumor that Schalk also fought with Risberg, the catcher steadfastly denied it throughout his life. Ed Burns, "Unforgettable Memory Left With Schalk," *The Sporting News*, November 28, 1940.

50. "Statements of the Rival Managers," *Detroit Free Press*, October 3, 1919; James Crusinberry, "Gleason's Squad Unlucky, But Not Hopeless Yet," *Chicago Tribune*, October 3, 1919.

51. Joe S. Jackson, "Strolling Through Sportland's By-Ways," *Detroit Free Press*, October 8, 1919.

52. "Statements of the Rival Managers," *Detroit Free Press*, October 3, 1919.

53. *Ibid.*

54. Lawrence S. Ritter, *The Glory of Their Times* (New York: Vintage Books, 1984), pp. 218–219.

55. *Ibid*, p. 219.

56. Yardley, *Ring*, p. 214.

57. Dan Gutman, *Baseball Babylon* (New York: Penguin Books, 1992), pp. 176–177. In his testimony regarding the Series, Joe Jackson seconded Gandil's sentiment, stating: "At lot of these sporting writers have been talking about the third game of the World Series being square. Let me tell you something. The eight of us did our best to kick it. Little Dick Kerr won the game for us by his pitching. Because he won it, those gamblers double-crossed us for double-crossing them." *New York Times*, September 29, 1920.

58. "Reds Lose Third Game to Chicago," *New York Times*, October 4, 1919.

59. *Ibid.*

60. "White Sox Win 3–0 Behind Kerr," *Chicago Tribune*, October 4, 1919.

61. Harry Bullion, ""Kerr Restores Sox Confidence with a Shutout," *Detroit Free Press*, October 4, 1919.

62. "White Sox Win 3–0 Behind Kerr," *Chicago Tribune*, October 4, 1919.

63. *Ibid.*

64. Gutman, *Baseball Babylon*, p. 177.

65. *Ibid.*

66. "Record Betting Cause of Alarm; Starts Scandal," *Chicago Tribune*, October 5, 1919.

67. *Ibid.*

68. "Cincinnati Takes Fourth Game of Series," *New York Times*, October 5, 1919.

69. Reichler (ed.), *The World Series*, p. 147.

70. Honig, *Baseball America*, pp. 109–110.

71. James Crusinberry, "Cicotte Loses, But 'Arm Gone' Pipe Burns Out," *Chicago Tribune*, October 5, 1919.

72. *Ibid*; "Statements of Rival Managers," *Detroit Free Press*, October 5, 1919.

73. Crusinberry, "Cicotte Loses, But 'Arm Gone' Pipe Burns Out," *Chicago Tribune*, October 5, 1919.

74. Joe S. Jackson, "Sidelights of the Game," *Detroit Free Press*, October 5, 1919.

75. Harvey T. Woodruff, "Sox Not Playing Game That Won Pennant," *Chicago Tribune*, October 6, 1919.

76. *Ibid.*

77. *Ibid.*

78. "Rain at Chicago Halts Series," *New York Times*, October 6, 1919.

79. Ritter, *The Glory of Their Times*, p. 219.

80. *Ibid.*

81. *Ibid*; Frommer, *Shoeless Joe and Ragtime Baseball*, p. 111. Covering the 1939 World Series, Dan Daniel wrote that this confrontation occurred before the eighth game, but all evidence indicates his recollection was incorrect. Dan Daniel, "Over the Fence," *The Sporting News*, October 5, 1939.

82. Frommer, *Shoeless Joe and Ragtime Baseball*, p. 110.

83. "Cincinnati Again Beats White Sox," *New York Times*, October 7, 1919.

84. Frommer, *Shoeless Joe and Ragtime Baseball*, p. 110.

85. *Ibid.*

86. Harry Bullion, "Only a Baseball Miracle Can Save Sox," *Detroit Free Press*, October 7, 1919.

87. Harry Bullion, "Eller a Hero in Red Triumph," *Detroit Free Press*, October 7, 1919.

88. Christy Mathewson, "Eller's Work was a Marvel," *Detroit Free Press*, October 7, 1919.

89. "Eller Tames Sox," *Chicago Tribune*, October 7, 1919; "How Managers View It," *Detroit Free Press*, October 7, 1919.

90. James Crusinberry, "What is Wrong with White Sox? Gleason Asks," *Chicago Tribune*, October 7, 1919.

91. *Ibid.*

92. *Ibid.*

93. *Ibid.*

94. "White Sox Rally and Defeat Reds," *New York Times*, October 8, 1919.

95. "Gift of Cincinnati K.C.'s to Moran Stolen," *Chicago Tribune*, October 9, 1919.

96. "Statements of Rival Managers," *Detroit Free Press*, October 8, 1919.

97. James Crusinberry, "Sudden Change in Sox Causes Woe in Cincy," *Chicago Tribune*, October 8, 1919.

98. *Ibid.*

99. Gutman, *Baseball Babylon*, p. 177.

100. "White Sox Again Beat Cincinnati," *New York Times*, October 9, 1919.
101. James Crusinberry, "Cincy Prepares to Dress Up in Mourning Robes," *Chicago Tribune*, October 9, 1919.
102. Gutman, *Baseball Babylon*, pp. 177–178.
103. "$2,000,000 Bet on Series," *New York Times*, October 10, 1919.
104. "Schoor, *The World Series*, p. 84; Frommer, *Shoeless Joe and Ragtime Baseball*, p. 113.
105. "Reds Defeat Sox in Eighth Game and Win Series," *New York Times*, October 10, 1919.
106. Asinof, *Eight Men Out*, p. 115.
107. "Reds Defeat Sox in Eighth Game and Win Series," *New York Times*, October 10, 1919.
108. Harry Bullion, "World Title Goes to Reds in Eighth Game," *Detroit Free Press*, October 10, 1919.
109. "Sox Were Outclassed," *New York Times*, October 10, 1919.
110. *Ibid.*
111. Asinof, *Eight Men Out*, p. 119; James Crusinberry, "Greatest Team Beaten by Reds, Says Gleason," *Chicago Tribune*, October 10, 1919.
112. Asinof, *Eight Men Out*, p. 123.
113. Williams (ed.), *The Joe Williams Baseball Reader*, p. 43. Weaver played clean ball, batted .324, and made no errors, either physical or mental during the Series; his guilt was knowing about the plot and not reporting it to anyone.
114. Frommer, *Shoeless Joe and Ragtime Baseball*, p. 114.
115. Joe Vila, "Reds Won Fair and Square," *The Sporting News*, October 16, 1919.
116. Ralph S. Davis, "Better Leader and Better Sportsman," *The Sporting News*, October 16, 1919.
117. James C. O'Leary, "Denounces Scandal Peddlers," *The Sporting News*, October 16, 1919.
118. Oscar C. Reichow, "Mitchell Will Not Lose Out With the Cubs," *The Sporting News*, October 16, 1919.
119. Benedict Cosgrove, *Covering the Bases* (San Francisco: Chronicle Books, 1997), p. 32, 34.
120. Frommer, *Shoeless Joe and Ragtime Baseball*, p. 115.
121. *Ibid*, p. 119.
122. Honig, *Baseball America*, p. 110.
123. Asinof, *Eight Men Out*, pp. 128–129.
124. "Rumors Arouse Comiskey," *New York Times*, October 11, 1919. Ever miserly, Comiskey later swore before the grand jury that he had only a $10,000 reward." "Grand Jury Hears World Series Plot," *New York Times*, September 25, 1920.
125. Reichow, "Mitchell Will Not Lose Out With the Cubs," *The Sporting News*, October 16, 1919.
126. Fountain, *Sportswriter*, p. 177.
127. Isaminger's story was reprinted in *Baseball Digest* (October–November, 1959), pp. 9–13.
128. Durso, *Baseball and the American Dream*, p. 128.
129. *Ibid.*
130. *Ibid*; "White Sox Players are Indicted," *New York Times*, September 29, 1920.
131. Durso, *Baseball and the American Dream*, p. 128, 130; Reichler, *The World Series*, p. 147.
132. Durso, *Baseball and the American Dream*, p. 130; "White Sox Players are Indicted," *New York Times*, September 29, 1920.
133. "White Sox Players are Indicted," *New York Times*, September 29, 1920; Reichler, *The World Series*, p. 147.
134. "White Sox Players are Indicted," *New York Times*, September 29, 1920.
135. Durso, *Baseball and the American Dream*, p. 130.
136. *Ibid.*
137. Gutman, *Baseball Babylon*, p. 179.
138. Reichler, *The World Series*, p. 147.
139. Reidenbaugh, *Baseball's 25 Greatest Pennant Races*, p. 215. The White Sox, who trailed Cleveland by 1½ games when the grand jury convened, finished two lengths behind the Indians with a 96–58 record.
140. Asinof, *Eight Men Out*, p. 212.
141. *Ibid*, p. 220.
142. Gutman, *Baseball Babylon*, p. 180.
143. Asinof, *Eight Men Out*, p. 272.
144. *Ibid.*
145. *Ibid*, p. 273.
146. *Ibid.*
147. Frederick G. Lieb, "Black Sox Forty Year Plague on Chicago," *The Sporting News*, September 30, 1959.
148. *Ibid.*
149. Asinof, *Eight Men Out*, p. 192.

Chapter 8 — 1929

1. Babe Ruth, "Athletics Good Defensive Club," *St. Louis Post-Dispatch*," October 1, 1929.
2. Golenbock, *Wrigleyville*, pp. 212, 214. Wrigley and club president William Veeck also instituted weekly fifty-cent admission Ladies' Day games.
3. Joe McCarthy, "Date With Mack at Dinner in 1925," *St. Louis Post-Dispatch*, October 1, 1925.
4. Connie Mack, "Cubs are Strangers," *St. Louis Post-Dispatch*, October 4, 1929.
5. *Ibid.*; "Athletics to Leave for Chicago Sunday Night," *St. Louis Post-Dispatch*, October 4, 1929.
6. "Everything in Chicago Ready for World Series," *St. Louis Post-Dispatch*, October 5, 1929.
7. Joe McCarthy, "Team Confident, Not Cocky," *St. Louis Post-Dispatch*, October 6, 1929.
8. *Ibid.*; "Good Series? Surely!" *Detroit Free Press*, October 8, 1929.
9. Ed Burns, "Root, Earnshaw Nice People, But Foes Today," *Chicago Tribune*, October 8, 1929.
10. Westbrook Pegler, "A's Confident of Victory," *Chicago Tribune*, October 8, 1929.
11. "The Business of the Day," *Chicago Tribune*, October 8, 1929.
12. Williams (ed.), *The Joe Williams Baseball Reader*, pp. 90–91; Connie Mack, "Athletics Have Big Edge Now," *St. Louis Post-Dispatch*, October 9, 1929. While many versions of this story exist, the one related here comes from accounts of Eddie Collins and Connie Mack.
13. John P. Carmichael (ed.), *My Greatest Day in Baseball* (New York: Grosset and Dunlap, 1951), pp. 127–131.
14. *Ibid.*; Lieb, *The Story of the World Series*, p. 198; Allen, *The World Series*, p. 122.
15. Grantland Rice, "Ehmke Merits Faith His Boss Placed in Him," *Detroit Free Press*, October 9, 1929.
16. Charlie Grimm, *Grimm's Baseball Tales* (South Bend: Diamond Communications, 1968), p. 71.
17. *Ibid.*
18. Arthur J. Daley, *Inside Baseball* (New York: Grosset and Dunlap, 1950), p. 143.
19. Carmichael, *My Greatest Day in Baseball*, p. 131.
20. "Athletics, Too, Have Words of Praise for Root," *Chicago Tribune*, October 9, 1929.
21. *Ibid.*

22. "What Connie and Joe Think About First Game," *Chicago Tribune*, October 9, 1929.

23. *Ibid.*

24. Joe McCarthy, "Praises Root for Fine Work," *St. Louis Post-Dispatch*, October 9, 1929; "What Connie and Joe Think About First Game," *Chicago Tribune*, October 9, 1929.

25. *Ibid.*

26. Westbrook Pegler, "Pat's Bluff Called by Foxx and Simmons," *Detroit Free Press*, October 10, 1929.

27. *Ibid.*

28. Grantland Rice, "Junior League Now Has Mark of Ten Straight," *Detroit Free Press*, October 10, 1929.

29. *Ibid.*

30. Joe McCarthy, "Cubs Not Out of It Yet," *St. Louis Post-Dispatch*, October 10, 1929.

31. Ed Burns, "Athletics Win Second in a Row, 9–3," *Chicago Tribune*, October 10, 1929.

32. Nick Altrock, "Cubs' Experience Seems to Come in Waving at Three," *St. Louis Post-Dispatch*, October 10, 1929.

33. *Ibid.*

34. Rice, "Junior Circuit Now Has Mark of Ten Straight," *Detroit Free Press*, October 10, 1929.

35. Lieb, *The Story of the World Series*, p. 200; Schoor, *The History of the World Series*, p. 132.

36. John Kieran, "Sports of the *Times*," *New York Times*, October 11, 1929; "Notables Advance on Philadelphia," *New York Times*, October 11, 1929. The *New York Times* of October 11, 1929 also ran a story relating how the Cubs were treated like royalty by the staff of the Ben Franklin Hotel. The National League champions were given an entire floor, a private dining room, three private chefs, a private elevator, a personal gymnasium, and in-room radios.

37. John Drebinger, "Cubs Undaunted, Hope to Get Breaks," *New York Times*, October 11, 1929.

38. *Ibid.*

39. Grantland Rice, "Old Guard of National League Admits Only Miracle Can Save Cubs," *Detroit Free Press*, October 11, 1929.

40. "Women Ushers Added," *New York Times*, October 11, 1929; "Rooftop Support Packed Bleachers," *New York Times*, October 12, 1929; John Drebinger, "Cubs Triumph, 3–1," *New York Times*, October 12, 1929. Most of the women hired were married because an Athletic official explained: "We feel that married women are most entitled to the $5 a day wage the job pays." "Notes on the World Series," *Chicago Tribune*, October 11, 1929.

41. "Rooftop Support Packed Bleachers," *New York Times*, October 12, 1929; Harry Bullion, "Weather Fine, But There Is No Band," *Detroit Free Press*, October 12, 1929.

42. "Rooftop Support Packed Bleachers," *New York Times*, October 12, 1929.

43. John Kieran, "Sports of the *Times*," *New York Times*, October 12, 1929.

44. Grantland Rice, "A's Sluggers are Stopped," *Detroit Free Press*, October 12, 1929.

45. *Ibid.*; "World Series," *Time*, October 21, 1929.

46. Drebinger, "Cubs Triumph, 3–1," *New York Times*, October 12, 1929.

47. *Ibid.*

48. Roscoe McGowen, "Victory Restores Cub Confidence," *New York Times*, October 12, 1929.

49. Ed Burns, "Hear That Din?" *Chicago Tribune*, October 12, 1929.

50. McGowen, "Victory Restores Cub Confidence," *New York Times*, October 12, 1929.

51. J. Roy Stockton, "Wilson Makes Leaping Catch of Boley's Fly," *St. Louis Post-Dispatch*, October 12, 1929.

52. *Ibid.*

53. McGowen, "Victory Restores Cub Confidence," *New York Times*, October 12, 1929.

54. Nick Altrock, "Parade of Wooden Soldiers With Glass Arms," *St. Louis Post-Dispatch*," October 13, 1929.

55. Ty Cobb, "Most Thrilling Game in World Series History," *St. Louis Post-Dispatch*, October 13, 1929.

56. Carmichael (ed.), *My Greatest Day in Baseball*, p. 64; Jimmie Dykes, "Greatest Rally, 10 Runs in '29," *Baseball Digest*, October–November, 1959, p. 16.

57. John Drebinger, "Athletics' Ten Runs in Seventh Defeats Cubs," *New York Times*, October 13, 1929.

58. Grimm, *Grimm's Baseball Tales*, p. 72.

59. Golenbock, *Wrigleyville*, p. 217; Altrock, "Parade of Wooden Soldiers With Glass Arms," *St. Louis Post-Dispatch*, October 13, 1929.

60. Drebinger, "Athletics' Ten Runs in Seventh Defeats Cubs," *New York Times*, October 13, 1929.

61. Altrock, "Parade of Wooden Soldiers With Glass Arms," *St. Louis Post-Dispatch*, October 13, 1929.

62. "Calm Old Connie Shaken by Triumph," *Detroit Free Press*, October 13, 1929.

63. *Ibid.*

64. *Ibid.*

65. John Kieran, "Sports of the *Times*," *New York Times*, October 13, 1929.

66. *Ibid.*

67. Anthony J. Connor, *Voices From Cooperstown* (New York: Collier Books, 1982), pp. 193–194; Harvey Frommer, *Baseball's Greatest Managers* (New York: Franklin Watts, 1985), p. 192; Joseph L. Reichler (ed.), *The World Series* (New York: Simon and Schuster, 1978), p. 155; Lieb, *The Story of the World Series*, p. 203.

68. Golenbock, *Wrigleyville*, pp. 217–218.

69. "Calm Old Connie Shaken by Triumph," *Detroit Free Press*, October 13, 1929.

70. Donald Honig, *The Man in the Dugout* (Lincoln: University of Nebraska Press, 1995), pp. 82–83.

71. Hack Wilson, "How I Became 'Sunny Boy,'" *Baseball Digest*, October–November, 1959, p. 17–18; Charles C. Alexander, *Rogers Hornsby* (New York: Henry Holt and Co., 1995), p. 157; Irving Vaughan, "Cubs Tell How Macks Scored Ten Runs in Fatal Seventh Inning," *Chicago Tribune*, October 13, 1929.

72. *Ibid.*

73. Al Stump, "Why They Freeze Up in the Big Series," *Baseball Digest*, October–November, 1960, p. 43.

74. Irving Vaughan, "I'm the goat," Hack Says, "Let it go at that," *Chicago Tribune*, October 14, 1929.

75. *Ibid.*

76. Cobb, "Most Thrilling Game in World Series History," *St. Louis Post-Dispatch*, October 13, 1929; Babe Ruth, "Thankful for Erasing Yankee Record," *St. Louis Post-Dispatch*, October 13, 1929; "Wrigley Field Blues," *Chicago Tribune*, October 13, 1929; John Kieran, "Sports of the *Times*," *New York Times*, October 14, 1929.

77. "Wrigley Field Blues," *Chicago Tribune*, October 13, 1929.

78. Ed Burns, "Athletics Rout Cubs, 10–8," *Chicago Tribune*, October 13, 1929.

79. *Ibid.*

80. John Drebinger, "Athletics Expect to Win Title Today," *New York Times*, October 14, 1929.

81. Grantland Rice, "Hoover Seeks Thrill and He Isn't Denied," *Detroit Free Press*, October 15, 1929.

82. Lieb, *The Story of the World Series*, p. 202; "President

Hoover Sees Athletics Win Title," *St. Louis Post-Dispatch*, October 14, 1929.

83. Harry Bullion, "Shibe's Canned Music Stirs President Hoover," *Detroit Free Press*, October 15, 1929.

84. "Crowd Astonished by Connie Mack," *New York Times*, October 15, 1929.

85. Connor, *Voices from Cooperstown*, p. 194; Lieb, *The Story of the World Series*, p. 203; Honig, *The Man in the Dugout*, p. 284.

86. *Ibid.*

87. "Crowd Astonished by Connie Mack," *New York Times*, October 15, 1929.

88. Westbrook Pegler, "Then the Mayor Left the President," *Detroit Free Press*, October 15, 1929.

89. Rice, "Hoover Seeks Thrill and He Isn't Denied," *Detroit Free Press*, October 15, 1929.

90. *Ibid.*

91. Pegler, "Then the Mayor Left the President," *Detroit Free Press*, October 15, 1929.

92. Rice, "Hoover Seeks Thrill and He Isn't Denied," *Detroit Free Press*, October 15, 1929.

93. Pegler, "Then the Mayor Left the President," *Detroit Free Press*, October 15, 1929.

94. Honig, *The Man in the Dugout*, p. 281.

95. *Ibid.*

96. Rice, "Hoover Seeks Thrill and He Isn't Denied," *Detroit Free Press*, October 15, 1929.

97. J. Roy Stockton, "9th Inning Rally Enables Athletics to Capture World Series," *St. Louis Post-Dispatch*, October 15, 1929.

98. Lieb, *The Story of the World Series*, 203; Edward J. Neil, "Rally in Ninth Inning Fools Calm Old Connie," *Detroit Free Press*, October 15, 1929; Schoor, *The History of the World Series*, p. 134.

99. Lieb, *The Story of the World Series*, p. 203; Honig, *The Man in the Dugout*, p. 281; Daley, *Inside Baseball*, p. 164.

100. Honig, *The Man in the Dugout*, p. 281; Reichler (ed.), *The World Series*, p. 155; Frommer, *Baseball's Greatest Managers*, p. 192.

101. Sam Murphy, "Why Mack Used Grove Sparingly in Title Clash," *The Sporting News*, October 24, 1929.

102. Neil, "Rally in Ninth Fools Calm Old Connie," *Detroit Free Press*, October 15, 1929.

103. *Ibid.*

104. *Ibid.*

105. Golenbock, *Wrigleyville*, p. 218.

106. Neil, "Rally in Ninth Fools Calm Old Connie," *Detroit Free Press*, October 15, 1929; Ed Burns, "Well, It's Over," *Chicago Tribune*, October 15, 1929. Mack lived long enough to see McCarthy win seven world championships (1932, 1936, 1937, 1938, 1939, 1941, 1943), all with the New York Yankees.

107. Ed Burns, "Well, It's Over," *Chicago Tribune*, October 15, 1929.

108. *Ibid.*

109. Alexander, *Rogers Hornsby*, p. 163.

110. Grimm, *Grimm's Baseball Tales*, p. 75.

111. Golenbock, *Wrigleyville*, p. 225; Eugene Murdock, *Baseball Players and Their Times* (Westport: Meckler, 1991), p. 295.

112. "Glum and Heartsick Cubs Reach Chicago," *Detroit Free Press*, October 16, 1929.

113. Irving Vaughan, "Cubs Disband; McCarthy Blames None," *Chicago Tribune*, October 16, 1929.

114. *Ibid.*

115. *Ibid.*; "Glum and Heartsick Cubs Reach Chicago," *Detroit Free Press*, October 16, 1929.

116. Honig, *The Man in the Dugout*, p. 281. The Athletics followed their 1929 Series triumph with a 102–52 record in 1930 and defeated the St. Louis Cardinals, who had dethroned the Cubs by two games, in a six game World Series. In 1931, the A's improved their record to 107–45, but lost to the Cardinals four games to three in the World Series. The Cubs slipped to third in 1931, finishing a distant seventeen games behind the Cardinals.

117. Gies and Shoemaker, *Stars of the Series*, p. 108.

118. Golenbock, *Wrigleyville*, p. 219.

119. Bob Wray, "Wray's Column: The Lost Art," *St. Louis Post-Dispatch*, October 16, 1929.

Chapter 9 — 1932

1. Nick Altrock, "McCarthy, Koenig Know Lowdown on Rivals," *Detroit Times*, September 26, 1932.

2. Frank Menke, "Grimm Flays Critics," *Detroit Times*, September 27, 1932.

3. John Drebinger, "Stellar Pitching Gives Cubs Edge on Defense Over Yankees," *New York Times*, September 24, 1932.

4. *Ibid.*

5. Altrock, "McCarthy, Koenig Know Lowdown on Rivals, *Detroit Times*, September 26, 1932.

6. "The Late Unpleasantness," *Chicago Tribune*, October 4, 1932.

7. Altrock, "McCarthy, Koenig Know Lowdown on Rivals," *Detroit Times*, September 26, 1932.

8. John Drebinger, "Yankees' High Power Offense Overshadows Attack of Cubs," *New York Times*, September 26, 1932.

9. John Kieran, "Sports of the *Times*," *New York Times*, September 27, 1932.

10. John Drebinger, "McCarthy's Shrewd Experience Gives Yanks Managerial Edge," *New York Times*, September 27, 1932.

11. Marshall Smelser, *The Life That Ruth Built* (New York: Quadrangle, 1975), p. 445.

12. "Landis Awaits Hornsby Protest," *New York Times*, September 23, 1932; "Hornsby Protests Action of Cubs," *New York Times*, September 25, 1932; Alexander, *Rogers Hornsby*, p. 180. Hornsby believed that his removal was engineered by Grimm, whom he claimed would regularly "carry tales to the front office about what was going on in the clubhouse." Rogers Hornsby, "I Always Kept My Bags Packed," *Sport*, September 1955; Grimm, *Grimm's Baseball Tales*, p. 81. Hornsby, whose protest was subsequently dismissed by Landis, was so enraged that he not only refused to attend the World Series, but also would not listen to it on the radio. "Hornsby Not Interested," *New York Times*, September 30, 1932.

13. Smelser, *The Life That Ruth Built*, p. 446. Cub players voted Frank Demaree, who played in twenty-three games in the regular season and batted .304, a quarter share. This led Babe Ruth to remark after the Series: "Jesus, I wish I had known they only voted that kid Demaree a quarter share. Would I have burned them on that one." Creamer, *Babe: The Legend Comes to Life*, pp. 359–360.

14. Smelser, *The Life That Ruth Built*, p. 446.

15. Ed Burns, "Home Runs By Ruth and Gehrig Beat Cubs," *Chicago Tribune*, October 2, 1932.

16. William E. Brandt, "Yankees Hold Drill at Series' Scene," *New York Times*, September 27, 1932. Schmeling knocked out Walker in the eighth round before 45,000 spectators at the Garden.

17. *Ibid.*

18. "Chicago Ticket Sales Boom Despite Defeat," *New York Times*, September 29, 1932.

19. "McCarthy Banks on Ruth to Lead to Victory," *New York Times*, September 28, 1932; Joe Vila, "Bambino Reported Weak Due to Layoff," *The Sporting News*, September 29, 1932.

20. "McCarthy Banks on Ruth to Lead to Victory," *New York Times*, September 28, 1932; "What Rival Pilots Say," *The Sporting News*, September 29, 1932.

21. William E. Brandt, "Rival Clubs Relax on Eve of Battle," *New York Times*, September 28, 1932; John Kieran, "Sports of the *Times*," *New York Times*, September 29, 1932.

22. John Drebinger, "World Series Opens at Stadium Today," *New York Times*, September 28, 1932.

23. John Drebinger, "Yanks Rout Cubs," *New York Times*, September 29, 1932.

24. *Time*, October 10, 1932, p. 19; Drebinger, "Yanks Rout Cubs," September 29, 1932.

25. Joe Sewell, "Game Held Two Breaks," *New York Times*, September 29, 1932.

26. Grantland Rice, "Gehrig Teams With Ruth to Crush Rivals," *Detroit Free Press*, September 29, 1932.

27. Donald Honig, *The October Heroes* (New York: Simon & Schuster, 1979), p. 247; Creamer, *Babe: The Legend Comes to Life*, p. 359.

28. Creamer, *Babe: The Legend Comes to Life*, p. 359.

29. Rice, "Gehrig Teams With Ruth to Crush Rivals," *Detroit Free Press*, September 29, 1932.

30. Woody English, "Cubs Will Improve Play," *New York Times*, September 29, 1932.

31. Gayle Talbot, "Yanks Promise to Win in Four Straight," *Detroit Free Press*, September 29, 1932.

32. *Ibid*; "Koenig Injures Wrist in Slide," *Detroit Free Press*, September 29, 1932. Koenig did not play in the remainder of the Series.

33. Talbot, "Yanks Promise to Win in Four Straight," *Detroit Free Press*, September 29, 1932.

34. *Ibid.*

35. "Yanks Exuberant Over Easy Victory," *New York Times*, September 29, 1932.

36. *Ibid*; Talbot, "Yanks Promise to Win in Four Straight," *Detroit Free Press*, September 29, 1932.

37. Davis J. Walsh, "Warneke Out to Even Up Series," *Detroit Times*, September 29, 1932; William E. Brandt, "Pitching of Gomez Impresses Grimm," *New York Times*, September 30, 1932; Gayle Talbot, "Charlie Grimm Praises Yankees' Star Southpaw," *Detroit Free Press*, September 30, 1932.

38. John Kieran, "Sports of the *Times*," *New York Times*, September 30, 1932.

39. *Ibid.*

40. *Ibid.*; Grantland Rice, "Yanks Profit by Wild Spell A Second Time," *Detroit Free Press*, September 30, 1932.

41. Kieran, "Sports of the *Times*," *New York Times*, September 30, 1932.

42. John Drebinger, "Yankees Defeat Cubs, 5–2," *New York Times*, September 30, 1932.

43. Rice, "Yankees Profit by Wild Spell a Second Time," *Detroit Free Press*, September 30, 1932.

44. *Ibid.*

45. Brandt, "Pitching of Gomez Impresses Grimm," *New York Times*, September 30, 1932; Talbot, "Charlie Grimm Praises Yankees' Star Southpaw," *Detroit Free Press*, September 30, 1932.

46. Talbot, "Charlie Grimm Praises Yankees' Star Southpaw," *Detroit Free Press*, September 30, 1932.

47. *Ibid.*

48. *Ibid.*

49. *Ibid.*

50. *Ibid.*

51. William E. Brandt, "McCarthy Advises Yanks to be Calm," *New York Times*, October 1, 1932.

52. John Drebinger, "Yankees and Cubs Ready for Third Game," *New York Times*, October 1, 1932.

53. Lieb, *The Story of the World Series*, p. 220; Creamer, *Babe: The Legend Comes to Life*, p. 359; Smelser, *The Life That Ruth Built*, p. 447.

54. Frederick G. Lieb, "Joy and Misery, Laughter and Groans Mingle," *The Sporting News*, September 29, 1932.

55. Brandt, "McCarthy Advises Yanks to be Calm," *New York Times*, October 1, 1932.

56. "Yank Homers Owe Much to West Wind," *New York Times*, October 2, 1932.

57. *Ibid.*; Creamer, *Babe: The Legend Comes to Life*, p. 360; *This Great Game* (New York: Rutledge Books, 1971), p. 160; John M. Rosenburg, *The Story of Baseball* (New York: Random House, 1968), p. 94.

58. "Ruth Visits Youth Injured in Bombing," *New York Times*, October 2, 1932.

59. "Babe Makes Cubs Sad With Big Bat and Chatter," *Detroit Free Press*, October 2, 1932.

60. Burns, "Home Runs by Ruth and Gehrig Beat Cubs," *Chicago Tribune*, October 2, 1932.

61. Smelser, *The Life That Ruth Built*, p. 447.

62. John Drebinger, "Yankees Beat Cubs 7–5 for Third in Row," *New York Times*, October 2, 1932; Burns, "Home Runs by Ruth and Gehrig Beat Cubs," *Chicago Tribune*, October 2, 1932; Creamer, *Babe: The Legend Comes to Life*, p. 359.

63. *This Great Game*, p. 160; Smelser, *The Life That Ruth Built*, p. 448.

64. *This Great Game*, p. 160. Ruth said after the game: "I didn't mind no ball players yelling at me, but the trainer cutting in—that made me sore." Creamer, *Babe: The Legend Comes to Life*, p. 360.

65. Honig, *The October Heroes*, p. 247.

66. Burns, "Home Runs by Ruth and Gehrig Beat Cubs," *Chicago Tribune*, October 2, 1932.

67. *Ibid.*; Creamer, *Babe: The Legend Comes to Life*, p. 361.

68. Creamer, *Babe: The Legend Comes to Life*, p. 362; Burns, "Home Runs by Ruth and Gehrig Beat Cubs," *Chicago Tribune*, October 2, 1932. Tom Manning, who was announcing the game on radio, called the scene for his listeners: "Oh, oh. Babe Ruth has stepped out of the batter's box, and he steps about two feet away from home plate. Now he steps toward the Cubs' dugout! We thought for a moment that he was going over and toss his bat at them or something! No, he's smiling at them! He takes off his hat. He holds up two fingers with his right hand. Now he drops his bat and he's indicating that the count is ball two and strike two. He gets back into the batter's box. The umpire warns the Cubs. Charlie Root gets his signal, and Babe Ruth steps out of the batter's box again. He's holding up two and two. Oh, oh. Now Babe Ruth is pointing out to center-field and he's telling the Cubs that the next pitch is going into center-field." Curt Smith, *Voices of the Game* (South Bend: Diamond Communications, 1987), p. 41.

69. Creamer, *Babe: The Legend Comes to Life*, p. 362; *This Great Game*, p. 160.

70. Creamer, *Babe: The Legend Comes to Life*, p. 362; *Time*, October 10, 1932, p. 19.

71. Creamer, *Babe: The Legend Comes to Life*, p. 366;

Donald Honig, *The World Series* (New York: Crown Publishers, 1986), p. 86; Lawrence S. Ritter and Mark Rucker, *The Babe: The Game That Ruth Built* (New York: Total Sports, 1997), p. 181.

72. Murdock, *Baseball Players and Their Times*, p. 292; George Castle, "Cubs' Glory Days in 1930s Recalled by Woody English," *Baseball Digest*, September, 1994, pp. 83–84.

73. Lawrence S. Ritter and Mark Rucker, *The Babe: A Life in Pictures* (New York: Ticknor & Fields, 1988), p. 180; Donald Honig, *Baseball When the Grass Was Real* (Lincoln: University of Nebraska Press, 1993), p. 139.

74. Ritter and Rucker, *The Babe: A Life in Pictures*, p. 181; Allen, *The World Series*, p. 133; Grimm, *Grimm's Baseball Tales*, p. 90.

75. Ritter and Rucker, *The Babe: A Life in Pictures*, p. 181; Honig, *The Man in the Dugout*, p. 49; Connor, *Voices From Cooperstown*, p. 195; Ritter and Rucker, *The Babe: The Game That Ruth Built*, p. 180.

76. Golenbock, *Wrigleyville*, p. 236.

77. Ritter and Rucker, *The Babe: A Life in Pictures*, p. 180.

78. *Ibid*; Walter M. Langford, *Legends of Baseball* (South Bend: Diamond Communications, 1987), p. 19; Connor, *Voices From Cooperstown*, p. 195.

79. Ritter and Rucker, *The Babe: A Life in Pictures*, p. 180.

80. Ray Robinson, *Iron Horse* (New York: HarperCollins, 1990), p. 27.

81. Carmichael (ed.), *My Greatest Day in Baseball*, pp. 184–186; Creamer, *Babe: The Legend Comes to Life*, p. 365.

82. Frank Graham, "Ford Frick Explains: What the World Series Means to All of Us," *Sport*, November, 1961, p. 76. Frick began ghosting for Ruth in 1933.

83. Golenbock, *Wrigleyville*, pp. 238–239.

84. Creamer, *Babe: The Legend Comes to Life*, p. 363; Williams (ed.), *The Joe Williams Baseball Reader*, p. 79; Ritter and Rucker, *The Babe: The Game That Ruth Built*, p. 180.

85. Golenbock, *Wrigleyville*, p. 238.

86. *Ibid*.

87. Creamer, *Babe: The Legend Comes to Life*, p. 365.

88. Burns, "Home Runs by Ruth and Gehrig Beat Cubs, "*Chicago Tribune*, October 2, 1932.

89. "All Over But The Shouting," *Detroit Free Press*, October 2, 1932; Lee Greene, "Babe Ruth's Ten Greatest Days," *Sport*, September, 1963, p. 76.

90. Murdock, *Baseball Players and Their Times*, p. 157.

91. William E. Brandt, "Cub Fans Faithful in Spite of Defeat," *New York Times*, October 2, 1932.

92. "All Over But The Shouting," *Detroit Free Press*, October 2, 1932.

93. Brandt, "Cub Fans Faithful in Spite of Defeat," *New York Times*, October 2, 1932.

94. *Ibid*.

95. "All Over But The Shouting," *Detroit Free Press*, October 2, 1932.

96. "Deal Denied by McGraw," *New York Times*, October 4, 1932.

97. Honig, *The October Heroes*, p. 249.

98. Ed Burns, "Yanks Win World Title," *Chicago Tribune*, October 3, 1932.

99. Charles Dunkley, "Yanks Begin Celebrating With Praise for Manager," *Detroit Free Press*, October 3, 1932.

100. *Ibid*.

101. Irving Vaughan, "Injuries Bring Downfall of Bush and Warneke," *Chicago Tribune*, October 3, 1932.

102. *Ibid*.

103. *Ibid*.

104. *Ibid*.

105. *Ibid*.

106. Smelser, *The Life That Ruth Built*, p. 450; "The Late Unpleasantness," *Chicago Tribune*, October 4, 1932.

107. John Kieran, "Sports of the *Times*," *New York Times*, October 4, 1932.

108. Davis J. Walsh, "Wobbly Infield Seen as End of Yanks," *Detroit Times*, October 5, 1932.

109. Grantland Rice, "Cubs Demoralized by Power of Yanks," *Detroit Free Press*, October 3, 1932.

110. "The World Series," *The Sporting News*, October 6, 1932.

111. Westbrook Pegler, "Mischievous Yanks Menace to Game," *Detroit Times*, October 3, 1932.

112. Babe Ruth, "Enjoyed the Series With Chicago," *Detroit Times*, October 3, 1932.

Chapter 10 — 1935

1. Gregory, *Diz* (New York: Viking, 1992), p. 210.

2. John Drebinger, "Tigers, Cubs Ready for Series' Opener, *New York Times*, October 1, 1935.

3. Bob Murphy, "Bob Tales," *Detroit Times*, October 1, 1935.

4. Mickey Cochrane, "Tigers Will Win," *Detroit Times*, September 29, 1935; Mickey Cochrane, "Experience Favors Us," *Detroit Times*, September 30, 1935.

5. Bud Shaver, "All Tiger Players Reported Ready," *Detroit Times*, September 30, 1935; "Tigers Count on Rowe to Subdue Cubs," *New York Times*," October 1, 1935.

6. Davis J. Walsh, "Tigers Have to Stop Hartnett to Win," *Detroit Times*, October 1, 1935.

7. Bill Corum, "Tigers Have More Hitting Strength," *Detroit Times*, September 30, 1935.

8. John Drebinger, "Heavy Hitters Dominate Tigers" *New York Times*, October 1, 1935; "To Play in Fifth Series," *New York Times*, October 2, 1935.

9. "Dean Now Favors Tigers," *New York Times*," October 2, 1935.

10. Drebinger, "Tiger's Cubs Ready for Series' Opener," *New York Times*, October 1, 1935.

11. "Writers Pick the Cubs," *New York Times*, October 2, 1935.

12. Leo Macdonell, "Grimm Fears Slugging Trio," *Detroit Times* September 29, 1935; Leo Macdonell, "Must Beat a Very Good Ball Club," *Detroit Times*, October 1, 1935; "No Ball Club Can Beat Cubs," *Detroit Times*, October 1, 1935; Irving Vaughan, "Bruins Rely on Warneke," *Chicago Tribune*, October 1, 1935.

13. "Tickets Hunted as 250,000 Seek 50,000 Seats," *Detroit Times*, October 1, 1935.

14. Shaver, "All Tiger Players Reported Ready," *Detroit Times*, September 29, 1935; James P. Dawson, "Detroit Thronged on Eve of Classic," *New York Times*, October 1, 1935.

15. Bud Shaver, "No Healthy Boys," *Detroit Times*, October 1, 1935.

16. Bob Murphy, "In the Tigers' Dugout," *Detroit Times*, October 2, 1935.

17. *Ibid*.

18. Golenbock, "*Wrigleyville*, p. 256.

19. "Cub Pitchers See Greenberg Bat," *Chicago Tribune*, October 2, 1935; Ira Berkow (ed.), *Hank Greenberg: The Story of my Life* (New York: *Times* Books, 1989), p. 82.

20. John Kieran, "Tooth and Claw in Detroit," *New York Times*, October 2, 1935.

21. John Drebinger, "Warneke of Cubs Downs Tigers 3–0 in Series' Opener," *New York Times*, October 3, 1935.

22. Bill Corum, "Looks Like Detroit Needs Nine of Joe Louis," *Detroit Times*, October 3, 1935.

23. Berkow (ed.), *Hank Greenberg: The Story of my Life*, p. 82.

24. "No Ball Club Can Beat Cubs," *Detroit Times*, October 1, 1935.

25. Richard Bak, *Cobb Would Have Caught It* (Detroit: Wayne State University Press, 1991), pp. 248–249.

26. Grimm, *Grimm's Baseball Tales*, 112.

27. Bob Murphy, "In the Tigers' Dugout," *Detroit Times*, October 4, 1935.

28. Berkow (ed.), *Hank Greenberg: The Story of my Life*, pp. 82–83.

29. *Ibid*; "Cubs Storm Clubhouse and Take It Apart," *Chicago Tribune*, October 3, 1935.

30. "The World Series," *Detroit Times*, October 3, 1945.

31. *Ibid*; Corum, "Looks Like Detroit Needs Nine of Joe Louis," *Detroit Times*, October 3, 1935.

32. "Cubs Storm Clubhouse and Take It Apart," *Chicago Tribune*, October 3, 1935; "'Greatest Ever,' Grimm Says of Rowe, Warneke," *Detroit Times*, October 3, 1935.

33. "Charlie Grimm, "Lauds Rowe's Hurling," *Detroit Times*, October 3, 1935.

34. "'Greatest Ever,' Grimm Says of Rowe, Warneke," *Detroit Times*, October 3, 1935.

35. "Warneke's Joy," *Detroit Times*, October 3, 1935.

36. "Cubs Storm Clubhouse and Take It Apart," *Chicago Tribune*, October 3, 1935; W.W. Edgar, "Bridges Called by Pilot," *Detroit Free Press*, October 3, 1935; Fred Lieb, "Gossip of the First Game," *The Sporting News*, October 10, 1935.

37. "Edgar, "Bridges Called by Tiger Pilot," *Detroit Free Press*, October 3, 1935; Mickey Cochrane, "Praise of Warneke," *Detroit Times*, October 3, 1935.

38. James P. Dawson, "Root of Cubs to Oppose Bridges," *New York Times*, October 3, 1935; Berkow (ed.), *Hank Greenberg: The Story of My Life*, p. 83.

39. Berkow (ed.), *Hank Greenberg: The Story of My Life*, p. 83.

40. *Ibid*, p. 84.

41. "Yanks Boss Bets Tigers," *Detroit Times*, October 3, 1945.

42. Drebinger, "Warneke of Cubs Downs Tigers 3–0 in Opener," *New York Times*, October 3, 1935.

43. Corum, "Looks Like Detroit Needs Nine of Joe Louis," *Detroit Times*, October 3, 1935.

44. John C. Manning, "46,742 See Tigers Win Second Game," *Detroit Times*, October 3, 1935.

45. John Drebinger, "Tigers Crush Cubs," *New York Times*, October 4, 1935; Berkow (ed.), *Hank Greenberg: The Story of My Life*, p. 84; James P. Dawson, "Fans Huddle in Navin Field Stands," *New York Times*, October 4, 1935; John Kieran, "Caught in the Ice Pack at Navin Field," *New York Times*, October 4, 1935; Bob Murphy, "In the Tigers' Dugout," *Detroit Times*, October 3, 1935.

46. Kieran, "Caught in the Ice Pack at Navin Field," *New York Times*, October 4, 1935.

47. *Ibid*.

48. *Ibid*.

49. *Ibid*.

50. Damon Runyon, "Grimm's Sentimental Gesture Whips Cubs," *Detroit Times*, October 4, 1935.

51. "Ruth in Press Box," *New York Times*, October 4 1935; Babe Ruth, "Knew Root Wouldn't Last," *Detroit Times*, October 4, 1935.

52. Kieran, "Caught in Ice Pack at Navin Field," *New York Times*, October 4, 1935; Runyon, "Grimm's Sentimental Gesture Whips Cubs," *Detroit Times*, October 4, 1935.

53. Grantland Rice, "Bengal Batters Come to Life With a Bang," *Detroit Free Press*, October 4, 1935.

54. Doc Holst, "That's the Way to Lose a Ball Game," *Detroit Free Press*, October 4, 1935; "We're Hitting, Watch Us Go," *Chicago Tribune*, October 4, 1935; James P. Dawson, "Cochrane Sees Tigers Back in Hitting Stride," *New York Times*, October 4, 1935.

55. Holst, "That's the Way to Lose a Ball Game," *Detroit Free Press*, October 4, 1935.

56. *Ibid*.

57. *Ibid*.

58. *Ibid*; "We're Hitting, Watch Us Go," *Chicago Tribune*, October 4, 1935; Rice, "Bengal Batters Come to Life With a Bang," *Detroit Free Press*, October 4, 1935; Charlie Grimm, "Took Good Licking," *Detroit Times*, October 4, 1935.

59. "We're Hitting, Watch Us Go," *Chicago Tribune*, October 4, 1935; W.W. Edgar, "Four Straight is Aim of Rejuvenated Tigers," *Detroit Free Press*, October 4, 1935.

60. Edgar, "Four Straight is Aim of Rejuvenated Tigers," *Detroit Free Press*, October 4, 1935.

61. "Dugout Debate Favors Tigers," *Detroit Free Press*, October 4, 1935.

62. Warren Brown, *The Chicago Cubs* (Carbondale: Southern Illinois University Press, 2001), pp. 145–146. Reprint of 1946 edition.

63. Bak, *Cobb Would Have Caught It*, p. 271.

64. Edgar, "Four Straight is Aim of Rejuvenated Tigers," *Detroit Free Press*, October 4, 1935; Bob Murphy, "Auker to Face Lee," *Detroit Times*, October 4, 1935; Dawson, "Cochrane Sees Tigers Back in Hitting Stride," *New York Times*, October 4, 1935.

65. Richard Farrington, "Fanning with Farrington," *The Sporting News*, October 24, 1935; Berkow (ed.), *Hank Greenberg: The Story of My Life*, p. 85; "Greenberg's Wrist Fractured," *New York Times*, October 10, 1935.

66. Dawson, "Cochrane Sees Tigers Back in Hitting Stride," *New York Times*, October 4, 1935. Greenberg did not see action during the remainder of the Series.

67. Babe Ruth, "Greatest Game I've Ever Seen," *Detroit Times*, October 5, 1935.

68. John Drebinger, "Tigers Beat Cubs 6–5 in Eleventh Inning," *New York Times*, October 5, 1935.

69. John Kieran, "Sports of the *Times*," *New York Times*, October 5, 1935.

70. Grimm, "*Grimm's Baseball Tales*, p. 112; Fred Lieb, "Gossip of the Third Game," *The Sporting News*, October 10, 1935.

71. Grimm, *Grimm's Baseball Tales*, p. 112; Ed Burns, "Landis Investigates Cub Feud with Umpire," *Chicago Tribune*, October 5, 1935; "The World Series, *Time*, October 14, 1935, p. 71.

72. Charlie Grimm, "Misses Men Chased from Bench," *Detroit Times*, October 5, 1935. Grimm's ghostwriter was Warren Brown.

73. "The World Series," *Time*, p. 72.

74. *Ibid*.

75. Burns, "Landis Investigates Cub Feud with Umpire," *Chicago Tribune*, October 5, 1935.

76. "The World Series," *Time*, p. 72; "Landis Investigates Wrangle," *New York Times*, October 5, 1935.

77. Burns, "Landis Investigates Cub Feud with Umpire," *Chicago Tribune*, October 5, 1935.

78. Fred Lieb, "Case Before Landis," *The Sporting News*, October 10, 1935.

79. *Ibid*; "Landis Will Defer Action on Dispute," *New York Times*, October 6, 1935.

80. Fred Lieb, "Gossip of the Fifth Game," *The Sporting News*, October 10, 1935.

81. Grimm, *Grimm's Baseball Tales*, p. 113.

82. "W.W. Edgar, "Mickey Feels Cubs Are Lost," *Detroit Free Press*, October 5, 1935.

83. "My Toughest Game," *Chicago Tribune*, October 5, 1935; Mickey Cochrane, "Tigers Finally Show Folks They're a Money Ball Club," *Detroit Times*, October 5, 1935.

84. James P. Dawson, "Fans Combat Cold With Winter Garb," *New York Times*, October 6, 1935.

85. John Kieran, "Sports of the *Times*," *New York Times*, October 6, 1935.

86. John C. Manning, "Smart Good Guy Crowder Slow Pitches Cubs to Fury," *Detroit Times*, October 6, 1935.

87. Fred Lieb, "Gossip of the Fourth Game," *The Sporting News*, October 10, 1935; Bob Murphy, "Bob Tales," *Detroit Times*, October 7, 1935.

88. Kieran, "Sports of the *Times*," *New York Times*, October 6, 1935.

89. W.W. Edgar, "Mike Praises Gen's Pitching," *Detroit Free Press*, October 6, 1935.

90. *Ibid*. .

91. *Ibid*; Mickey Cochrane, "I think We're in Now," *Detroit Times*, October 6, 1935. Cochrane's ghostwriter was Bud Shaver.

92. "Tiger Pilot Praises Flea," *Detroit Times*, October 6, 1935 .

93. Leo Macdonell, "Grimm Peps UP Cubs After Third Defeat," *Detroit Times*, October 6, 1935; "Four Games in a Row Forecast by Tigers," *New York Times*, October 6, 1935.

94. *Ibid*; Charlie Grimm, "Pin Hopes on Warneke," *Detroit Times*, October 6, 1935.

95. Macdonell, "Grimm Peps Up Cubs After Third Defeat," *Detroit Times*, October 6, 1935.

96. *Ibid*.

97. *Ibid*.

98. *Ibid*.

99. John Drebinger, "Klein Hits Homer as Cubs Win 3–1," *New York Times*, October 7, 1935.

100. "Warneke Mum," *Chicago Tribune*, October 7, 1935; James P. Dawson, "Warneke is Acclaimed by Cubs," *New York Times*, October 7, 1935.

101. "Warneke Mum," *Chicago Tribune*, October 7, 1935; Charlie Grimm, "Two Bad Hops Cost Cubs Shutout," *Detroit Times*, October 7, 1935.

102. Dawson, "Warneke is Acclaimed by Cubs," *New York Times*, October 7, 1935. Warneke recovered and pitched another ten seasons, compiling a career record of 198–121 with a 3.18 earned run average. He then had a successful career as a highly respected National League umpire.

103. "Warneke Mum," *Chicago Tribune*, October 7, 1935.

104. *Ibid*.

105. Dawson, "Warneke is Acclaimed by Cubs," *New York Times*, October 7, 1935.

106. Bill Corum, "Winning Run Belongs to Mike," *Detroit Times*, October 8, 1935.

107. John Kieran, "Sports of the *Times*," *New York Times*, October 8, 1935.

108. Grimm, *Grimm's Baseball Tales*, p. 114.

109. Walter M. Langford, *Legends of Baseball* (South Bend: Diamond Communications, 1987), p. 82.

110. Honig, *Baseball When the Grass was Real*, p. 144.

111. Honig, *The October Heroes*, p. 222.

112. Lawrence Ritter, *The Glory of Their Times* (New York: Macmillan, 1966), p. 288 .

113. Honig, *Baseball When the Grass was Real*, p. 144.

114. Honig, *The October Heroes*, p. 222.

115. *Ibid*.

116. Smith (ed.), *Voices of the Game*, p. 42.

117. Irving Vaughan, "Young Chicago Team Puts Up Gallant Fight," *Chicago Tribune*, October 8, 1935; James P. Dawson, "Wild Celebration Takes Place in Tigers' Dressing Room," *New York Times*, October 8, 1935; Doc Holst, "Cubs Praise Their Conquerors But Shower Scathing Words," *Detroit Free Press*, October 8, 1935.

118. Dawson, Wild Celebration Takes Place in Tigers' Dressing Room," *New York Times*, October 8, 1935; Holst, "Cubs Praise Their Conquerors But Shower Scathing Words," *Detroit Free Press*, October 8, 1935.

119. *Ibid*.

120. Holst, "Cubs Praise Their Conquerors But Shower Scathing Words," *Detroit Free Press*, October 8, 1935. The 1935 World Series was the first Fall Classic to be broadcast by three radio networks: CBS, NBC, and Mutual. Smith (ed.), *Voices of the Game*, p. 549.

121. Holst, "Cubs Praise Their Conquerors But Shower Scathing Words," *Detroit Free Press*, October 8, 1935; Dawson, "Wild Celebration in Tigers' Dressing Room," *New York Times*, October 8, 1935.

122. Holst, "Cubs Praise Their Conquerors But Shower Scathing Words," *Detroit Free Press*, October 8, 1935.

123. *Ibid*. Herman claimed the 1935 Cubs "had everything. It was one of the two best clubs I ever played on — the '41 Dodgers was the other." Honig, *Baseball When the Grass was Real*, p. 144. Phil Cavarretta echoed Herman's sentiment, saying: "The infield we had on the Cubs in '35 was the best ever in Chicago. Yes, sir, better even than the Tinker to Evers to Chance infields." Honig, *The October Heroes*, p. 223. Even Grimm claimed: "The Cubs we put together in 1935 were the best group I ever managed." Grimm, *Grimm's Baseball Tales*, p. 105.

124. W.W. Edgar, "Wild Scenes are Enacted in Tigers' Dressing Room," *Detroit Free Press*, October 8, 1935; Dawson, Wild Celebration Takes Place in Tigers' Dressing Room," *New York Times*, October 8, 1935; Bob Murphy, "150 Pounds of Guts," *Detroit Times*, October 8, 1935.

125. Murphy, "150 Pounds of Guts," *Detroit Times*, October 8, 1935.

126. Corum, "Winning Run Belongs to Mike," *Detroit Times*, October 8, 1935. The winner's share was $6,545 apiece, while the losers received $4,199 per man.

127. Dawson, "Wild Celebration Takes Place in Tigers' Dressing Room," *New York Times*, October 8, 1935.

128. John C. Manning, "Tommy Bridges Tells of Ninth Inning," *Detroit Times*, October 8, 1935.

129. "Series Adds Two Million Dollars in Business," *Detroit Times*, October 8, 1935. Chicago officials estimated a similar amount of revenue came into the Windy City.

130. Edgar, "Wild Scenes are Enacted in Tigers' Dressing Room," *Detroit Free Press*, October 8, 1935.

131. "In the Wake of the News," *Chicago Tribune*, October 9, 1935.

132. Warren Brown, "Chicago Scribe Lauds Play of Tigers," *Detroit Times*, October 10, 1935.

133. "Winning Series not all Honey says Tiger Owner

Navin," *Detroit Times*, October 9, 1935; Lieb, *The Story of the World Series*, p. 242.

134. Lieb, *The Story of the World Series*, p. 242.

135. John Kieran, "The Sports of the *Times*," *New York Times*, October 9, 1935.

136. Damon Runyon, "Old Missus Luck Set Stage for Hero," *Detroit Times*, October 10, 1935.

137. "Scribbled by Scribes," *The Sporting News*, October 17, 1935.

Chapter 11 — 1938

1. John Hoffman, "Scribbled by the Scribes," *The Sporting News*, September 29, 1938. The Yankees had easily disposed of the New York Giants in six and five games respectively in the Series of 1936 and 1937.

2. *Ibid.*

3. Jack B. Moore, *Joe DiMaggio* (New York: Praeger, 1987), p. 36; Gies and Shoemaker, *Stars of the Series*, p. 156.

4. John Drebinger, "Yanks Hold Big Edge in Teamwork," *New York Times*, October 3, 1938.

5. Irving Vaughan, "Chicago Rates Yanks' Equal in Defensive Play," *Chicago Tribune*, October 3, 1938.

6. *Ibid.*; "Yankee Batting Power Worries Chicago Staff," *Chicago Tribune*, October 4, 1938.

7. Dan Daniel, "Over the Fence," *The Sporting News*, October 13, 1938.

8. Drebinger, "Yanks Hold Big Edge in Teamwork," *New York Times*, October 3, 1938.

9. *Ibid.*

10. Ed Burns, "Ball Fans Pay In $659,000," *Chicago Tribune*, October 4, 1938; "300,000 Hail Conquering Cubs," *New York Times*, October 4, 1938.

11. "300,000 Hail Conquering Cubs," *New York Times*, October 4, 1938.

12. *Ibid.*

13. *Ibid.*

14. Grimm, *Grimm's Baseball Tales*, p. 132; "Grimm Departs for his Home," *Detroit Times*, October 5, 1938.

15. "Grimm Off Air for Series," *New York Times*, October 5, 1938.

16. *Ibid.*

17. "300,000 Hail Conquering Cubs," *New York Times*, October 4, 1938; Burns, "Ball Fans Pay in $659,000," *Chicago Tribune*, October 4, 1938.

18. "300,000 Hail Conquering Cubs," *New York Times*, October 4, 1938.

19. "Park's Facilities Taxed to Utmost," *New York Times*, October 6, 1938.

20. Charles Bartlett, "Bleacher Fans Wait All Night to Buy Tickets," *Chicago Tribune*, October 5, 1938; James P. Dawson, "World Series Spirit Grabs Chicago," *New York Times*, October 5, 1938.

21. Bartlett, "Bleacher Fans Wait All Night to Buy Tickets," *Chicago Tribune*, October 5, 1938.

22. *Ibid.*

23. John Drebinger, "World Series Jinx No Worry to Yanks," *New York Times*, October 4, 1938; Dawson, "World Series Spirit Grabs Chicago," *New York Times*, October 5, 1938; Gregory, *Diz*, p. 353.

24. Dawson, "World Series Spirit Grabs Chicago," *New York Times*, October 5, 1938; John Drebinger, "Yanks Start Bid for Third Straight World Title," *New York Times*, October 5, 1938.

25. Dawson, "World Series Spirit Grabs Chicago," *New York Times*, October 5, 1938; Fred Lieb, "Timely Hits Decide Opener," *The Sporting News*, October 13, 1938.

26. "Park's Facilities Taxed to Utmost," *New York Times*, October 6, 1938.

27. Lieb, *The Story of the World Series*, p. 255.

28. John Drebinger, "Yanks Top Cubs 3–1," *New York Times*, October 6, 1938.

29. Arthur "Bugs" Baer, "Lee's Next Start to be for New York," *Detroit Times*, October 6, 1938.

30. *Ibid.*

31. James P. Dawson, "Hartnett Says Yanks Were Lucky to Win," *New York Times*, October 6, 1938; "Hartnett Still Hopeful," *Chicago Tribune*, October 6, 1938.

32. "Hartnett Still Hopeful," *Chicago Tribune*, October 6, 1938; Dawson, "Hartnett Says Yanks Were Lucky to Win," *New York Times*, October 6, 1938.

33. "Hartnett Still Hopeful," *Chicago Tribune*, October 6, 1938.

34. *Ibid.*

35. Ed Burns, "Cubs Send Dean Against Gomez Today," *Chicago Tribune*, October 6, 1938.

36. *Ibid.*

37. "Hartnett Still Hopeful," *Chicago Tribune*, October 6, 1938; Dawson, "Hartnett Says Yanks Were Lucky to Win," *New York Times*, October 6, 1938.

38. Dawson, "Hartnett Says Yanks Were Lucky to Win," *New York Times*, October 6, 1938.

39. "Combs 'Tipped' Lee's Pitches," *Detroit Times*, October 7, 1938. Fred Lieb claimed Combs was getting tipped by Lee's grip on the ball, not from Hartnett's signs. Combs, Lieb said, would yell "There it is!" for a curve and "Get hold of it!" for a fastball. Fred Lieb, "Gossip of the First Game," *The Sporting News*, October 13, 1938.

40. Charles P. Ward, "Cubs Turn to Diz Dean After Yanks Win Opener," *Detroit Free Press*, October 6, 1938.

41. John Kieran, "Sports of the *Times*," *New York Times*, October 7, 1938.

42. Ward, "Cubs Turn to Diz Dean After Yanks Win Opener," *Detroit Free Press*, October 6, 1938.

43. Gregory, *Diz*, p. 354.

44. *Ibid.*, pp. 354–355.

45. Kieran, "Sports of the *Times*," *New York Times*, October 7, 1938.

46. *Ibid.*

47. Gregory, *Diz*, p. 355.

48. *Ibid.*

49. *Ibid.*

50. *Ibid.*

51. *Ibid*; Daley, *Inside Baseball*, p. 96; Allen, *The World Series*, p. 145; Golenbock, *Wrigleyville*, p. 264; Smith, *Voices of the Game*, p. 44; Bob Broeg and Bob Burrill, *Don't Bring THAT Up* (New York: A.S. Barnes, 1946), p. 55. This exchange, although accepted even by Cub players in the game, may never have occurred. Its source was Dean, and Crosetti later admitted: "If Dizzy yelled something at me, I didn't hear it, and I didn't say anything back to him." Gregory, *Diz*, p. 357.

52. Irving Vaughan, "Cubs, Beaten Twice, Off for New York," *Chicago Tribune*, October 7, 1938.

53. Henry McLemore, "Head Up, Chin Out, Diz Walks That Last Mile," *Detroit Free Press*, October 7, 1938.

54. *Ibid.*

55. James P. Dawson, "McCarthy Applauds Dean's Courage," *New York Times*, October 7, 1938; Golenbock, *Wrigleyville*, p. 264.

56. John Drebinger, "70,000 Will See World Series Resume," *New York Times*, October 8, 1938; Dawson, "McCarthy Applauds Dean's Courage," *New York Times*, October 7, 1938; Moore, *Joe DiMaggio*, p. 36; Gregory, *Diz*, p. 356.

57. Dawson, "McCarthy Applauds Dean's Courage," *New York Times*, October 7, 1938; Vaughan, "Cubs, Beaten Twice, Off for New York," *Chicago Tribune*, October 7, 1938. Dean pitched two more years for the Cubs , compiling a 9–7 record, before being released.

58. Arthur "Bugs" Baer, "Cubs Deader Than a Fish on a Plate," *Detroit Times*, October 7, 1938.

59. Dawson, "McCarthy Applauds Dean's Courage," *New York Times*, October 7, 1938. Gehrig was singled out by the sports editor of the *Detroit Free Press* as proof that the Yankees were an aging, overrated club. "The Yankees are definitely on their way over the hill, and Herr Gehrig is leading the way," he wrote, ignorant of Gehrig's physical problems. "The tip-off on Gehrig came in the opening game when he tried to stretch a single to right into a two-base hit. To those watching the game, Lou seemed to spend a great deal of time running in one place, and at least one guy was heard to remark that 'if he doesn't get out of there pretty soon he'll dig a hole with his spikes, and they'll have to call out the PWA [Public Works Administration] so the game can continue.'" Charles P. Ward, "Ward to the Wise," *Detroit Free Press*, October 11, 1938.

60. Dawson, "McCarthy Applauds Dean's Courage," *New York Times*, October 7, 1938; Chester Youll, "'It's All Over Now,' Chant Yankees," *Detroit Times*, October 7, 1938.

61. Youll, "'It's All Over Now,' Chant Yankees," *Detroit Times*, October 7, 1938.

62. Fred Lieb, "Gossip of the Second Game," *The Sporting News*, October 13, 1938.

63. Baer, "Cubs Deader Than a Fish on a Plate," *Detroit Times*, October 7, 1938.

64. Dawson, "McCarthy Applauds Dean's Courage," *New York Times*, October 7, 1938.

65. John Kieran, "Sports of the *Times*," *New York Times*, October 9, 1938.

66. Damon Runyan, "Bats Impotent, Cubs Almost Try Fisticuffs," *Detroit Times*, October 9, 1938.

67. Kieran, "Sports of the *Times*," *New York Times*, October 9, 1938.

68. "Injured Umpire Will Work Today," *New York Times*, October 9, 1938.

69. Kieran, "Sports of the *Times*," *New York Times*, October 9, 1938.

70. Arthur "Bugs" Baer, "Gordon Earned Perfect Day," *Detroit Times*, October 9, 1938.

71. Kieran, "Sports of the *Times*," *New York Times*, October 9, 1938.

72. Baer, "Gordon Earned Perfect Day," *Detroit Times*, October 9, 1938.

73. James P. Dawson, "Victory Shouts Fill Yankee Dressing Quarters," *New York Times*, October 9, 1938.

74. *Ibid.*

75. *Ibid.*

76. *Ibid*; "Pilot Hartnett Benches Gabby, Reynolds, Too," *Detroit Free Press*, October 9, 1938.

77. Dawson, "Victory Shouts Fill Yankee Dressing Quarters," *New York Times*, October 9, 1938.

78. Baer, "Gordon Earned Perfect Day," *Detroit Times*, October 9, 1938.

79. *Ibid.*

80. Dawson, "Victory Shouts Fill Yankee Dressing Quarters," New York Times, October 9, 1938.

81. Ed Burns, "Hartnett Sums It Up," *Chicago Tribune*, October 10, 1938.

82. Dawson, "Victory Shouts Fill Yankee Dressing Quarters," *New York Times*, October 9, 1938.

83. *Ibid.*

84. Fred Lieb, "Gossip of the Third Game," *The Sporting News*, October 13, 1938.

85. Fred Lieb, "McCarthy Shoots the Works to Win Fourth Straight," *The Sporting News*, October 13, 1938; "Yanks Calm About Victory," *Detroit Free Press*, October 10, 1938.

86. "Yanks Calm About Victory," *Detroit Free Press*, October 10, 1938.

87. John Kieran, "Sports of the *Times*," *New York Times*, October 10, 1938.

88. Fred Lieb, "Gossip of the Fourth Game," *The Sporting News*, October 13, 1938.

89. *Ibid.*

90. James P. Dawson, "McCarthy Calls Yanks Best Ever," *New York Times*, October 10, 1938.

91. *Ibid.*

92. "Yanks Calm About Victory," *Detroit Free Press*, October 10, 1938.

93. Dawson, "McCarthy Calls Yanks Best Ever," *New York Times*, October 10, 1938.

94. *Ibid.*

95. *Ibid.*

96. Lieb, "Gossip of the Fourth Game," *The Sporting News*, October 13, 1938.

97. Robinson, *Iron Horse*, p. 241.

98. "Cubs Heap Blame on Own Heads for Series Collapse," *Chicago Tribune*, October 10, 1938; Dawson, "McCarthy Calls Yanks Best Ever," *New York Times*, October 10, 1938.

99. Dawson, "McCarthy Calls Yanks Best Ever," *New York Times*, October 10, 1938; Burns, "Hartnett Sums It Up," *Chicago Tribune*, October 10, 1938.

100. Lieb, "Gossip of the Fourth Game," *The Sporting News*, October 13, 1938.

101. Dawson, "McCarthy Calls Yanks Best Ever," *New York Times*, October 10, 1938; "Cubs Heap Blame on Own Heads for Series Collapse," *Chicago Tribune*, October 10, 1938.

102. Golenbock, *Wrigleyville*, p. 265.

103. *Ibid.*

104. John Kieran, Sports of the *Times*," *New York Times*, October 11, 1938.

105. *Ibid.*

106. *Ibid.*

107. "Baseball Exit," *Time*, October 17, 1938.

108. John Drebinger, "Yanks Win Series," *New York Times*, October 10, 1938.

109. Burns, "Hartnett Sums It Up," *Chicago Tribune*, October 10, 1938.

110. *Ibid.*

111. John Drebinger, "No Means in Sight for Halting Yanks," *New York Times*, October 11, 1938.

112. "Mightiest of them All," *The Sporting News*, October 13, 1938.

113. Drebinger, "Yanks Beat Cubs 5–2," *New York Times*, October 9, 1938; Gregory, *Diz*, p. 352.

114. "Mightiest of them All," *The Sporting News*, October 13, 1938.

Chapter 12 — 1945

1. Berkow (ed.), *Hank Greenberg: The Story of My Life*. p. 155.

2. Irving Vaughn, "Tigers Finally Cash Pennant Check Made Out in June," *Chicago Tribune*, October 1, 1945.

3. Arthur Daley, "Sports of the *Times*," *New York Times*, October 1, 1945.

4. "Our Champions," *Detroit News*, October 1, 1945. Detroit drew 1,280,321 patrons; the Cubs finished third behind Brooklyn and New York in the National League with 1,037,026 spectators.

5. Arthur Daley, "Sports of the *Times*," *New York Times*, October 7, 1945. In actuality, Cramer was forty-two, Webb, thirty-six, and Mayo thirty-five.

6. Rogers Hornsby, "Look at Pitchers," *Detroit News*, October 2, 1945.

7. Arthur Daley, "Sports of the *Times*," *New York Times*, October 3, 1945.

8. H.G. Salsinger, "The Umpire," *Detroit News*, October 1, 1945.

9. "Cubs Spurn Beds on Boats," *Detroit Times*, October 3, 1945.

10. "Golenbock, *Wrigleyville*, p. 309; Ed Burns, "Grimm Names Former Yankee to Face Tigers," *Chicago Tribune*, October 2, 1945; "Crowded Detroit in Balancing Act," *New York Times*, October 3, 1945; James P. Dawson, "O'Neill, Grimm See Six Game Series," *New York Times*, October 3, 1945.

11. "Golenbock, *Wrigleyville*. p. 309.

12. Arthur Daley, "Sports of the *Times*," *New York Times*, October 6, 1945. Some writers, however, were housed on the steamers. When one was asked how his hotel was, he replied: "I don't know; my room hasn't docked yet." "Cubs Easy for Southpaws, *St. Louis Post-Dispatch*, October 2, 1945.

13. Dawson, "O'Neill, Grimm See Six Game Series," *New York Times*, October 3, 1945; Sam Greene, "Series Facts," *Detroit News*, October 3, 1945; "Gossip of the First Game," *The Sporting News*, October 11, 1945.

14. Dawson, "O'Neill, Grimm See Six Game Series," *New York Times*, October 3, 1945.

15. "Newhouser, Borowy to Pitch in Opening Game," *St. Louis Post-Dispatch*, October 1, 1945.

16. "World Series Highlights," *St, Louis Post-Dispatch*, October 3, 1945.

17. Leo Macdonnel, "Hal in Series Action for First Time," *Detroit Times*, October 3, 1945; Paul Richards, "Lowdown on Tiger Pitching," *Detroit Times*, October 3, 1945. Richards did own and operate a newspaper in his hometown.

18. Irving Vaughn, "Borowy Draws Newhouser as Pitching Rival," *Chicago Tribune*, October 3, 1945; Oscar Fraley, "Two Oft-Fired Managers are Pilots in World Series," *Detroit News*, October 2, 1945.

19. Charles P. Ward, "Chicago Cubs in Town," *Detroit Times*, October 3, 1945.

20. Dawson, "O'Neill, Grimm See Six Game Series," *New York Times*, October 3, 1945.

21. Watson Spoelstra, "Hank Borowy Welcomed Chance at Tigers—Old Cousins," *Detroit News*, October 3, 1945; David M. Jordan, *A Tiger in His Time* (South Bend: Diamond Communications, 1990), p. 157.

22. "World Series Highlights," *St. Louis Post-Dispatch*, October 3, 1945; Greene, "Series Facts," *Detroit News*, October 3, 1945.

23. "World Series Highlights," *St. Louis Post-Dispatch*, October 3, 1945.

24. George W. Stark, "The Day's Winning Battery: Weatherman and Greensman," *Detroit News*, October 3, 1945.

25. *Ibid*.

26. "Happy Won't Pick Winner," *Detroit Times*, October 4, 1945; "Truman Too Busy to Attend Series," *Chicago Tribune*, October 2, 1945.

27. "Series Notes," *Detroit News*, October 4, 1945.

28. "A Paving Brick Helps Cubs Win!" *Chicago Tribune*, October 4, 1945; James P. Dawson, "Margin of Victory Surprise to Cubs," *New York Times*, October 4, 1945.

29. *Ibid*; Charles P. Ward, "Hal's Fastball, Cubs Meet," *Detroit Times*, October 5, 1945.

30. Dawson, "Margin of Victory Surprise to Cubs," *New York Times*, October 4, 1945; Arthur Daley, "Sports of the *Times*," *New York Times*, October 4, 1945.

31. "A Paving Brick Helps Cubs Win," *Chicago Tribune*, October 4, 1945.

32. *Ibid*.

33. "I'll Get 'em Next Time, Says Hal," *St. Louis Post-Dispatch*, October 4, 1945; Dawson, "Margin of Victory Surprise to Cubs," *New York Times*, October 4, 1945; Watson Spoelstra, "Hot Bricks for Hank Borowy's Cold Feet," *Detroit News*, October 4, 1945; Jordan, *A Tiger in His Time*, p. 158.

34. Jordan, *A Tiger in His Time*, p. 158; Spoelstra, "Hot Bricks for Borowy's Cold Feet," *Detroit News*, October 4, 1945; "I'll Get 'em Next Time, Says Hal," *St. Louis Post-Dispatch*, October 4, 1945; "A Paving Brick Helps Cubs Win," *Chicago Tribune*, October 4, 1945.

35. Dawson, "Margin of Victory Surprise to Cubs," *New York Times*, October 4, 1945; "A Paving Brick Helps Cubs to Win," *St. Louis Post-Dispatch*, October 4, 1945.

36. Dawson, "Margin of Victory Surprise to Cubs," *New York Times*, October 4, 1945.

37. Sam Greene, "Just Write It Off," *Detroit News*, October 4, 1945.

38. "Series Notes," *Detroit News*, October 4, 1945.

39. "Dan Daniel, "Yankees Site Second Camp," *The Sporting News*, October 18, 1945.

40. "Series Notes," *Detroit News*, October 4, 1945.

41. Bob Murphy, "Bob Tales," *Detroit Times*, October 4, 1945.

42. H.G. Salsinger, "The Umpire," *Detroit News*, October 5, 1945.

43. Bill Corum, "They Can Run Fast, But Only Up and Down," *Detroit Times*, October 4, 1945.

44. *Ibid*.

45. John Drebinger, "Tigers Tie Series," *New York Times*, October 5, 1945.

46. Ed Burns, "Cubs Lose," *Chicago Tribune*, October 5, 1945.

47. "Hank's Homers End if History Rules," *New York Times*, October 5, 1945.

48. Drebinger, "Tigers Tie Series," *New York Times*, October 5, 1945.

49. "Bob Wray, "Wray's Column," *St. Louis Post-Dispatch*, October 5, 1945.

50. "Greenberg, Trucks Draw Tigers' Postgame Applause," *Chicago Tribune*, October 5, 1945; James P. Dawson, "Tigers Show Joy for Their Heroes," *New York Times*, October 5, 1945.

51. "Greenberg, Trucks Draw Tigers' Postgame Applause," *Chicago Tribune*, October 5, 1945.

52. Bob Murphy, "Bob Tales," *Detroit Times*, October 5, 1945.

53. Dawson, "Tigers Show Joy to Their Heroes," *New York Times*, October 5, 1945; "Greenberg, Trucks Draw Tigers' Postgame Applause," *Chicago Tribune*, October 5, 1945; Arthur Daley, "Sports of the *Times*," *New York Times*, October 5, 1945; Daley wrote that Trucks' curve balls "had sharper bends than pretzels." *Ibid*.

54. Arch Ward, "In the Wake of the News," *Chicago Tribune*, October 5, 1945.

55. Dawson, "Tigers Show Joy to Their Heroes," *New York Times*, October 5, 1945.

56. *Ibid;* "Greenberg, Trucks Draw Tigers' Postgame Applause," *Chicago Tribune,* October 5, 1945.

57. "Greenberg, Trucks Draw Tigers' Postgame Applause," *Chicago Tribune,* October 5, 1945.

58. Dawson, "Tigers Show Joy to Their Heroes," *New York Times,* October 5, 1945.

59. Sam Greene, "Grimm's Appraisal," *Detroit News,* October 5, 1945; "Greenberg, Trucks Draw Tigers' Postgame Applause," *Chicago Tribune,* October 5, 1945; "Gossip of the Second Game," *The Sporting News,* October 11, 1945.

60. "Daley, "Sports of the *Times,*" *New York Times,* October 5, 1945; "Gossip of the Second Game," *The Sporting News,* October 11, 1945.

61. "Men with Mad-Ons," *Detroit Times,* October 6, 1945.

62. Bob Murphy, "Bob Tales," *Detroit Times,* October 6, 1945.

63. Jordan, *A Tiger in His Time,* p. 156.

64. Rex G. White, "Fans Give Tickets to Wounded," *Detroit News,* October 4, 1945.

65. *Ibid.*

66. *Ibid.*

67. *Ibid;* "Wounded Vets Guests of Fans at Series," *Chicago Tribune,* October 6, 1945.

68. Arthur Daley, "Sports of the *Times,*" *New York Times,* October 6, 1945.

69. *Ibid.*

70. Rogers Hornsby, "Break for Cubs," *Detroit News,* October 6, 1945.

71. Irving Vaughan, "Cubs Win 3-0," *Chicago Tribune,* October 6, 1945.

72. James P. Dawson, "Both Teams Hail Work of Passeau," *New York Times,* October 6, 1945.

73. *Ibid;* "Passeau Keeps Calm in Midst of Victory Din," *Chicago Tribune,* October 6, 1945; Watson Spoelstra, "Dipsy-Doodlers Do It," *Detroit News,* October 6, 1945; Norman L. Macht, "Claude Passeau: He Pitched a World Series One-Hitter," *Baseball Digest,* November, 1993, p. 75. During his career Passeau also pitched under the names of Newman, Newburn, and his real name Passo. H.G. Salsinger, "The Umpire," *Detroit News,* October 6, 1945.

74. Dawson, "Both Teams Hail Work of Passeau," *New York Times,* October 6, 1945; "Gossip of the Third Game," *The Sporting News,* October 11, 1945.

75. Macht, "Claude Passeau: He Pitched a World Series One-Hitter," p. 76. Eddie Mayo later claimed that Passeau had sandpaper in his glove to doctor the ball. Bak, *Cobb Would Have Caught It,* p. 320.

76. Spoelstra, "Dipsy-Doodlers Do It," *Detroit News,* October 6, 1945.

77. *Ibid;* Dawson, "Both Teams Hail Work of Passeau," *New York Times,* October 6, 1945.

78. Sam Greene, "Pattern Changed," *Detroit News,* October 6, 1945; "Passeau Keeps Calm in Midst of Victory Din," *Chicago Tribune,* October 6, 1945; Dawson, "Both Teams Hail Work of Passeau," *New York Times, October 6, 1945.*

79. H.G. Salsinger, "The Umpire," *Detroit News,* October 6, 1945.

80. Dawson, "Both Teams Hail Work of Passeau," *New York Times,* October 6, 1945.

81. "World Series Highlights," *St. Louis Post-Dispatch,* October 7, 1945; Arch Ward, "In the Wake of the News," *Chicago Tribune,* October 7, 1945; "TNT and Trumps," *Time,* October 15, 1945, p. 60.

82. Ward, "In the Wake of the News," *Chicago Tribune,* October 7, 1945.

83. *Ibid.*

84. *Ibid.* Legend has it that when the goat was not permitted to remain at the game and was refused entrance for future contests that Sianis cursed the Cubs, vowing that they would never get into another World Series. As of the 2005 season, his "curse" has been effective.

85. "Trout Recalls Time Cubs Rejected Him," *Chicago Tribune,* October 7, 1945.

86. Ed Burns, "Tigers, Trout Triumph 4-1," *Chicago Tribune,* October 7, 1945.

87. H.G. Salsinger, "Diz Makes Good Boast," *Detroit News,* October 7, 1945.

88. John Drebinger, "Tigers Beat Cubs 4-1," *New York Times,* October 7, 1945.

89. Bob Murphy, "Bob Tales," *Detroit Times,* October 7, 1945.

90. Daley, "Sports of the *Times,*" *New York Times,* October 7, 1945; "Gossip of the Fourth Game," *The Sporting News,* October 11, 1945.

91. *Ibid.*

92. Sam Greene, "Diz Just Took His Time," *Detroit News,* October 7, 1945; Bob Murphy, "Roy, Dizzy are Happiest," *Detroit Times,* October 7, 1945; James P. Dawson, "Trout Gives Credit to his Atom Ball," *New York Times,* October 7, 1945; Arthur P. Daley, "Sports of the *Times,*" *New York Times,* October 8, 1945.

93. Dawson, "Trout Gives Credit to his Atom Ball," *New York Times,* October 7, 1945.

94. *Ibid.*

95. Murphy, "Roy, Diz are Happiest," *Detroit Times,* October 7, 1945; "O'Neill Now Says His Club Has Definite Edge," *St. Louis Post-Dispatch,* October 7, 1945.

96. *Ibid;* Dawson, "Trout Gives Credit to his Atom Ball," *New York Times,* October 7, 1945.

97. Charles P. Ward, "Borowy, More Hits Cure — Grimm," *Detroit Times,* October 7, 1945; "O'Neill Now Says His Teams Has Definite Edge," *St. Louis Post-Dispatch,* October 7, 1945; Dawson, "Trout Gives Credit to his Atom Ball," *New York Times,* October 7, 1945.

98. Ward, "Borowy, More Hits Cure — Grimm," *Detroit Times,* October 7, 1945.

99. Daley, "Sports of the *Times,*" *New York Times,* October 8, 1945.

100. Bill Corum, "Tall Men Beat the Fat Men," *Detroit Times,* October 8, 1945.

101. Jerome Holtzman and George Vass, *Baseball Chicago Style* (Chicago: Bonus Books, 2001), p. 71.

102. *Ibid.*

103. "Gossip of the Fifth Game," *The Sporting News,* October 11, 1945.

104. Daley, "Sports of the *Times,*" *New York Times,* October 8, 1945.

105. Bob Murphy, "Bob Tales," *Detroit Times,* October 8, 1945.

106. *Ibid;* Jordan, *A Tiger in His Time,* p. 161.

107. Daley, "Sports of the *Times,*" *New York Times,* October 8, 1945.

108. Bob Murphy, "Greenberg Biggest Series Hero," *Detroit Times,* October 8, 1945.

109. *Ibid.*

110. Murphy, "Bob Tales," *Detroit News,* October 8, 1945.

111. *Ibid.*

112. H.G. Salsinger, "The Umpire," *Detroit News,* October 10, 1945.

113. James P. Dawson, "Detroit's Batting Balance Slips Up," *New York Times,* October 8, 1945; Sam Greene, "Riding Back in the Bus," *Detroit News,* October 8, 1945.

114. Arch Ward, "In the Wake of the News," *Chicago*

Tribune, October 8, 1945; John Drebinger, "Tigers Defeat Cubs 8–4," *New York Times*, October 8, 1945.

115. Ed Burns, "Cubs Win, Tie Series in Twelve Inning Game," *Chicago Tribune*, October 9, 1945.

116. J. Roy Stockton, "Borowy and Hack Star," *St. Louis Post-Dispatch*, October 9, 1945.

117. Bak, *Cobb Would Have Caught It*, p. 312.

118. Burns, "Cubs Win, Tie Series in Twelve Inning Game," *Chicago Tribune*, October 9, 1945. Stockton was cynical as well about the first scoring reversal in World Series history, writing: "Hank spent three years in the army air force. Hank is good to his folks. Besides that, Hank had hit that eighth inning homer that tied the score at seven all. It was tough to make Hank the goat of the game, and so the official scorers reconsidered and decided to change their scoring." Stockton, "Borowy and Hack Star," *St. Louis Post-Dispatch*, October 9, 1945.

119. Walter Byers, "Sportswriters 'Save' Greenberg," *Detroit Times*, October 9, 1945.

120. "Series Notes," *Detroit News*, October 9, 1945.

121. "TNT and Trumps," *Time*, October 15, 1945, p. 60; James P. Dawson, "Scorers Reverse Decision on Play," *New York Times*, October 9, 1945.

122. Dawson, "Scorers Reverse Decision on Play," *New York Times*, October 9, 1945.

123. Caswell Adams, "Tigers Believe Passeau Uses Illegal Pitch," *Detroit Times*, October 9, 1945.

124. "World Series Notes," *Detroit News*, October 9, 1945; Dawson, "Scores Reverse Decision on Play," *New York Times*, October 9, 1945; Daley, "Sports of the *Times*," *New York Times*, October 10, 1945.

125. H.G. Salsinger, "The Umpire," *Detroit News*, October 10, 1945.

126. *Ibid.*

127. Stockton, "Borowy and Hack Star," *St. Louis Post-Dispatch*, October 9, 1945.

128. Arch Ward, "In the Wake of the News," *Chicago Tribune*, October 10, 1945.

129. John Drebinger, "Tigers Rated Edge Over Cubs Today," *New York Times*, October 10, 1945.

130. Daley, "Sports of the *Times*," *New York Times*, October 10, 1945.

131. "Series Notes," *Detroit News*, October 11, 1945.

132. *Ibid.*

133. J. Roy Stockton, "Hal Had It, Borowy Didn't," *St. Louis Post-Dispatch*, October 11, 1945.

134. Arthur P. Daley, "Sports of the *Times*," *New York Times*, October 11, 1945.

135. *Ibid.*

136. Berkow (ed.), *Hank Greenberg: The Story of My Life*, p. 157; Bob Murphy, "Hank Hid Injury in Final," *Detroit Times*, October 12, 1945.

137. *Ibid*; Sam Greene, "Cubs Walk Greenberg Twice Never Realizing He Could Hardly Hold a Bat," *Detroit News*, October 11, 1945.

138. Golenbock, *Wrigleyville*, p. 311.

139. *Ibid*, p. 312.

140. Grimm, *Grimm's Baseball Tales*, pp. 172–173.

141. Golenbock, *Wrigleyville*, p. 311.

142. *Ibid.*

143. James P. Dawson, "Six Tigers Called Heroes of Series," *New York Times*, October 11, 1945; Hal Newhouser, "I'll Never Forget That Final Game," *Detroit Times*, October 12, 1945.

144. Murphy, "Hank Hid Injury in Final," *Detroit Times*, October 12, 1945.

145. Ed Burns, "Bruised Wrist May Cramp Greenberg's Style Today," *Chicago Tribune*, October 10, 1945.

146. Schoor, *The History of the World Series*, p. 203.

147. Charles P. Ward, "Tigers Stage Show for Photographers," *Detroit Times*, October 12, 1945.

148. Dawson, "Six Tigers Called Heroes of Series," *New York Times*, October 11, 1945.

149. Honig, *The October Heroes*, p. 227; Golenbock, *Wrigleyville*, p. 311.

150. Golenbock, *Wrigleyville*, p. 311.

151. "Record Hangover," *Time*, October 22, 1945.

152. Golenbock, *Wrigleyville*, p. 312; Dawson, "Six Tigers Called Heroes of Series," *New York Times*, October 11, 1945; Grimm, *Grimm's Baseball Tales*, pp. 172–173; Arch Ward, "In the Wake of the News," *Chicago Tribune*, October 11, 1945.

153. Arthur P. Daley, "Sports of the *Times*," *New York Times*, October 12, 1945.

154. John Drebinger, "Newhouser Pivot of Tiger Triumph," *New York Times*, October 12, 1945.

155. Bingay, *Detroit is My Own Home Town*, p. 148.

156. "The World's Champions," *Detroit Times*, October 12, 1945.

157. "The Came Through," *Detroit News*, October 12, 1945. The "Arsenal of Democracy" had suffered through a tragic race riot in 1943 and during the late summer and fall of 1945 was in the throes of massive post-war labor unrest and strikes.

158. Bill Corum, "Tigers Backed to Title," *Detroit Times*, October 12, 1945.

159. *Ibid.*

160. J. Roy Stockton, "Hal Had It, Borowy Didn't," *St. Louis Post-Dispatch*, October 11, 1945.

Chapter 13 — 1959

1. Arthur Daley, "Sports of the *Times*," *New York Times*, October 1, 1959.

2. *Ibid.*

3. Red Smith, *On Baseball* (Chicago: Ivan R. Dee, 2000), p. 247.

4. Roy Terrell, "A Series of Strange Events," *Sports Illustrated*, October 12, 1959.

5. "Drysdale, Donovan Mound Foes," *Flint Journal*, October 4, 1959; John Drebinger, "Record 92,000 to attend Series Today," *New York Times*, October 4, 1959.

6. Daley, "Sports of the *Times*, *New York Times*, October 1, 1959.

7. *Ibid.* Bill Veeck in *'59: The Summer of the Sox* echoed Daley's assessment, saying: "A typical White Sox rally consisted of two bloopers, an error, a passed ball, a couple of base on balls, and, as a final crusher, a hit batsman. Never did a team make less use of the lively ball." Mark R. Callum, "The 1959 World Series," *www.accessatlanta.com/shared/sports/mlb/post/ws/1959.html*.

8. John Drebinger, "Dodgers' Craig to Oppose Wynn of White Sox in World Series Opener Today," *New York Times*, October 1, 1959.

9. *Ibid.*

10. "'I get jump, I go'—Luis," *Flint Journal*, October 1, 1959; "It's Wynn Versus Craig," *Flint Journal*, October 1, 1959.

11. "'I get jump, I go'—Luis," *Flint Journal*, October 1, 1959.

12. "Veeck Gets Even with Perini," *Chicago Tribune*, October 2, 1959.

13. *Ibid*; "No Bunting," *The Sporting News*, October 14, 1959; Terrell, "A Series of Strange Events," *Sports Illustrated*, October 12, 1959.

14. "No Bunting, *The Sporting News*, October 14, 1959.

15. "Stengelese to Get Innings as Live Language," *New York Times*, October 2, 1959; "Veeck Gets Even With Perini," *Chicago Tribune*, October 2, 1959.

16. "No Worries for Wynn," *The Sporting News*, October 14, 1959. Veteran New York scribe Dan Daniel noted sadly, however: "The club owners of 1959 lack appreciation of the romance of baseball. How else may be absence of the Hall of Fame stars in the Clean Sox from the Series be explained?" Dan Daniel, "Over the Fence," *The Sporting News*, October 14, 1959; John Drebinger, "White Sox Rout Didgers in Series Opener, 11–0," *New York Times*, October 2, 1959.

17. "Mom Climbs Pole to Free Flag," *The Sporting News*, October 14, 1959. After the contest, Sox officials were rebuffed in eight attempts to hire a steeplejack to free the flag. A ninth call, to Mrs. Roni Weaver, resulted in success as, to the amazement of male onlookers, the twenty-nine year old steeplejack shinnied up the pole easily and repaired the pulley. *Ibid.*

18. Arthur Daley, "Sports of the *Times*," *New York Times*, October 2, 1959.

19. "No Worries for Wynn," *The Sporting News*, October 14, 1959.

20. Robert Cromie, "Could Have Happened to Us," *Chicago Tribune*, October 2, 1959.

21. Terrell, "A Series of Strange Events," *Sports Illustrated*, October 12, 1959.

22. "Los Angeles Grins and Bears It," *Flint Journal*, October 2, 1959; Danny Peary (ed.), *We played the Game* (New York: Hyperion, 1994), p. 458.

23. "Los Angeles Grins and Bears It," *Flint Journal*, October 2, 1959.

24. *Ibid.*

25. Richard Dozer, "Losers Await New Day," *Chicago Tribune*, October 2, 1959.

26. "Los Angeles Grins and Bears It," *Flint Journal*, October 2, 1959; Dozer, "Losers Await New Day," *Chicago Tribune*, October 2, 1959; Louis Effrat, "White Sox Restrained After Victory, While Hopeful Dodgers Plan Comeback," *New York Times*, October 2, 1959; Terrell, "A Series of Strange Events," *Sports Illustrated*, October 12, 1959.

27. Effrat, "White Sox Restrained After Victory, While Hopeful Dodgers Plan Comeback," *New York Times*, October 2, 1959.

28. "'We'll Win,' Says Podres," *Flint Journal*, October 2, 1959.

29. Arthur Daley, "Sports of the *Times*," *New York Times*, October 3, 1959.

30. "Griffith Denies Report of Shift," *New York Times*, October 3, 1959. Griffith relocated the Senators to Minneapolis for the 1961 season.

31. Daley, "Sports of the *Times*," *New York Times*, October 3, 1959.

32. "That's All Right, Mr. Alston; Our sox were Very Different, Too," *Chicago Tribune*, October 3, 1959. After the game, Cole explained: "Singing the most powerful song in the world to such a large crowd frightened me a little, and I blew the line." Edward Prell, "Surprise Visitors," *The Sporting News*, October 14, 1959.

33. Daley, "Sports of the *Times*," *New York Times*, October 3, 1959.

34. Larry Sherry, "Everybody Loves the Series Hero," *Sport*, October, 1960, p. 94.

35. "That's All Right, Mr. Alston; Our Sox Were Very Different, Too," *Chicago Tribune*, October 3, 1959.

36. Richard Dozer, "Neal A Bit Puzzled, But Happy," *Chicago Tribune*, October 3, 1959.

37. "Cocky Dodgers Edge Chicago 4–3," *Flint Journal*, October 3, 1959.

38. *Ibid.*

39. *Ibid*; ":Podres Isn't Impressed by the White Sox," *Chicago Tribune*, October 3, 1959.

40. "That's All Right, Mr. Alston; Our Sox Were Very Different, Too," *Chicago Tribune*, October 3, 1959.

41. *Ibid.*

42. *Ibid.*

43. David Condon, "In the Wake of the News," *Chicago Tribune*, October 3, 1959; Lieb, *The Story of the World Series*, p. 393.

44. Louis Effrat, "Cuccinello Takes Blame for Waving Lollar Home," *New York Times*, October 3, 1959; George Vass, "Top Baserunning Feats, Blunders in World Series," *Baseball Digest*, October, 1985, p. 21; Robert Cromie, "Cuccinello Signaled Lollar," *Chicago Tribune*, October 3, 1959.

45. "United Airlines Flies 410 in Biggest Sports Caravan," *The Sporting News*, October 14, 1959.

46. "Picked Up on First Bounce," *The Sporting News*, October 14, 1959; "Campy's Record Stands," *The Sporting News*, October 14, 1959; "Red Cross Gives Advice to Dodger Fans," *Chicago Tribune*, October 4, 1959.

47. "Red Cross Gives Advice to Dodger Fans," *Chicago Tribune*, October 4, 1959.

48. "Picked Up on First Bounce," *The Sporting News*, October 14, 1959.

49. Ibid; Edward Prell, "White Sox Inspect Coliseum," *Chicago Tribune*, October 4, 1959.

50. Prell, "White Sox Inspect Coliseum," *Chicago Tribune*, October 4, 1959.

51. Joe Trimble, "Lopez Warns Sox to Resist Temptation," *New York Daily News*, October 4, 1959.

52. *Ibid.*

53. Drebinger, "Record 92,500 to Attend Series Today," *New York Times*, October 4, 1959.

54. Arthur Daley, "Sports of the *Times*," *New York Times*, October 5, 1959.

55. "Alston Denies Slur," *New York Times*, October 5, 1959; Richard Dozer, "It's Wynn Versus Craig Again Today in Number Four," *Chicago Tribune*, October 5, 1959.

56. Richard Dozer, "Alston: Furillo was Right Man for Job," *Chicago Tribune*, October 5, 1959; Bill Becker, "Bad Hop Good Break for Furillo," *New York Times*, October 5, 1959.

57. Edward Prell, "Winning Hit Opens Series Controversy," *Chicago Tribune*, October 5, 1959.

58. *Ibid.*

59. David Condon, "In the Wake of the News," *Chicago Tribune*, October 5, 1959.

60. *Ibid.*

61. *Ibid.*

62. *Ibid.*

63. *Ibid.*

64. Arthur Daley, "Sports of the Times," *New York Times*, October 6, 1959.

65. *Ibid.*

66. David Condon, "In the Wake of the News," *Chicago Tribune*, October 6, 1959.

67. Richard Dozer, "Winning Hit Not Genuine, Claims Smith," *Chicago Tribune*, October 6, 1959.

68. Ibid; Condon, "In the Wake of the News," *Chicago Tribune*, October 6, 1959; "Dodgers Steal Sox Script," *Flint Journal*, October 6, 1959; Bill Becker, "Dodgers are Quietly Confident," *New York Times*, October 6, 1959; "No Early Celebration," *Flint Journal*, October 6, 1959.

69. Condon, "In the Wake of the News," *Chicago Tribune*, October 6, 1959; "No Early Celebration," *Flint*

Journal, October 6, 1959; "Name Koufax to End Series in Fifth Game," *Flint Journal*, October 6, 1959.

70. "Los Angeles Aware of Yankees' Comeback," *Flint Journal*, October 6, 1959.

71. *Ibid*.

72. "White Sox Change Luck With Black Stockings," *New York Times*, October 7, 1959; "Chisox Discard White Socks," *The Sporting News*, October 14, 1959.

73. Edgar Munzel, "Go-Go Sox Slowed to a Crawl," *The Sporting News*, October 14, 1959.

74. *Ibid*.

75. "Crowds at the Coliseum," *The Sporting News*, October 14, 1959.

76. Arthur Daley, "Sports of the *Times*," *New York Times*, October 7, 1959.

77. *Ibid*.

78. *Ibid*; "Superstition in 'Must' Victory," *Chicago Tribune*, October 7, 1959.

79. "Superstition in 'Must' Victory," *Chicago Tribune*, October 7, 1959.

80. David Condon, "In the Wake of the News," *Chicago Tribune*, October 8, 1959.

81. Daley, "Sports of the Times," *New York Times*, October 7, 1959.

82. David Condon, "In the Wake of the News," *Chicago Tribune*, October 7, 1959.

83. *Ibid*; "Alston Lauds Lopez for Rivera Shift," *Chicago Tribune*, October 7, 1959.

84. "Alston Lauds Lopez for Rivera Shift," *Chicago Tribune*, October 7, 1959.

85. Richard Dozer, "Picks Wynn to Square Big Series," *Chicago Tribune*, October 7, 1959; Bill Becker, "Lopez Happy After Strategy Succeeds," *New York Times*, October 7, 1959; Condon, "In the Wake of the News," *Chicago Tribune*, October 7, 1959.

86. Condon, "In the Wake of the News," *Chicago Tribune*, October 7, 1959.

87. "Crowds at the Coliseum," *The Sporting News*, October 14, 1959.

88. "Donovan, Rivera Liberate Sox 1–0," *Flint Journal*, October 7, 1959.

89. Peary (ed.), *We Played the Game*, p. 458.

90. "Wynn Clutch Choice of Lopez," *The Sporting News*, October 14, 1959.

91. Richard Dozer, "Wynn Lets Off Steam," *Chicago Tribune*, October 8, 1959.

92. "Woman Fan, 53, Circles Bases; Fails to Score," *Chicago Tribune*, October 8, 1959; "Counterfeit Job Pains Ticket Men," *New York Times*, October 9, 1959; "20,000,000 to see Movies," *The Sporting News*, October 14, 1959.

93. Honig, *The October Heroes*, p. 205.

94. In the 1934 Series, St. Louis Cardinal outfielder Joe Medwick, who had spiked Detroit third-baseman Marv Owen, was removed by Commissioner Kenesaw Mountain Landis "for his own safety," as the left-fielder was being pelted with vegetables by Tiger fans in the bleachers.

95. Robert L. Burnes, "Dodgers Lower Boom," *The Sporting News*, October 14, 1959; "Profanity Cost Chuck $200, and an Extra $100 for Showboating," *The Sporting News*, October 21, 1959.

96. Smith, *On Baseball*, p. 247.

97. Arthur Daley, "Sports of the Times," *New York Times*, October 9, 1959.

98. *Ibid*.

99. Smith, *On Baseball*, p. 248.

100. Louis Effrat, "Nearly Every Dodger Has a Theory to Explain Triumph," *New York Times*, October 9, 1959.

101. "L.A. Dodgers are Happy, But Chisox Aren't Blue," *Flint Journal*, October 9, 1959.

102. Effrat, "Nearly Every Dodger Has a Theory to Explain Triumph," *New York Times*, October 9, 1959.

103. *Ibid*; "L.A. Dodgers are Happy, But Chisox Aren't Blue," *Flint Journal*, October 9, 1959.

104. Effrat, "Nearly Every Dodger Has a Theory to Explain Triumph," *New York Times*, October 9, 1959.

105. "One of Those Days," *Flint Journal*, October 9, 1959.

106. Effrat, "Nearly Every Dodger Has a Theory to Explain Triumph," *New York Times*, October 9, 1959; Robert Cromie, "World Championship to Los Angeles," *Chicago Tribune*, October 9, 1959.

107. John Carmichael, "World Series Post-Mortems," *The Sporting News*, October 21, 1959; "20,000,000 to see Movies," *The Sporting News*, October 14, 1959.

108. "One of Those Days," *Flint Journal*, October 9, 1959; David Condon, "Condonsations," *The Sporting News*, October 21, 1959; Cromie, "World Championship to Los Angeles," *Chicago Tribune*, October 9, 1959.

109. Cromie, "World Championship to Los Angeles," *Chicago Tribune*, October 9, 1959; Herb Fagen, "Jim Landis: He Played Center Field in Classic Style," *Baseball Digest*, July, 1994, p. 78.

110. "Sixth Game," *The Sporting News*, October 14, 1959.

111. Oliver Kuechle, "World Series Post-Mortems," *The Sporting News*, October 21, 1959.

112. Til Ferdenzi, "World Series Post-Mortems," *The Sporting News*, October 21, 1959.

113. Lou Smith, "World Series Post-Mortems," *The Sporting News*, October 21, 1959.

114. Joe Williams, "World Series Post-Mortems," *The Sporting News*, October 21, 1959.

115. "Dodgers Bums to Flatbush Fans," *Flint Journal*, October 9, 1959.

116. David Condon, "In the Wake of the News," *Chicago Tribune*, October 10, 1959.

117. Jimmy Cannon, "World Series Post-Mortems," *The Sporting News*, October 21, 1959.

118. "Estimated 42,000,000 Watched Each Series Tilt on NBC-TV," *The Sporting News*, October 14, 1959.

119. "No Worries for Wynn," *The Sporting News*, October 14, 1959.

120. John Drebinger, "92,294 See Dodgers Win 3–1," *New York Times*, October 5, 1959; Oscar Kahn, "Dodgers and White Sox Split Richest Melon in Series History," *The Sporting News*, October 21, 1959.

121. Jimmy Powers, "World Series Post-Mortems," *The Sporting News*, October 21, 1959.

Chapter 14 — 2005

1. *Athlon Sports Baseball 2005 MLB Preview*, p. 97; "White Sox, Astros are Odd Men In," *Port Huron Times Herald*, October 21, 2005; Michael Hirsley, "Las Vegas Expects Sox to Capture World Series, *Chicago Tribune*, October 18, 2005.

2. Mark Gonzales, "Sox Motto: 1 More Run," *Chicago Tribune*, October 22, 2005.

3. *Athlon Sports Baseball 2005 MLB Preview*, p. 35: "White Sox, Astros are Odd Men In," *Port Huron Times Herald*, October 21, 2005.

4. "White Sox, "Astros are Odd Men In," *Port Huron Times Herald*, October 21, 2005; Rick Morrissey, "Sox's 2005 Journey is no Miracle," *Chicago Tribune*, October 22, 2005.

5. Greg Couch, "Sox Magic Starts with Blend of Global Warming," *Chicago Sun-Times*, October 20, 2005.

6. *Ibid.*

7. "A World Series City!" *Chicago Tribune*, October 17, 2005.

8. Thomas Condon, "Voice of the People," *Chicago Tribune*, October 14, 2005.

9. Brian Hiatt, "Can Cub Fans Suck It Up?" *Chicago Tribune*, October 18, 2005.

10. Maura Kelly Lannan, "Cubs Fan Blagojevich Wants White Sox to Win but Won't Wear Sox Hat," *Chicago Tribune*, October 21, 2005.

11. David Thigpen, "Every Year, a Miracle," *Time*, October 31, 2005, p. 75.

12. Mary Ann Fergus, "Chicago vs. Houston," *Chicago Tribune*, October 21, 2005.

13. Steve Dahl, "Avoid Shooting my TV like Elvis," *Chicago Tribune*, October 21, 2005; Mike Downey, "Everything turns Gold," *Chicago Tribune*, October 22, 2005.

14. Howard Witt, "Astros may help polish this city's grimy image," *Chicago Tribune*, October 22, 2005.

15. *Ibid.*

16. Downey, "Everything turns Gold," *Chicago Tribune*, October 22, 2005.

17. Rick Morrissey, "Guillen Tries to win it all for his hero Carrasquel," *Chicago Tribune*, October 21, 2005.

18. *Ibid.*

19. Richard Justice, "Only Choice for Astros is this Designated Hero," *Houston Chronicle*, October 22, 2005.

20. *Ibid.*

21. Julia Keller, "The Rocket's Dread Glare," *Chicago Tribune*, October 23, 2005; Jay Mariotti, "Ooohs, Oz and Clemens: The spectacle is ours," *Chicago Sun-Times*, October 22, 2005.

22. Keller, "The Rocket's Dread Glare," *Chicago Tribune*, October 23, 2005.

23. *Ibid.*

24. Jay Mariotti, "Fates seemingly align for destiny's darlings," *Chicago Sun-Times*, October 23, 2005.

25. Dan McGrath, "Crede, Bullpen Deliver," *Chicago Tribune*, October 23, 2005.

26. Keller, "The Rocket's Dread Glare," *Chicago Tribune*, October 23, 2005.

27. David Haugh, "'Big Boy' shows he's a man now," *Chicago Tribune*, October 23, 2005.

28. *Ibid*; Mariotti, "Fates seemingly align for destiny's darlings," *Chicago Sun-Times*, October 23, 2005.

29. Rick Morrissey, "Country hardball at its best," *Chicago Tribune*, October 23, 2005.

30. Dave van Dyck, "Feared effect of layoff is no factor for Sox," *Chicago Tribune*, October 23, 2005.

31. Tyler Kepner, "White Sox Look Spry as Clemens Shows His Age," *New York Times*, October 23, 2005; Mariotti, "Fates seemingly align for destiny's darlings," *Chicago Sun-Times*, October 23, 2005.

32. Haugh, "'Big Boy' shows he's a man now," *Chicago Tribune*, October 23, 2005.

33. Phil Rogers, "No time for sentiment in opener," *Chicago Tribune*, October 23, 2005.

34. Richard Justice, "With an ailing Clemens, Astros can't get a leg up," *Houston Chronicle*, October 23, 2005.

35. John P. Lopez, "A little bit of second guesswork," *Houston Chronicle*, October 23, 2005.

36. Brian McTaggart, "It's the same song, but a different verse," *Houston Chronicle*, October 23, 2005.

37. *Ibid*; Lopez, "A little bit of second guesswork," *Houston Chronicle*, October 23, 2005.

38. McTaggart, "it's the same song, but a different verse," *Houston Chronicle*, October 23, 2005.

39. Kepner, "White Sox Look Spry as Clemens Shows His Age," *New York Times*, October 23, 2005; Jose deJesus Ortiz, "Moment ripe for greatness doesn't end in fairy tale," *Houston Chronicle*, October 23, 2005.

40. *Ibid.*

41. Dale Robertson, "Clemens' future in World Series uncertain," *Houston Chronicle*, October 23, 2005.

42. Steve Campbell, "Despite rally in 9th inning, Astros fail to even Series," *Houston Chronicle*, October 24, 2005.

43. Phil Rogers, "Sox hitting greatness groove," *Chicago Tribune*, October 24, 2005.

44. Thomas Boswell, "The Last Row Critic's Corner," *Chicago Tribune*, October 24, 2005.

45. Jay Mariotti, "Podsednik's magic moment a Houstunner," *Chicago Sun-Times*, October 24, 2005.

46. Anthony McCarron, "Scott's shocker is one good call," *New York Daily News*, October 24, 2005.

47. *Ibid*; Mariotti, Podsednik's magic moment a Houstunner," *Chicago Sun-Times*, October 24, 2005.

48. David Haugh, "As weeks go, this is as grand as they come," *Chicago Tribune*, October 24, 2005.

49. *Ibid.*

50. Melissa Isaacson, "things changed radically in 24 hours ... and a few minutes," *Chicago Tribune*, October 24, 2005.

51. Tyler Kepner, "Slam-Bang Victory puts White Sox in Command," *New York Times*, October 24, 2005.

52. Campbell, "Despite rally in 9th inning, Astros fail to even Series," *Houston Chronicle*, October 24, 2005; Sam Borden, "Shockin' Sox snare a pair," *New York Daily News*, October 24, 2005.

53. Campbell, "despite rally in 9th inning, Astros fail to even Series," *Houston Chronicle*, October 24, 2005.

54. Kepner, "Slam-Bang Victory puts White Sox in Command," *New York Times*, October 24, 2005; Richard Justice, "More heartbreak for Lidge," *Houston Chronicle*, October 24, 2005.

55. Rick Morrissey, "Behold, the Incredibles," *Chicago Tribune*, October 23, 2005; Jose deJesus Ortiz, "Lightning strikes twice," *Houston Chronicle*, October 24, 2005.

56. Paul Sullivan and Mark Gonzales, ""Guillen: Everett not owed explanation," *Chicago Tribune*, October 24, 2005.

57. James Janega and Mark Gonzales, "Astros angered by attack report," *Chicago Tribune*, October 25, 2005.

58. *Ibid.*

59. *Ibid.*

60. Morgan Ensberg, "It's nice to back at home, sweet home," *Houston Chronicle*, October 25, 2005.

61. *Ibid*; Jose deJesus Ortiz, "Biggio's wife slapped at White Sox's ballpark," *Houston Chronicle*, October 25, 2005.

62. Morgan Ensberg, "Here's hoping for a closed Juice Box," *Houston Chronicle*, October 25, 2005; Adam Caldarelli, "From the Cubicle," *Chicago Tribune*, October 26, 2005.

63. Mike Downey, "Almost feeling sorry for the Astros," *Chicago Tribune*, October 26, 2005.

64. *Ibid.*

65. John P. Lopez, Astros' dream fades on longest of nights," *Houston Chronicle*, October 26, 2005.

66. Murray Chass, "A Fine Line 'Twixt Glory and Shame," *New York Times*, October 27, 2005.

67. Lisa Olson, "Astros finish on Scrap Iron heap," *New York Daily News*, October 27, 2005; Richard Justice,

"Nothing to show for a long night's work," *Houston Chronicle*, October 26, 2005; Tyler Kepner, "Marathon Victory puts White Sox on Brink of Title," *New York Times*, October 26, 2005; Dale Robertson, "Garner gets hot over Astros' cold bats," *Houston Chronicle*, October 26, 2005.

68. Rick Morrissey, 3–0? Nighty night Houston," *Chicago Tribune*, October 27, 2005.

69. Justice, "Nothing to show for a long night's work," *Houston Chronicle*, October 26, 2005.

70. Rick Morrissey, "After 88 years, there's joy in Soxville," *Chicago Tribune*, October 27, 2005.

71. Steve Campbell, "Astros out at home," *Houston Chronicle*, October 27, 2005; Dan McGrath, "South Siders end 88-year drought," *Chicago Tribune*, October 27, 2005.

72. Brian McTaggart, "Despite Series losses, Lidge has no regrets," *Houston Chronicle*, October 27, 2005; Jose deJesus Ortiz, "Great year ends on downer," *Houston Chronicle*, October 27, 2005.

73. Anthony McCarron, "Sox win it in a whitewash," *New York Daily News*, October 27, 2005; Tyler Kepner, "White Sox End 88-Year Wait for Series Title," *New York Times*, October 27, 2005.

74. Fran Blinebury, "Astros' offense lays one big goose egg," *Houston Chronicle*, October 27, 2005.

75. Richard Justice, "No tricks left in a magical season," *Houston Chronicle*, October 27, 2005.

76. John P. Lopez, "First taste of Series well worth the wait," *Houston Chronicle*, October 27, 2005.

77. Morrissey, "After 88 years, there's joy in Soxville," *Chicago Tribune*, October 27, 2005.

78. *Ibid.*

79. Paul Sullivan, "Guillen savors his players' joy," *Chicago Tribune*, October 27, 2005.

80. Jack Curry, "A Year After Cursed Red Sox End Drought, Unsung White Sox Do the Same," *New York Times*, October 27, 2005; McCarron, "Sox win it in a whitewash," *New York Daily News*, October 27, 2005.

81. Curry, "A Year After Cursed Red Sox End Drought, Unsung White Sox Do the Same," *New York Times*, October 27, 2005.

82. *Ibid*; McCarron, "Sox win it in a whitewash," *New York Daily News*, October 27, 2005.

83. Bill Madden, "They can do without," *New York Daily News*, October 27, 2005.

84. *Ibid.*

85. Gary Washburn, "Daley savors Sox victory and team's 'life lessons,'" *Chicago Tribune*, October 28, 2005

BIBLIOGRAPHY

Periodicals

Athlon Sports Baseball 2005 MLB Preview
Baseball Digest 1959–2005
Chicago Sun Times 2005
Chicago Tribune 1906–2005
Detroit Free Press 1906–2005
Detroit News 1935, 1945
Detroit Times 1935, 1945
Flint Journal 1935, 1945, 1959, 2005
Houston Chronicle 2005
New York Daily News 2005
New York Times 1906–2005
Port Huron (MI) Times Herald 2005
Sport 1959–1961
Sports Illustrated 1959, 2005
St. Louis Post-Dispatch 1935–1945
The Sporting News 1906–2005
Time 2005

Books

Alexander, Charles C. *John McGraw.* New York: Viking, 1988.

_____. *Rogers Hornsby.* New York: Henry Holt and Co., 1995.

_____. *Ty Cobb.* New York: Oxford University Press, 1984.

Allen, Lee. *The World Series: The Story of Baseball's Annual Championship.* New York: Putnam, 1969.

Asinof, Eliot. *Eight Men Out: The Black Sox and the 1919 World Series.* New York: Henry Holt, 1963.

Bak, Richard. *Cobb Would Have Caught It.* Detroit: Wayne State University Press, 1991.

_____. *A Place for Summer.* Detroit: Wayne State University Press, 1998.

Berkow, Ira (ed.). *Hank Greenberg: The Story of My Life.* New York: Times Books, 1989.

Bingay, Malcolm. *Detroit Is My Own Home Town.* New York: Bobbs-Merrill, 1946.

Broeg, Bob, and Bob Burrill. *Don't Bring THAT Up: Skeletons in the Sports Closet.* New York: A.S. Barnes, 1946.

Brown, Warren. *The Chicago Cubs.* Carbondale: Southern Illinois University Press, 2001; reprint of 1946 edition.

Carmichael, John P. (ed.). *My Greatest Day in Baseball.* New York: Grosset and Dunlap, 1951.

Cobb, Ty. *My Life in Baseball.* Lincoln: University of Nebraska Press, 1993; reprint of 1961 Doubleday edition.

Connor, Anthony J. *Voices from Cooperstown: Baseball's Hall of Famers Tell It Like It Was.* New York: Collier Books, 1982.

Cosgrove, Benedict. *Covering the Bases: The Most Unforgettable Moments in Baseball in the Words of the Writers and Broadcasters Who Were There.* San Francisco: Chronicle, 1997.

Creamer, Robert W. *Babe: The Legend Comes to Life.* New York: Simon and Schuster, 1974.

Townsend, Doris (ed.). *This Great Game.* New York: Rutledge, 1971.

Daley, Arthur. *Inside Baseball: A Half Century of the National Pastime.* New York: Grosset & Dunlap, 1950.

Durso, Joseph. *Baseball and the American Dream.* St. Louis: The Sporting News, 1986.

Falls, Joe. *The Detroit Tigers: An Illustrated History.* New York: Walker, 1989.

Fitzgerald, Ed (ed.). *The American League.* New York: Grosset & Dunlap, 1955.

_____. *The National League.* New York: Grosset & Dunlap, 1955.

Fleming, G.H. *The Unforgettable Season: 1908: The Cubs, Giants, and Pirates in the Greatest Race of All Time.* New York: Fireside, 1981.

Fountain, Charles. *Sportswriter: The Life and Times of Grantland Rice.* New York: Oxford University Press, 1993.

Frommer, Harvey. *Baseball's Greatest Managers.* New York: Franklin Watts, 1985.

_____. *Shoeless Joe and Ragtime Baseball*. Dallas: Taylor, 1992.

Gies, Joseph, and Robert H. Shoemaker. *Stars of the Series: A Complete History of the World Series*. New York: Thomas Y. Crowell, 1964.

Golenbock, Peter. *Wrigleyville: A Magical History Tour of the Chicago Cubs*. New York: St. Martin's, 1996.

Graham, Frank. *McGraw of the Giants*. New York: Putnam, 1944.

Gregory, Robert. *Diz: The Story of Dizzy Dean and Baseball in the Great Depression*. New York: Viking, 1992.

Grimm, Charlie. *Grimm's Baseball Tales: Jolly Cholly's Story*. South Bend IN: Diamond Communications, 1983; reprint of 1968 edition.

Gutman, Dan. *Baseball Babylon: From the Black Sox to Pete Rose, the Real Stories Behind the Scandals That Rocked the Game*. New York: Penguin, 1992.

Harwell, Ernie. *Diamond Gems*. Ann Arbor: Momentum, 1991.

Holtzman, Jerome. *No Cheering in the Press Box*. New York: Henry Holt, 1995.

_____, and George Vass. *Baseball Chicago Style: A Tale of Two Teams, One City*. Chicago: Bonus, 2001.

Honig, Donald. *Baseball America*. New York: Galahad, 1985.

_____. *Baseball When the Grass Was Real: Baseball From the Twenties to the Forties Told by the Men Who Played It*. Lincoln: University of Nebraska Press, 1993.

_____. *The Man in the Dugout*. Lincoln: University of Nebraska Press, 1995.

_____. *The October Heroes: Great World Series Games Remembered by the Men Who Played Them*. New York: Simon & Schuster, 1979.

_____. *The World Series: An Illustrated History from 1903 to the Present*. New York: Crown, 1986.

Hynd, Noel. *The Giants of the Polo Grounds: The Glorious Times of Baseball's New York Giants*. Dallas: Taylor, 1995.

Jordan, David M. *A Tiger in His Time: Hal Newhouser and the Burden of Wartime Baseball*. South Bend IN: Diamond Communications, 1990.

Langford, Walter M. *Legends of Baseball: An Oral History of the Game's Golden Age*. South Bend IN: Diamond Communications, 1987.

Lieb, Frederick G. *The Baseball Story*. New York: Putnam, 1950.

_____. *The Story of the World Series*. New York: Putnam, 1965.

Mathewson, Christy. *Pitching in a Pinch*. New York: Stein & Day, 1977.

McCollister, John. *The Tigers and Their Den: The Official Story of the Detroit Tigers*. Shawnee Mission, KS: Addax Publishing Group, 1999.

Moore, Jack B. *Joe DiMaggio: Baseball's Yankee Clipper*. New York: Praeger, 1987.

Mosedale, John. *The Greatest of Them All*. New York: Dial, 1974.

Murdock, Eugene C. *Ban Johnson*. Westport CT: Greenwood, 1982.

_____. *Baseball Players and Their Times*. Westport: Meckler, 1991.

Okrent, Daniel, and Harris Lewine. *The Ultimate Baseball Book*. Boston: Houghton Mifflin, 1988.

Peary, Danny (ed.). *We Played the Game: 65 Players Remember Baseball's Greatest Era, 1947–1964*. New York: Hyperion, 1994.

Reichler, Joseph L. (ed.). *The World Series: A 75th Anniversary*. New York: Simon & Schuster, 1978.

Reidenbaugh, Lowell. *Baseball's 25 Greatest Pennant Races*. St. Louis: The Sporting News, 1987.

Ritter, Lawrence S. *The Glory of Their Times: The Story of the Early Days of Baseball as Told by the Men Who Played It*. New York: Vintage, 1984.

Ritter, Lawrence S., and Mark Rucker. *The Babe: A Life in Pictures*. New York: Ticknor & Fields, 1988.

_____, and _____ *The Babe: The Game That Ruth Built*. New York: Total Sports, 1997.

Robinson, Ray. *Iron Horse: Lou Gehrig in His Time*. New York: HarperCollins, 1990.

Rosenburg, John M. *The Story of Baseball*. New York: Random House, 1968.

Ruth, George Herman. *Ruth, Babe's Own Book of Baseball*. Lincoln: University of Nebraska Press, 1992; reprint of 1928 edition.

Schoor, Gene. *The History of the World Series: The Complete Chronology of America's Greatest Sports Tradition*. New York: William Morrow, 1990.

Smelser, Marshall. *The Life That Ruth Built: A Biography*. New York: Quadrangle, 1975.

Smith, Curt. *Voices of the Game: The First Full-Scale Overview of Baseball Broadcasting, 1921 to the Present*. South Bend IN: Diamond Communications, 1987.

Smith, Ken. *Baseball's Hall of Fame*. New York: Grosset & Dunlap, 1952.

Smith, Red. *On Baseball: The Game's Greatest Writer on the Game's Greatest Years*. Chicago: Ivan R. Dee, 2000.

Stump, Al. *Cobb: A Biography*. Chapel Hill: Algonquin, 1996.

Williams, Peter (ed.). *The Joe Williams Reader: The Glorious Game, from Ty Cobb and Babe Ruth to the Amazing Mets: 50 Years of Baseball Writing by the Celebrated Newspaper Columnist*. Chapel Hill: Algonquin, 1989.

Yardley, Jonathan. *Ring: A Biography of Ring Lardner*. New York: Random House, 1977.

Zingg, Paul J. *Harry Hooper*. Urbana: University of Illinois Press, 1993.

INDEX

Numbers in *bold italics* indicate photographs.